SECOND EDITION

READINGS IN MANAGEMENT AND ORGANIZATIONS

193 - 200
218 - 227
288 - 299

Monique A. Pelletier
Professor of Management
San Francisco State University

KENDALL/HUNT PUBLISHING COMPANY
2460 Kerper Boulevard   P.O. Box 539   Dubuque, Iowa 52004-0539

CONTENTS

DECISION MAKING

ORGANIZING

STAFFING

PART FOUR ■ ORGANIZATIONAL LEADERSHIP 287

MOTIVATION

LEADERSHIP

COMMUNICATION

CULTURE AND CHANGE

PREFACE

The importance of the basic management course that is part of the core curriculum is most schools and colleges of business cannot be overemphasized. In most cases, the theories, concepts, and principles disseminated in this course constitute the only formal knowledge on this subject that the student will receive in his or her program of studies. Regardless of the career path chosen by the student, basic managerial concepts and theories will be a part of the work environment. Whether functioning as a manager or an employee, as a leader or a follower, the student will be required to have a working knowledge of the concepts and theories presented in this foundation course. This knowledge will assuredly make the student a more productive and satisfied employee. It will also work to facilitate promotion into the ranks of management in fulfillment of higher levels of aspiration. As management is the key to success for any organization, so a knowledge of management is the key to becoming and remaining a successful manager. This book of readings is directed toward this end.

There are many textbooks available for use in the basic management course. The orientation of these books will differ depending upon the academic background of the author. In spite of many individual differences, most of the theories, concepts and principles of management are generic in that they are found in almost any textbook. Examples include objectives, planning, organizing, staffing leading, decision making and controlling which speak to the overall process of management along with a complement of behavioral subjects such as motivation, communication and conflict which relate to the people who are being managed.

The comprehensive selection of readings in the 2nd edition is adaptable to a wide range of pedagogies and will complement and extend the content and approach of most textbooks and other learning aids employed by instructors. Examples include supplemental readings, term paper assignments, managerial case assessments, individual or team presentations or, simply, intellectual inquiry into selected subjects. This book can also be used in the absence of a textbook on management as the center piece of short courses, workshops, or institutes dealing with specialized aspects of management. The writings contained in this book of readings have been selected with great care and reflect the recent research done in the area of management and organizational behavior.

The book is divided into five major parts. Each major part contains several subparts arranged to facilitate a logical progression of subjects designed to enhance the learning process by linking the theory of management with its application in a wide variety of organizational settings.

M. A. P.

PART ONE

MANAGERIAL PERSPECTIVES

The first set of readings in this book provides the student with several broad perspectives on the management of different types of organizations in a variety of settings. By definition, management involves working with and through people to accomplish the work of the organization. Managers also perform certain basic functions that distinguish them from other people in the organization. For example, managers set objectives for the entire organization and then develop and implement plans to ensure that the objectives are accomplished within time and cost constraints. Managers also determine the kinds of activities and the number and qualifications of people to perform these activities within a formal structure of organization. Working through the organizational structure, managers provide leadership in committing resources to accomplish planned activities that will fulfill the mission of the organization. Finally, managers control the direction and momentum of activities by ensuring that people perform in accordance with the operating standards derived from the managerial objectives. Managers provide the initiative for all of the work of the organization. Indeed without managers there is not organization.

The significance of management in the success of any organization is the major point of emphasis in this part of the book. Managerial values and ethics as the primary determinants of managerial behavior and actions are accorded a primary focus here. In recognition of the growing realization that managers in the United States must come to know more about the management practices in other countries, two articles put an emphasis on significance of international business. America's competitiveness in international business is directly dependent upon a renewed appreciation by managers in the United States of managerial thinking and actions abroad.

Within the past few years there has been a resurgence of interest in and emphasis on entrepreneurship in the United States. Entrepreneurs are individuals who are managing businesses that they have founded. As America's large corporations in its basic industries have come under increasing competitive pressures in foreign markets and in domestic markets from foreign producers, most of the slack has been taken up by new industries or new businesses in established industries. Successful entrepreneurs enjoy much the same recognition and status that the managers of large corporations have received for several decades. This section of the book focuses on several key aspects of entrepreneurship in America.

The Half Truths of Management

E. Frank Harrison
San Francisco State University

Monique A. Pelletier
San Francisco State University

Managers tend to base much of their decision making and many of their actions on principles and precepts that are presumed to embody the conventional wisdom of the whole truth. Actually this conventional wisdom is founded on numerous overt half truths which provide an incomplete basis for managerial behavior. A complete foundation for managerial actions includes both overt and covert half truths—i.e., the actual whole truth. In combination, these half truths constitute an essential union by which to guide managerial decision making in organizations of all types.

Managers tend to be guided in most of their actions by their experience and what they perceive to be correct. Much of the conventional wisdom that prompts the behavior of managers is founded on knowledge that is incomplete or only partially true. Managers place great store in half truths. Most of these half truths have evolved out of organizational folklore. Generally they are adduced and rationalized to deal with a specific problem or as a reaction to a particular situation. In many cases the half truths of management are sufficient to dissipate the dilemma at hand. In many other cases, the half truths tend to compound the negative consequences of incomplete or inappropriate managerial actions.

These half truths tend to be passed on from one generation of managers to another. The accumulative beliefs of successive generations of managers tend to perpetuate the half truths. Incomplete knowledge tends to obscure the whole truth. Inaccurate knowledge reduces the marginal value of the half truth. Managerial behavior consistently vectors and revectors from one crisis to another based on actions taken in pursuit of half truths. The seemingly unending reliance on the half truths of management adds greatly to the difficulties experienced by managerial practitioners in organizations of all types. Opportunities tend to be overlooked or are bypassed; problems develop and deepen; and necessary improvements and changes are not made as management clings tenaciously to an untenable set of half truths. In the private sector, organizations managed in this mode tend to disappear or are

Reprinted with permission from The International Journal of Management Vol. 6, No. 2, pp. 168–174, June 1989.

absorbed by other organizations. In the public sector, organizations managed with half truths tend to survive at the general expense of the common good.

This paper presents and discusses seven common half truths of management that guide the daily decision making of managers in formal organizations of all types. These seven half truths are not represented as being exhaustive of all possibilities. Rather they are intended to illustrate that managers tend to rely for guidance on policies, procedures, principles, and practices that reflect only a fraction of the variables underlying the situation at hand. These are the overt half truths of management. Managerial actions and decisions will be greatly improved by proceeding on the basis of the whole truth. The whole truth includes those variables not readily apparent to management. The reciprocality of the overt and covert parts of the whole truth seems unassailable. All that remains is for management to bring the covert half truth into full view and to combine it with the overt half truth preparatory to action based on a perceived whole truth. By this means, managerial performance and organizational effectiveness will be greatly furthered.

CONFLICT

Conflict is endemic to all forms of human interaction which, by definition, includes all types of formal organization. The unity of conflict is typically bifurcated as follows:

Overt Half Truth: Conflict harbors numerous negative consequences for the organization.

Covert Half Truth: Conflict harbors numerous positive consequences for the organization.

Proceeding on the basis of the overt half truth, management typically goes to incredible lengths to deny the presence of conflict. This overemphasis on the divisive, disruptive, and destructive aspects of conflict is dysfunctional to the organization for at least two reasons: (1) Conflict cast in a negative image becomes a spectre against which to array resources that could be employed more productively elsewhere and (2) conflict is denied the opportunity to reveal its full potential as an agent of change and a source of innovation. In truth an organization without conflict would be complacent, stagnant, and devoid of the dynamism that frequently stems from disagreement and dissonance. It is unlikely that such an organization would accommodate the innovation and adaptiveness necessary to survive in a social structure marked by inevitable change and a technology marked by continuous permutation (Harrison 1979 and 1980). Fusing the overt and covert half truths of conflict into multidimensional unity can lead to a more effective treatment and use of this interactional phenomenon in formal organizations.

2. EFFECTIVENESS

Managers in organizations of all types are concerned with effectiveness. In a fairly recent survey of 6,000 executives and managers conducted under the auspices of the American Management Association, the 1,460 respondents rated the effectiveness of their respective organizations as their most important goal. Effectiveness is the ultimate measure of exemplary organizational performance. It is the ideal state toward which good managers strive. In this context, effectiveness refers to the ability of an organization "to mobilize its centers of power for action, production and adaption. Effective organizations are those that produce more and higher quality outputs and adapt more (readily) to environmental and internal problems than do other similar organizations" (Mott, 1972, p. 17).

The half truth of effectiveness stems from the tendency to use *effectiveness* as a synonym for *efficiency* in many organizations. The whole truth of the relationship between effectiveness and efficiency is encapsulated in the following duality:

Overt Half Truth: Managers can't be effective without being efficient.

Covert Half Truth: Managers can be efficient without being effective.

Drucker (1973) notes that effectiveness is concerned with doing the right things and efficiency is concerned with doing things right. Etzioni (1964) avers that effectiveness is achieved when the organization attains its desired outcome; and efficiency refers to the expenditure of resources in pursuit of this outcome. These definitions indicate that effectiveness is an end state and efficiency is the means to gain the sought end. If efficiency by definition is embodied in effectiveness, then it must be truth that managers can't be effective without being efficient. Indeed efficiency is essential for the effective management of almost any formal organization. Conversely efficiency does not axiomatically result in effectiveness. It is entirely possible to do the wrong things the right way. A given manager can, at least in the short run, be enormously efficient without being completely effective. Many managers expend considerable time, intellect, and energy pursuing ends that are not in the best long-term interests of the organization. By focusing on the whole truth of effectiveness rather than the overt relationship of this concept with efficiency, the performance of management and the organization will be greatly enhanced.

³ PLANNING AND CONTROL

Planning looks to the future; control checks the past. Both concepts provide perspectives for the manager who makes decisions in the present (Harrison, 1978). "A plan describes the way in which something is to be done. Control is that managerial activity that tells you how well you are doing what you planned" (Cleland and King, 1972, p. 396). Planning and control exist in a kind of reciprocal relationship that is only partially reflected in the conventional wisdom of the overt half truth of management. It is only through the addition of the covert half truth that shadow becomes sunlight and the whole truth is revealed as an indivisible unity. This unity is as follows:

Overt Half Truth: In the absence of control, the attainment of the managerial objectives contained in the long-range plan is pure happenstance.

Covert Half Truth: In the absence of a long-range plan, the organization is already out of control.

In the absence of a long-range plan there is nothing to control. A plan provides a foundation and a direction through which the managerial objectives are attained and the organizational mission is fulfilled. Indeed an organization without a long-range plan is like a ship without a rudder. It is directionless and drifting on a sea of impoverished purpose. In this case, the overt half truth of management addresses that part of the reciprocality in which the managerial objectives contained in the long-range plan is the end and control is the means to obtain this end. Control is also an end in its own right in that it is attainable only through the guidance provided by a long-range plan. In this part of the reciprocality, the plan is the means to keep the organization under control. It is through the whole truth of this essential and indivisible unity that management is most likely to accomplish its intended outcomes.

⁴ MANAGEMENT AND LEADERSHIP

There is probably a more extensive literature on the subject of leadership than on any other aspect of management (Harrison, 1976). There is an inordinate fascination with this "doing" part of the manager's job. Management theorists and practitioners seem intent on finding the ideal model of leadership. This preoccupation presumably stems from the obvious fact that leadership involves working with and through people—which, by definition, allows for infinite variables. The key to leadership is influence. In a somewhat simplistic fashion, leadership may be defined as "the relationship in which one person, or the leader, influences others to work together willingly on related tasks to obtain that which the leader desires (Terry, 1972, p. 458).

Directing operations requires leadership on the part of the manager. It is appropriate here to distinguish between leadership and management, since the two terms are often, and incorrectly, used interchangeably. It is this incorrect usage that gives rise to the following half truths of management

Overt Half Truth: One can be a leader without being a manager. ✓

Covert Half Truth: One cannot be a manager without being a leader. ✓

It is, for example, entirely possible to be an effective leader without being an effective manager, but effective management is not possible without effective leadership. Leadership is an *interpersonal* process; management is an *organizational* process (Harrison, 1978, p. 170). Leadership is part of management but not all of it. A manager is required to plan and organize; but he is also required to elicit performance from subordinates to attain the objectives contained in the plans. Leadership is an integral part of management. It is the interactional part of the manager's job. The whole truth is that leadership outside of an organizational context has no direct relationship with management. Within the organization, however, management cannot be accomplished without the attributes of leadership. In this context leadership is a subset of management. In any other context, leadership must survive on its own merits.

⊦ PARTICIPATIVE DECISION MAKING

Participation refers to the active involvement of subordinates or followers in the making of decisions that directly affect them in the workplace. Participation in decision making is generally regarded as a sign of enlightened and democratic management. Through the use of participation, individual members of the organization are involved in a broad range of objective-setting, problem-solving, and decision-making activities of the organization. Participation in these activities is held to contribute to the effective integration of the individual's goals and the organization's objectives.

The tendency in discussing participative decision making in formal organizations is to focus on its alleged benefits to the virtual exclusion of its covert costs. For this reason the half truths of participation are as follows:

Overt Half Truth: The advocacy of participative decision making is based on several alleged benefits.

Covert Half Truth: The proponents of participative decision making seldom consider its potentially significant costs.

Participation in decision making can be justified on several grounds. Along with an assumed moral obligation to manage democratically, participation is usually justified on the basis of increased productivity and greater employee satisfaction. Participation in decision making is said to produce (1) generally favorable employee attitudes toward management, (2) better relations between superiors and subordinates, (3) better upward communication, and (4) greater subordinate acceptance of superiors as their representatives. All of these factors are said to lead to greater employee satisfaction, heightened motivation, and higher levels of productivity. Participation by employees also tends to result in greater subordinate acceptance of decisions. This is one of the principal arguments in favor of participative decision making.

There are several disadvantages to participative decision-making. First, unless it is genuine in intent, participation can be perceived as tokenism with attendant undesirable effects. Because it usually involves some type of group effort, participative decision making can be very time-consuming. Moreover, many decisions are highly confidential in nature which tends to work against participation. Other decisions require high levels of specialized knowledge which also militates against broad participation. Finally, the most signficant potential disadvantage of participation is the diffusion of accountability for results. Participation in decision making is highly situational and is largely a matter of degree. Depending upon the preferences of higher levels of management, the competencies of lower levels of management, the motive of the decision at hand, and the time and cost constraints of the moment, it seems reasonable to posit a continuum of participation in decision making. This is the whole truth of management.

6 MOTIVATION

There are a few generally accepted definitions of motivation. Psychologists tend to speak of motivation in terms of specific motives related to a need or desire that causes an individual to act. Motivation theory attempts to explain how behavior originates and is energized, sustained, directed and stopped, and what kind of subjective reaction is present in the individual while this is going on (Jones, 1959). Motivation has been defined as "a process governing choices made by persons . . . among alternative forms of voluntary activity" (Vroom, 1964, p. 6). Another view of motivation is based on the broad assumption that all behavior is motivated behavior (Sikula, 1971). This latter view contributes directly to the half truths of management as they relate to motivation. These half truths are set forth below:

Overt Half Truth: There are many ways to energize motivatable employees.

Covert Half Truth: There are few techniques for energizing unmotivatable employees.

If we assume, as does Maslow (1943), that human beings are motivated by a hierarchy of needs, it seems unrealistic to further assume infinite motivation. At the lower levels of Maslow's hierarchy are such needs as food, water, sex, and security. These needs must be satisfied before those at the higher levels can be met. The highest level need, self-actualization, may take many forms and be pursued with varying intensity. And the satisfaction of what is a lower-level need for one individual may represent a kind of ultimate fulfillment for another individual. In other words, some individuals may not aspire in the workplace to reach beyond the lower-level needs of Maslow's hierarchy. Such individuals may be characterized as unmotivatable simply because, according to Herzberg (1966) and others, the lower-level needs in Maslow's hierarchy are not motivators in their own right. These basic or biogenic needs constitute hygiene factors, maintenance items, or dissatisfiers depending upon your preference. The hygiene factors must be satisfied before management can employ selected techniques such as recognition, advancement or achievement. However, many employees don't seek recognition, strive for advancement or aspire to achievement. Such employees are seldom discussed in the management or social science literature, but they exist in large numbers, conceivably larger than the total number of motivatable employees. If this state of affairs prevails in the workplace then management must focus on the whole truth which concentrates on the motivatable employees while acknowledging the unmotivatables.

7   MANAGERIAL CONTROL

Timing is doubtless the most important element in achieving and sustaining managerial control. Timing is a special subset of control usually related to the need for corrective action when it becomes apparent that actual performance is deviating from standard performance. Succinctly, timing is concerned with when corrective action should be taken. The need for good timing in the overall process of managerial control begins with the measurement and evaluation of actual performance. The time for management to prepare for corrective action is when it becomes apparent that actual performance will deviate to an unacceptable degree from standard performance. Timely corrective action, therefore, depends on the accurate measurement of current indicators of actual performance. There is not only a need for timely corrective action, but there is a more compelling need to anticipate the need for timely corrective action. The whole truth of management in this regard is as follows:

Overt Half Truth: There is a need for timely corrective action.

Covert Half Truth: There is a need to anticipate the need to take timely corrective action.

There is a discernible tendency on the part of practicing managers to overlook the covert half truth of managerial control and to take corrective action when only it is painfully apparent and long overdue. If management would only broaden its level of awareness to transform the whole truth of managerial control from its present hybrid state to a completely overt anticipation of recurring variations from standard performance, the control process would be much more likely to achieve its objective. A heightened level of awareness by management would result in less hasty and drastic overcorrection which, in many cases, must be undone at great expense to avert consequences worse than if no correction had been made at all.

Management needs to accept the notion that reality and cost demand the acceptance of some variance from standard performance. Performance that exceeds the range of acceptable variance in either direction is unacceptable and calls for timely corrective action. The time to take the corrective action is when actual performance gives a clear indication that if something isn't done, the range of acceptable variable will be ruptured and drastic corrective measures may be required to restore equilibrium within standard performance. The establishment of control tolerances around a standard level of performance followed by anticipation of the need for corrective action before variations from the standard become serious is the whole truth of managerial control in any type of formal organization (Harrison, 1986).

SUMMARY

This article has presented seven half truths of management that guide the daily decision making of managers in organizations of all types. Managers tend to proceed on the basis of the overt half truths in management to the exclusion of the reciprocal covert half truths. This article asserts that managerial performance and organizational effectiveness will be greatly enhanced if practicing managers sharpen their awareness to encompass the whole truth. More often than not what is immediately apparent constitutes only one half of the equation. Additional reflection, analysis, and evaluation will reveal the other half. Management can then proceed to take timely and appropriate action with a much higher level of confidence in a favorable outcome. ■

REFERENCES

Cleland, D. J. and W. R. King, 1972, *Management: A Systems Approach*, New York: McGraw-Hill.

Drucker, P. F., 1973, *Management Tasks—Responsibilities—Practices*, New York: Harper & Row.

Etzioni, A., 1964, *Modern Organizations*, Englewood Cliffs, N.J.: Prentice-Hall.

Harrison, F., 1980, "A Conceptual Model of Organizational Conflict". *Business and Society*, 19–2 and 20–1: 30–40.

Harrison, F., 1976, "Dimensions of Leadership". *Journal of General Management*, 4: 59–65.

Harrison, F., 1978, *Management and Organizations*, Boston: Houghton Mifflin Co.

Harrison, F., 1986, *Policy, Strategy, and Managerial Action*, Boston: Houghton Mifflin Co.

Harrison, F., 1979, "The Management of Organizational Conflict". *University of Michigan Business Review*, 31: 18–23.

Herzberg, F., 1966, *Work and the Nature of Man*, Cleveland World Publishing Co.

Jones, M. R., ed. 1959, *Nebraska Symposium on Motivation*, Lincoln Nebraska University Press.

Maslow, A. H., 1943, "A Theory of Human Motivation". *Psychological Review,* 50: 370–396.

Mott, P. E., 1972, *The Characteristics of Effective Organizations,* New York: Harper & Row.

Posner, B. Z., and Schmidt, W. H., 1984, "Values and the American Manager: An Update". *California Management Review,* 26: 202–216.

Sikula, A. F., 1971, "Values and Value Systems: Importance and Relationship to Managerial and Organizational Behavior". *Journal of Psychology,* 78: 277–286.

Terry, G. R., 1972, *Principles of Management,* 6th ed., Homewood, Ill.: Irwin.

Vroom, V. H., 1964, *Work and Motivation,* New York: Wiley.

When Good Management is Not Enough

Julien R. Phillips

Conventional good management cannot cope with the demanding organizational requirements of adapting major corporations to changing market conditions, the author argues. Many who try find their efforts frustrated by the inertial pull to revert to business-as-usual methods before the change is fully in place. In this article he shows how successful "change managers" take bold, unconventional steps to announce new priorities, change procedures, ensure everyone understands the change, and play a highly visible part in orchestrating the organizational learning process.

Changing times have always spelled opportunity for aggressive, innovative competitors while threatening the strength, even the survival, of those too slow to respond. Today, turbulent economic, technological and behavioral changes are challenging companies in virtually every sector of the economy.

The historical record of industries facing major discontinuities would lead us to expect that only one in three of current industry leaders will retain their leadership 10 years from now. The thought may be encouraging to those companies that are now mounting challenges to established leaders, but it should be unsettling to others.

What will differentiate the present and future industry leaders from those other companies that fall by the wayside? In my view, a key factor will be their ability to adopt approaches to managing change that differ profoundly from the way they have habitually managed business as usual. All too often, good managers of ongoing businesses—even very good ones—fail to adjust their established managerial approach sufficiently.

Reprinted with permission from *The Mckinsey Quarterly,* Summer 1986, pp. 19–33.

Julien Phillips is a Principal in the San Francisco office and a co-leader of the Firm's change management practice. This article is drawn from a talk before the Medical Marketing Association in Monterey, California earlier this year.

THE CONVENTIONAL WAY

What does a conventionally good top manager do when he becomes aware of a problem or challenge that he doesn't understand? First, he will try to learn about it. If he graduated from a major business school in the past 15 years, he will almost certainly commission a few top managers to study it analytically. He probably won't want to get too many people involved, but because he doubts that many people in the organization really can contribute very much, and because he doesn't want to confuse the organization unduly until he knows where he wants to go.

At some point, our CEO will commit a new strategy that appears to be suited to the emerging competitive circumstances. At the same time, he will often decide that in order to execute the new strategy well, the company's organization will have to be changed. Such organizational shake-ups are a very common (and sensible) aspect of conventional management responses to a change challenge. "Structure follows strategy" is the well-known maxim. He may even decide to bring in a new executive or two in order to add new perspective and new skills, but more often he sticks with the team he has built over the years to execute his old strategy.

Having made these decisions—"That's what I get paid for, tough decisions," he says to himself, or perhaps to his human resources manager who has been his confidant during this period—the top manager announces the changes. Often he follows them up with a series of talks, which he gives all around the company, about the new competitive environment and the company's response. For the next few months, he may continue to provide active leadership for the change, monitor implementation actions, and push the process forward. But as soon as he feels it prudent or senses other priorities, he figuratively steps aside to let his line managers get on with it.

Then, all too frequently, the thrust toward major change peters out. It peters out because the conventional approach to management is not suited to dealing with three key obstacles:

1. *Habits of thinking and working.* The second-third-fourth level managers have certain questions that they routinely ask of the people who report to them. How are we doing relative to budget? Are shipments up? Where can we squeeze a few dollars out on the cost side? If, after the change process is launched, subordinates keep hearing these same old questions again and again, they are likely to believe that expectations really haven't changed. Moreover, it's futile to expect people to change their working habits unless they are reminded constantly of the new and different approaches that are required.

2. *Shared values and expectations.* People in the organization are attentive to explicit strategies and agreed on objectives. But they also carry around a set of shared values in their heads—more or less unspoken beliefs about what is

important: Which customers count most? What is distinctive about the way we serve them? What are management's most important expectations? What's the easiest way to get into hot water? Such shared values are almost as deeply ingrained as a conscience, and people change them only slowly. Even if the new strategy is so seemingly straightforward as designing new products that are simple, inexpensive and reliable, development engineers who have grown up in the belief that technological sophistication counts most will have a tough time adapting.

3. *Distribution of power and influence.* Suppose the company's response to new competitive circumstances requires the marketing function to play a much stronger role in setting product development and manufacturing priorities. The manufacturing and R & D heads are very likely to behave in a way that undermines marketing's new initiatives—not necessarily because they are trying to torpedo the overall change, but because they are convinced that they must retain their authority and influence to ensure that what they see as the most important considerations are properly weighed when important decisions are at issue.

Changing habits, shared values, and distribution of power and influence is a slow task, and it is all too easy for initial understandings and good intentions to disappear as the old realities are allowed to reassert themselves.

RECEIVED WISDOM

What is it about conventional ideas of good management that makes them ineffective in dealing with such obstacles? Consider these bits of received wisdom:

- *Sound Analysis.* When faced with a perplexing problem a senior executive should pull some smart people together to analyze it thoroughly and figure out how to respond most effectively.
- *Touch-minded decision making.* The most important responsibility of senior managers is to make tough decisions.
- *Delegation.* Down-the-line managers are in a much better position to interpret and adapt top management decisions to their particular circumstances. Furthermore, only if down-the-line managers have ample autonomy will they exercise owner-like initiative and judgment.
- *Management by exception.* Since the top executive can't possibly manage everything that's going on in the organization, he must watch for exceptions: failure of subordinates to execute decisions; failure by the organization to achieve agreed objectives or to adhere to policies, norms, standards and expectations; failure of outside actors—customers, competitors, or others—to behave as they have in the past.

What's wrong with these tenets? Very little in stable times, though they are a bit narrow even then. But they can inhibit top executives from exercising the extent of intensity of leadership that is needed to meet one of the central managerial challenges presented by strategic discontinuities—namely, overcoming deeply ingrained habits, core beliefs, shared values, and entrenched political positions.

THE CHANGE MANAGERS' WAY

How do successful managers of major change cope with these obstacles? The differences between what conventionally good managers do and what successful change managers do at the point of launching a major change program are easiest to describe, but there are important differences before and after the launch as well.

At first glance, the actions of successful change managers do not seem much different. Normally they announce the intended new direction with a good deal of fanfare and accompany it with a substantial organizational shake-up. But on closer examination there are some important differences, even at this early stage. The central message is generally more clear-cut, and is supported by carefully orchestrated drama and symbolism. But people are not just told about the change; they are actively involved in launching it.

Take the example of a major chemical company. Although it was the market-share leader and reasonably profitable, its new product development had virtually dried up. Competitors were gaining an edge with new, high profit-margin specialty chemicals that were taking a large and growing share of the total relevant market. At the same time, the tariff barriers that had protected commodity chemicals were being eroded and imports were gaining ground. To make matters worse, field interviews revealed that the company was distinctly unpopular with many of its customers. It had a history of arrogance in exercising its market power, and the customers welcomed the foreign competition.

The CEO, having spent a good deal to time learning about the problem and pondering what to do about it, made up his mind that a profound change was needed. The company had to raise its sights from maintaining volume to achieving leadership in the growing specialty chemical segment. The shift would require far-reaching changes in managerial approach.

Proclaiming the Goal

To launch the change, the CEO first announced a new objective: "We are going to get close to our customers by offering top service. By understanding their needs better, we will gain leadership in tailor-made, high-margin chemicals."

To reinforce people's understanding of the new objective, the CEO ran a contest for the best slogan to describe the new mission. The winning entry, "The key to our profitability fits our customers' door," made it clear to everyone—including hitherto arrogant engineers—that they would have to collaborate with customers in ways they had never done before.

Next, the CEO, like a conventional manager, shook up his organization. It had been dominated by an old guard of product managers, mainly engineers, who spent most of their time on production logistics and little on marketing. Although this CEO didn't, like some change managers, bring in new managers from the outside or fire his old ones, he did profoundly change the composition of his senior management team. Having identified a group of aggressive, market-aware young managers who were chafing at the loss of customer opportunities through hidebound product management, he created a new group of market-manager positions—organized around industries, not products—put his young Turks into those new slots, and gave them bottom-line accountability, along with authority for new product development and pricing. The old product managers stayed on, but in staff rather than line positions.

Then the CEO went one bold step further. He made his top manufacturing manager the new head of marketing, and shifted his head of marketing into the top manufacturing slot. (There were plenty of knowledgeable manufacturing managers at the second level to keep things running smoothly while the new boss learned his job; and the challenge facing the new marketing head had more to do with determined pursuit of well-defined initiatives with customers than with sophisticated marketing techniques.) Both men objected vehemently, but ambition impelled them to accept the challenge. The former head marketer was soon at home (and well regarded) in his new job, and today the former head of manufacturing runs the company's new-business division and is considered a marketing whiz.

DRAMA AND SYMBOLISM

The CEO's changes had forced a fundamental shift in organizational focus and the power structure. But he did not stop there. At the point of launch—and this is one of the hallmarks of effective change managers—he deliberately used drama and symbolism to drive home the change message. Once the new organization structure had been worked out, and the managers who were slated for new jobs duly informed, he invited the top 75 managers to a "mad-hatters" party at corporate headquarters. As each manager entered, he was given a funny hat somehow befitting his old job. Everyone was then encouraged to trade (or steal) hats until a whistle blew and a draw was held with prizes matching the number hats.

After explaining the symbolism of the changing hats, the CEO distributed a new picture directory, the first the company had ever issued. It opened with a chart of the new organization structure, followed by a half-page for each manager with his photo, a one-line summary of his responsibilities, and his direct phone number.

The CEO mailed his directory to all the company's customers with a personal letter encouraging them to call on anyone in the company any time they needed help. The program, which he dubbed "Operation Access," was a great success with customers. In a blind survey done a year later, 47 percent said they had noticed a significant improvement in service.

The leaders of companies that achieve successful change, then, approach the launch much as a conventionally good manager might do. But they generally go much further to:

- Make it clear to everyone exactly what the new objectives are and how the organization is going to change in order to achieve them.
- Explicitly and unmistakably contrast the old and the new.
- Dramatize the change, in order to increase the probability of emotional as well as intellectual understanding.
- Decisively shift the power structure.

The most interesting and important differences between more and less successful managers to change, however, are evident in the periods before and after the launch.

EARLIER INITIATIVES

In general, successful change managers give a great deal more attention to *how* the need for change is perceived, and *who* becomes involved in the process. Soon after they sense the possibility of a decisive shift in economic and technological forces, they begin calling attention to what they see. The chemical company CEO, for example, began talking about new chemicals that had been developed and marketed competitors.

Even when signs of impending problems are unmistakable, conventional managers often shrink from their implications, hesitating to call attention to them for fear of confusing or demotivating people. The successful change manager, on the other hand, instinctively knows that his people can help him figure out what is really going on with customers and competitors, product technologies and process technologies, and how his company can respond in a winning way. It's obvious to him that he should begin expressing his concerns, focusing other people's attentions on matters that need thought and initiative, and stirring up open and constructive dialogue throughout the organization.

Successful change managers tend to start exploring possible shifts in the competitive environment earlier than conventional managers, and in a wider-ranging way. An industrial goods company sent delegations from its unionized workforce to visit Japanese factories. A frozen food manufacturer, intent on converting its commodity potatoes into a branded good that would command a price premium, picked out one city and conducted intensive market tests of branded products. An electronics company, faced with puzzling consumer reactions in a new market, tried out focus groups for the first time, and asked each of its development engineers to spend at least half a day observing these focus groups live or on videotape. In another company, the CEO invited some important dissatisfied customers to lunch with several members of his management team who had remained unconvinced that they were facing serious problems.

These successful change managers faced up to worrisome phenomena, rather than trying to ignore them. They sought understanding through direct exposure to customers and the market-place rather than relying on detached data-gathering and analysis. They involved large numbers of their people directly, and they shared their concerns and the insights they were gaining with virtually everyone in their companies.

The most striking contrast between the successful change leaders and the conventional managers, however, showed up in the period subsequent to the launching of the change and the concomitant shake-up. Six distinctive differences were particularly marked:

SPREADING THE WORD

First, the successful companies we have studied worked very hard to ensure that key employees, way beyond top management, understood what needed to be done differently. For example, the head of one of the major business groups in a bank pursuing major change held a series of "cascading workshops" down the organizational hierarchy. At the first of these, he and his 10 direct subordinates met off-site for four days. They began by reviewing their new strategy—the result of a year of study, discussion and experimentation. They looked first at those activities in which the bank would have to excel its competitors and decided where they would have to work hardest to develop new organizational capabilities.

Since most of these capabilities would be exercised several levels down in the organization, they next had to figure out how they, the senior management, could best support the new focus and activities. They considered what changes would be required in their planning and control processes, in their information and measurement systems, in their personal approaches to direction and supervision, and in other organizational arrangements. Then each of them, including the top executive, translated the resulting common understanding of their collective role into a personal action plan for the next one, three and nine months. They ended by exchanging personal work plans and, in essence, contracting together to support the shift to the new managerial approach.

Next, each of the 10 held a similar 3-day workshop with his or her own direct subordinates. Again, they worked from an understanding of the new strategy to a concrete definition of how key activities would have to be performed to a superior standard, and then to how each person would have to do his own job differently. In turn, these third-level people drew their direct reports together in 2-day workshops. And so on. In this way everyone gained a keen awareness of precisely what changes in organizational performance were called for, and what each person's role would be in bringing them about.

Another company, an electronic equipment manufacturer, focused immediately on the three key front-line jobs that would be most critical in actually delivering value to the customer under its new vertical-marketing strategy: (1) account representatives for major customers, (2) service supervisors, and (3) project managers for high-priority systems development projects.

This company put together project teams to translate its overall value proposition for each vertical-market segment into specific values to be delivered by people in each of the three key positions. To deliver the new value, what would people in each key job do differently? Whom should they be working with? How should they be using their time? What were the main activities in which they should engage? What new skills did they need?

With the answers in hand, the project teams then identified the main influences on the performance of those jobs—compensation approach, objective-setting processes, supervisory direction and support, training, information, and so on. For each, the teams designed the specific changes that would be necessary in order to influence and support front-line job holders to do their jobs in the desired way.

In this way the chief executive made sure that his new strategy would be executed as intended. He took the trouble to ensure that people on the front line of value delivery to the customer understood the new strategy, knew what they were expected to do to make it work, and work appropriately directed, influenced and supported in their redesigned jobs.

SHOWCASING THE CHANGE

Second, the successful companies sought early opportunities to demonstrate how they intended to work differently. One company put together a special team, protected from normal organizational influences and controls, to work with three customers in a new way.

Another created a pilot region in which it began realizing its new vision in practice. A third began redesigning jobs in one plant for radically increased flexibility. It eliminated an entire level of supervision so as to encourage self-management and involve people intensively in identifying and implementing ideas for improving productivity.

Such early initiatives enable an organization to learn from real experience how best to modify and adapt its new approach. But they serve another critically important purpose: Most people, if they are to envision concretely what is being asked of them, let alone abandon their tried-and-true approaches in favor of new work patterns, need to see and feel the possibility of success through doing things differently.

To permit effective experimentation and demonstration, these early initiatives were always carefully insulated or "cocooned" from normal organizational processes that might have forced the participants back into the old patterns. In most cases, those involved later played a major part in rolling out the new approaches among their peers across the organization.

The basic point here is that successful change managers seem to reject, or at least go beyond, the conventional "trickle-down" theory of hierarchical management in favor of directly engaging the people—regardless of their organization level—who will actually have to do things differently. Intensive direct influence is often necessary in order to replace deep-set patterns of thinking and action. Otherwise, there is likely to be a progressive waterdown of vision and commitment at each level of the hierarchy.

SHAKING UP STRUCTURES

Third, successful companies worked very aggressively to change standard operating procedures—"the way we do things around here." Unlike many conventional managers, their leaders understood that no single model of good management applies everywhere; that organizational and managerial approaches, as well as strategies and objectives and actual make-and-sell activities must change, if people are to be led actually to do things differently.

The successful companies went much farther than most others, therefore, to influence people's behavior through extensive organizational redesign, usually with widespread participation of those involved:

- *Structure:* They not only altered top management reporting relationships, but also took pains to change the actual content of jobs at almost every level of the organization. And they tended to worry not just about the formal organizational structure, but also about informal mechanisms such as cross-functional work teams, special project approaches, and routine use of special assignments.

- *Systems:* Because they understood that the pattern of management systems and processes largely shapes what people actually do, they tended to invest substantial effort in redesigning compensation systems, information systems, performance review processes, planning and budgeting and control processes, and the like.
- *Staff:* Quite often the successful companies replaced managers in key positions, often bringing in outsiders. In doing so, they were remarkably attentive to professional values and working styles as well as to managerial and technical competence; they looked not just for new expertise, but for mentors and capability-builders.

LEADING TO CHARGE

Fourth, top managers in the successful companies played remarkably active, visible roles in the change process for extended periods, rather than backing off after a few months in order to let their subordinates "get on with it." Typically, they built trusted teams of up to six top managers who collectively led the effort, but they themselves kept close to the action.

For example, in each of the first three years after launching a major change program, the CEO and president of an industrial equipment manufacturer each made 50 visits to plants, distribution centers and other work sites. After walking around and talking individually with front line workers at least five management levels below them, they got all the employees together at shift changes, beginning each such meeting with the statement, "We are in business to make money for our shareholders." A provocative assertion, perhaps, to make before a highly unionized workforce; but successful change managers play absolutely straight with their people, and—as the speaker would go on to point out—since most workers were shareholders, this objective was in their interest.

More straight talk followed, on automation. "It's clear now that we're in a war for jobs, and there will be winners and losers. Will our foreign competitors win our jobs, or will we hold on to them?" Winning the war would require major automation and therefore major investment. If the company started now and pushed very aggressively, it could accomplish this automation without having to put any of its current workers on the street, though ultimately the workforce would be much reduced. But the company could win only if workers kept examining their jobs and operations for opportunities to reduce costs and raise productivity. Many improvements could and would be accomplished in familiar ways, through work reorganization, equipment modifications and the like. But others would involved extensive automation. To start his audience thinking about concrete opportunities for improvement, the top executive would then get down to specifics—inventory costs, labor costs per unit of output, and so on.

The reasoning behind this effort was simple. For a company to achieve fundamental change—e.g., succeed in achieving major productivity improvements through automation that would profoundly affect processes and jobs everywhere—the people on the front line, like those above them, need to think and act very differently from before. But it is rarely possible to accomplish this pervasive change by fully transforming the top level first, translating that into change at the next level, and so on. Everyone needs to change more or less simultaneously. Moreover, in an important sense the intervening layers of management are no more than facilitating devices for the value generation and delivery that is occurring on the front line. And often the best way to get change at the intermediate levels as well as on the front line is to push change strongly at the bottom as well as at the top.

Yet another reason for intensive top management involvement is that only by being in touch with the front line—observing and listening for ideas he can use to reinforce, redirect and revitalize the organization—can the CEO really know how the change is going.

PROVIDING INCENTIVES

Fifth, these top managers made real efforts to help people feel good about the change process. They established awards and other incentives; for example, when someone in the chemical company went an extra mile for a customer, his name and picture were posted at the main office and entrance, he received dinner or theater tickets. They looked for "small wins"—a first-time sale to an attractive target customer, development of an early prototype of a new product designed to meet emerging market needs, even a meeting held in a desired new way—and broadcast their success widely.

REWRITING THE AGENDA

Sixth, in successful companies managing the change program actually becomes the top management agenda. Once they have launched a change program, conventional managers will continue to talk it up from time to time. But since they still have to keep costs down, find new customers, and run a business that is expected to generate quarterly earnings, the change program soon takes a back seat to other, seemingly more pressuring concerns. Soon, business-as-usual topics—shipments, run rates, downtimes, unit costs—are again the main focus of top managers' regular operating meetings and conversations with subordinates and others in the field.

In successful companies, by contrast, top managers not only continue to talk up the change program. They constantly emphasize it as the most important priority in the company, they find ways to highlight what is new and contrast it with what used to be, and they tie expectations of future success to effective adoption of the new ways. Moreover, they seem to devote at least half, and often more, of their time and attention to meetings to the progress of the change program—reviewing the progress of each specific change project, asking whether it fully reflects the spirit of the needed changes, and what needs to be done to push it forward. Have the people in the Milwaukee plant "brought" the change program? What can we do to clear up misunderstanding and resistance in the field sales force? Are there any signs yet that our System K customers notice the difference? Is the problem in R & D simply a reflection of poor project management, or does it signal a fundamental misunderstanding of what we're trying to accomplish?

This mental set, reaching far beyond regular operating reviews, seems a common focus among successful change managers. Often they temporarily jettison standard planning or budgeting approaches in order to focus on issues critical to the success of the change program. Usually they set up a parallel management structure, making specified people responsible for bringing about specific changes in support of the overall program. Some even introduce a formal change-monitoring system:

- Are our top managers doing what they should to lead this change effort? What are they spending time on? What is the pattern of their decisions?
- Are others getting the idea—first-level and middle management and then the front line? Are they starting to change what they are doing? How far? What is the next step? Are there pockets of incomprehensive or resistance?
- Are customers noticing? What do they think? Are their attitudes toward us changing?
- Are we beginning to see a tangible impact on cooperation with customers, on new product development, on sales to new customers, on profitability?

This final feature of successful change management is the critical distinction which, in effect, encapsulates all the others. In a company that is changing successfully, the dominant management approach shifts, in effect, from the "standard operating procedure" mode of business-as-usual to something very like the mega-project management mode of a company like Bechtel or Fluor or Boeing.

ORGANIZATIONAL LEARNING

There is, however, one significant difference: Bechtel, Fluor and Boeing already know now to orchestrate the massive, complex, extended, one-time projects that are the mainstays of their business. In contrast, the successful change manager is not only a mega-project manager, but the leader of a giant organizational learning process. He is guiding the organization as it figures out what is going on in its changing environment, how it can change what it is doing in order to compete successfully in that environment, what lessons it can draw from each attempt to do something differently, and how these lessons can be translated into effective new patterns of activity. At the same time, along with the others he enlists, he is trying to help people to understand their work environment in a new way—to set aside old perspectives, old habits of thinking, and old approaches to their work in favor of new ones.

Few successful change managers seem to be satisfied that they have done all the direction-setting—all the planning and specifying and prescribing—that is needed. Most of them seem confident that they know broadly how their competitive environment is going to change, and where and how their organizations will be able to compete successfully, but they are less clear about how to translate broad direction into specifics. They know that they must constantly and aggressively seek deeper insights into the competitive environment, into what customers value and will respond to, what competitors and suppliers will do in the new circumstances, what their own organization is capable of achieving, and so on. Equally, most of them seem much more attuned than the conventional good manager to helping their people, as individuals, to learn to see things in new ways, to break old habits and try out new patterns of behavior. This kind of learning orientation, it seems to me, is the essential basis for changing successfully and winning in the face of really profound changes in competitive circumstances.

In counterposing "conventionally good management" and "successful change management," I have tried in interpret fairly what I have observed in a large number of companies that were facing truly profound change after a long period of good performance, achieved by conventionally good management in more or less stable times. But even in times of stability or evolutionary change, I believe that the best managerial model is closer to the "learning approach" that I have described as successful change management. In my view, most companies today—whether or not they are yet under pressure from emerging discontinuities—would be wise to recast their managerial approaches along these lines. Even in a stable environment, the change might enable them to manage more effectively, and it could prove their salvation in more turbulent times. ■

Do Your Managers Really Manage?

Charles R. Day Jr.

Too often, managers duck decisions and neglect people as they shuffle papers and crunch numbers. Too few are held accountable for their actions, critics say. And too many fear responsibility.

Is the company to blame?

The episode has been forever branded in Robert Grasing's memory. A management consultant, Mr. Grasing had presented his corporate client with 15 specific recommendations to improve its operations. After reviewing them, a senior executive agreed that at least ten were sound ideas.

"But he quickly made it clear that he wasn't about to adopt any of them, because they would require taking some risks," recounts Mr. Grasing, vice president of Robert E. Nolan Co., Simsbury, Conn. He vividly remembers the executives telling him: "I got to where I am today by not making mistakes. I survived."

Surviving, though isn't managing. Neither is the paper shuffling and the number crunching that fill many a managerial agenda. And when confronted with the broader question—*Are managers really managing today?*—the response of a host of respected critics is all too crisp:

No.

"Obviously, they are not, and you know that as well as I do," snaps Dr. Ray O. Werner, professor of economics at Colorado College, Colorado Springs. "What's needed today are managers who can ask: *What do people want? How can you deliver it? And what happens if you don't?* We don't have managers who ask that," he insists.

Not everyone is guilty as charged, of course. The dozen experts who addressed the issue can readily point to shining examples of executive action. All told, though, their appraisals stand as compelling evidence that too many managers today aren't worthy of the title. The ineffective managers stand accused of:

- Lacking the skills necessary to motivate, train, and communicate with people.
- Failing to fully understand their business operations.
- Perpetuating and responding to an outdated reward system that discourages innovation and risk-taking.
- Wallowing in oceans of data that seldom tell managers what they really need to know.

ROSEN
"People will respond to high targets, and respect each other more when they are held to them."

INSUFFICIENT

The technical skills and "staff expertise" that managers possess is widely praised. But that's not enough, contends Dr. Warren Bennis, professor of management at the University of Southern California, because the emphasis on such skills has given birth to a "generation of incrementalists—people who are good at the routine. But they fail to motivate people to do better," he says.

Dr. Bennis, who has advised the last four Administrations in Washington, recently complete a study of chief executives of 90 major U.S. companies. He concludes that "no more than 20%" are truly leading their companies.

To charge managers with failing to get the best out of their people is a stinging indictment. After all, motivating employees is their premier task. Yet, of some 125 shortcomings identified by IW sources, 77 (over 61%) are people-related. (The others have to do with organizational problems, technical skills, and the tendency to seek quick fixes.)

One cause of this problem stems, perhaps, from a shift in the nation's workday collars from blue to white. For example, the auto industry's whitecollar staffs doubled from 1950 to 1980, while the number of production workers fell 16%. David Kearns, president and CEO of Xerox Corp., Stamford, Conn., suggests that managements have neither recognized nor responded to the *attitudinal* changes—toward work, organizational life, and bosses—extant among better-educated workers.

As a result, managers face a decidedly different workforce today, one that often challenges traditional managerial axioms, Workers' unwillingness to blindly follow orders is but one reflection of the difference. Thus, veteran managers are simply being overwhelmed, while younger ones schooled in specific disciplines—law, finance, technology—are not much better equipped.

But some leaders, aware of the problem, are attempting credible solutions. One, a direct result of mushrooming whitecollar employment, is the two-career ladder. "It's a professional ladder" which serves as an alternative to the traditional management ladder, explains Richard D. Calmes, vice president for personnel and industrial relations at American Motors Corp., Southfield, Mich. Technical and professional employees climb it by honing their skills and increasing their knowledge, earning recognition, and sometimes pay, equal to that in management.

Not long ago, for instance, Mr. Calmes asked a young personnel analyst to present a study to the automaker's board. "Just doing that was a big thing for that individual. It brought him recognition, helped his career, and stimulated others," he says. "And it didn't cost [the company] a nickel."

However, too many companies neglect the recognition factor, and cling to the notion that money alone motivates people. In truth, money may not even be No. 1. The former co-director of the White House Conference on productivity, I. William Seidman, determined that the leading motivator is personal satisfaction—not dollars.

ARCHAIC, CREAKING CONTRAPTIONS

Critics of management fire some of their most scathing denouncements at the ultimate citadel of management: the board of directors.

Retired ITT Corp. CEO Harold Geneen dismisses it as an "archaic, creaking contraption" that seldom does what it's charged with doing: review company operations and pass judgment on management's performance. Instead, he declares in his book, *Managing,* boards have become "captives" of the very executives they are supposed to audit.

"The vitality and juices seem to have seeped out of the top layer of management and are being replaced by dry rot and procedures that smack of plodding bureaucracy," he charges. All in all, "boards of directors of U.S. companies include numerous first-rate people doing what amounts to a second-rate job."

Lee Iacocca, too, chides the former board of Chrysler Corp. for allegedly standing idly by while a giant corporation came apart at the seams. As he relates in his autobiography, he could only wonder what in the world the directors were doing before he took over the automaker's reins.

Mr. Geneen suggests a simple remedy for what he sees as a crippled corporate machine: Get rid of all internal directors—including the CEO. Top executives should attend board meetings, he submits, but only to advise and answer questions. Even his own tenure as both board chairman and CEO of ITT, he says in retrospect, "was not fair to the interests of the stockholders."

TOO LITTLE PARTICIPATION

Bringing employees into the decision-making process is one method that some managers are using as a motivational tool. Yet, many others "make decisions beforehand, and seek opinions afterward," laments Paul R. Sullivan, senior vice president, Harbridge House Inc., a Boston-based consulting firm. There was sad evidence of that not long ago in Detroit when an eager executive was admonished that "people get ahead in this company by waiting to hear what their supervisors think, then working to support that decision."

That tack just won't fly anymore, nor should it, reasons Lee Iacocca in his recent autobiography. Employees, he reminds, strive "to help achieve goals they helped shape." Yet, he says, "too few executives let their people run with the ball."

Adds Mr. Seidman, now Dean of Arizona State's College of Business Administration: "There are still too many companies that see workers as either the enemy or a commodity item. That's simply the wrong approach."

Both individual managers and their organizations must shoulder the blame for the malaise they find themselves in today, contends Mr. Sullivan. "Many managers fear responsibility," he states flatly. "They don't understand how their decisions will impact other facets of the business because they don't fully understand the business itself."

Colorado College's Dr. Werner, who heartily concurs, holds graduate business school facilities responsible, castigating them for drumming nothing but financial expertise and short-term thinking into their students.

Dean Seidman also fears that too little attention has been paid to such functions as "purchasing, logistics, material handling, and the like, which tie up a bundle of money." And Harold Geneen, the former legendary—if controversial—CEO of ITT Corp., faults business schools for spending too much time on mechanics and too little on the "emotional values of good management."

For whatever reason, failure to grasp the entire corporate picture often paralyzes managers. They delay decisions or "delegate them 'up' to a higher level, when, in fact, the decisions should be made then and there," says Harbridge House's Mr. Sullivan.

Managers are afraid to make mistakes, adds Robert MacAvoy, a partner with Easton Consulting Inc., Stamford, Conn., in part because "they aren't allowed to be wrong very often, if at all. This stems, he believes, from the unfounded notion that management is a "science." According to that approach, he says, "anything not in the equations is ignored. And when things don't go the way they are supposed to on paper, someone is blamed."

OF LITTLE FAITH

Unwillingness to take risks is often a sign that the organization lacks trust in its managers and won't let them manage. Mr. Sullivan also believes. Moreover, senior executives often are reluctant to delegate "because they feel they must be involved in many decisions, so they can report to *their* bosses." In turn, second-guessing flourishes, adds Mr. MacAvoy.

The budgeting ritual is a case in point, consultant Mr. Grasing says. Managers are annually expected to present accurate budgets, "after which they are told by others not close to the situation to cut them by 15%. So budgeting becomes a game in itself," he concludes. "Yet, even after a budget has been approved, managers still have to undergo more scrutiny for any expenditure over a given sum of money." Why? The answer escapes him. "If the budget has been approved, why does there have to be yet another set of controls?"

One answer, theorizes Mr. Sullivan, may be found in the history of the U.S. space program. "Major contractors had to live in a 100% failproof environment. There was absolutely no room for errors," he points out. "For many, I suspect, it looked like a good way to run *any* business."

Another reason why managers are stifled: there are too many of them: Xerox's Mr. Kearns notes that the U.S. has by far the highest ratio of managers to workers. "Business always tries to solve problems by throwing more managers at them," he says "What's needed is not more, but better."

SULLIVAN

"I remember an engineering executive who felt that he had no time for people concerns, that his job was purely a technical one. The truth is, his job was to make sure he had the right people on board doing the right things to get the technical job done."

CALMES

"We still too often have a narrow view of what turns people on. In many cases, it's not money, and managers don't realize (there are) other ways to motivate."

Building layer upon flabby layer of management has squeezed innovation out of corporations and clogged communications channels. "To succeed today, you must be able to articulate clearly your goals throughout your organization," stresses Edward I. Rosen, co-founder, president, and CEO of Ziyad Inc., a Denville, N. J. manufacturer of computerized office products. Multilayered managements make that terribly difficult, if not impossible—and they waste money.

Not only do these layers swell operating costs, but they also give rise to what USC's Dr. Bennis calls the *Pinocchio effect.* Just as storyland's Geppetto crafted the marionette Pinocchio, uncertain of what he would look like upon completion, creators of ideas seldom recognize the final results—simply because communications become tangled.

"Not only that," says Colorado College's Dr. Werner, "many ideas are never even acted upon, because someone along the line thinks the short-term costs aren't worth it."

SOUR SYSTEMS

Reward systems themselves, critics further charge, continue to beget "short-term thinking" and decisions, despite vows to the contrary. Compensation systems based on the "bell curve," for instance, typically allow a manager to properly reward only a select few employees, says Mr. Grasing. "To take care of other equally deserving people, he has to create overtime, or concoct other devices, which everyone can see through."

Other pay systems, like those based on a manager's "span of control" (i.e., the number of workers reporting to him), discourage managers from streamlining operations. "A manager may be able to cut the number of positions he controls and still achieve the desired results—to improve profits and productivity," he explains. "But that will effectively cut; his compensation, so he doesn't.

Results themselves are another sore spot with management's critics. Too often, managers aren't held accountable when goals aren't attained, mainly because "nobody makes them do it," chides Mr. Geneen in his book *Managing*, published by Doubleday in 1984. "Explanations and rationalizations are too readily accepted," he says. "Indeed, they are even expected." Thus, companies set lofty goals even though everyone knows that hitting just 80% of them will be acceptable. "Even if someone exceeds that 80%, sales will be hidden so that they can be used next year," Mr. Geneen observes.

Ziyad's Mr. Rosen believes that such practices are counterproductive. "People will respond to high targets, and respect each other more when they are held to them."

The lack of good "qualitative measures" of managerial performance is lamented by others. At the very least, appraisals should consider the long-term effects of executive decisions, but almost none do. Too few managers, in fact, accept the idea that there even are qualitative aspects to an evaluation, consultant Mr. MacAvoy believes.

That reflects, in part, poor corporate recruiting efforts, contends Colorado College's Dr. Werner. Industry is not getting the talent it needs, he says. Instead, it just accepts what it is getting. He suspects that company recruiters don't know what top management really wants. He recalls a recent visit by a

U.S. Steel Corp. recruiter to his campus. The recruiter refused to talk with anyone except business administration majors. "But those types are too narrow to deliver the broad-based skills and understanding that business now needs," Dr. Werner believes.

Corporate recruiting and promotion practices are weak, agrees consultant Mr. Grasing. But weaker still are the training programs available to managers once they're hired, if they're available at all. "In too many cases," Mr. Grasing says, "managers are put in a position and it is simply hoped that they will do well."

NEGLECTED TASK

Some observers suspect that business is putting far too much faith in M.B.A. degrees and college training, while managers themselves "misunderstand" their responsibilities as teachers, says Harbridge House's Mr. Sullivan. "I remember an engineering executive who felt that he had no time for people concerns, that his job was purely a technical one. The truth is, his job was to make sure he had the right people on board doing the right things to get the technical job done."

Managers might have more time for people if they weren't, as Mr. Iacocca says, "so weighted down with information."

That's one of the real problems, Dean Seidman believes. "We are measuring everything today, but we have to better manage the ability to gather information. Measures alone are just a barometer." The sheer volume of information today, adds USC's Dr. Bennis, "often obscures the meaning."

Xerox CEO Kearns blames management as a whole for the numbers glut. "There's no clear purpose of sense of mission in the office," he says. "Offices are not organized to produce or manage information in a meaningful way." (Lest one think that Mr. Kearns has a particular ax to grind, he also stresses that automation for its own sake leads to disaster.)

Even Mr. Geneen, who possessed a capacious appetite for numbers, says numbers themselves aren't important. Their real value is what they reveal about the business and what needs to be done.

At some point, states Mr. Iacocca, managers have got to put numbers aside "and take that leap of faith." They have to act.

Mr. Geneen puts it another way—forcefully: "Managing means to manage! You must be in control of your operations. If something goes wrong, you probe until you find the cause, and if one solution does not work, you try another, and another, and another. . . ."

A story told by Mr. Geneen about an ITT European manager makes one wonder if the same initiative and common sense would have prevailed in a U.S. manager. The overseas manager was struggling to rein in soaring inventory costs. After a variety of sophisticated measures had failed, the manager appointed someone to stand at the company loading dock. His instructions were simple and non-computerized: Reject any item that had not been ordered.

It worked like a charm. ■

The Decline and Fall of Business Ethics

Myron Magnet

Beyond Ivan Boesky and Dennis Levine, a profit-at-any-price malaise is spreading through investment banking and reaching into other industries as well.

Perhaps a $100-million SEC penalty—the biggest ever—doesn't make arbitrager Ivan Boesky the all-time biggest crook. Yet a special contempt attaches to an insider trader who had strutted round the business schools and even published a respectfully received book claiming not just that his takeover-related predations were a high public service but also that they required an insight bordering on clairvoyance. Some crystal ball he had. Properly appalled, the business community anxiously wonders how much corruption lies beyond Boesky, how rotten is the investment banking trade that fed him his tainted secrets, and how riddled with wrong-doing is today's business world.

What is this—the business news or the crime report? Turn over one stone and out crawls Boesky's tipster, investment banker Dennis Levine, dirt clinging to his $12.6-million insider-trading profits. Turn over another and there's a wriggling tangle of the same slimy creatures, from minute grubs like the Yuppie Gang to plump granddads like jailed former Deputy Defense Secretary Paul Thayer. A shovel plunged into the ground above General Electric recently disclosed a bustling colony industriously faking time sheets to overcharge the government on defense contracts. Almost everywhere you look in the business world today, from the E. F. Hutton check-kiting scheme to the Bank of Boston money-laundering scandal, you glimpse something loathsome scuttling away out of the corner of your eye.

It's not just illegality. As if trapped by a thermal inversion, the ethical atmosphere of business, some executives mutter, is growing acrid. Says private investor and Fordham business school dean Arthur Taylor: "I can't do transactions on the telephone any more because people do not keep their word." Adds leverage-buy out panjandrum Jerome Kohlberg of Kohlberg

Reprinted with permission from *Fortune*, Vol. 114, pp. 65 ff., December 8, 1986.
REPORTER ASSOCIATE *Margaret A. Elliot*

Kravis Roberts: "Agreements have got to be in writing, and writing is itself subject to interpretation." Laments Merle J. Bushkin, president of an investment banking boutique bearing his name: "I used to think that I could tell good guys from bad guys, and wouldn't deal with people I thought dishonest or unethical. But I've learned that I can't tell the difference. They look alike."

Not that Boy Scouts have always run American business: The Robber Barons didn't earn that name through philanthropy. But some eras are faster and looser than others, and in this one—at least in matters concerning the vast restructuring of U.S. industry now under way—the business climate has become less ethical than it was in the relatively aboveboard period from the Depression's end until the mid-Seventies.

No place have standards dropped more vertiginously than in the investment banking trade that is presiding over this restructuring. While other areas of business are in most respects no more unethical than ever, wrongdoing in this central arena makes a crisis of business ethics seem in full swing. And with investment banking now largely manned by the young, is the erosion of ethics here an early warning of imminent trouble elsewhere in business as this generation rises to power?

Insider trading is investment banking's most widely publicized sin, and since extrasensory perception alone doesn't explain why the stock price of takeover targets regularly rises in advance of official announcement, doubtless plenty of insider traders besides Boesky's confederate Levine remain uncaught. But much more pervasive, if less heralded, is the unscrupulousness that now infects relations with clients. Says Herbert A. Allen Jr., president of the Allen & Cop. Inc., investment banking firm: "A major disquieting factor is the loss of confidentiality, well short of illegality. Important clients can find out anything about other important clients."

Formerly circumspect investment bankers now routinely trade confidential information, hoping to glean tips leading to new business. Information seeps out to other clients, too. In one example, a company preparing to go public to raise capital suddenly found itself faced with an unwelcome tender offer from another client of the investment banker arranging the stock offering.

Company chiefs are becoming understandably skittish about entrusting themselves to such leaky vessels. One divisional chief executive, hoping to buy his company out from its corporate parent, almost *froze* with fear when the time came to hire investment bankers to help structure the deal. If his boss discovered his plans before he could present the proposal in detail, he feared he'd be thought a traitor and get fired. "Here I am being asked to put my life in the hands of these people," he confided to Emory University business school professor Joseph McCann, "and for all I know the guy on the other end of the line is Dennis Levine."

This was no idle worry: such leaks have proven catastrophic. When management was trying to take U.S. Industries private in 1984, one of the investment bankers in the deal let out word that the company was for sale before the management group had lined up financing. The stock began to rise, and ultimately Britain's Hanson Trust snatched the company from under its astonished managers, compounding the injury by firing most of them as an economy move. A knowledgeable insider believes that the leaky banker, fearing that management might yet back off from the deal and assured by contract that the board would pay his firm if the company was sold to *anybody,* deliberately put U.S. Industries in play to guarantee the fee.

Perhaps, or maybe it was just an accident. But in many instances investment bankers haven't scrupled to work against their clients by putting them in play when that looked more profitable than working for them. A veteran of one august firm says of his colleagues: "When they speak ethics, you'd think they've worn white gloves all their lives. But these days they'll sell their clients out for a couple of million bucks in fees." Typically, says this veteran, you look over your client list, picking out a company that appears vulnerable. Somebody's going to put him in play, you sign philosophically, so we'd better do it first—and accordingly you shop his company around his back.

A senior member of a more demonic firm reports a common variation on this technique. You tell a client who has come to you for some simple bankerly service that a raider is about to put his company in play and he'd better be scared; you gallantly offer your services in his defense: and then you look for a buyer yourself. "They take a healthy patient that walks in and make a cadaver," says this investment banker. "It happens so quick that the victim doesn't even know it's going on." Rather than snatching a client's company an investment banker might merely snatch his deal. Former ITT chief Harold Geneen and ex-Norton Simon chairman David Mahoney, for instance, recently came to Drexel Burnham Lambert to get financing for their proposed purchase of a W. R. Grace retail unit. To Geneen's outrage, another group—with close ties to Drexel and financed by the firm—ended up with the unit instead, after seeing, Geneen believes, the voluminous analysis of the unit's value that he had prepared and given to Drexel. (FORTUNE was unable to reach Drexel for comment.)

Clients contribute to the appearance of conflict of interest that hangs over some routine investment banking practices. When they hire firms to give fairness opinions on the terms of a deal, they conventionally pay a small retainer, with the bulk payable when the fairness letter is put into the proxy statement—where only a favorable letter can appear if the deal is to succeed. Or they hire firms to advise on whether to do a particular deal and how to structure it, with the fee contingent on the successful completion of the very deal whose wisdom is at issue.

Troubling, too, in terms of the appearance of conflict of interest is the investment banker's increasing propensity to turn up on all sides of a deal. In the pending sale of an equity stake in Western Union to Pacific Asset Holdings, Drexel not only advised the seller but also raised the financing for the buyer, and outfit, moreover, that includes among its partners Drexel junk bond start Michael Milken and other present and former Drexel employees, It's all perfectly legal, of course.

For potential buyers, the auction process by which companies often get sold has become what one leveraged-buyout specialist calls "a nightmare of back-room dealing." Lucky you, you're the high bidder for Transylvania Airlines, and the investment banker running the auction says, "You've won, but you just need to sweeten your bid a little to make it totally palatable to the seller." So you up your offer, and regardless of what he's told you, the banker invites another high bidder to top it, and so on, all with jet speed and steam-engine pressure. "You can't believe anything anyone tells you in the process," says the leveraged-buyout specialist; who, like some other former participants, refuses to play the auction game again. Sums up Lazard Freres partner Felix Rohatyn: "The big business community views all investment bankers now as a bunch of samurais who will do anything for money."

What happened to turn a once sedate, gentlemanly business into such a free-for all? The takeover movement fueled the change by pouring great gouts of money into investment banking and attracting hordes of aspirants to hold their buckets under the golden shower. The huge and numerous deals in turn produced such lightning stock appreciation that some quiet trading on your insider knowledge could make you seriously rich.

Changes in the structure of the business also have eroded standards of behavior. When clients pushed investment banks to buy up whole issues of their securities for later resale, most of the major private firms of 15 years ago gained access to the need capital by going public or selling out to big public companies. With that, each lost a measure of its distinctive character, along with the proprietary willingness to identify self-interest with the firm's interest, a willingness that used to characterize partners and those who knew that behaving like a partner was a good way to become one. Now even bigger and more bureaucratic, firms inspire still less loyalty. "Conscience is a fragile thing," says Dr. Abraham Zaleznik, a psychoanalyst and Harvard Business School professor. "It needs support from institutions, and that support is weakening.

With hopping from firm to firm becoming common employees often think of their mission as doing as well for themselves as they can in the three to five years they spend on average at any given place. "These people see themselves as baseball free agents, not as belonging to anything larger than themselves that they feel a responsibility to protect," says Samuel L. Hayes

III, investment banking professor at the Harvard Business School. Most junior investment bankers don't care what their firm's relationship with Mega Inc. will be two years hence. Their goals is to get the Mega deal done now, without worrying how Mega, or their own firm's reputation, will fare thereafter.

Loyalty between firms and clients has weakened no less conspicuously. Fifteen years ago, corporations still had long-term relationships with one or perhaps two investment bankers. The chief executive—often a company founder—dealt directly with the investment bank's chief, himself often a founder of his firm and frequently a member of his client's board. But when the SEC's adoption of self registration in 1982 made it possible to issue securities almost in a rote manner, which in turn allowed clients to force investment banks to compete on price, all that began to change.

The clients' focus moved from the relationship to the individual transaction: who could do it cheapest, and since investment banks have different areas of expertise, who could do more complicated deals best? As had already happened with their commercial bankers, companies pushed to have loose connections with five or six investment banks, from whom, they would buy particular services, depending on the particular deal. "The ethical equation has changed, because neither the adviser nor the client sees himself committed and held to the same standards as he did when the relationship was different," says Lazard's Rohatyn. Of course, not just honor kept you from behaving unethically in the days of stable relationships. Says Jerome Kohlberg of the black sheep: "Nobody would do business with you. Misconduct would hit you right in the pocketbook."

Twenty years ago, when investment bankers started at $9,000 a year, firms also felt less goaded to keep their new hires in perpetual motion than these days, when their numbers are legion and they start at up to $100,000. "There weren't the same hungry mouths needing a worm stuffed down them every day," says Harvard's Samuel Hayes. What's more, the deal being done now is much likelier to be a hostile takeover than two decades ago, when aggression in takeovers was less respectable. "Taking the gloves off," says Hayes, "creates an environment in which corners can be cut."

Because investment banking has become so competitive, so dependent on innovation, it has had to open itself to talent more than in the past, when a genteel oligarchy manned it. "The bottom quarter of the Yale class wasn't so bright," says Fordham's Arthur Taylor, "but it did share a sense of family and a sense of obligation." One mustn't romanticize this class's gentlemanly code—this wasn't a bunch of Sir Galahads, and few expansively lived out the ideals Groton or Exeter tried to teach them. But for all the oligarchy's snobbish exclusivity, it did promote a measure of probity and honor. The recruits that investment banking has attracted to its new meritocracy truly are the talented: business is this generation's hot career, and investment banking the hottest part of it. What they often lack is the ethic that belonged not to the business but to the class that once ran it.

They have their own ethic, and it centers on money, as is increasingly true for the ethic off the culture at large. "Where we saw the Eighties money is the thing," says Hayes. For the get-rich-quick mergers and acquisitions generation, it sometimes seems that money is the only value. "The people with the most money are admired regardless of how they achieved it," says James Schreiber, a New York Lawyer who specializes in cases involving securities fraud. The investment banking boom gives these people their chance to be rich, and they are taking it. "For them, it's money *now,*" says one of their elders in the business. "It's Las Vegas."

It's hard to know where they would get what used to be thought of as mainstream values, given schools that strive to be so inoffensively value-neutral that they shrink from telling pupils that it was God the Pilgrims were giving thanks to, or colleges that teach—when they teach anything beyond their preprofessional curriculum—that everything is relative, or a television culture celebrating instant gratification. It's hard to know where the new people would acquire a strong sense of responsibility for their actions when two of the chief social ideas they have been raised with are that the cause of wrongdoing is the economic or psychological environment of the wrongdoer and that it is right to hire and promote people not because of their personal merit but because they come from a particular group.

The ethic they have, half articulate but deeply felt, takes the idea of the free market and turns an economic theory into a personal moral code, making nonsense of reasonable propositions by exaggeration and distortion. "Okay," the rising generation says, "the mechanism of the market insures that each individual, pursuing his own interest in his own way, will augment the wealth of the nation, thereby advancing the public interest by self-interest. That means that whatever I do in my own race for wealth—spill this company's secrets or put that one into play or lie to a third—is fine. It is only mistaken sentimentality to say that these things are wrong." Observes Getty Foundation chief and ex Norton Simon C. E. O. Harold Williams: "The concept of 'Let the market govern' relieves one of one's sense of responsibility."

Members of the post-1975 generation of investment bankers don't sense that what they do advances the common weal only in some abstract, distant way. In fact, in their view they directly confer a vital social benefit. American industry fell behind in the Seventies, they reasonably argue, because overregulation and a national emphasis on redistribution rather than production of wealth shackled competitiveness. But then they expand this point—and pervert it. "Rejecting talk of small is beautiful and eras of limitations," they argue, "our generation stuck with this mess, rolled up its sleeves. Now, directed by investment bankers like us, and often opposed by contemptible entrenched managements whose barren stodginess and porcine presumption helped make the country uncompetitive, U.S. industry is restructuring to be lean and strong, as changed conditions require. Only the strong and realistic survive in this competitive world—and you have to be strong and realistic as a nation, a company, and an individual."

But here the ethic turns into social Darwinism, and an appropriate tough-mindedness becomes mere hardness. "Part of the ethic is that the strong were meant to prevail over the weak, and the strong just do not have responsibility," says Fordham's Taylor. They can do what they want, and their success proves they were right to do it.

And how can what they do be wrong when they work so hard, with such virtuous self-denial? For the ethic of this new generation of investment bankers retains a nub of the Protestant ethic in its emphasis on hard work and dedication, if not to calling," at least to a career. Paradoxically, that virtue can turn into a license to misbehave. The 100-hour weeks, the lack of time for social or family life, the continual pressure, all breed resentment. "It's an inhuman way of life. You're at the firm's beck and call," says Dr. Mary Ann Goodman, a New York psychoanalyst. "There comes to be a feeling that they owe you—there's no way that they can repay what you've given up." Adds Harvard's Zaleznik, "This leads to a sense of entitlement that weakens the conscience."

This may well be part of what drives people beyond the unethical into the illegal. But psychoanalysts think that what pushes some insider traders over the line, beyond mere greed, is a more primitive wish to flirt with danger, like stunt drivers. "As long as they're winning, they don't feel there's anything to stop them," says Goodman. "Clinically speaking," adds Zaleznik, "these people are fighting off major depressions" stemming from the "fear of being unloved, unlovable, and worthless."

Even their greed isn't always simple, as in the recent case of Kidder Peabody superbroker Peter Brant, a Great Gatsby for the Eighties. Like F. Scott Fitzgerald's character, Gatz who reinvented himself according to his own ideal. Buffalo-born Brant rejected the name Bornstein in favor of something he apparently thought evoked Cary Grant, and went on to transform himself into a millionaire Racquet Clubman and polo player of swank Locust Valley, Long Island. To protect all this when his talent for picking stocks faltered, he induced *Wall Street Journal* reporter R. Foster Winans to disclose, prior to publication, what that paper's stock-tip column would be saying about individual companies, at least according to Winan's book, *Trading Secrets*. Like Gatsby trying to reveal his innermost soul by throwing open his wardrobe and pouring out the profusion of his handmade shirts—

the outer surface he longed to make his identity—Brank needed the money to preserve not just his possessions but the sense of self tied up in them.

Because the Eighties ethic now seems so pervasive, top executives in many businesses increasingly fear that wrongdoing could break out in their companies too. Executives worry that the industrial restructuring process could lower the standards of employee behavior by its relentless pressure to squeeze budgets and raise profits, by its fanning of fright and resentment among the survivors whenever employees are fired, and by its shredding of the corporate culture in which standards are embedded.

One of the worried is American Can Chairman William Woodside, a champion restructurer who over the last five years has sold off most of his original company and put together a new one. "Two or three years ago," he says, "I thought, 'We're disassembling the culture we grew up in and spinning it off, and we're acquiring a lot of different cultures, but we have not the vaguest idea of what the underpinnings of those cultures are. We don't know how our family was brought up'."

He decided to administer an ounce of prevention. Mindful that you shouldn't buy entrepreneurial companies and force them to conform to your corporate culture, Woodside instead put every middle manager at the newly constituted enterprise through an ethics course and outfitted him with an ethics manual. Equally uneasy, scores of other chief executives have tried the same remedy, making a boomlet for ethics consultants.

But the ethics experts who write such tomes and teach MBA students often aren't really sure what is ethical. Listen to Vernon Henderson, a retired minister who is an ethics consultant to the Arthur D. Little consulting firm: "Ethical behavior is always a function of a context. It is relative to a culture, an era, to the pressures exerted in a given job." Standards, moreover, are in constant flux, he says. "In a society like ours," he asks, "who's going to decide what's right and wrong?" One looks in vain in this kind of talk for anything that would prevent a person from pulling the lever at Auschwitz.

The result of such moral relativism is that every situation becomes a problem that every manager is expected to solve as if no one had ever faced it before. And the solutions become fairly zany, as in an example reported to Barbara L. Toffler, a professor of ethics at the Harvard Business School. When an employee came back to work at AT & T after a dangerous illness, he was a man transformed: formerly by far the worst of his superior's subordinates, he was now much the best. AT & T, then undergoing its breakup, had devised a new performance evaluation, requiring each manager to list subordinates in order of excellence. Should the manager rank her born-again subordinate first, as he deserved? Wouldn't this be unfair to her three other subordinates, she agonized, since higher-ups were bound to think them awful if she ranked them beneath an employee known to be the bottom of the barrel?

Her long-meditated solution: gradually improve the best employee's ranking, waiting several more quarters before anointing him No. 1. Toffler presents this case to her students approvingly; it takes a while for a visitor to get her to see that what the manager did was *lie.*

In the end, the business school ethicists may be as much a part of the problem as of the solution. Their main message starts off with the reasonable exhortation that the future managers in their classes must prevent the creation of cultures of corruption at the outfits they'll help run. Corporate cultures powerfully affect employee behavior, students rightly are told, so you mustn't have reward systems that encourage misreporting of revenue and expenses or that promote cheating on government contracts. But in practice all this talk about how employees are creatures of their culture ends up by tacitly accepting the notion that the individual employee really can't be held personally responsible for his actions. The result is to genuflect piously to the idea of ethics without requiring any person to be ethical.

The corporate employees in most danger nowadays are chief executives, for they are most susceptible to the contagion bred of corporate restructuring. In them it produces symptoms like questionably ethical golden parachutes, dealmaking in which C. E. O.'s don't always keep their word to each other, leveraged buyouts in which the management team that arguably hasn't maximized return so far acts as both seller and buyer of the shareholders' assets, not to mention the host of company-bruising contortions chief executives have used to evade raiders and save their jobs.

Critics of restructuring fear that the process may not prove quite the panacea its supporters foresee, which makes the unethical behavior of the participants seem not just sordid but sinister. These critics admit that mismanagement bloated many companies that then needed shaping up. But by now, certain investment bankers and business leaders believe, it is not just poorly run companies that are being put through the wringer.

Some critics worry that the restructuring of mere financial manipulation. "The advent of junk bonds," says Felix Rohatyn, "took mergers and acquisitions away from where the industrial or business logic guided the merger to where the availability of finance beamed the guiding force." Companies have been brought simply to be broken up, here argues, not for any larger, constructive purpose. "We're not going to look back on this period and think that Boone Pickens performed a great service to U.S. interests or to the energy industry.

The vaunted restructuring may be making companies more profitable to shareholders, but that isn't necessarily the same thing as making them stronger global competitors. Their cultures destroyed, they may be stripped down not for competitive action but to pay off their new, restructuring-imposed burden of debt, a burden that could prove unsustainable when business turns down.

Presiding over all this, increasingly as instigators rather than mere intermediaries, are the investment bankers, saying, "Trust us, it's all for the best—trust us." But the steady barrage of their ethical lapses makes trusting them hard to do. ■

Whistle-Blowing: Individual Morality in a Corporate Society

Nancy R. Hauserman
*Associate Professor of Industrial
Relations and Human Resources
University of Iowa*

*An earlier version of this editorial was delivered in July 1985 as part
of a conference on business and ethics. The conference held at the
University of Iowa, was cosponsored by the National Endowment for
the Humanities, the Iowa Humanities Board, and the College of Business
Administration, University of Iowa.*

Whistle blowers need to be protected against employer retaliation. Why?
Because whistle blowers are reasserting the individual will and a sense of
individual values that go *beyond* the value structure maintained by corporate
America. If we wish society in the future to reflect the ideals of democracy
and personal commitment, it is crucial for the social community (as distinct
from the business community) to commit itself to protecting this individual
will.

THE INDIVIDUAL CONSCIENCE IN A CORPORATE SOCIETY

It is imperative that our society move to recapture a concept of the individual conscience and reestablish the idea of community morality beyond
the community of the "corporate society." In the pursuit and largely successful attainment of the goals of productivity and consumption, we have
failed to preserve individual and community values. The individual has been
reduced to a cog in the corporate wheel, a capital investment, a corporate
property. The values of the corporation, the goals of the society.

For example, Kenneth Schneider points to the growth of an educational
system that is structured to teach the technical rudiments but does little to
foster personal or social worth.[1] Certainly those of us who teach in Colleges
of Business are familiar with this trend. Our curricula usually offer only one
course on ethics, and even that may be taught as a readings course.

The concept of national or local citizenry appears to have been replaced
with the idea of a corporate citizenship. As members of this "corporate

From *Business Horizons* © 1986 by the Foundation for the School of Business at Indiana
University. Reprinted by permission.

society," we are not, in Schneider's words, "socially or economically independent of [our] bureaucratic identity."[2]

This process of changing allegiance must be considered in conjunction with the movement from smaller communities to the massive complex of American cities and their sterile suburbs. We have isolated ourselves physically from any sense of community beyond the corporate community.

Our concerns are often material and self-centered to the exclusion of concern for others. Too often we have no sense of responsibility for the rest of society.

This isolation, this loss of a sense of social responsibility, at least permits—and may, at worst, foster—an environment in which Kitty Genovese could be killed while her neighbors ignored her pleas for aid and failed to call the police. An environment in which a young woman could be raped in the middle of a crowded New Bedford bar.

I am not equating corporate misconduct with rape and murder. What I do equate, however, is the unwillingness of society to take responsibility for the victimization, let alone the criminal actions, of others. Although the New Bedford atrocity and the Kitty Genovese murder may generate a public outcry, although they may move us to assert that *we* would have acted differently, I wonder if we would be so sure of acting differently, of taking responsibility, if the wrongdoing that went unreported were a corporate wrongdoing.

I suggest that failure to protect the person who *does* report corporate malfeasance—in other words, failure to protect the whistle blower—is a failure to take responsibility. We sanction moral turpitude when we not only tolerate corporate malfeasance but also permit employees to be fired for reporting illegal acts of the employer.

This failure to protect those among us who came to *our* aid attests to our skewed sense of priorities. We exalt the aims of business and deny the moral and cultural values of the individuals within that business.

THE WHISTLE BLOWER

Let me define my use of "whistle blower." A person who reports a real or perceived wrongdoing of her or his employer is called a "whistle blower."[3]

Whistle-blowing can arise in several contexts. For example, an employee may learn of an illegality committed by her or his superiors or coworkers. Knowledge of the illegality can be obtained directly—for example, where the employee's participation in the illegality is requested or coerced.[4] Or this knowledge may be gained indirectly—for example, through the employee's access to company records.[5] The employee initially may report this illegality internally, either to her or his superiors or to an appropriate government agency. Or the report may be made externally, directly to the press and hence to the public.[6]

A whistle blower can also be an employee who believes that a company official has acted immorally or contrary to company policy—but not necessarily illegally. The term "whistle blower" can refer to any employee who disagrees with an employer on general policy matters or finds an employer's actions contrary to the employee's own morals. The employee may object, for example, to the company's investment or business dealings in South Africa. Or perhaps the employee takes exception to a utility company's active development of nuclear power.

Frankly, I think "whistle blower" should be replaced with a more descriptive term.[7] Regardless of the particular facts of a given situation, when the term "whistle blower" is used, the implication seems to be that the reporting employee is right or correct in her or his allegation and that the employer is in fact guilty of some wrongdoing.[8] Surely this assumption of guilt is not always correct.

The implication of guilt is likely to exacerbate an employer's defensive reaction to the individual whistle blower specifically and the concept of whistle-blowing generally. The much needed discussion between business and society is deterred even further by the hardened positions that defensive posturing tends to create.

Furthermore, the term "whistle-blower" often seems a polite synonym for familiar epithets like "squealer," "rat," and "snitch." Such terms do not reflect well on the reporting employee. Because they are likely to discourage reporting, they sustain the autonomy of business.

In any event, lacking a better term, I will use "whistle blower" to describe the person who reports a real illegality—a narrow definition of whistle-blowing.

TERMINATION AT WILL

For years, private sector employment has, at least in this country, been considered the prerogative of the employer and the employee. In 1877, America adopted the rule of termination at will for employment contracts. The termination-at-will doctrine, according to judicial interpretation, presumed that all employment contracts, unless there were explicit provisions to the contrary, were for an indefinite length of time. They could be terminated by either party at any time without any notice.[9] The practical effect of this new rule was a substantial decrease in the duties of the employer owed to the employee.

The adoption of the American rule corresponded to the rapid growth of industry in the nation. Termination at will reflected the emerging public policy that favored and encouraged the growth and development of new business enterprises and fostered a risk-taking attitude in industry. The termination-at-will doctrine effectively demonstrated government support and promotion of business. A legal framework that protected employers would, it was presumed, minimize industry risks and encourage further expansion.

When the at-will doctrine was established, the United States was in the early stages of economic development. The interests of both the employer and the employee, it was thought, were amply protected by the concept of freedom of contract and the supporting concept of mutuality. In the late nineteenth century, when the doctrine was first established, less than one half of all employed people were wage and salary workers. Today, more than 90 percent of those employed earn a wage or salary.[10]

Twenty-five years ago one author put it this way:

We have become a nation of employees. We are dependent upon others for our means of livelihood, and most of our people have become completely dependent upon wages. If they lose their jobs they lose every resource, except for the relief supplied by the various forms of social security. Such dependence of the mass of the people upon others for all of their income is something new in the world. For our generation, the substance of life is in another man's hands.[11]

Since the nineteenth century there has been a tremendous growth in the number of businesses and a corresponding growth in the scope of their economic power. This fact, coupled with the concern for the consumer generated in the 1960s and the continued high rate of unemployment, has shifted consideration from strict adherence to freedom-of-contract theory to a greater concern for the protection of an employee's job security.

Employees cannot freely transfer between jobs. The relative lack of employee mobility is due in part to the increasing rate of unemployment and the consequent decrease in the availability of alternate employment. The situation is further complicated by the increasing employment specialization that results from continued advances in modern technology. In another time, employees might have been more inclined to risk their jobs rather than to go along with the seemingly unreasonable demands of an employer. Under present employment conditions, however, employees are more likely to silently put up with unfavorable treatment rather than risk the possibility of finding another job—or looking for another job with the sigma of a dismissal on their employment record.

In spite of these economic changes in the absence of legislation to the contrary most courts continue to follow the termination-at-will principle. In a time of high unemployment, coupled with inflation, the suggestion that termination at will is desirable for employees seems ludicrous at best. This is not to suggest that employees do not quit their jobs. But the effects of *quitting* are hardly comparable to the consequences of *being fired.*

What are the implications when we, as a society, allow an employee to be fired for reporting the illegal action of his or her employer? Permitting employers to retaliate supports the notion that loyalty to the corporation outweighs—and presumably *should* outweigh—any loyalty to societal rules or laws and personal morals.

The question of an employee's "loyalty" suggests the need to consider the question, To whom or to what is a person to be loyal? One response might be that people must be loyal to themselves. But in fact, what does such a statement mean? Does it, as Aristotle suggested, mean loyalty *only* to oneself? Surely personal loyalty might also imply a need to eat or to provide for a family. If, instead, we assert that loyalty is to society, then people are presumably responsible for carrying out the rules and regulations of that society and for seeing that others do the same. Yet another approach—and one that I think we implicitly sanction by failing to protect the whistle blower—is that loyalty is owed *only* to one's employer.

When considering these choices, shouldn't we question the extent to which any of these loyalties are or should be maintained independently of each other? Why should a person have to choose between loyalty to self, to society, and to employer? Although we live in a pluralistic society, surely certain values are *shared.* For instance, while recognizing a concept of civil disobedience, our culture supports adherence to law. It values honesty. These maxims of honesty and law are not exclusive to the individual, the society, or the corporate society.

What happens, then, when we permit the whistle-blowing employee to be fired for reporting an illegal action, or an action that the employee reasonably believes to be illegal? We are forcing the employee to choose between the three loyalties and in some sense to relinquish his or her loyalty to self and society. When we allow the corporation to "banish" the whistle blower, we are essentially revoking that person's corporate citizenship. We are punishing the employee as we might punish a traitor.

Yet imagine our revoking the citizenship of Americans who report a criminal activity! Law enforcement agencies make frequent use of such informants. Often they reward the informant with money, and in some cases they furnish the informant with an entirely new identity—*and new employment.*

The failure to appreciate the merit of encouraging—or at least not punishing—corporate whistle-blowing is certainly not confined to some amorphous notion of "society at large." The precedent provided by the judiciary dramatically illustrates the extent to which an exclusive or absolute corporate loyalty is supported. Most courts repeatedly have decline to recognize whistle-blowing as falling within the scope of "public policy," a concept that permits an exception to the termination-at-will doctrine.

PROTECTION IN THE PUBLIC INTEREST

The public policy argument suggests that there are circumstances when the employer's motive for discharging an employee harms or interferes with an important interest of the community. This policy, therefore, justifies compensation to the employee. It is difficult to define succinctly the term "public policy." The consideration of what constitutes public policy is likely to change a society changes. It is perhaps more useful to focus on the factors involved in making such a determination.

To assess public policy, the courts consider public mores, attitudes, and sentiments as expressed in federal and state constitutions, statutes, and judicial decisions. In sum, the courts attempt to assess the values of society upon which our democracy is formed and maintained.

Several cases illustrate this public policy exception. In one case, the court held that public policy was violated when the plaintiff employee was discharged by his employer for refusing to give perjured testimony before a committee of the legislature.[12] In another case, the plaintiff employee claimed she was the subject of harassment by her foreman because she refused to go out on a date with him. His hostility, the claimant continued, resulted in her discharge. The court found in favor of the plaintiff.[13]

Courts have also allowed recovery when an employee was dismissed because she accepted jury duty.[14] In addition, some court decisions have indicated that an employee may not be discharged for refusing to act contrary to a recognized code of professional ethics, the rationale being that such a breach would be contrary to public policy.[15]

In two other cases, however, courts found that no public policy existed that protected the right of an employee to sue his employer as a fiduciary or in a stockholder's derivative suite.[16]

What distinguishes these public policy cases? In the latter two cases, where employees were stockholders in the employer-company, the court found that the interest of the employee was purely private and not of general public concern. The courts look to the specific facts and circumstances of each case to determine if the community's interest is so substantial that an employer should be required to compensate his or her employee for any damages suffered from the discharge. In such cases, the court is not protecting the employee's interest in continuing employment but instead is protecting some public interest, like the jury system.

I submit that the protection of whistle blowers is also in the public interest.

The public interest concern is not raised just because one individual loses a job. Nor does it have anything to do with the motives for whistle-blowing, nothing to do with making whistle blowers into heroes. It has to do with the public's interest in keeping its citizenry, including corporations, accountable to the law. In light of the pressure to conform with corporate loyalty, public recognition of the whistle blower's honesty in some cases may be justified, but this is irrelevant. The point of the public interest argument is that, as citizens of a lawful society, we are responsible for maintaining our laws. Protecting whistle blowers is one way to do this.

THE WHISTLE BLOWER AS PARIAH

Certain obvious common elements occur in most of the autobiographical and biographical information about whistle blowers. Although the incidents that prompted the whistle-blowing vary, virtually all of the whistle blowers were terminated in some way disciplines (retaliated against) by the employer. In almost every case where the employment was terminated, the whistle blower had little if any luck in securing new employment.

This factor might not be particularly noteworthy if employees were fired for stealing from or lying to their employers. But we are not talking about employees who committed an illegality and who might therefore be thought of, from an honesty standpoint, as poor employment risks. Whistle blowers, assuming "good faith" reporting, are obviously honest employees.

They are not, however, likely to be considered "game players", not part of the corporate "team". Although these employees might have been adequate or even highly successful in actual job performance, they violated an unwritten rule or job requirement: They asserted a loyalty that went beyond—or did not place primary emphasis on—the corporate employer.

In essence, the whistle blower becomes the pariah of corporate society. The issue does not center around who actually committed a legal wrong but rather siblings for some transgression, *everybody* got in trouble: the erring sibling for his or her prohibited acts, and the reporter for "tattling."

It is little wonder, then, that an employee might be well advised to weight seriously the consequences of corporate tattling. We continue to espouse democracy as this country's political philosophy. Yet we insist upon complete and unswerving corporate loyalty. The punishment for not adhering to corporate loyalty is banishment from the corporate society. Our actions produce and maintain a powerful totalitarian structure.

Kenneth Schneider has pointed out the price we will pay if we sacrifice the whistle blower at the altar of corporate society:

If modern [men and women] in the age of development can reaffirm [their] human purposes in society, and imprint them on all human institutions, then the faith that [people] have put in technological progress is likely to be rewarding. However, should corporations follow a course of institutional self-interest, expressed in unlimited striving for profits, growth, and social power, and if these interests command the primordial position in society, material progress will likely be achieved at the expense of traditional values and rights centered on the individual.[17]

As citizens of a lawful society, we must take some responsibility for maintaining that society. The continued assertion of individual morality provides an imperative congruity between the values and ethics of the social community and those of the corporate or business community. Protecting the whistle blower is one way of reasserting individual morality in the corporate structure. ∎

NOTES

1. Kenneth Schneider, *Destiny of Change* (New York: Holt Rinehart and Winston, 1968): 33.
2. Schneider: 20.
3. Ralph Nader et al., eds., *Whistle Blowing* (New York: Bantam Books, 1972): viii.
4. See, for example, *Petermann v. International Brotherhood of Teamsters, Local 396,* 174 Cal. App. 2d 184, 344 P.2d 25 (Ct. App. 1959).
5. See, for example *Harless v. First National Bank in Fairmont,* 246 S.E. 2d 270 (1978).
6. See, for example, *Rozier v. St. Mary's Hospital,* 88 Ill. App. 3d 994, 411 N.E. 2d 50 (1980).
7. I have, in fact, struggled—to date, unsuccessfully—to find such a term. Because my position is that the whistle blower functions as a citizen loyal to her of his society, any term specific to the *corporate* setting may be superfluous.
8. In a session on "Law and Society," I discussed the concept of whistle-blowing with the thirty executives in attendance at 1983 Executive Development Program at the University of Iowa's College of Business. The discussion was generated by consideration of *Nixon v. Fitzgerald,* 50 College of U.S.L.W. & 797 (1982). Without exception, the executives felt that, although "blowing the whistle" had merit, the term "whistle blower" immediately and definitively suggested corporate malfeasance.
9. C. Summers "Individual Protection Against Unjust Dismissal: Time for a Statute," *Virginia Law Review,* 62 (1976): 481–485.
10. See *Work in America,* Report of Special Task Force to Secretary of HEW (1973): 20–23.
11. Frank Tannenbaum, *A Philosophy of Labor* (New York: Knopf, 1951): 9.
12. *Petermann v. International Brotherhood of Teamsters,* Local 396. 174 Cal. App. 2d 184, 344P.2d 25 (Ct. App. 1959).
13. *Monge v. Beebe Rubber Co.* 114 N. H. 130, 316 A.2d 549 (1974).
14. *Nees v. Hocks* 279 Ore. 210, 536 P.2d 512 (1975).
15. See, for example, *Pierce v. Orth. Pharmaceutical Corp.,* 84 N.J. 58 417 A.2d 505 (1980).
16. *Becket v. Welton Becket & Associates,* 39 Cal. App. 3d 815, 114 Cal. Rptr. 531 (1974) and *Campbell v. Ford Industries,* Inc., 274 Or. 243, 546 P.2d 141 (1974).
17. Schneider (note I): 32.

The Foundations of Business Ethics: Exploring the Relationship Between Organization Culture, Moral Values, and Actions

Charles R. Stoner

*Associate Professor of
Business Management,
Bradley University, Peoria, Illinois.*

Expressing a widespread concern, a national news magazine suggested in May 1987 that the United States was in the throes of moral disarray.[1] As highly visible evidences of corporate misconduct heighten public awareness, corporate America has been targeted as a key culprit in the downward ethical spiral. Not surprisingly, surveys over the past few years reveal that large numbers of Americans are cynical and distrustful of the ethics practiced by business and its leaders.[2]

Increasingly, contemporary organizations realize that ethics and profits are not conflicting concerns. Top executives note that good ethics is a prime corporate asset.[3] They understand that a solid ethical foundation is one of the important components for long-term corporate success.

However, ethics is a troublesome issue for many managers. Their uneasiness stems partially from an uncertainty about what ethics actually is and how it fits into the realm of business.

Business ethics is deeply concerned with both moral values and moral actions. Moral values are basic ideals that are considered desirable or worthwhile for human interaction.[4] Moral actions are the overt expressions and applications of these underlying values. Therefore, the notion that, as businesspersons, we should not deceive or mislead our customers is a moral value. Behaving honestly and fairly toward our customers is a moral action. Business ethics is called into question when the moral values or the accompanying moral actions or organizational decisionmakers conflict with the commonly accepted standards of society.

Reprinted by permission, *SAM Advanced Management Journal,* December 1989, Society for Advancement of Management, Vinton, VA 24179.

Dr. Stoner is an active consultant to business ad service organizations and author of the recent textbook, Strategic Planning in the Small Business.

Although a variety of explanations have been offered for the perceived decline in the state of business ethics, few have emphasized, in a comprehensive manner, the overwhelming impact of organizational culture on ethics. The dynamics of organizational culture not only opens new theoretical perspectives and understanding of organizational ethics, it is crucial to a full understanding of the forces that permit or, at times, prompt unethical behavior and to our ability to structure remediations for encouraging stronger organizational ethical responses.

THE GENERAL RELATIONSHIP BETWEEN ETHICS AND CULTURE

In testimony before the Senate subcommittee investigating the Iran-Contra affair, Fawn Hall said that she willingly carried out document alteration and destruction. Her boss, Lt. Col. Oliver North, had indicated that such actions were necessary. Accordingly, she engaged in these activities without apparent consideration of the ethical or legal ramifications. Many outside observers were appalled at such "blind" acceptance and loyalty. Yet, Ms. Hall retorted that Lt. Col. North was a good boss, that she trusted him, and that it was her job to do what he asked. Her response is neither an indication of moral ambivalence nor a lack of willingness to wrestle with important ethical considerations. Rather, the organization culture, and the strength and general pervasiveness of the values it supported, demanded that Ms. Hall behave exactly as she did.

Strong moral directives can be a key component of the organization's culture, and thereby define for members appropriate moral actions. However, many cultures do not encompass such moral values. While some may actually condone immoral acts, others simply fail to consider them. As Carroll notes, many organizational cultures are neither moral or immoral, but amoral.[5]

DEFINING ORGANIZATION CULTURE

Organization culture is a broad, powerful and definitionally complex concept. Shafritz and Ott view culture as "the unseen and unobservable force that is always behind organizational activities that can be seen and observed."[6] Essentially, this force or culture is comprised of the dominant underlying assumptions commonly shared and accepted by organization members.[7] In order to understand culture, three facets of this definition must be examined. First, assumptions are considered dominant and underlying if they are of primary importance to the organization as it operates day-to-day. Second, these assumptions are made up of beliefs and values which indicate what is desirable and acceptable by organizational members. Finally, the common sharing and acceptance of these assumptions implies that organization members "take them for granted"[8] and internalize them to the extent that they become "congruent with corresponding personal beliefs and values."[9]

The critical moral values of the organization are included in this conception of organization culture. These moral values dictate standards or norms of conduct that guide members in their daily routine.[10] To the extent that moral values are integrated into and represented throughout the culture, organization members will respond with moral force and conviction when confronted with difficult or ambivalent ethical situations. Of course, this condition represents an ideal—a normative pattern that is easier to state than to enact. Therefore, it is important to consider how an organization goes about embracing moral values within its culture.

THE LEVELS OF CULTURE AND ETHICS

It is useful to realize the existence of three separate, yet interrelated, levels of organization culture.[11] The first and most visible level of culture deals with the observable behavioral manifestations of the culture. Although these are the things we seek, we are not sure why they occur as they do. The customary words and phrases peculiar to a given organization, the physical layout of the executive offices, and the actions and decisions made by management would all be examples of this first level.

The second level of culture refers to its overt, espoused values. These values—often representing the convictions of the organization's leaders—are views about what "ought" to be. These values are debated and tested through organizational experience. Thus, a small manufacturing company experiencing depressed markets may find it imperative to slash costs. However, the CEO asserts that he views his employees as family and intends to treat them as such. Therefore, while hours may be cut, no layoffs will occur and no jobs will be lost. Here, the CEO has taken a definite action based on an espoused value. Again, this action and its underlying value base may be questioned (most likely privately and introspectively) by a number of organizational members. Over time, as values guide actions that lead to successful experiences, they gradually evolve into dominant, underlying assumptions, are taken for granted, and are commonly accepted, shared, internalized, and used by organization members. Thus, these values become habitual, unconscious, automatic, nonconfrontable, and nondebatable. These values represent the third level of culture and, accordingly, most implicitly and forcefully guide member perceptions, feelings, and actions.

Although quite powerful and pervasive, cultures are not rigid and inflexible. They are evolutionary and may be challenged as situations and needs change. Although organizational members are guided by the prevailing culture, their daily actions influence and contribute to an evolving culture.

Organizational members may refuse to accept and use espoused values. This act of refusal represents adherence to new values, thereby fostering the development of new cultural perspectives.

Ethics, as a cultural question, must be approached on three levels. As an outside observer of organizational life, all one sees are ethical outcomes— first-level behavioral manifestations or actions which are then evaluated on moral or ethical grounds. Of course, the acts are overt representations of some moral values (second level) that may or may not be culturally based (third level). It is in considering the interplay of these levels that the complexity and difficulty of organizational ethical response emerges. Consider the following example.

Corporate and industry codes of ethics have been popular approaches for encouraging moral business behaviors. Similarly, formal statements and pronouncements by organizational leaders that support ethical behavior presumably enhance the likelihood of ethical behaviors. Codes and statements are to be encouraged, as these efforts may yield positive ethical orientations and outcomes. Yet, one should recognize that corporate codes and statements are merely starting points in the search for moral directives and ethical organizational behavior. The problem is that what these codes and statements express may not indicate how the organization actually operates and makes decisions. Organizations with elaborate ethical codes and inspiring ethical pronouncements are not always the ones demonstrating the strongest moral actions.

The conflict here is between "espoused" and "enacted" moral values. Espoused values are those the organization is formally and explicitly committed to.[12] These espoused values (typically explained through formal codes and statements) are expressions (first level of culture) of the moral values (second level of culture) of key individuals within the organization. Enacted values are those the organization and its general membership actually believe in and are willing to apply. The outcomes derived from these enacted values reflect the underlying, pervasive third level of organization culture.

It is relatively easy for an organization to present second-level espoused moral values. However, it is more significant for these to evolve into third-level enacted moral values. Stated simply, the day-to-day actions of decision makers constitute a more precise picture of the organization's ethical tone than anything said or written. Espoused values may serve external image and publicity purposes, but enacted values guide member behaviors. Again, we reiterate that an ethical firm must possess an ethical culture.

Interestingly, many companies contend that their cultures are deeply moral and that questionable ethical acts come from isolated deviants who break a clear pattern of organizational expectation. To a large extent, E. F.

Hutton and others have used this argument to explain their ethical shortcomings. Apparently, in these situations, moral commitment had not evolved into a third-level culture, as an internalization of espoused values did not take place. While these organizations may hope to explain their ethical problems by attributing blame to individual, isolated, moral deviators, such superficial attempts fail to explain why the evolved culture differs so markedly from their public positions. Of course, espoused values need not differ from enacted values. As noted earlier, the third level of culture may logically evolve from the second level of culture. Yet, to assume that espousing moral values will easily lead to the desired cultural evolution is foolish and naive. The organization must go further to build a true moral culture.

BUILDING A MORAL ORGANIZATIONAL CULTURE

One must always keep in mind that organization culture evolves over time. It does not spring into existence, full-grown, because some top level executive deems it appropriate and proper. Organization culture must be nurtured and developed.

In order to build a moral culture, four distinct, yet related processes must be present. Each is complex and can be laden with implementation difficulties.

I. Establishing Clear Moral Values

Initially, clear moral values must be established within the organization. Certainly, corporate codes of conduct and executive pronouncements help establish these values. Yet, one must recognize clearly their limitations. Generally, they seek to present broad clarifications of company intentions and expectations. As Saul notes, these approaches address major issues and rarely are capable of specifying the subtleties that provoke true ethical conflicts for organization members.[13]

One must keep in mind that the attempt here is to establish values and not simply to enumerate a series of moral directives. This distinction is critical. A moral directive says, "Our managers will not accept gifts from vendors." A moral value says, "Any gesture or action that comprises a manager's ability to make decisions based on the objective quality of the choices involved is wrong." Thus, moral directives are specific elements of more general moral values. A manager can adhere to the specific directive (i.e., "The gifts were given directly to my spouse, not me.") and still violate the intent of the value. However, one cannot comply with the value unless this directive is obeyed.

Instilling appropriate moral values, then, must involve more than codes and statements. The organization must develop a series of on-going steps that augment the important moral values. Logically, the consideration of underlying moral values begins with initial orientation training and may be included as a component of the corporate orientation program. The author recently interviewed the president of a large manufacturing firm who met with each newly-hired manager to personally convey moral value expectations, stress their significance, and clearly delineate the costs of deviation.

Additionally, on-going discussion of moral values should be encouraged. For each major decision—ethical as well as strategic—ramifications must be addressed. In this way, moral considerations become ritualized and underlying values are solidified. Ethics seminars have grown in popularity as a means of helping bring key concerns to the forefront and presenting a forum of their discussion.

Open discussion of ethical issues must not be seen as the exclusive purview of special training sessions. Rather, it must be part of staff meetings, group decision making, strategic planning and development. Perhaps "ethics circles"—drawing from the blueprint of quality circles—can be established to provide debate and guidance for particularly sticky or troublesome ethical quandaries. All these efforts are part of a complementary series of steps to bring ethics to high levels of consciousness for organizational members and, thereby, establish clearer notions of the moral values the organization believes in and wishes to guide member actions.

Although always present, the need for elaborating and clarifying moral values is intensified as firms struggle through the challenges of pervasive organizational change. For example, mergers and acquisitions often have the effect of disrupting, obscuring, or markedly altering existing cultures and inherent values. As merger and acquisition activity grows, cultural integration declines and key values are often lost. Similarly, recent movements toward corporate downsizing create an atmosphere of questioning and ambivalence toward organizational moral values. The new, "streamlined," downsized firm may have lower costs and stronger competitive muscle, but its traditional values and expectations may be disrupted. Recently, General Motors announced plans to eliminate 40,000 white-collar employees (more than a quarter of its salaried staff) over the next two years. Here, historic perspectives of loyalty and security are shattered, and key values are called into question as members begin to ask, "What's going on here?" and "What really counts anymore?" In short, the need for continually addressing, clarifying, and reinforcing organizational moral values may be greater today than ever.

II. Moral Values Must Be Given High Priority

Not only must moral values be clearly and firmly established, they must be seen by organizational members as significant, high priority values for the firm and its operations. Of course, paying regular attention to these values helps demonstrate their importance. However, the relative ranking of moral values in relation to other business values is revealed by the actions taken when relevant values conflict. For example, is the company willing to sacrifice access to a new market area rather than pay a bribe? The answer to this and similar quandaries establish in the minds of organizational members the place and significance of moral values to the organization.

III. Moral Values Must Be Consistently Maintained

It is hard to differentiate between priority and consistency. Certainly, as consistency is maintained, priority becomes more clear. Likewise, as values are accorded higher priority, they are more likely to be consistently maintained.

Consistency of moral values occurs on two levels: consistency throughout the organization and consistency through a variety of situations. First consistency throughout the organization asserts that the values professed at one level of the organization are the same as those accepted at other (typically lower) levels. Therefore, those in the executive suite do not live by different moral values than those on the shop floor. Perhaps even more important is that the moral values of first-line, middle-level, and upper-level leaders are consistent. Realistically, consistency can be developed only by specific organizational actions. Generally, some type of "checks and balances" system must be in place. Recent advances such as special ethics ombudsman, ethics "hotlines," and more liberal "whistle-blowing" legislation help promote an increased atmosphere of consistency.

Consistency in a variety of situations asserts that the company adheres to the same moral values and standards regardless of any situational stresses. One of the best ways to determine true culture and underlying values is to observe how the organization responds to emergency or crisis situations. For example, Johnson & Johnson for years espoused the moral value of customer care. In short, they suggested that customer well-being and safety were more important to the company than profits. Their implementation of this value in the Tylenol crisis demonstrated its significance, consistency of application, and no doubt went a great way toward embedding this value within the overall organization culture.

IV. Internalizing Moral Values

The final component for building a moral culture is internalizing moral values in organization members. As noted earlier, internalizing must occur if the third level of culture is to evolve. Since this process is individually-oriented and occurs slowly and subconsciously, organization leaders cannot dictate or control it. However, leaders can take actions which are likely to affect the degree to which moral values are internalized.

When organization members identify with, accept as their own, and are willing to apply the moral values espoused by the organization, the values are internalized. For this to happen, organization members must believe that it is in their self-interest to accept and adhere to the organizationally-prescribed moral values. This condition occurs only when the organizational reward and disciplinary system clearly reinforces the desired moral values.

Unfortunately, the lack of such support has been a major stumbling block to value internalization and a key deterrent to the development of a moral culture. Often, organization members are rewarded for performance and results, regardless of how they are achieved.[14] Thus, a commitment to produce, to demonstrate financially-oriented returns, and to do so quickly and consistently is reinforced. The emphasis on results is heightened by bitter internal competition for an ever-shrinking number of lucrative advances. Not surprisingly, some managers feel compelled to abandon values in favor of more expedient means of "getting the numbers" and getting ahead. Although few organizations would espouse "results at the expense of moral values," the climates they have created may foster such outcomes. For example, a business may express its commitment to a series of lofty moral values. Organization members will challenge and test the efficacy of these moral standards. Ambitious, achievement-oriented workers may feel that they must demonstrate consistently outstanding performance to succeed in an increasingly competitive arena. Accordingly, they may displace ethical values if adherence to them is perceived as complicating the attainment of performance expectations. If the resulting performance outcomes are accepted and rewarded, a new culture, supporting counter-value positions, has been reinforced.

Organizations must reward those who adhere to moral values, even if this reflects negatively on short-run financial results. Organizations should go even further and include ethical behavior as part of formal performance evaluations. Certainly, incorporating ethics into performance evaluation offers unique methodology and implementation challenges. Yet, such a focus highlights moral issues and promotes the motivation and commitment necessary for employees to take moral values seriously.

Likewise, disciplinary emphasis must be refocused. Top management must promptly and strictly discipline those who violate moral standards.[15] Formal procedures for monitoring and addressing moral shortcomings must be implemented. In 1985, the Center for Business Ethics at Bently College reported that only 14% of firms with formal ethics policies had ethics committees and only 1% had ethics panels to sit in judgment of violators. Such situations must be remedied.

THE CHALLENGE

Corporate America will behave morally only when contemporary business incorporate key moral values into their organization cultures. However, the most popular, current methods of addressing ethical concerns frequently fall short of providing the necessary depth of cultural evolution. As highlighted here, organizational efforts must focus on establishing clear moral values, giving these values high priority, visibility, and consistency, and making sure organization members internalize them.

Such procedures are tough. They require top-down energy and commitment. Required changes will not occur quickly or easily. But the challenge is clear. Organizations must undertake systematic, concerted action aimed at "building" a moral organization culture. The moral culture is the route for stemming current ethical criticisms and refocusing attention toward the positive qualities of American business. The payoffs—for both the organization and society—are worth the struggle. ■

NOTES

1. "Looking To Its Roots", *Time,* May 5, 1989: 26–29.
2. Two informative surveys were conducted by *The Wall Street Journal* in November, 1982 and the *New York Times* in June, 1985.
3. *Corporate Ethics: A Prime Business Asset,* published by the Business Roundtable, 1988.
4. Vijay Sathe, *Culture and Related Corporate Realties* (Homewood, Illinois: Richard D. Irwin, Inc., 1985): 11.
5. Archie B. Carroll, "In Search of the Moral Manager", *Business Horizons,* March–April, 1987: 7–15.
6. Jay M. Shafritz and J. Steven Ott, "The Organization Culture School", in *Classics of Organization Theory* (Chicago: The Dorsey Press, 1987); 373–380.
7. Excellent overviews of organization culture are provided by T. E. Deal and A. A. Kennedy, *Corporate Cultures* (Reading, Massachusetts: Addition-Wesley Publishing, 1982); Edgar H. Schein, *Organizational Culture and Leadership* (San Francisco: Jossey-Bass Publishers); and Caren Siehl and Joanne Martin, "The Role of Symbolic Management: How Can Managers Effectively Transmit Organizational Culture?", in J. G. Hunt and others, *Leaders and Managers: International Perspectives on Managerial Behavior and Leadership* (New York: Permagon Press, 1984): 227–239.
8. Schein: 18–21.
9. Sathe: 12–13.
10. A nice explanation of these issues and relationships is provided by Vincent Barry, *Moral Issues in Business* (Belmont, California: Wadsworth Publishing, 1979).
11. This distinction is developed by Schein and is thoroughly outlined in *Organizational Culture and Leadership.*
12. Chris Argyris and D. A. Schon, *Organizational Learning* (Reading, Massachusetts: Addison-Wesley Publishing, 1978).
13. George K. Saul, "Business Ethics: Where Are We Going?", *The Academy of Management Review,* April, 1981: 269–276.
14. Robert Jackall, "Moral Mazes: Bureaucracy and Managerial Work," *Harvard Business Review,* September–October 1983: 118–130.
15. J. G. Kaikati and W. A. Label, "American Bribery Legislation: An Obstacle to International Marketing", *Journal of Marketing,* Fall 1980: 38–43.

The Silent Language in Overseas Business

Edward T. Hall

With few exceptions, Americans are relative newcomers on the international business scene. Today, as in Mark Twain's time, we are all to often "innocents abroad," in an era when naivete and blundering in foreign business dealings may have serious political repercussions.

When the American executive travels abroad to do business, he is frequently shocked to discover to what extent the many variables of foreign behavior and custom complicate his efforts. Although the American has recognized, certainly, that even the man next door has many minor traits which make him somewhat peculiar, for some reason he has failed to appreciate how different foreign businessmen and their practices will seem to him.

He should understand that the various peoples around the world have worked out and integrated into their subconscious literally thousands of behavior patterns that they take for granted in each other.[1] Then, when the stranger centers, and behaves differently from the local m = norm, he often quite unintentionally insults, annoys, or amuses the native with whom he is attempting to do business. For example:

- In the United States, a corporation executive knows what is meant when a client lets a month go by before replying to a business proposal. On the other hand, he senses an eagerness to do business if he is immediately ushered into the client's office. In both instances, he is reacting to subtle cues in the timing of interaction, cues which he depends on to chart his course of action.

  Abroad, all this changes. The American executive learns that the Latin Americans are casual about time and that if he waits an hour in the outer office before seeing the Deputy Minister of Finance, it does not necessarily mean he is not getting anywhere. There people are so important that nobody can bear to tear himself away; because of the resultant interruptions and conversational detours, everybody is constantly getting behind.

What the American does not know is the point at which the waiting becomes significant.

- In another instance, after traveling 7,000 miles an American walks into the office of a highly recommended Arab businessman on whom he will have to depend completely. What he sees does not breed confidence. The office is reached by walking through a suspicious-looking coffeehouse in an old, dilapidated building situated in a crowded non-European section of town. The elevator, rising from dark, smelly corridors, is rickety and equally foul. When he gets to the office itself, he is shocked to find it small, crowded, and confused. Papers are stacked all over the desk and table tops—even scattered on the floor in irregular piles.

The Arab merchant he has come to see had met him at the airport the night before and sent his driver to the hotel this morning to pick him up. But now, after the American's rush, the Arab is tied up with something else. Even when they finally start talking business, there are constant interruptions. If the American is at all sensitive to his environment, everything around him signals, "What am I getting into?"

Before leaving home he was told that things would be different, but how different? The hotel is modern enough. The shops in the new part of town have many more American and European trade goods than he had anticipated. His first impression was that doing business in the Middle East would not present any new problems. Now he is beginning to have doubts. One minute everything looks familiar and he is on firm ground; the next, familiar landmarks are gone. His greatest problem is that so much assails his senses all at once that he does not know where to start looking for something that will tell him where he stands. He needs a frame or reference—a way of sorting out what is significant and relevant.

That is why it is so important for American businessmen to have a real understanding of the various social, cultural, and economic differences they will face when they attempt to do business in foreign countries. To help give some frame of reference, this article will map out a few areas of human activity that have largely been unstudied.

The topics I will discuss are certainly not presented as the last word on the subject, but they have proved to be highly reliable points at which to begin to gain an understanding of foreign cultures. While additional research will undoubtedly turn up other items just as relevant, at present I think the businessman can do well to begin by appreciating cultural differences in matters concerning the language of time, of space, of material possessions, of friendship patterns, and of agreements.

LANGUAGE OF TIME

Everywhere in the world people use time to communicate with each other. There are different languages of time just as there are different spoken languages. The unspoken languages are informal; yet the rules governing their interpretation are surprisingly *ironbound.*

In the United States, a delay in answering a communication can result from a large volume of business causing the request to be postponed until the backlog is cleared away, from poor organization, or possibly from technical complexity requiring deep analysis. But if the person awaiting the answer or decision rules out these reasons, then the delay means to him that the matter has low priority on the part of the other person—lack of interest. On the other hand, a similar delay in a foreign country may mean something altogether different. Thus:

- In Ethiopia, the time required for a decision is directly proportioned to its importance. This is so much the case that low-level bureaucrats there have a way of trying to elevate the prestige of their work by taking a long time to make up their minds. (Americans in that part of the world are innocently prone to downgrade their work in the local people's eyes by trying to speed things up.)
- In the Arab East, time does not generally include schedules as Americas know and use them. The time required to get something accomplished depends on the relationship. More important people get fast service from less important people, and conversely. Close relatives take absolute priority; non relatives are kept waiting.

In the United States, giving a person a deadline is a way of indicating the degree of urgency or relative importance of the work. But in the Middle East, the American runs into a cultural trap the minute he opens his mouth. "Mr. Aziz will have to make up his mind in a hurry because my board meets next week and I have to have an answer by then," is taken as indicating the American is overly demanding and is exerting undue pressure. "I am going to Damascus tomorrow morning and will have to have my car tonight," is a sure way to get the mechanic to stop work, because to give another person a deadline in this part of the world is to be rude, pushy, and demanding.

An Arab's evasiveness as to when something is going to happen does not mean he does not want to do business; it only means he is avoiding unpleasantness and is side-stepping possible commitments which he takes more seriously than we do. For example:

The Arabs themselves at times find it impossible to communicate even to each other that some processes cannot be hurried, and are controlled by built-in schedules. This is obvious enough to the Westerner but not to the Arab. A highly placed public official in Baghdad precipitated a bitter family dispute because his nephew, a biochemist, could not speed up the complete analysis of the uncle's blood. He accused the nephew of putting other less important people before him and of not caring. Nothing could sway the uncle, who could not grasp the fact that there is such a thing as an inherent schedule.

With us the more important an event is, the further ahead we schedule it, which is why we find it insulting to be asked to a party at the last minute. In planning future events with Arabs, it pays to hold the lead time to a week or less because other factors may intervene or take precedence.

Again, time spent waiting in an American's outer office is a sure indicator of what one person thinks of another or how important he feels the other's business to be. This is so much the case that most Americans cannot help getting angry after waiting 30 minutes; one may even feel such a delay is an insult, and will walk out. In Latin America, on the other hand, one learns that it does not mean anything to wait in an outer office. An American businessman with years of experience in Mexico once told me, "You know, I have spent two hours cooling my heels in an executive's outer office. It took me a long time to learn to keep my blood pressure down. Even now, I find it hard to convince myself they are still interested when they keep me waiting."

The Japanese handle time in ways which are almost inexplicable to the Western European and particularly the American. A delay of years with them does not mean that they are building up to something. They have learned that Americans are vulnerable to long waits. One of them expressed it. "You Americans have one terrible weakness. If we make you wait long enough, you will agree to anything."

Indians of South Asia have an elastic view of time as compared to our own. Delays do not, therefore, have the same meaning to them. Nor does indefiniteness in pinpointing appointments mean that they are evasive. Two Americans meeting will say, "We should get together sometime," thereby setting a low priority on the meeting. The Indian who says, "Come over and see me, see me anytime," means just that.

Americans make a place at the table which may or may not mean a place made in the heart. But when the Indian makes a place in his time, it is yours to fill in every sense of the word if you realize that by so doing you have crossed a boundary and are now friends with him. The point of all this is that time communicates just as surely as do words and that the vocabulary of time is different around the world. The principle to be remembered is that time has different meanings in each country.

LANGUAGE OF SPACE

Like time, the language of space is different wherever one goes. The American businessman, familiar with the pattern of American corporate life, has no difficulty in appraising the relative importance of someone else, simply by noting the size of his office in relation to other offices around him:

- Our pattern calls for the president or the chairman of the board to have the biggest office. The executive vice president will have the next largest, and so on down the line until you end up in the "bull pen." More important offices are usually located at the corners of buildings and on the upper floors. Executive suites will be on the top floor. The relative rank of vice presidents will be reflected in where they are placed along "Executive Row."
- The French, on the other hand, are much more likely to lay out space as a network of connecting points of influence, activity, or interest. The French supervisor will ordinarily be found in the middle of his subordinates where he can control them.

Americans who are crowded will often feel that their status in the organization is suffering. As one would expect in the Arab world, the location of an office and its size constitute a poor index of the importance of the man who occupies it. What we experience as crowded, the Arab will often regard as spacious. The same is true in Spanish cultures. A Latin American official illustrated the Spanish view of this point while showing me around a plant. Opening the door to an 18-by-20-foot office in which seventeen clerks and their desks were placed, he said, "See, we have nice spacious offices. Lots of space for everyone."

The American will look at a Japanese room and remark how bare it is. Similarly, the Japanese look at our rooms and comment, "How bare!" Furniture in the American home tends to be placed along the walls (around the edge). Japanese have their charcoal pit where the family gathers in the *middle* of the room. The top floor of Japanese department stores is not reserved for the chief executive—it is the bargain roof!

In the Middle East and Latin America, the businessman is likely to feel left out in time and overcrowded in space. People get too close to him, lay their hands on him, and generally crowd his physical being. In Scandinavia and Germany, he feels more at home, but at the same time the people are a little cold and distant. It is space itself that conveys this feeling.

In the United States, because of our tendency to zone activities, nearness carries rights of familiarity so that the neighbor can borrow material possessions and invade time. This is not true in England. Propinquity entitles you to nothing. American Air Force personnel stationed there complain because they have to make an appointment for their children to play with the neighbor's child next door.

Conversation distance between two people is learned early in life by copying elders. Its controlling patterns operate almost totally unconsciously. In the United States, in contrast to many foreign countries, men avoid excessive touching. Regular business is conducted at distances such as 5 feet to 8 feet; highly personal business, 18 inches to 3 feet—not 2 or 3 inches.

In the United States, it is perfectly possible for an experienced executive to schedule the steps of negotiation in time and space so that most people feel comfortable about what is happening. Business transactions progress in stages from across the desk to beside the desk, to the coffee table, then on to the conference table, the luncheon table, or the golf course, or even into the home—all according to a complex set of hidden rules which we obey instinctively.

Even in the United States, however, an executive may slip when he moves into new and unfamiliar realms, when dealing with a new group, doing business with a new company, or moving to a new place in the industrial hierarchy. In a new country the danger is magnified. For example, in India it is considered improper to discuss business in the home on social occasions. One never invites a business acquaintance to the home for the purpose of furthering business aims. That would be a violation of sacred hospitality rules.

LANGUAGE OF THINGS

Americans are often contrasted with the rest of the world in terms of material possessions. We are accused of being materialistic, gadget-crazy. And, as a matter of fact, we have developed material things for some very interesting reasons. Lacking a fixed class system and having an extremely mobile population, Americans have become highly sensitive to how others make use of material possessions. We use everything from clothes to houses as a highly evolved and complex means of ascertaining each other's status. Ours is a rapidly shifting system in which both styles and people move up or down. For example:

- The Cadillac ad men feel that not only is it natural but quite insightful of them to show a picture of a Cadillac and a well-turned out gentleman in his early fifties opening the door. The caption underneath reads, "You already know a great deal about this man."
- Following this same pattern, the head of a big union spends an excess of $100,000 furnishing his office so that the president of United States Steel cannot look down on him. Good materials, large space, and the proper

surroundings signify that the people who occupy the premises are solid citizens, that they are dependable and successful.

The French, the English, and the Germans have entirely different ways of using their material possessions. What stands for the height of dependability and respectability with the English would be old-fashioned and backward to us. The Japanese take pride in often inexpensive but tasteful arrangements that are used to produce the proper emotional setting.

Middle East businessmen look for something else—family, connections, friendship. They do not use the furnishing of their office as part of their status system; nor do they expect to impress a client by these means or to fool a banker into lending more money than he should. They like good things, too, but feel that they, as persons, should be known and not judged solely by what the public sees.

One of the most common criticisms of American relations abroad, both commercial and governmental, is that we usually think in terms of material things. "Money talks," says the American, who goes on talking the language of money abroad, in the belief that money talks the *same* language all over the world. A common practice in the United States is to try to buy loyalty with high salaries. In foreign countries, this maneuver almost never works, for money and material possessions stand for something different there than they do in America.

LANGUAGE OF FRIENDSHIP

The American finds his friends next door and among those with whom he works. It has been noted that we take people up quickly and drop them just as quickly. Occasionally a friendship formed during schooldays will persist, but this is rare. For us there are few well-defined rules governing the obligations of friendship. It is difficult to say at which point our friendship gives way to business opportunism or pressure from above. In this we differ from many other people in the world. As a general rule in foreign countries friendships are not formed as quickly as in the United States but go much deeper, last longer, and involve real obligations. For example:

It is important to stress that in the Middle East and Latin America your "friends" will not let you down. The fact that they personally are feeling the pinch is never an excuse for failing their friends. They are supposed to look out for your interests.

Friends and family around the world represent a sort of social insurance that would be difficult to find in the United States. We do not use our friends to help us out in disaster as much as we do as a means of getting ahead—or, at least, of getting the job done. The United States systems work by means of a series of closely tabulated favors and obligations carefully doled out where they will do the most good. And the least that we expect in exchange for a favor is gratitude.

The opposite is the case in India, where the friend's role is to "sense" a person's need and do something about it. The idea of reciprocity as we know it is unheard of. An American in India will have difficulty if he attempts to follow American friendship patterns. He gains nothing by extending himself in behalf of others, least of all gratitude, because the Indian assumes that what he does for others he does for the good of his own psyche. He will find it impossible to make friends quickly and is unlikely to allow sufficient time for friendships to ripen. He will also note that as he gets to know people better, they may become more critical of him, a fact that he finds hard to take. What he does not know is that one sign of friendship in India is speaking one's mind.

LANGUAGE OF AGREEMENTS

While it is important for American businessmen abroad to understand the symbolic meanings of friendship rules, time, space, and material possessions, it is just as important for executives to know the rules for negotiating agreements in various countries. Even if they cannot be expected to know the details of each nation's commercial legal practices, just the awareness of and the expectation of the existence of differences will eliminate much complication.

Actually, no society can exist on a high commercial level without a highly developed working base on which agreements can rest. This base may be one or a combination of three types:

1. Rules that are spelled out technically as law or regulation.
2. Moral practices mutually agreed on and taught to the young as a set of principles.
3. Informal customs to which everyone conforms without being able to state the exact rules.

Some societies favor one, some another. Ours, particularly in the business world, lays heavy emphasis on the first variety. Few Americans will conduct any business nowadays without some written agreement or contract.

Varying from culture to culture will be the circumstances under which such rules apply. Americans consider that negotiations have more or less ceased when the contract is signed. With the Greeks, on the other hand, the contract is seen as a sort of way station on the route to negotiation that will cease only when the work is completed. The contract is nothing more than a charter for serious negotiations. In the Arab world, once a man's word is given in a particular kind of way, it is just as binding, if not more so, than most of our written contracts. The written contract, therefore, violates the Moslem's sensitivities and reflects on his honor. Unfortunately, the situation is now so hopelessly confused that neither system can be counted on to prevail consistently.

Informal patterns and unstated agreements often lead to untold difficulty in the cross-cultural situation. Take the case of the before-and-after patterns where there is a wide discrepancy between the American's expectations and those of the Arab:

- In the United States, when you engage a specialist such as a lawyer or a doctor, require any standard service, or even take a taxi, you make several assumptions: (a) the charge will be fair; (b) it will be in proportion to the services rendered; and (c) it will bear a close relationship to the "going rate."

   You wait until after the services are performed before asking what the tab will be. If the charge is too high in the light of the above assumptions, you feel you have been cheated. You can complain, or can say nothing, pay up, and take your business elsewhere the next time.
- As one would expect in the Middle East, basic differences emerge which lead to difficulty if not understood. For instance, when taking a cab in Beirut it is well to know the going rate as a point around which to bargain and for settling the charge, which must be fixed before engaging the cab.

   If you have not fixed the rate *in advance,* there is a complete change and an entirely different set of rules will apply. According to these rules, the going rate plays no part whatsoever. The whole relationship is altered. The sky is the limit, and the customer has no kick coming. I have seen taxi drivers shouting at the top of their lungs, waving their arms, following a redfaced American with his head pulled down between his shoulders, demanding for a two-pound ride ten Lebanese pounds which the American eventually had to pay.

It is difficult for the American to accommodate his frame of reference to the fact that what constitutes one thing to him, namely, a taxi ride, is to the Arab two very different operations involving two different sets of relationships and two sets of rules. The crucial factor is whether the bargaining is done at the beginning or the end of the ride! As a matter of fact, you cannot bargain at the end. What the driver asks for he is entitled to!

One of the greatest difficulties Americans have abroad stems from the fact that we often think we have a commitment when we do not. The second complication on this same topic is the other side of the coin, i.e., when others think we have agreed to things that we have not. Our own failure to recognize binding obligations, plus our custom of setting organizational goals ahead of everything else, has put us in hot water far too often.

People sometimes do not keep agreements with us because we do not keep agreements with them. As a general rule, the American treats the agreement as something he may eventually have to break. Here are two examples:

- Once while I was visiting an American post in Latin America, the Ambassador sent the Spanish version of a trade treaty down to his language officer with instructions to write in some "weasel words." To his dismay, he was told, "There are no weasel words in Spanish."
- A personnel officer of a large corporation in Iran made an agreement with local employees that American employees would not receive preferential treatment. When the first American employee arrived, it was learned quickly that in the United States he had been covered by a variety of health plans that were not available to Iranians. And this led to immediate protests from the Iranians which were never satisfied. The personnel officer never really grasped the fact that he had violated an iron-bound contract.

Certainly, this is the most important generalization to be drawn by American businessmen from this discussion of agreements: there are many times when we are vulnerable *even when judged by our own standards.* Many instances of actual sharp practices by American companies are well known abroad and are giving American business a bad name. The cure for such questionable behavior is simple. The companies concerned usually have it within their power to discharge offenders and to foster within their organization an atmosphere in which only honesty and fairness can thrive.

But the cure for ignorance of the social and legal rules which underlie business agreements is not so easy. This is because:

- The subject is complex.
- Little research has been conducted to determine the culturally different concepts of what is an agreement.
- The people of each country think that their own code is the only one, and that everything else is dishonest.
- Each code is different from our own; and the farther away one is traveling from Western Europe, the greater the difference is.

But the little that has already been learned about this subject indicates that as a problem it is not insoluble and will yield to research. Since it is probably one of the more relevant and immediately applicable areas of interest to modern business, it would certainly be advisable for companies with large foreign operations to sponsor some serious research in this vital field.

A CASE IN POINT

Thus far, I have been concerned with developing the five check points around which a real understanding of foreign cultures can begin. But the problems that arise from a faulty understanding of the silent language of foreign custom are human problems and perhaps can best be dramatized by an actual case.

A Latin American republic had decided to modernize one of its communication networks to the tune of several million dollars. Because of its reputation for quality and price, the inside track was quickly taken by American company "Y."

The company, having been sounded out informally, considered the size of the order and decided to bypass its regular Latin American representative and send instead its sales manager. The following describes what took place.

The sales manager arrived and checked in at the leading hotel. He immediately had some difficulty pinning down just who it was he had to see about his business. After several days without results, he called at the American Embassy where he found that the commercial attache had the up-to-the-minute information he needed. The commercial attache listened to his story. Realizing that the sales manager had already made a number of mistakes, but figuring that the Latins were used to American blundering, the attache reasoned that all was not lost. He informed the sales manager that the Minister of Communications was the key man and that whoever got the nod from him would get the contract. He also briefed the sales manager on methods of conducting business in Latin America and offered some pointers about dealing with the minister.

The attache's advice ran somewhat as follows:

1. "You don't do business here the way you do in the States; it is necessary to spend much more time. You have to get to know your man and vice versa.
2. "You must meet with him *several times* before you talk business. I will tell you at what point you can bring up the subject. Take your cues from me. [Our American sales manager at this point made a few observations to himself about "cookie pushers" and wondered how many payrolls had been met by the commercial attache.]
3. "Take that price list and put it in your pocket. Don't get it out until I tell you to Down here price is only one of the many things taken into account before closing a deal. In the United States, your past experience will prompt you to act according to a certain set of principles, but many of these principles will not work here. Every time you feel the urge to act or to say something, look at me. Suppress the urge and take your cues from me. This is very important.
4. "Down here people like to do business with men who *are* somebody. In order to be somebody, it is well to have written a book, to have lectured at a university, or to have developed your intellect in some way. The man you are going to see is a poet. He has published several volumes of poetry. Like many Latin Americans, he prizes

poetry highly. You will find that he will spend a good deal of business time quoting his poetry to you, and he will take pleasure on this.

5. "You will also note that the people here are very proud of their past and of their Spanish blood, but they are also exceedingly proud of their liberation from Spain and their independence. The fact that they are a democracy, that they are free, and also that they are no longer a colony is very, very important to them. They are warm and friendly and enthusiastic if they like you. If they don't they are cold and withdrawn.

6. "And another thing, time down here means something different. It works in a different way. You know how it is back in the States when a certain type blurts out whatever is on his mind without waiting to see if the situation is right. He is considered an impatient bore and somewhat egocentric. Well, down here, you have to wait much, much longer, and I really mean *much, much* longer before you can begin to talk about the reason for your visit.

7. There is another point I want to caution you about. At home, the man who sells takes the initiative. Here, *they* tell you when they are ready to do business. But, most of all, don't discuss price until you are asked and don't rush things."

The Pitch

The next day the commercial attache introduced the sales manager to the Minister of Communications. First, there was a long wait in the outer office while people kept coming in and out. The sales manager looked at his watch, fidgeted, and finally asked whether the minister was really expecting him. The reply he received was scarcely reassuring, "Oh yes, he is expecting you but several things have come up that require his attention. Besides, one gets used to waiting down here." The sales manager irritably replied, "But doesn't he know I flew all the way down here from the United States to see him, and I have spent over a week already of my valuable time trying to find him?" "Yes, I know," was the answer, "but things just move much more slowly here."

At the end of about 30 minutes, the minister emerged from the office, greeted the commercial attache with a *double abrazo,* throwing his arms around him and patting him on the back as though they were long-lost brothers. Now, turning and smiling, the minister extended his hand to the sales manager, who, by this time, was feeling rather miffed because he had been kept in the outer office so long.

After what seemed to be an all too short chat, the minister rose, suggesting a well-known cafe where they might meet for dinner the next evening. The sales manager expected, of course, that, considering the nature of their business and the size of the order, he might be taken to the minister's home, not realizing that the Latin home is reserved for family and very close friends.

Until now, nothing at all had been said about the reason for the sales manager's visit, a fact which bothered him somewhat. The whole set-up seemed wrong; neither did he like the idea of wasting another day in town. He told the home office before he left that he would be gone for a week or ten days at most, and made a mental note that he would clean this order up in three days and enjoy a few days in Acapulco or Mexico City. Now the week had already gone and he would be lucky if he made it home in ten days.

Voicing his misgivings to the commercial attache, he wanted to know if the minister really meant business, and, if he did, why could they not get together and talk about it? The commercial attache by now was beginning to show the strain of constantly having to reassure the sales manager. Nevertheless, he tried again:

> *"What you don't realize is that part of the time we were waiting, the minister was rearranging a very tight schedule so that he could spend tomorrow night with you. You see, down here they don't delegate responsibility the way we do in the States. They exercise much tighter control than we do. As a consequence, this man spends up to 15 hours a day at his desk. It may not look like it to you, but I assure you he really means business. He wants to give your company the order; if you play your cards right, you will get it."*

The next evening provided more of the same. Much conversation about food and music, about many people the sales manager had never heard of. They went to a night club, where the sales manager brightened up and began to think that perhaps he and the minister might have something in common after all. It bothered him, however, that the principal reason for his visit was not even alluded to tangentially. But every time he started to talk about electronics, the commercial attache would nudge him and proceed to change the subject.

The next meeting was for morning coffee at a cafe. By now the sales manager was having difficulty hiding his impatience. To make matters worse, the minister had a mannerism which he did not like. When they talked, he was likely to put his hand on him; he would take hold of his arm and get so close that he almost "spat" in his face. As a consequence, the sales manager was kept busy trying to dodge and back up.

Following coffee, there was a walk in a nearby park. The minister expounded on the shrubs, the birds, and the beauties of nature, and at one spot he stopped to point at a statue and said: "There is a statue of the world's greatest hero, the liberator of mankind!" At this point, the worst happened, for the sales manager asked who the statue was of and, being given the name of a famous Latin American patriot, said, "I never heard of him," and walked on.

The Failure

It is quite clear from this that the sales manager did not get the order, which went to a Swedish concern. The American, moreover, was never able to see the minister again. Why did the minister feel the way he did? His reasoning went somewhat as follows:

> *"I like the American's equipment and it makes sense to deal with North Americans who are near us and whose price is right. But I could never be friends with this man. He is not my kind of human being and we have nothing in common. He is not simpatico. If I can't be friends and he is not simpatico, I can't depend on him to treat me right. I tried everything, every conceivable situation, and only once did we seem to understand each other. If we could be friends, he would feel obligated to me and his obligation would give me some control. Without control, how do I know he will deliver what he says he will at the price he quotes?"*

Of course, what the minister did not know was that the price was quite firm, and that quality control was a matter of company policy. He did not realize that the sales manager was a member of an organization, and that the man is always subordinate to the organization in the United States. Next year maybe the sales manager would not even be representing the company, but would be replaced. Further, if he wanted someone to depend on, his best bet would be to hire a good American lawyer to represent him and write a binding contract.

In this instance, both sides suffered. The American felt he was being slighted and put off, and did not see how there could possibly be any connection between poetry and doing business or why it should all take so long. He interpreted the delay as a form of polite brushoff. Even if things had gone differently and there had been a contract, it is doubtful that the minister would have trusted the contract as much as he would a man whom he considered his friend. Throughout Latin America, the law is made livable and contracts workable by having friends and relatives operating from the inside. Lacking a friend, someone who would look out for his interests, the minister did not want to take a chance. He stated this simply and directly.

CONCLUSION

The case just described has of necessity been oversimplified. The danger is that the reader will say, "Oh, I see. All you really have to do is be friends." At which point the expert will step in and reply:

"Yes, of course, but what you don't realize is that in Latin America being a friend involves much more than it does in the United States and is an entirely different proposition. A friendship implies obligations. You go about it differently. It involves much more than being nice, visiting, and playing golf. You would not want to enter into friendship lightly."

The point is simply this. It takes year and years to develop a sound foundation for doing business in a given country. Much that is done seems silly or strange to the home office. Indeed, the most common error made by home offices. Once they have found representatives who can get results, is failure to take their advice and allow sufficient time for representatives to develop the proper contacts.

The second most common error, if that is what it can be called, is ignorance of the secret and hidden language of foreign cultures. In this article I have tried to show how five key topics—time, space, material possessions, friendship patterns, and business agreements—offer a starting point from which companies can begin to acquire the understanding necessary to do business in foreign countries.

Our present knowledge is meager, and much more research is needed before the businessman of the future can go abroad fully equipped for his work. Not only will he need to be well versed in the economics, law, and politics of the area, but he will have to understand, if not speak, the silent languages of other cultures. ∎

NOTES

1. For details, see my book, *The Silent Language* (New York, Doubleday & Company, Inc., 1959).

The European Market in 1992: Strategies for U.S. Companies

James Catoline
*Associate Professor of
International Management*

John Chopoorian
*Professor of Marketing
both at Southeastern
Massachusetts University*

AN OVERVIEW

The advent of a single, unified European market in 1992 is in the news daily in Europe. The 12 member states representing 320 million people and a 4.1 trillion dollar economy are committed by the end of 1992 to eliminating physical, technical and fiscal barriers to the free movement of goods, services, equipment, capital, and people.[1]

The U.S. with an already serious trade deficit—currently 1.48 billion dollars with the European Economic Community—is particularly vulnerable. No longer in the simpler world of bilateral or GATT agreements, what is shaping up is a "Triadian" grouping of the Pacific Rim, North American, and European nations. Unless there is a measured strategic response by both the government and private sector, the U.S. will drift into the 21st century with growing pressures for isolationism and the specter of trade wars that those pressures usually bring.[2]

Until recently, there was little awareness in the U.S. of these important events. The trade debate over hormones in beef, feverish activity by U.S. multinationals on the European merger and acquisition scene, and corresponding interest by European mergers and acquisition participants in the U.S. have finally begun to attract the attention of the business community and media. Numerous recent conferences and professional meetings are building awareness, and 1992 is becoming a hot area of endeavor.[3]

To address the subject of strategic response by U.S. companies, we conducted an exploratory study early in 1989 with a task force comprised of the

Reprinted by permission, *SAM Advanced Management Journal*, Spring 1990, Society for Advancement of Management, Vinton, VA 24179.

Dr. Catoline has worked for GTE, DEC, and most recently as director of Human Resources for Data General in Europe; Dr. Chopoorian formerly held management positions with American Cynamid and Union Carbide.

author and 30 graduate and undergraduate management students. Data were collected through an extensive literature search at the London School of Economics and University of London libraries, covering British and other European periodicals, newspapers, and working papers. We conducted in-depth personal interviews with executives at ten British and U.S. corporations which have European operations, the Chamber of British Industries and the Department of Trade and Industry, several British academic experts, and a Member of the European Parliament. The content of our interviews spanned strategic responses as well as a wide range of environmental factors including political, social, cultural, economic, technological, and governmental. The object of our study was to assess the following.

1. The extent to which European political and economic integration will occur;
2. The degree of preparation of U.S. films for this event; and
3. The likelihood that a "Fortress Europe" will develop.

Our study revealed both a strong likelihood that a single European market will occur and a surprising lack of preparation by all but the largest firms. Even in the case of large multinational corporations, it is tempting to conclude that preparations consist of "buying" positions through joint ventures with local partners—a strategy of preventing exclusion. We believe that this may not lead to the desired result. While the political process is creating an infrastructure of a single market, markets will be established not by politicians but by the entrepreneurial efforts of business people who correctly perceive the dynamics of needs, trends, directions, and niches. Few U.S. or British firms appear to be looking at the realities of 1992 at a product market level and doing the needed marketing research to take advantage of its opportunities. It is by no means certain that merely choosing a European joint venture partner will automatically provide this capability.

Depending on the specific industry, product, or market at issue, it is late in the game. Firms will need not only primary and secondary market data, but also an understanding of the importance of cross cultural influences, especially for consumer products such as foods and apparel. For more industrial products, such as computer systems, software, and office landscape architecture, advantages of operating on a market-wide basis in Europe may be quickly attained.

EUROPEAN INTEGRATION AT THE MACROECONOMIC LEVEL

A major EC goal is the "harmonization" of fiscal policies and technical standards. This means that major differences among the European nations' tax systems, including revenue, excise, and value-added taxes will be eliminated to avoid competition for business investment or skilled labor based on tax rates. Manufactured products from farm machinery to pharmaceuticals would have to meet minimum industry standards to be marketed in any of the member countries.

Steps to permit the free movement of services include abolishing restrictions in insurance and banking, deregulation and increased competition in the airline industry, and the uniform licensing of legal, medical, consulting, and other professional services. Insurance companies will be able to sell commercial and other policies in any EC country by 1990. Businesses and individuals in one country will be able to establish relationships with banks in other countries. Residence requirements for professionals would be standardized, insuring the right of lawyers, doctors, accountants, and therapists to practice in any EC country. The establishment of uniform employment policies would insure the free flow of labor among the countries.

The creation of ECU (European Currency Unit) and the elimination of exchange rate fluctuations within the European Currency Union represent important steps toward monetary unity. Without the monetary manipulations of individual countries, there will be greater efficiency in business transactions, investment, pricing and credit, as well as more stability in interest rates. An inevitable, though controversial, next step is the creation of a central European Bank.

All of these measures point to the establishment of one vast internal market, increasing the economic and political clout of Europe and enabling powerful European and multinational companies to compete and achieve great economies of scale.

There are several barriers to this ideal of an economic union, not the least of which is the need for the member nations to surrender a great measure of their national sovereignty. For 2000 years, European history has advanced the notion of the supreme power and autonomy of the nation-state; now the concept of "Europe sans frontieres" may threaten the independence, prestige, and self-determination of some member states, giving rise to strong opposition by some political leaders. Economic differences will arise between the affluent, industrial Northern Europe and the poorer, agricultural South, and political differences between free enterprise-oriented governments and more socialistic systems. The expansion of EC membership has hindered its decision-making ability, and the original industrialized member nations fear that admitting more particulary under-developed, countries may "overload" the community system and create internal competition. Some fear the cultural homogenization of Europe, which occurred in the Balkans after World War II. Europeanists stress that the benefits from a more integrated European Community far outweigh the losses. They point out that economic integration is necessary and inevitable and cite the 18th century American philosopher, Benjamin Franklin, to the effect that, "If we do not hang together, we will surely hang separately."

European executives take the view that the politicians may argue indefinitely about why, whether, and when complete European integration will occur. The fact is that industry leaders believe in it and will make it happen. Some economists have suggested that European economic unity has two separate aspects: corporate integration and institutional integration, which run parallel but at different rates of speed.[4]

Trade Blocs and "Trade Blocs and "Triadian Marketing"

The Single European Act of 1987 has provided challenges and opportunities to European companies. They are aware that a "fortress Europe" may protect them from external competitive attack and foreign dumping, but at the same time restrict their competitive advantage outside the Great Market. The strength of Western Europe in world trade would consequently be decreased, which would be devastating to a continent whose world market share has been eroding over the last 20 years.

Since the mid-1980s, distinct trade blocs have emerged. This is an historically interesting development, as the nation-state appears to be giving way to the supranational trade group. Three such groups dominate the world economic picture—the European Community, North America, and the East Asia/Pacific Rim—resulting in a "Triad" of economic powers. While trade within each of those blocs is accelerating, trade among them is declining.[5] According to one recent statistical study, trade among EC member countries has increased nearly 15% since 1985, while in the same period the EC's trade with all non-member countries decreased approximately 10%. In the first nine months of 1988, the EC's trade with North America grew only some 5%, but trade in the same period among the U.S., Mexico, and Canada grew almost 20%. This trend is expected to increase dramatically in the 1990s as a result of the new Free Trade Agreement between Canada and the U.S.[6] An Asian-Pacific common market seems to be emerging, including Japan, the "four dragons" of Singapore, Hong Kong, Taiwan, and South Korea, as well as Indonesia, Thailand, Malaysia. Although currently in political turmoil, the Philippines and China seek to be included. Trade among these ten nations grew at 32% in the first nine months of 1988, compared with a 17% growth with North America and 10% with Europe in the same period.[7]

Some believe that protectionism is the shadowy figure responsible for these developments in world trade, and that the effect of the "Triadian" economy will be an end to international trade as we know it and the growth of economically self-sufficient "fortresses." From the perspective of many U.S. businesses, the ED, by passing laws to remove internal trade barriers, is erecting external ones, designed to keep foreign businesses out of Europe.

European companies stress that they should be out in front in their own turf, and if they cannot make it in the European market, they will not be able to make it anywhere. They want to have a competitive edge, but at the same time believe they can handle foreign competition. Some industrial leaders have said that they do not want to keep American goods out of Europe, but fear that U.S. companies will become transhipment points for Japanese products.[8] They point out that because of increasing offshore manufacturing in the U.S. by Japanese companies, America, in insisting on open trade abroad, will in fact be exporting Japanese products to Europe, to the detriment of its own and European economies.

In fact, Japanese companies may not even find such strategies necessary, as many, like SONY and several camera manufacturers, have been setting up manufacturing bases and entering into free trade agreements with regional economic development agencies in European countries (e.g., the Alsace region of France in 1984).

Reciprocity represents a crucial concept for the EC. Essentially it means that countries that want to trade in Europe will have to open up their own markets to potential EC trading partners. Banks, for example, that wish to market their products and services in Europe will be issued banking licenses by member nations only if European banks are permitted to conduct business in the non EC country. According to Malcom Levitt, an executive consultant in the London office of Ernst & Whinney, "EC states want a guarantee that, if by abandoning their public procurement policies they risk having their markets cleaned by non-EC countries, they at least want a full opportunity to market their own products in those countries."[9]

The key question is whether the EC will act as a bloc in this matter, barring entry to countries that do not freely import European goods, or whether individual member states will be able to negotiate separate trade agreements with non-EC countries, particularly as a way of selling off the quantities of surplus goods not disposed of under the Common Agricultural Policy.

The new frontier of trade for EC countries is Eastern Europe and the Soviet Union. Glasnost and Perestroika in the Soviet Union have opened up the possibility of greater political and economic cooperation, and Western European politicians and entrepreneurs see that the EC has a vast new market in Eastern Europe and the Soviet Union.[10] The opening of borders in Hungary and East Germany in the fall of 1989, and the inevitable reunification of Germany, pose major threats and opportunities for European integration.

In the 1990s, the U.S. may seek to reduce its budgetary burden and put pressure on a stronger and richer Europe to take over a greater share of its own defense spending. The EC needs to decide whether to build its nuclear arsenal, invest in conventional weapons, or to establish a neutral Europe. European leaders fear that President Gorbachev's efforts for change could fail, resulting in either a return to conservative old-guard policies or social upheaval in the Soviet Union either of which would have severe repercussions in Europe. Because of this fear, several European governments and financial institutions are actively seeking to support the Soviet leader by providing loans and economic aid. To encourage the opening and liberalizing of Eastern bloc markets a kind of Marshall Plan for economic aid to Poland, Czechoslovakia, Hungary, Romania, and East Germany is being planned by the EC.[11] Western European companies are already very actively engaged in bartering and countertrade deals with Eastern block governments. In addition, EC countries are exporting their food surpluses, including grain, dairy products, beef, oil, and wine, at bargain prices to the Soviet Union and the Eastern bloc (the famous "wine lakes and butter mountains"). Such dumping practices could lead to trade wars with the U.S. South American countries, and New Zealand over the sale of agricultural products to Eastern Europe. At the same time, it is likely that the Soviet Union will follow China's example and launch an export campaign to penetrate Western markets. It is possible that the USSR and Eastern Europe will form a fourth coalition, perhaps in conjunction with Asian countries, or seek a closer partnership with Europe.

U.S. and Japanese companies must set up operations in the EC now to position themselves as European.[12] The decline of production and productivity in the U.S., coupled with its rising trade and budget deficits, compel America to be more competitive overseas.

Inevitably, the three trade giants will be host competition on each other's turf as well as for other potential markets in Africa, Latin America, Asia, Australia, and Eastern Europe. Hence the concept of "Triadian Marketing" (i.e., the increasing need for companies in the three blocs to compete for markets, seek new investment and technology-transfer opportunities, and off-shore production bases.)

THE CLIMATE FOR FOREIGN BUSINESS IN THE EC

The French press has coined the sardonic phrase, "L'Europe a pulsieurs vitesses" (Europe at different speeds). The new Europe's global clout is limited by cultural, linguistic, legal, and political differences. Foreign companies doing business or seeking to enter the European market may be exasperated by the lack of common business practices: differences in accounting practices in payment practices (some countries like Italy and France have accounts payable delays of normally up to 180 days) and in marketing practices (Germany has strict laws governing promotional techniques and giveaways.)

One of the major obstacles to free trade within Europe and to marketing by foreign companies is the maze of standards which individual countries have for various products, from appliances to food products to pharmaceuticals. France is more liberal than other countries about regulating the potency of over-the-counter drugs and itemizing the ingredients of canned and processed foods. The U.K. has a different system of electrical currents than the rest of Europe. Some countries use three-pronged plugs, while others use two-pronged. Germany has strict consumer-protection laws. There are two different systems for television reception in Europe.

The EC has adopted some Europe-wide standards, and others will go into effect by 1992 and after. These include guidelines on machine tools, TV sets, telephones, health and safety products, prescription drugs, automobiles and automotive equipment. In the case of food and beverages, products licensed in one country can be sold in all the others. How all this will work in practice, however, is not clear, and standardization in production and marketing is still far away. Reforms in customs procedures and product standards are necessary for the bottom line health of both European and American multinationals. Some of these, like Philips, are planning a strategy of centralized manufacturing and assembly plants.[13]

European companies are taking advantage of deregulation to enter into a host of cross-border mergers, and the industrial giants are rushing to acquire smaller companies to create pan-European industrial and financial mega-corporations capable of successfully blocking Japanese and American competitors.

A number of foreign businesses are hurrying to get in the elevator before it goes up. In order to position themselves as local companies, insure their access to local markets, or comply with "local content" regulations (see the later section Product and Production), they are increasingly establishing manufacturing plants. Several Japanese microchip and camera companies, Korean auto makers, and Hong Kong textile manufacturers are already producing in Western Europe.

Some large U.S. companies have begun to take the initiative. IBM, responding perhaps to aggressive merger and acquisition strategies of European competitors like Siemens, Olivetti and Honeywell-Bull, has started setting up joint ventures with European firms, including two French banks, Credit Agricole, and Paribas to develop data transmission services for financial institutions.[14] Companies that provide telecommunications services like electronic mail, tele-conferencing, tele-faxing, and data networks (NYNEX has recently signed a contract with the Dutch telephone company) are aggressively penetrating the European market. AT&T also has entered into a joint venture with Phillips Telecommunications, and the two have formed an alliance with a third company, the Spanish electronics producer Amper.[15]

With a multimillion dollar contract to sell equipment to the Spanish telephone company, this foothold in Southern Europe represents a major strategic position for the American and Dutch multinationals.

In addition to telecommunications companies, banks and securities firms are also expected to reap big profits. Because of planned legislation, like the single banking license valid in all EC countries or the plan of some countries like Spain and France to allow foreign financial institutions to acquire local brokerage firms, a number of mergers between European and American banks have already occurred. U.S. financial institutions, like J. P. Morgan, are moving to portfolio management, brokerage, and marketing of foreign stocks in Europe and European stocks in other countries. American Express is attempting to be seen as more European, attracting local corporate and individual clients through its travel, banking, and credit card services as well as investments through its Shearson Lehman Hutton division.[16]

THE MICROLEVEL: IMPLICATIONS FOR MANAGEMENT STRATEGY

What are individual firms doing to prepare for 1992? Dr. John Owens, deputy director general of the Chamber of British Industries (CBI) states, "British companies are sleep walking towards 1992. Many of them will go out of business in the early 1990s unless they start to prepare." A survey conducted by the CBI revealed the following about British firms:

- 80% are not reviewing strategy;
- 90% are not conducting marketing research on the continent;
- 93% are not taking initiatives to train employees in languages;
- 95% do not have sales agents in the rest of the EEC; and
- 1% are opening any new manufacturing plants on the continent.[17]

The vast majority of the 12,000 firms included in the CBI, which represent over $18 billion in sales, are making little effort to plan for the coming single market in 1992. In 1989, the Department of Trade and Industry launched a national campaign to create awareness of the opportunities for British companies in Europe.

We are conducting a similar study of U.S. firms in four product areas including consumer and industrial markets. Preliminary results show that except for the largest firms most U.S. companies are showing a similarly passive response to 1992.

U.S. firms and the U.S. government need a major stimulus to promote open trade policy and competitiveness. They need to prepare now or be left behind. Management consultant Christopher Cook, who has advised a number of European clients on their strategic planning, suggests the matrix shown in Table 1 as a starting point. As an example, we show market size for the auto industry, with shares held by North America-U.S., EC, Japan, and others (including USSR, Eastern Europe, Latin America, Africa, Asia, and China). Unless firms understand their business in terms of markets, supplier shares, technologies, and customers, it will be difficult to identify the opportunities and challenges that lie ahead.

While market data are clearly understood and available for the automotive industry, agricultural products, chemicals, and metals, other industries require the gathering of primary data through surveys, interviews, and focus groups in concert with available secondary data. This is especially true for emerging markets.

Doing business in the Single Market will mean major changes in the competitive position and selling strategies of U.S. companies. New regulations now being established affect a broad range of products and services, as well as manufacturing, sourcing, distribution, pricing strategies, advertising, standardization, and product positioning. Let us examine the implications for management in each of these areas.

PRODUCTION AND PRODUCT DEVELOPMENT

In January, 1989, the European Commission enacted strict "local content" rules which will directly affect foreign manufacturers in Europe. Specifically designed to restrict the imports of integrated circuits, these rules will likely force leading U.S. and Japanese microchip suppliers to build manufacturing plants in the EC to ensure market access. Until now, most Japanese and some U.S. semiconductor manufacturers have had final assembly and test facilities in Europe for finishing the circuits imported from their home-based plants. In an effort to eliminate these "screwdriver plants," the new regulations require that integrated circuits be *completely* manufactured in the EC, and that foreign companies obtain a certificate of origin to have free access to the markets of the 12 members states. Also 60–80% of the components used in the finished product must be EC-made.

Most large U.S. companies, like Texas Instruments, had begun to set up factories in Europe prior to the ruling. But Japanese companies have generally preferred to export products and components. If Japanese companies step up their investments in Europe in response to the new rules of origin they could cut into the market share of, the very European electronics companies that pressed for the rules in the first place. Some of these companies, like Siemens and Philips, could mount a very aggressive campaign to boost their sales, emphasize their European image, and thwart foreign competitors. Since, as is widely believed, these new regulations are aimed primarily at the Japanese, large European companies may seek joint ventures with American manufacturers.

It is likely that local content rules will ultimately apply to all manufacturing industries, so that foreign suppliers lacking EC-based operations are going to have to invest $100 to $200 million within the next couple of years to build factories in Europe and hire local labor, or face losing their European market altogether. According to our research, smaller and medium-sized U.S. companies unable to make such an investment are looking to partnerships and joint ventures with European companies. Two promising venues for manufacturing operations of foreign companies are Spain and Portugal. Tax incentives, liberal profit repatriation plans, low labor and construction costs, and pro-business attitudes (unexpected from Socialist governments) all constitute attractive features of these countries.

Another result of the move by foreign companies to establish a European manufacturing presence will be an increase in local product development and the establishment of a separate and independent R&D function in Europe. Indeed, having a European image will be an important strategic goal for U.S. companies: European consumers will consider foreign-owned companies with local manufacturing and R&D facilities as full-fledged European companies. They will be seen as contributing to the development of the European economy and employment, selling a product made by and for Europeans. These concerns can thus take advantage of pan-European marketing. They may also need to consider entering into collaborative arrangements to develop new products, e.g., with other firms needing to make the same changes required by the market, with universities and technology institutes, with European trade associations, or with E.C.R.&D programs and research consortiums.

New, more liberal merger policies under consideration by the European Commission would accelerate cross-border mergers and acquisitions and increase the pressure on companies from outside the community to acquire more operations in Europe.

Interestingly, some of the larger European auto manufacturers are adopting a Japanese strategy and, through acquisitions and restructuring, are transforming themselves into diversified conglomerates. West Germany's Daimler-Benz, maker of the Mercedes, is getting into the aerospace business, while Italy's Fiat has started a medical equipment division, and Sweden's Volvo also has a large food company.[18] These trends will bolster the automobile industry through cross-subsidization and provide a further competitive challenge to U.S. auto manufacturers.

Exploiting new markets and responding to competition may require radical changes to products and processes. Common technical standards in all EC countries should help companies rationalize production if they can satisfy local content requirements. Moreover, they will have to assess opportunities to relocate their plants as national boundaries become less important.

DISTRIBUTION

These changes in policy, competitive strategy, and customer attitudes will have an impact on distribution structure and approach. More destinations, more buyers, new transport routes, speed and frequency of delivery, new services and different types of channels will all pose distribution challenges.

Multinationals will need to decide whether to extend a standardized distribution strategy throughout the EC or adapt their distribution approach to each national market. They will need to identify new destinations to be served, estimate the increased volume of products, and decide between direct delivery and the need for warehousing. They will also need a new organizations structure to support their distribution, particularly in view of new information handling requirements and problems of control of remote locations.

Service companies will need to decide whether they can provide service from one EC country (and which one) or if they need a presence in each local market. They will have to consider the relative advantages and costs of establishing a subsidiary or branch, using an agent or broker, or linking with local firms.

PRICING

Pricing an international marketing has always been problematic because of the idiosyncrasies of legal, competitive, and buyer behavior environments in foreign markets. Pricing strategy of foreign companies doing business in the EC may, in fact, be more complex after 1992 than before.

Companies will be expected to go to market in most if not all of the 12 countries, and barring the unlikely event that a single European currency is in effect by the mid '90s, they will face the challenge of dealing with different currencies subject to floating exchange rates. Even when one standard currency is in effect, demand and competitive situations will vary in the target markets, so that companies may aim for standardized marketing and even standardized advertising but not standardized pricing. Some European multinationals, like Saint-Gobain-Pont-a-Mousson, have already decided to use the ECU (European Currency Unit) for cross-border billing purposes in order to reduce foreign exchange risks and simplify accounting. The benefits for Saint-Gobain have been lower exchange losses and the sharing of both gains and losses between exporter and importer.

Distribution margins, taxes, transport and handling costs will affect pricing. Manufacturing in an EC country will be a plus in terms of pricing and may even be a necessity to meet the competition. Local manufacturing will eliminate transfer pricing from a domestic product division to subsidiaries via an international division. One real possibility will be frequent price wars between European and foreign companies doing business in Europe, particularly in consumer products and services.

U.S. firms will face a problem that most of their European competitors will not have, i.e., needing a variety of transfer pricing strategies that permit their European subsidiaries to price equitably and competitively in their respective markets, while satisfying both headquarters' demands and EC constraints. The challenge is maintaining varying transfer prices and remaining both legal and competitive. Joint ventures may enable U.S. companies to price their products more competitively by avoiding transfer costs.

PROMOTION

Several important trends in Europe will critically impact the promotional strategies of foreign companies.

1. Standardization of regulations on advertising. Until now, European countries have had widely different laws and customs pertaining to print and media advertising. Some countries, like Belgium, have limited institutional advertising and no brand or product advertising. Many countries prohibit television advertising of certain products, like tobacco (Germany), alcohol (U.K.), and computers (France). Banking, financial and insurance services can be advertised on television in the U.K. but in few other EC countries.

Cable and household TV penetration varies widely, from zero ad minutes per day in Denmark to 740 ad minutes per day in Italy, with the average being 40–80 minutes per day in West Germany, France and Spain.[19] Private commercial television stations have existed alongside public channels for several years in Italy, offering viewers a wide variety of programming and a choice of 8 to 10 channels. As in America, private channels interrupt their programming with frequent commercials. Only in 1986 did France permit a commercial and a cable channel alongside its three government-sponsored channels, where commercials are grouped together prior to or following the programs. By its geographic position, Belgium benefits from 15 or more channels transmitted from the U.K., France, the Netherlands and Germany, so despite their own country's restrictions, Belgians presumably are highly sensitized to TV advertising. As a result of standardization in many areas, common regulations regarding the nature and frequency of TV advertising will be forthcoming.

But national tastes and customs are another matter. The major newspapers, like the *London Times, Le Monde, Frankfurter Allgemeine* and *Corriere della Sera,* have little or no advertising and few pictures. Yet respectable magazines like *Paris Match, Epoca,* and *Bunte* are packed with ads and sensational photography. France is a country of billboards, yet few are found in Germany; are the French more visually attuned? A long-running bloc of creative and entertaining commercials is common before the start of the feature in French cinemas. In both France and Germany, nudity and sex are used to sell all kinds of products, but such advertising would be shocking if not illegal in Spain, Greece, or Ireland. As satellite TV, commercial and cable TV become more common, will advertising practices of one country prevail in the others, or will standardized advertising be the result?

2. International TV will have fewer governmental constraints than domestic TV, therefore, it will be difficult to control the kind or frequency of advertising. Television advertising will in fact become the chief form of consumer-product advertising in Europe, and European consumers like their American counterparts, will become more brand-conscious and less quality-conscious than in the past.[20] All EC countries will have to accept the same regulation of ads, or none at all. Expansion of commercial time on TV will be inevitable. One strategy that advertising agencies are already selling to consumer product manufacturers is standardized multi-lingual TV advertising, i.e., using the same ad, transmitted in different languages with voice-over dubbing. Dannon Yogurt and Pepsi are examples of this.

3. As in the U.S., advertising of professional service businesses—investment, insurance, banks, law firms, medical and health services, education and consulting—will become common in the EC and will go hand in hand with the expansion of these sectors for foreign companies.

4. European integration seems to be encouraging the concentration of certain industries, and business sectors in certain cities. Hence London's stock market shows signs of becoming Europe's principal international financial market; Frankfurt will be the EC's high tech center and "silicon valley"; Brussels will be the political capital as well as locus for multinational corporate headquarters and management consulting; Milan is becoming the capital of the fashion industry; Luxembourg specializes in finance and insurance. It is no surprise that Paris will emerge the European center of the $60 billion per-year advertising business, with several of the top 20 worldwide agencies located there, including Ogilvy & Mather, the Eurocom Group, Publicists International, and Roux Seguela Cayzac and Godard. The domination of international advertising by American agencies is waning, as multinational accounts consolidate in relatively few agencies.

5. Changes in product positioning. Products which are now common household items in one country will become novelty items in another, while prestige-brand products in one national market will lose their image or need to reposition themselves in another market. American exporters may have an advantage here over European manufacturers. Increased advertising of pharmaceutical products will trigger a number of changes, including the packaging and labelling of products, the use of generic drugs, and radically

different distribution of pharmaceutical products, likely resulting in American-style drug stores competing with traditional pharmacies.

TABLE 1
International Context: Strategic Scoping Suppliers/Market Share Example-Not a Forecast 1989 to 2000

Case: Automobile Units	Suppliers				
Markets	U.S.	EEC	Japan	Other	Total
U.S.	60%	15%	25%	NIL	100%
EEC	17%	60%	23%	NIL	100%
Japan	10%	5%	85%	NIL	100%
Other	25%	20%	30%	25%	100%
Supplier %	36.4%	28.7%	30.5%	4.4%	100%

CONCLUSION

The following is a summary of our conclusions. These are based on our analysis of current development, surveys of EC and multinational companies; and our considered opinion.

1. European economic integration is necessary and inevitable and will result in political and economic unity in the EC.
2. A protectionist "Fortress Europe" is feared by European companies as restricting their competitive advantage and further eroding Europe's world market share. They do not want to keep American goods out of Europe, nor do they want their markets deluged by Japanese products manufactured in the U.S. The EC is interested in reciprocity in trade agreements with non-member countries.
3. The trend toward economic integration will produce three large trade blocks—the EC, North America, and the Pacific Rim. The need for off-shore manufacturing, technology transfer, and new market opportunities will promote the concept of "Triadian Marketing" or increased presence and penetration by multinationals of foreign markets.
4. The opening up of Eastern Europe and the Soviet Union will pave the way for increased trade and integration with the EC.

5. U.S. industry in general is not preparing for the opportunities or challenges of the single European market. Because of "local content" legislation in the EC, the rush toward mergers and acquisitions by large European firms, and the need for companies to market themselves as European, U.S. companies wishing to penetrate the European market of 1992 must establish a presence now, either in manufacturing or marketing, before barriers or competition preclude entry.

6. Establishing a European manufacturing presence by foreign companies will increase local product development and R&D.

7. U.S. banks, financial management and brokerage firms, and insurance companies are in a good position to benefit from opportunities to market their services in Europe as well as enter joint ventures with EC counterparts.

8. Doing business in the Single Market will necessitate changes in the competitive strategies of U.S. companies, particularly marketing research, sourcing, distribution, pricing, promotion, and positioning. ■

NOTES

1. Cecchini, Paolo. *The European Challenge 1992: The Benefits of a Single Market,* p. 37.
2. "A New Landscape Takes Shape," *The Financial Times—London,* January 11, 1989, p. 20.
3. "Europeans to Offer Plan to Ease Trade Dispute with U.S." *The New York Times,* January 4, 1989, p. D20.
4. Remarks of Fulbright Scholar Paul Teague quoted from the Southeastern Massachusetts University International Seminar, "The Single European Market in 1992: Impact on U.S. Trade." February 23, 1989.
5. Finn, Edwin A. "Sons of Smoot-Hawley." *Forbes,* February 6, 1989, p. 38–40.
6. Ibid.
7. Ibid.
8. "The '90s and Beyond." *The Wall Street Journal,* February 13, 1989, p. 1.
9. Milmo, Sean. "Are You Ready for 1992?" *Business Marketing,* September 1988, p. 74.
10. Ibid.
11. "A 'Marshall Plan' to Rescue Poorer Regions." *The Boston Globe,* March 12, 1989.
12. Magee, John F. "1992: Moves Americans must Make." *The Harvard Business Review.* May-June 1989, p. 78.
13. Tully, Shawn. "Europe Gets Ready for 1992." *Fortune,* February 1, 1989, p. 81–82.
14. Ibid.
15. Ibid.
16. Julian Oliver, Managing Director of American Express-London, quoted from address to SMU Field Seminar in London, "The Changes in Financial Markets Due to EEC Integration in 1992." January 11, 1989.
17. "Firms Not Awake to 1992 Says CBI." *The Times,* January 9, 1989.
18. Tully, Shawn. "Europe Gets Ready for 1992." *Fortune,* February 1, 1988, p. 81–82.
19. *International Advertiser.* September, 1985, p. 8.
20. Ibid.

Profiling the Entrepreneur
John G. Burch

Entrepreneurs are the darlings of news anchors, talk show hosts, politicians, and academicians. But just who are the entrepreneurs? And what makes them tick?

The term *entrepreneur* is a derivative of the French word *entreprendre,* which means "to undertake". The entrepreneur is the one who undertakes a venture, organizes it, raises capital to finance it, and assumes all or a major portion of the risk. Entrepreneurs also appear to be the prime change agents in a society. Who are the entrepreneurs? And what makes them tick?

ENTREPRENEURS: SOME EXAMPLES

Columbus, a true entrepreneur, started America's development with backing from Queen Isabella, a venture capitalist. From all over the world, aspiring entrepreneurs—many of them penniless—representing different religions, cultures, and ethnicities, came to America and played a major role in its development. The entrepreneurial thread is tightly woven into the fabric of American society.

Today the entrepreneurial beat goes on. Entrepreneurs abound: Edson de Castro, founder of Data General; George Mitchell, founder of Mitchell Energy and Development Corporation; An Wang, founder of Wang Laboratories; Steven Jobs, cofounder of Apple Computer; L. J. Sevin, founder of Compaq Computers; Ted Turner, founder of Turner Broadcasting Systems; Samuel Walton, founder of Wal-Mart; Fred Smith, founder of Federal Express; and Trammell S. Crow, developer. Literally thousands of other successful entrepreneurs could be mentioned.

The point is that these people, and others like them, create change, provide a variety of job opportunities, and also serve as role models to inspire new generations of entrepreneurs. Moreover, they have reaped huge rewards

From *Business Horizons* © 1986 by the Foundation for the School of Business at Indiana University. Reprinted by permission.

John G. Burch is a professor of accounting and information systems at the University of Nevada in Reno. His most recent books are *Entrepreneurship* and the fourth edition of *Information Systems: Theory and Practice*, both published by Wiley this year.

for themselves and the venture capitalists who had the foresight to back them.

The advent of personal computers opened up a vast software market, and young computer wizards developed marketable computer software packages while sitting at their home computer terminals. William Gates III, cofounder of Microsoft, and Mitchell D. Kapor, founder of Lotus Development Corporation, exemplify a budding group of entrepreneurs—the new tinkerers and "in-the-garage" inventors.

Many hardware niches remain to be filled. Kevin Jenkins, an accounting graduate, and two friends founded Hercules Computer Technology with $32,000. The company quickly grew from nothing to a $30 million enterprise by providing graphics boards for retailers who sell IBM personal computers.

Furthermore, personal computers create a number of supplementary niches, Users need training, computers require maintenance and repair, and soon there will be a vast used-computer market. The same situation exists in any new industry, such as biotechnology, telecommunications, and robotics. These industries all generate the need for thousands of small new businesses to fill niches in the marketplace.

On the lighter side, Rich Tennant makes a profit by poking fun at computers and serious users. His quirky cartoons and illustrations are displayed in a number of computer magazines. A group of entertainers wrote and presented a comedy show called *Up You Computer!* for a consumer electronics convention. Also, some enterprising publishers gave birth to *Confuserworld, a Computerworld* parody. They were sued, however, by a humorless IBM when Mark Florant, one of the founders wrote a story called "IBM Calls It Quits," where the giant corporation decides to pull out because business is too successful and boring.

It is not all high-tech entrepreneurship and its spinoffs, however. Observe the niches produced by shopping centers. Special niches cater to the taste buds of hungry and thirsty shoppers. Entrepreneurs across the country offer these shoppers everything from specially prepared orange juice to delightfully stuffed potatoes. An entrepreneur can become a millionaire by setting up lemonade stands!

THE ENTREPRENEURIAL SUPPLY

Where do entrepreneurial talent, know-how, and dedication come from? Are people born with entrepreneurial skills? Can entrepreneurs be taught? What gives then the incentive and energy to exploit opportunities? All these questions are puzzling because entrepreneurs cannot be standardized and reduced to mechanical models.

The supply of entrepreneurial talent is subject to a number of both internal and external forces. Entrepreneurs are, to some extent, a product of genetics, family influences, peer pressure, cultural conditions, educational systems, religion, and strength of the work ethic. Moreover, the would-be entrepreneur must perform within and be motivated by, the same conditions in which entrepreneurship itself is embedded. Impediments to entrepreneurship—such as taxes, regulations, and other unfavorable conditions—tend to dry up the supply of entrepreneurs, while favorable conditions tend to spawn entrepreneurs. Still, entrepreneurship and vice versa. In environments hostile to entrepreneurship, underground economies usually develop. In friendlier climates, outsiders come in to exploit entrepreneurial opportunities.

The existence of a favorable environment will not be itself ensure entrepreneurial activity, any more than the existence of a soccer field guarantees soccer games and players.

ENTREPRENEURS AND INNOVATION

Simply being a caretaker or administrator of a business will not result in economic growth and diversification. Innovation is a major factor for meeting the changing needs of society. Clearly, an important tool of the entrepreneur is innovation.

There are six types of innovation:

- Introduction of a new product or service that improves the quality or decreases the price of the existing product or service;
- Implementation of a system or resource that differentiates an existing product or service (for example, American Airlines' Sabre System);
- Introduction of a new system that increases productivity (for example, robotics) and decision making (for example, artificial intelligence);
- The opening of a new market, particularly an export market in a new territory;
- The conquest of a new source of supply of raw materials, half-manufactured products, or alternative materials or methodologies; and
- The creation of a new organization.

The entrepreneur does not perform well in bureaucracies. Entrepreneurial innovation usually occurs, therefore, outside large corporations. For example, credit cards were not developed by banks; xerography was not created by a large office equipment company; Atari was not started by a computer vendor; and Weed Eater was not conceived by a lawn equipment manufacturer. These were the innovations of entrepreneurs who grasped an idea, developed it, and pursued its success with unflagging efforts.

Entrepreneurs are always looking for something unique to fill a need or want. They may or may not be inventors, but they have the ability to see the economic potential of an invention. They spend a lot of time asking "What if?" and "Why not?" Other people are exposed to the same opportunity, and yet none of them see it. Or if they recognize an opportunity, they may not have the ambition and guts to take advantage of it.

Innovation does not necessarily mean developing something earthshaking and profound; it does not always have to be a "new" gadget, tool, or service. A simple adjustment to something old can do the trick. For example, game rooms and penny arcades were flourishing before the turn of the century. Entrepreneurs saw an opportunity to convert this old idea into new whizbang electronic entertainment centers.

WHAT MAKES ENTREPRENEURS TICK?

Entrepreneurs are clearly the main actors in change and economic growth. But can they be defined? Can a person act entrepreneurially without going into business? What are the characteristics of entrepreneurs? What are their tendencies?

CHANGE AGENT

The entrepreneur is, indeed, the change agent, the source of innovation and creativity, the schemer, the heart and soul of economic growth. But the entrepreneur remains partly charted territory who cannot be fully defined. Why, for example, does one person see an opportunity when another does not? Why do some people have strong entrepreneurial tendencies when others have little to none? These questions intrigue scholars. Though mysteries remain, more has been learned about entrepreneurs in the past twenty or thirty years than in all previous history. What is known is informative and helpful; what is still unknown is tantalizing.

Typically, the entrepreneur is seen as an individual who owns and operates a small business. But simply to own and operate a small business— or even a *big* business—does not make someone an entrepreneur. If an individual is merely a caretaker involved in ordering, scheduling, and administration, then he or she should be considered a manager. If this person is a true entrepreneur, then new products are being created, new ways of providing services are being implemented.

The entrepreneur can be described as anyone who takes the risk to develop and implement an enterprise, be it a small, one-employee bicycle shop run on a part-time basis, a manufacturer of a new jogging shoe, or a new high-tech firm involved in biotechnology. Entrepreneurs can be the ramrod of innovation in large corporations, where they are sometimes called intrapreneurs. Entrepreneurs are often the ones who go where others fear to tread. By seeking out and accepting new and risky ventures, they often operate on the frontier of business.

Moreover, a number of people who are not considered business people can act entrepreneurially. Accountants and lawyers can offer new, innovative services to their clients; teachers can use and experiment with a number of techniques, such as video, sketches, role playing, and theatrical props, to enhance communications; pediatricians can dress in clown suits to gain better rapport with little patients. Malcolm Forbes flies balloons across continents and rides motorcycles into China and Russia. These exploits probably help to increase the circulation of *Forbes*, but also satisfy Malcolm Forbe's entrepreneurial yen. Certainly, one does not have to "open shop" to be entrepreneurial.

CHARACTERISTICS

A galaxy of personality traits characterize individuals who have a propensity to behave entrepreneurially. Nine of the more salient ones are:

1. **A desire to achieve.** All entrepreneurs must have the push to conquer problems and give birth to a successful venture.
2. **Hard work.** Most entrepreneurs are workaholics. In many instances they have to be to achieve their goals.
3. **Nurturing quality.** Entrepreneurs take charge of and watch over a venture until it can stand alone.
4. **Acceptance of responsibility.** Entrepreneurs accept full responsibility for their ventures. They are morally, legally, and mentally accountable.
5. **Reward orientation.** Entrepreneurs want to achieve, work hard, and take responsibility, but they also want to be rewarded handsomely for their efforts. And reward can come in forms other than money, such as recognition and respect.
6. **Optimism.** Entrepreneurs live by the philosophy that this is the best of times and that anything is possible.
7. **Orientation to excellence.** Entrepreneurs often desire to achieve something that is outstanding that they can be proud of—something first-class.
8. **Organization.** Most entrepreneurs are very good at bringing together all the components of a venture to make it achieve its goals. They are normally thought of as take-charge people.
9. **Profit orientation.** As surprising as it may seem, money takes a back seat to the desire to achieve and the nurturing quality. Entrepreneurs want to make a profit, but the profit serves primarily as a meter to gauge their degree of achievement and performance.

TENDENCIES

Tendencies toward entrepreneurial activity provide another way to show one more facet of the entrepreneur. The **Figure** shows a continuum of entrepreneurial activity, from almost no entrepreneurial tendencies to very strong ones.

In this schema, the *laborer* is the least entrepreneurial and the *inventrepreneur* is the most entrepreneurial. In fact, the inventrepreneur is the epitome of entrepreneurial activity. This special entrepreneur has the ability both to invent a new product or service and to bring it successfully to the marketplace. The *bureaucrat, lender* (bank loan officer), *professional,* and *manager* tend to be nonentrepreneurial. *Copycat entrepreneurs* simply imitate someone else's product or service and business. They have fairly strong entrepreneurial tendencies except in innovation. *Opportunistic entrepreneurs* have fairly strong overall tendencies toward entrepreneurial activity, especially the tendency toward spotting and exploiting opportunities. *Venture capitalists* are not entrepreneurs as such but are primary sources of equity financing for business ventures, especially for start-ups and early-stage expansion. They have a strong wealth-seeking tendency. Both the *innovative entrepreneur* and the *inventrepreneur* have very strong overall tendencies toward entrepreneurial activity.

ARE YOU AN ENTREPRENEUR?

If you seek independence, you want to be your own boss and self-governing, not subject to control by others or reliance on others for your livelihood. You are a loner, and individualist, someone who wants to do your own thing. You have a strong desire for freedom of choice to make your own decision. On the other hand, if you are dependent, you welcome influence and control from others. You are more comfortable in a subordinate role. You probably seek institutions and group affiliation. Clearly, these tendencies are anathema to entrepreneurial activity.

One of the key reasons to engage in entrepreneurial activity is to gain wealth. If you strive for wealth, abundance, and the so-called good life, then your tendency is clearly toward entrepreneurship. Subsistence-seeking has no entrepreneurial pull. Here you are interested in the minimum to support life. You work only for basic necessities and are completely satisfied with a day-to-day existence.

Entrepreneurs are alert to unnoticed opportunities. They make it a practice always to be on the lookout for an opportunity and a way to exploit it. People on the other end of the continuum do not look for entrepreneurial opportunities.

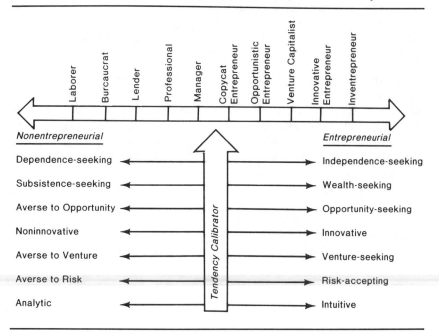

TENDENCIES TOWARD NONENTREPRENEURIAL OR
ENTREPRENEURIAL ACTIVITY

The tendency to innovate is a strong propensity to introduce new things, effect change, and broach bold ideas. The person who leans toward the non-innovative end of the continuum is lacking in new thoughts and ideas. A person, however, can become a successful entrepreneur without strong innovative tendencies. Innovation is desirable but not absolutely imperative. For example, copycat and opportunistic entrepreneurs do not have strong innovative tendencies.

Engaging an entrepreneurial activity, to a large extent, means venturing. So you should have a zeal for the new and a passion for novelty. You should be able to travel an uncharted course. If you abhor routine, are restless, and are drawn to new ventures and quests, you have a strong tendency toward entrepreneurial activity. Alternatively, if you automatically say no to almost anything new, thrive on routine, will not leave the tired and true, and are totally satisfied with the status quo, then your inclination toward entrepreneurial activity is weak.

Entering into an entrepreneurial activity is tantamount to accepting risk. Remember that being entrepreneurial means that you are irresistibly drawn to the unknown, the untried, the new quest, and the new venture. This clearly means risk. It is the lure of the new and the quest, however, that pulls the entrepreneur, not the risk itself. But the entrepreneur will accept risk. The tendency of nonentrepreneurs is toward risk-aversion. They are not willing to take a chance or to be exposed to loss, especially financial. They will not enter the tunnel until clear light can be seen at the other end.

A great deal of research indicates that persons who engage in entrepreneurial activity are quite logical but also possess ready insight and tend to rely on this insight more than on elaborate quantitative analysis.[1] They tend to have strong instincts and can readily make decisions in uncertain conditions. On the other hand, the tendency to depend on quantitative analysis and logic alone points away from entrepreneurial activity. The person who is extremely reluctant to guess, to make assumptions, to brainstorm, and to accept anything until all the boundaries are known and completely measured is going to feel insecure in venturing.

Of course, nothing is ironclad about the preceding analysis. For example, people other than entrepreneurs can make decisions under uncertain conditions—the laborer or the lender, for example. They also can and do bear risk whether they want to or not. Also, in specific cases, people who are on the nonentrepreneurial end of the continuum can move to the entrepreneurial end overnight. For example, a laborer can invent a construction tool and develop a successful business venture from it. Or a loan officer can create a new banking service. A manager can open a new market. A physician can develop and introduce a computer-based diagnostic system.

Entrepreneurs are the prime movers of the economy innovators of new products and services, and initiators of change and diversity. They come from all backgrounds, races, creeds, and religions. They are young and old, male and female. They flourish in countries that have conditions favorable to entrepreneurship.

Although entrepreneurs cannot be completely defined, certain characteristics and tendencies can be used to paint their profile. They want to achieve, are willing to work hard, able to nurture, and disposed to accept responsibility. Oriented toward reward, they are optimists, with an inclination toward excellence, a knack for organization, and a desire to make a profit. They seek independence, wealth, opportunity, innovation, and venture, accept risk, and rely on intuition. People who possess a preponderance of these characteristics and tendencies are already or can become strong entrepreneurs. ■

NOTES

1. See. John G. Burch, *Entrepreneurship* (New York: Wiley, 1986), pp. 30–33.

Why Managers Turn Entrepreneur

Richard Scase and Robert Goffee

Every large company has ambitious managers convinced that their talents are under-used. Don't hoard them: encourage would-be entrepreneurs to launch out on their own, benefiting the economy and freeing up corporate career channels.

Most government policies on small business are geared to encouraging start-ups among the unemployed. Managers and others in work, meanwhile, are given little incentive to start their own businesses. But a recent study of British managers, financed by the Economic & Social Research Council, has uncovered considerable enthusiasm for small business startups of all kinds. The research shows that many dissatisfied managers are more than keen to leave the shelter of corporate life and set up in business for themselves.

Failure to encourage these managers to make the break leaves pools of entrepreneurial energy untapped within many large corporations. These could provide the basis for the formation and growth of hordes of new enterprises. Numerous studies have revealed that people who start their own businesses often lack the managerial and supervisory skills necessary to convert successful start-up ventures into growing concerns. Market opportunities may be present, but founders often choose not to expand because they lack vital additional skills in financial and human resource management. Those who do decide to go for growth often get into financial difficulties. But if more experienced managers could be persuaded to start their own businesses, the potential for growth and job creation in the small business sector would be substantial.

People who choose a career in management might be expected to prefer to cooperate with others in the planned pursuit of corporate objectives rather than to take risks independently in volatile, unpredictable markets. The evidence shows the contrary to be true; many have well planned business proposals but are unsure of the path that leads from corporate life to the real world of the small business owner. They recognize that it would be fool-

Reprinted with permission from *Management Today*, pp. 44–47, August 1986.

Richard Scase is professor of sociology at the University of Kent, Canterbury. Dr. Robert Goffee is lecturer in organizational behavior at the London Business School.

hardy to jeopardize pensions, career prospects and job security by plunging headlong into a business start-up. Many are well aware of the perils and the one-in-three chance of failure. What they are looking for is advice; but they are reluctant to seek this openly because it would put into doubt their commitment to their employers.

Our survey covered more than 300 male managers, aged 25–65, in six large organizations. The firms chosen represent broad patterns of economic, technological and organizational change in British industry. They include both public and private companies, and their activities embrace traditional manufacturing; high electronic technology; finance and banking; hotel, leisure and recreational services; public administration; and the provision of a public utility. Functions included general administration, sales and marketing, finance and accounting, personnel, public relations and production management. (As part of a wider study, the career paths and expectations of women managers are being compared with those of their male colleagues.)

Among those interviewed, no fewer than 59% had seriously considered starting their own business. The proportion was highest in the private company providing hotel, leisure and recreation services and—perhaps not surprisingly—lowest in one of the public corporations. Age was an important factor, almost 70% of the under-35s had considered a start-up, compared with less than half of those over 45.

It is often said that when managers give up corporate jobs to start their own businesses, they are opting out: running guest houses in the West Country, tea shops in Sussex and garden centres in East Anglia. This is not the case—at least, not among the managers in the survey. On the contrary, they were attracted to starting businesses which would use their work-based skills and exploit the talents acquired in their corporate jobs. In fact, their major motive for starting businesses is to use their management skills more fully. More than 20% feel their companies are not making the best use of their managerial talents, and of these, two-thirds are thinking of setting up their own businesses. This response suggests that many corporations wasting managerial talent on a wide scale, which presumably has considerable repercussions on their financial performance.

The sort of manager who wants to start his own business has a strong need for self-fulfillment, creativity and opportunities for independent judgment. It is because this need isn't met that such people want to start their own businesses. Frustrations at work are often directed towards the immediate boss: of managers dissatisfied with their boss, no fewer than 75% HAD considered business proprietorship. Other motivators include the fact that "the cost of career pursuit greatly outweighs the benefits', 'employment inhibits personal growth', and 'small-scale organizations are more satisfying places to work than large ones'.

PLANTING THE SEEDS

Scottish-born Roger Bilmour jumped at the chance of starting up the Agricultural Genetics Company. As president of Griffith Laboratories in the US he wanted a new challenge and welcomed the chance to use his management skills in the UK. At 44, he enjoys building companies, and sought the combination of personal equity and an exciting, high-risk venture to create a significant new firm.

The brainchild of the British Technology Group, AGC followed on the same lines as the medical biotechnology company, Celltech. It was formed in 1983 to exploit the world=wide market opportunities in agricultural biotechnology which emerge from the research of the Agricultural and Food Research Council (AFRC). BTG head-hunted Gilmour to start up the company, which has first option to develop commercially the plant biotechnology discoveries made at the six AFRC institutes specializing in this field.

AGC has already established itself as a technology transfer company harnessing AFRC research in three main areas: non-conventional plant breeding, microbial inoculants and biological pest control products. The first areas is the most exciting research, but the latter two are likely to be the earliest sources of commercial revenues. The first significant products are being tested for market next year.

BLACKMAN HITS THE SCREEN

Ken Blackman, a former marketing executive with Intel, the silicon chip manufacturer, left to start up 01 Computers for a variety of reasons—including a desire for personal wealth, the wish not to work for anyone else and wanting to build something of his own 'rather than being a small cog in a large wheel'.

01 Computers was set up to supply microcomputer-based solutions to business users. There are three trading divisions: 01 Computers, supplying complete computer systems to business users, which won an IBM quality award in 1985; 01 Consultancy, offering comprehensive training course for personal computer users in programming and microcomputer applications; and Paradigm, which identifies and markets high-quality, leading-edge computer products to extend the capabilities of PCs.

Blackman, 30 aims to achieve a USM listing in 'as short a time as possible'. The group is growing fast—currently turnover is £5 million with profits of 10%. The target is turnover of £10 million, still with 10% profits, by 1988, by when Blackman would like to be publicly quoted. By continuing this spanking growth rate, he hopes to gain the confidence of the City. Once he has that, "I intend to use this to gear up to either a full listing, or to acquire further finance for other ventures."

These managers are not dissatisfied with the work itself; it is the organizational conditions which frustrate them. Two-thirds of those considering a business start-up see work (rather than family or leisure pursuits) as the major source of personal satisfaction in their lives. For most managers, proprietorship is a vehicle for opting in rather than out, an opportunity to pursue work more fully.

It seems that there are many square pegs in round holes in British management. Further, many companies do not appear to be making the most of the energies and talents of their managers—at all levels of seniority. How, then, is this problem to be resolved in ways that are beneficial to companies, to individual managers and to the economy as a whole?

Job redesign is one solution. The content and parameters of many managerial occupations are ill-defined. At the moment, there are a number of forces creating dissatisfaction at different levels within managerial hierarchies. Management education and training are becoming more widespread, and the quality of managers is improving as a result. At the same time, managers have heightened expectations of the intrinsic rewards of jobs.

However, opportunities to develop creative talents are diminishing. The tougher trading conditions of the 1980s reinforce the need to monitor closely the performance of managers against broad targets and tightly regulated budgets. More sophisticated management information systems make this easier. At the same time, the reward of promotion for doing a routine middle management job efficiently is becoming rarer as management structures are collapsed and organizations slimmed down. Organizations, technological and economic changes tend to heighten the level of frustration among managers and make unfulfilled ambition a common complaint.

Some large organizations are adapting to change and taking steps to improve the quality of managerial working life. The conversion of complex divisionalized structures into wholly-owned subsidiaries within new holding companies can encourage the development of risk-taking. Consequently, divisional managers who are part of a tightly controlled, hierarchical system, are being replaced by staff with greater autonomy who can take strategic initiatives as long as targets are met.

Similarly, many large companies are trying to reduce their dependence on rigid bureaucratic or mechanistic management procedures. Instead, they appoint task forces, project teams and forms of 'ad-hocracy' which encourage managerial creativity, flair and self-fulfillment. Such innovations depend on a variety of factors—the nature of the product, the market competition, for example. But the trends are growing stronger as companies recognize and respond to the needs of their managers by creating the right culture for optimum corporate performance.

Clearly, it is not to the advantage of any corporation to hoard dissatisfied managers—particularly if they want to become bosses in their own right. Apart from anything else, it restricts the career opportunities of those lower down the hierarchy. Moreover, it would be good for companies and the economy if these managers could be encouraged to pursue their ambition to leave corporate life. Many already possess some of the key skills required for starting commercial ventures; for example, detailed knowledge of specific markets, particular products and services, financial management, staff supervision, and so on. What they lack are some basic, but easily acquired, business techniques needed at start-up: for example, cash flow, forecasting, viability analysis, commercial negotiation, raising finance.

The transition from employment to self-employment needs to be made easier. Companies are already devoting resources to preparing executives for early retirement. Some offer intensive periods of 're-training', while others, as part of their management development policies, encourage a gradual and phased withdrawal from full-time employment. But as yet, few companies accept much responsibility for encouraging staff to start their own businesses. In some companies, that would be regarded as quite absurd. There is an understandable fear that such schemes would lead to the loss of their most able and creative managers. But managers who find their jobs challenging and fulfilling and are satisfied with career prospects are less attracted by the entrepreneurial lifestyle.

Perhaps, then, more companies should encourage their dissatisfied managers to start their own ventures. They hold sponsor programmes to equip them with the necessary skills and ease the transition to self-employment. If they did, many could benefit. Opportunities for promotion would open up for the enthusiastic and the committed. More managers moving outwards would lead to more managers moving inwards and upwards. Greater fluidity could increase the general level of managerial motivation and, hence, performance.

A further benefit would be job creation. Experienced managers often have the skills and ability to expand newly created enterprises where skilled craftsmen, technologists or engineers may not. Studies have shown that many small businesses fail to grow because of reluctance or inability to manage increasing numbers of staff, not because of limited market opportunities or suitable finance. Lack of managerial expertise is a severe impediment to growth and job creation. Experienced managers starting their own businesses are less likely to suffer from such inhibitions.

Further, it seems that managers who become entrepreneurs are more likely to set up wealth-creating enterprises. Business start-ups are currently concentrated in the retail and service sectors—restaurants, garden centres, consultancies, shops, professional services, etc. The study suggests that managers want to start businesses on the as is of their work-related skills— particularly those employed in traditional manufacturing and high technology. Many had ideas about how they could create manufacturing facilities which were technically more efficient than those which they were currently using. Others could identify highly profitable niches in the market. Of course, these things are easier said than done. But at least managers could be given greater inducement to put their ideas to the test. Indeed, because of their managerial expertise, venture capital could be more forthcoming.

Government, of course, also has a role to play. Pension schemes need modifying to smooth the transition from employment to independent proprietorship and eliminate inherent financial penalties. Further, the MSC could offer more start-up programmes geared to the specific needs of managers.

If, then, there are dissatisfied managers who want to start their own businesses, why not encourage them? It must surely be a more satisfactory use of highly trained human resources than managers counting the ways to early retirement. ■

CHAMBERLAIN'S NEW NUMBER

Peter Chamberlain became frustrated by the big company bureaucracy after a career with Xerox, Mars and finally British Telecom, where he was a sales operations director. When he came under pressure from venture capital companies eager to take advantage of Telecom's liberalization, 42 year old Chamberlain eventually decided to realize his long-held ambition to 'go it alone' (and make money).

He founded National Telephone Systems in 1978 with Robin Bailey, to develop and market a range of small to medium business telephone systems. The company sells through a range of dealers and distributors in the UK and is expanding rapidly abroad. All manufacturing is sub-contracted in the UK through Thorn Ericsson. For the future, relationships are being formed with Far East countries for certain products and markets.

NTS now turn over £-6 million, increasing to £-8 million by year-end March, 1987. If all goes to plan, turnover should be £21 million by 1988–89, with profits of £2–4 million. To do this, the company must 'continue the pace and development which has already made us the fastest-growing British telecoms company'. NTS aims to support the new emergent distribution channels in the UK and to secure a solid base in the home market while expanding internationally.

PLACING THE MARKER

After working as a manager for IBM, followed by an 'enjoyable spell' as a management consultant with McKinsey & Co., 36-year-old Stuart Evans decided to go back into general management. He was looking for a small company 'to get better control over my own destiny and to make money and build capital': and found it in Tag Radionics, which he joined in 1983 having been head-hunted by its directors who felt the firm needed good general management.

Since then Evans has raised over £2 million from venture capitalists and other sources. The company was relaunched in August 1984 as Cotag International. It designs and manufactures automatic identification systems using coded tags, which are used in markets such as hands-free access control and automatic vehicle identification. Evans regards existing markets as only 'the tip of an enormous iceberg'.

Cotag is, moreover, pioneering in a new, international high-tech market from a UK MANUFACTURING BASE ~ Our vision is clear and simple—we intend to be world=class, operating globally to achieve costs and volume leadership'. The company is on track—it has installed systems in over 20 countries including the US and Japan; well over half of sales are exported: "We are growing rapidly and sustaining an excellent competitive position.'

PART TWO

PLANNING AND DECISION MAKING

This part of the book presents writings dealing with some of the basic managerial functions performed in organizations of all types. Managerial objectives provide the foundation for any action taken by managers in fulfillment of the organization's mission. Objectives indicate what management intends to accomplish; and planning reveals who, where, when and how such accomplishment will take place. Both of these functions are included in the readings in this part. Once the objectives have been set and the plans have been made, management can begin to make decisions to commit resources toward the direction taken for the future.

Decision making is easily the most important thing managers do. Managers must carefully compare and evaluate alternatives before they commit the resources of the organization to particular courses of action. Good managers make good decisions. The success of the entire organization is directly dependent upon the quality of management's decisions. The writings in this part of the book deal with some key aspects of managerial decision making.

MBO and Performance Appraisal: A Mixture That's Not a Solution Part 1

Jeffrey S. Kane
Kimberly A. Freeman

Before examining the problems that performance appraisal and management by objectives (MBO) create for each other, let's examine the history of MBO and how it became a panacea. The concept of MBO first appeared as a formal system of management in Peter F. Drucker's 1954 book *The Practice of Management*. Although Drucker formalized the concept of MBO, he has never claimed credit for originating it. In fact, a number of influential management theorists before Drucker advocated the use of objectives as a basis for management. In his excellent article on the origins of MBO, entitled "Management by Objectives" (*Academy of Management Review*, 6, 1981), R. G. Greenwood provides references to a number of those predecessors, including Henry Fayol, James O'McKinsey, Chester I. Barnard, and Mary Parker Follett. Drucker's work also rests on a strong foundation of psychological theory and research in which objectives, usually referred to as goals, were studied for many years before the introduction of MBO. For example, the work of C. L. Hull, E. C. Tolman, and Kurt Lewin recognized the importance of goals in the organization, direction, and motivation of human behavior.

Perhaps it was this long-standing tradition, as well as the persuasiveness of Drucker's own writing, that allowed MBO to rapidly sweep aside competing management ideologies. By 1974 a survey of the Fortune 500 conducted by F. E. Schuster and A. F. Kindall showed that nearly 40% of these com-

Reprinted by permission of the publisher, from *Personnel,* December 1986 © 1986 American Management Association, New York. All rights reserved.

JEFFREY S. KANE is associate professor of management at the University of Massachusetts at Amherst. He received an M.A. in industrial relations from the University of Minnesota and a Ph.D. in organizational psychology from the University of Michigan. KIMBERLY A. FREEMAN received an M.B.A. from Indiana University, where she is currently a doctoral candidate in organizational behavior.

This first part of a two-part article explains the alternative types of MBO and their common problems with performance appraisal.

In Part 2 of this article, which will be published in the February 1987 issue of *Personnel*, the authors will discuss the problems involved in specific types of MBO appraisal system moaels and suggest a solution to the problems of MBO and performance appraisal.

(A reference list is available from the authors.)

panies currently had MBO programs. This trend toward widespread acceptance has continued, as evidenced by a 1980 survey of industrial firms that reported the use of MBO in 75% of such firms with more than 2,500 employees (Bureau of National Affairs, 1980).

The spread of MBO has been accompanied by a continuing spate of writing on the subject. The volume of this writing is revealed by George Odiorne's 1981 bibliography on the subject, in which he lists 81 books and 1,270 articles. This outpouring of writing includes some reports of empirical research on the effectiveness of MBO. These reports present a picture that is not altogether encouraging about the prospects for MBO. For example, while the majority of survey studies that have been conducted have reported positive effects of MBO, only one study of this type identified the use of MBO by strict criteria (Schuster and Kindall, 1974). Significantly, this study found that a majority of Fortune 500 firms with MBO-type programs rated such programs as less than moderately successful. J. N. Kondrasuk, in his 1981 review of MBO research entitled "Studies in MBO Effectiveness" (*Academy of Management Review,* 1981), found that the more rigorous the study, the more likely it was to show that MBO was not effective. Even when positive results were shown in rigorously conducted research, in some cases these positive effects began to disappear six to nine months after the program's initiation (John Ivancevich, 1972, 1977).

The search for the cause of the failures of MBO has led some writers to view performance appraisal as the major weakness of MBO. H. John Bernardin and Richard Beatty show this concern in this quotation from *Performance Appraisal: Assessing Human Performance at Work* (Kent, 1984):

> *MBO neither proposes nor provides a measurement system that permits a comparison of ratee's scores. Thus, any time PA [performance appraisal] data are to be used for the purpose of comparing ratee's performances, the management strategy of MBO has little (or nothing) to contribute. . . . [We] have no way of knowing whether the goalsetting framework might serve as the basis for an ongoing PA system that dictates important personnel decisions (e.g., regarding merit pay or promotion).*

INDICTMENT OF AN EXTREMELY HARMFUL MIXTURE

While these and other writers have intimated that performance appraisal might be the Achilles' heel of MBO (and vice versa), no one has ever drawn up the full indictment of the combination of performance appraisal with the rest of the MBO process within the typical MBO system. In this article we shall draw up this indictment. We believe that when the "bill of particulars" against this practice is delineated, there will be little doubt that instead of producing a solution, combining MBO and performance appraisal creates a mixture that is extremely harmful to any organization.

The first difficulty in defining the problems that MBO and performance appraisal create for each other stems from the variegated nature of MBO. In the years since Drucker first proposed MBO, his successors have produced a wide range of alternative incarnations of the concept. As far back as 1973 J. S. Hodgson, in his article "Management by Objectives: The Experience of a Federal Government Department" (*Canadian Public Administration*, 16, 1973), observed that "MBO, like ice cream comes in 29 flavors." This situation became exacerbated in the years that have followed. In his book *Work Motivation: Theory, Issues, and Applications* (Scott, Foresman, 1984), Craig Pinder put it this way: "In actual practice, there are almost as many varieties of MBO as there are organizations that claim to have adopted it."

The problem created by this diversity in the forms of MBO is that some criticisms of the use of MBO as the basis for performance appraisal only apply to a subset of the existing forms of MBO. Rather than trying to describe MBO systems to which each criticism applies, it would be far more efficient to devise a generalized taxonomy of MBO types. With such a taxonomy the criticisms of MBO-based appraisal systems could be grouped according to whether they apply to all types of MBO systems or only to a subset of them. We have found a classification scheme in a neighboring realm that we believe effectively fills the bill as the needed taxonomy.

THE THREE MODELS OF MBO

In our view the style of the objective-setting process in an MBO system is what makes it vulnerable to the criticisms of mixing MBO and performance appraisal. Since objective setting is essentially a governance process, it follows that the search for a useful classification scheme led us to those processes that have been used for leadership. We didn't have to search far before finding a scheme that seemed to embody the essence of the differences in objective-setting styles: the famous three-way classification of leadership styles proposed by Kurt Lewin, R. Lippitt, and R. K. White in "Patterns of Aggressive Behavior in Experimentally Created 'Social Climates' " (*Journal of Social Psychology*, 10, 1939). Accordingly, we propose to classify alternative forms of MBO into the categories of democratic, autocratic, and laissez faire. Each of these three styles of objective setting will be used as the identifying feature of a distinct model of MBO. The objective-setting process identified with each of these models is described below.

THE DEMOCRATIC MODEL

The democratic model employs a cyclical objective-setting process in which top management initially sets organization wide objectives that are broken down into objectives for successively lowering operating units. The manager of each unit is asked whether it would be feasible to attain the objectives derived for his or her unit. When a manager is able to convince his or her superior that the objectives proposed for his or her unit are infeasible to achieve, the two of them negotiate a set of revised objectives. The revised objectives are then communicated back up the hierarchy to all the units they affect; this communication exerts a ripple effect that may extend to the highest level of management. This repetitive process continues until all management levels have had input and all objectives have been adjusted to conform with what managers at all levels consider to be feasible.

THE AUTOCRATIC MODEL

In the autocratic model, top management (the CEO and his "team") determine the organization's goals, based partly on reality and partly on what will satisfy the board of directors. Objectives for time frames lasting more than one year are set only when pressure for near term (1 year) gains is low and/or pressure for longer term gains is high. Objectives for each successively lower operating unit are then logically derived from the objectives of the higher unit of which it is part. Little or no upward adjustment occurs, and any adjustments that do not occur remain localized, to prevent repercussions from upsetting established organizationwide objectives.

THE LAISSEZ-FAIRE MODEL

The laissez-faire objective-setting process is often found in the terminal stage of the life cycle of MBO systems. Upper management has lost interest in the system and each manager is left on his or her own to work out objectives for his or her work unit. Objectives typically are set vaguely enough to allow for a wide range of achievement while normally appearing to be coordinated between organizational levels.

We shall now describe the problems that arise when objectives are used for appraising performance. The only limitations we place on the MBO and MBO-like systems encompassed by our discussion is that they must employ one of the above three styles of objective setting and that the objectives thus set are used as the basis for performance appraisal. While some problems with mixing MBO and performance appraisal arise from specific features of the objective-setting processes that distinguish the three models of MBO, many are common to all three models. We shall first discuss the problems shared in common by all three models of MBO when they are used as the basis for appraisal. Then we shall consider the problems with mixing MBO and appraisal that affect only one or two of the three models of MBO. Finally, we will offer our recommendation for distilling a solution out of this troublesome mixture.

PROBLEMS COMMON TO ALL MBO-BASED APPRAISAL SYSTEM MODELS

In this section we shall bring to light the problems that are common to appraisal systems formulated within the frameworks of any of the MBO models. These problems are inherent flaws in any MBO-based appraisal system, not just remediable deficiencies in implementation.

The Rate-Setting Phenomenon

When the allocation of rewards is based on performance appraisals that assess the attainment of objectives, employees can be expected to adopt an economic rationality orientation toward their objectives. The principle of economic rationality holds that people should try to maximize the expected value of their outcomes. The best way of doing this within the context of an MBO-based appraisal system is to ensure that objectives are set, and maintained, at the lowest level possible in order to maximize the probability of attaining them. This means that during each appraisal period employees should avoid performing in a manner that either would undermine the validity of their arguments in favor of setting their objectives at the same or lower levels the next time around, or would justify the imposition of more difficult objectives where the autocratic MBO approach is used. Such performances to be avoided are those, in short, which exceed objectives. While exceeding objectives may maximize outcomes in the immediate term, the fear that such a performance will result in having to attain more difficult objectives in the future inevitably leads to the perception that one's long-term economic interests are best served by avoiding such performances. Objectives that are also used as appraisal standards tend to pressure individuals to maintain artificially low performance ceilings. These pressures are every bit as potent—and every bit as damaging to productivity—as those imposed by social forces in piece-rate situations.

Lack of Comparability in Performance Standards

In order for an appraisal system to be fair and effective, the standards it imposes for attaining each rating level must be comparable in difficulty, at least for jobs at comparable pay levels. This is a criterion that MBO-based appraisal systems find impossible to meet. For one thing, to the extent that employees participate in setting their own objectives, the difficulty level of these objectives is determined more by the relative bargaining skills of supervisor and employee than by a concern for equity. The objective-setting stage in systems employing one of the two nonautocratic MBO models also becomes a key point where supervisory bias can enter as a determinant of the difficulty of the objectives. Since the resulting objectives end up as performance standards in the appraisals based on such systems, the appraisals cannot help but reflect this bias.

In MBO systems using the autocratic model, in which each job's objectives are derived from the leadership's organizational objectives, comparability problems of equal magnitude occur but through a different, less personal phenomenon. To understand this phenomenon, one must realize that the difficulty of any objective is determined by the conditions under which it must be achieved. Objectives derived from the autocratic MBO model disregard the differences between jobs in the conditions under which their incumbents must achieve their objectives. The sole concern is to derive the objectives that each job must meet in order to achieve the organizational objectives imposed by leadership. Such a blind assignment process makes the objectives assigned to some jobs much more difficult to achieve, due to the conditions facing such jobs, than the objectives assigned to others. Thus, the degree to which jobs lack comparability in the difficulty of their performance standards will probably be as great for this model as it is for the others, even though an entirely different mechanism will have caused this result. However, in this case the impact will not come from pressures of personal influence.

The lack of comparability between jobs in performance standards for separate dimensions of performance will also be reflected in the overall scores on the appraisals. It cannot be assumed that the comparability problems will simply disappear in the process of computing a composite overall score. When bias or influence efforts cause the lack of comparability, their effects will probably color every dimension on which a person's performance is to be appraised. Similarly, the circumstances inhibiting performance on any one dimension will probably have the same effect on the other dimensions. This effect will occur either directly by restricting action to a narrow range on most job functions, or indirectly by making performance so difficult in one dimension that insufficient effort is invested in a job's other functions. Consequently, most of the dimensions on which performance in any given job are to be appraised will probably reflect a similar degree of noncomparability to the dimensions for other jobs in terms of the difficulty of the standards for their performance.

Procrustean Definition of Objectives

Procrustes was one of the less admirable characters in Greek mythology, a highwayman who robbed and then dispensed with his victims by leaving them bound spread-eagled on a bed reserved for this purpose. However, in many cases the limbs of his victims extended over the edge of the bed. In his penchant to force all his victims into a common mold, Procrustes solved this problem by lopping off the overhanging portions of their limbs. This myth is continuously recalled by processes that force-fit things into some preconceived mold. As a result, such processes have come to be referred to as Procrustean.

Basing performance appraisal on MBO results in the Procrustean forcing of objectives to fit within the boundaries of individual jobs. Such a force-fit results from the habitual designation of the individual performer (rather than the work group or an organizational subdivision) as the entity whose performance is to be appraised. Despite the fact that the individual frequently is not the best object of an appraisal (H. Levinson, 1970), the bias to make the individual the object (indeed, the necessity of doing so from an administrative standpoint) exists and must be reckoned with. However, breaking down the organization's objectives into the achievements needed from each individual is Procrustean in the fullest sense of the word. Such a practice undermines organizational performance to the extent that the building blocks for achieving an organization's objectives comes not from individuals but from groups of individuals working together. The derivation and assignment of objectives at the level of the individual performer almost always promote individualistic (if not competitive) work orientations toward the achievement of those objectives. Thus the sum of these "parts" will fall short of the whole that is sought, since the "glue" of cooperation needed to bind the parts into the sought-after whole has been lost. Consequently, the overall performance of the organization will suffer.

An Excessive Emphasis on Short-Term Accomplishment

This problem can also be considered Procrustean. The main purpose of performance appraisal is to generate data for use as the basis for personnel decisions; when appraisal results are used for this purpose these decisions will usually be of the reward allocation type (such as bonuses and awards, merit pay, and certain forms of promotion and retention). Reward allocation decisions are usually made annually or semiannually. This practice is dictated by tradition and by the need to keep pay rates in step with inflation, as well as by the need to reinforce worker's efforts at relatively frequent intervals. For these reasons, this practice must be viewed as essentially inviolable. Thus when MBO is implemented under the constraint of having to serve as the basis for an appraisal system that is to be used for reward allocation decisions, the organization must choose objectives that can be achieved (or for which significant milestones can be reached) within intervals of one year or less. The short-term perspective that consequently characterizes organizational planning under these conditions has become dominant in organizations that mix MBO and performance appraisal. This is the very same short-term perspective that has recently been widely lamented as the source of America's growing productivity deficit relative to countries like Japan. However, the difference between America and the countries it has fallen behind is not that the latter's industrial organizations don't use objective-based planning, for all planning must start with objectives. Rather, it is that the organizations in these countries have not held their planning processes hostage to the appraisal processes that provide the basis for annual (or even more frequent) personnel decisions.

The Substitution of Supervisory Discretion for Measurement

In order for a performance appraisal system to adequately satisfy any of the purposes it is expected to serve, it must first satisfy the requirements of a measurement system. Perhaps the most important requirement of a measurement system is that the rules governing the assignment of measurement levels to the phenomena being measured (such as work performance) must be complete. If cases can occur that are not covered by any of the assignment rules, the measurement process falls under the control of the subjective whims of the measurers. When this occurs, the process can no longer guarantee that any two qualified and equally informed observers will assign a given case to the same measurement level. This is the most important criterion (i.e., interobserver reliability) that any measurement process must satisfy; when it is not met, any hope of the process yielding accurate, unbiased measurements is lost.

There are two ways in which the measurement processes of MBO-based appraisal systems tend to promote incomplete assignment rules. First, the setting of objectives involves trying to predict the outcomes that will be considered satisfactory performance of an activity during some future period. However, often it is impossible to predict all aspects of an activity on which it turns out to be important to achieve satisfactory outcomes. This is especially true for jobs involving nonroutine demands and unforeseeable constraints on the conduct of their activities, as is the case for many managerial and technical jobs. Thus one may find at the end of an appraisal period that although the stated objectives for an activity were adequately achieved, some of that activity's unforeseen but significant aspects were not adequately dealt with. On the other hand, satisfactory outcomes might have been achieved on these unforeseen crucial aspects at the expense of adequately meeting the stated objectives. In either case the outcomes relating to the stated requirements for a rating level are accompanied by other unforeseen outcomes that justify giving the performer a higher or lower rating on the overall activity. In short, cases occur that are not covered by the assignment rules established in the course of setting objectives, and the rater is left to resolve the resulting rating dilemma according to his idiosyncratic, subjective devices.

Even if all the aspects of an activity's performance were explicitly specified in the statement of an objective, these aspects (e.g., quality, quantity, cost effectiveness, etc.) would themselves create the potential for incomplete assignment rules to occur in a second way. There are often trade-offs between these aspects, so that superior achievement on one aspect can compensate for deficient achievement on another. However, the statement of the objective often fails to specify all the combinations of achievement levels on the different aspects subsumed under each rating level. Those combinations let unspecified are consequently assigned to rating levels according to the whim of the rater.

Excessive supervisor discretion can also distort the measurement process when there is no standardized procedure for making "allowances" for the influence of factors beyond the performer's control on the outcome levels achieved. Such extraneous factors can either facilitate performance (e.g., being assigned to a high potential sales territory) or hinder it (e.g., suppliers failing to deliver materials need to meet production schedules). In either case, a given outcome level may represent higher or lower performance than originally thought because of the greater or lesser difficulty involved in achieving it. MBO-based appraisal systems attempt to control such influences either by letting objectives be changed after the fact or by allowing raters to assign outcomes to higher rating levels than they were originally specified to deserve. These provisions for "allowances" present two serious problems. First, it is impossible to determine who is using the provisions for legitimate reasons without elaborate justification procedures that are so demanding of time and effort as to discourage use of the provisions for legitimate reasons. Second, such provisions let the supervisor decide how much allowance to make in each case. There is no means of ensuring any comparability between supervisors in the use of such provisions, so it is unlikely that any two supervisors will arrive at the same allowance decision. This problem plagues virtually all other appraisal methods in conventional use, not just those based on MBO. However, we mention it here to emphasize that MBO-based systems do nothing to solve the problem.

Flexibility Lost; No Way to Shift Gears

Most organizations go through periods when it is almost impossible either to set future goals or to devise appropriate strategies for achieving their goals. These periods of high uncertainty are caused by such factors as organizational growth, economic decline, technological change, and increased competition. During such periods it is vital that an organization's employees be ready and willing to shift the nature or emphasis of their activities in response to contingencies that arise. In these circumstances the organization depends upon its employees to make the necessary adaptations at their own discretion rather than at managerial direction. However, responding to such contingencies usually diverts employees from attaining their formal objectives. This creates a problem when attaining objectives is the basis for the appraisal process, which in turn is typically the basis for distributing valued outcomes. Employees are bound to perceive that responding to contingencies at their own discretion is very risky. Acting at their own discretion to sacrifice progress toward their objectives in order to meet various contingencies runs the risk that the necessity of such actions won't be acknowledged after the fact, resulting in lowered appraisals.

Instead of responding to contingencies at their own discretion, employees are more likely to behave in one of two ways. Some employees will seek managerial approval for the adjustments to their objectives that will be necessary before taking such actions. This behavior slows their response time and adds to the cognitive overload that the manager is probably already experiencing in such a situation. Such approval-seeking behavior negates the delegation of authority at the very time when it is most needed. It is likely that under these conditions managers will be too overburdened to take the time to renegotiate their subordinates' objectives. Employees are then likely to proceed on the assumption that they should minimize the time they spend in dealing with the contingencies in order to maximize their chances of reaching their objectives, since for all they know, no adjustments to their objectives will be approved. Since the time needed to make the successive adjustments in each person's objectives is usually never found in such environments, the whole system of objectives and any appraisals based on them drift into irrelevance.

In the alternative scenario employees believe that any effort for the purpose of dealing with contingencies will be disregarded when the time comes to evaluate their performance against their objectives. Such employees will probably ignore any contingencies until management tells them to act, by which time it may be too late for them to be effective. Even after being directed to take the necessary actions, these employees will probably devote only minimal levels of effort to such actions because they feel they are being sidetracked from the activities that are really going to determine their rewards.

Accountability Distortion

In Drucker's own words in *The Practice of Management,* each manager's objectives ". . . should lay out what performance the man's own managerial unit is supposed to produce." Thus from the beginning, the philosophy of MBO has been that objectives should refer to the expected output levels of a manager's work unit, rather than to the expected effectiveness of the manager's performance of his or her job functions. Defining a manager's objectives in terms of his work unit's outputs can ensure that the manager's activities do not become ends in themselves (i.e., the proverbial activity traps) but rather are directed toward furthering the achievements of the work unit as a whole. But basing appraisal and its associated personnel decision-making and feedback functions on such objectives is highly dysfunctional. Appraisals based on work-unit objectives can completely misrepresent the manager's performance. Such misrepresentation occurs because the relationship between the effectiveness of managers' performance and the achievement levels of their work units is far from perfect. As a result, the following types of distortion in appraisals can occur:

1. Managers who were highly effective in carrying out their job functions can receive low appraisal ratings when their work units fail to achieve their objectives because of factors beyond the manager's control.
2. Managers who were grossly ineffective in carrying out their job functions can nevertheless receive high appraisal ratings when their work units achieve their objectives despite their manager's incompetence.

Basing appraisals on the objectives set for a manager's work unit can obviously lead to the wrong conclusions in appraisals of that manager's performance. The demoralizing effects of the inequities that result from such erroneous appraisals are likely to strongly counteract any motivational benefits of objective setting.

Uselessness as Predictive Input Into Promotion Decisions

"Past performance is the best predictor of future performance" is a statement that has become so widely accepted that it is a virtual axiom. Organizations have relied on this principle for many years as the basis for both their internal and their external selection programs. However, its truth must be qualified by the fact that performance is not a generic phenomenon but rather something that occurs in reference to specific activities or functions. Thus performance in a lower-level job can predict performance in a higher-level job only if the two jobs share common functions. Performance measurements on functions that two jobs do *not* have in common, or on functions that do not utilize common abilities, cannot be used as part of a valid selection process. Unfortunately, performance measurements on specific functions cannot be isolated when an MBO-based appraisal system is used. This is because an MBO system's objectives are established for work-unit outcomes or for assignments or projects that generally represent combinations of functions. Appraisals based on such objectives simply cannot be broken down into measurements of performance on the functions that had to be performed in order to attain them.

Another reason why MBO-based appraisals cannot be used to furnish useful input to promotion decisions is that according to the Drucker MBO philosophy, managerial objectives must be established in terms of the outputs of the work units being managed. Except for cases in which the individual worker and his work unit are synonymous, the degree to which such objectives are achieved probably reflects the performances of work-unit members at *their* functions more than it does the manager's performance. Consequently, measurements of performance on such objectives would be highly misleading as bases for promotion decision.

The Bottleneck Syndrome

Objectives must be established for every work unit at the outset of the organization's annual period of operation. Only in this way can the organization proceed into and through the annual period with the requisite degree of coordination among its work units. Because each work unit's objectives are established for a common annual period, they all "come due" at the same time. In other words, all workers must be appraised in relation to their objectives at the same point in time during the year. Since the end of one annual period marks the beginning of another, objective setting will also occur simultaneously for all employees who are subject to an organization's MBO-cum-appraisal system, an occurrence that creates a tremendous administrative bottleneck for managers and supervisors. So overwhelming is this workload in many organizations that managers and supervisors must choose between forsaking their operational activities or giving short shrift to the appraisal and objective-setting processes. Either choice is, of course, highly detrimental to the organization.

The above-mentioned appraisal bottleneck is always a problem for organizations seeking to appraise everyone at the same time. Simultaneous appraisals almost always create administrative problems that more than offset their desirability for such purposes as bonus determination. The obvious solution to such bottlenecks is to stagger the appraisals throughout the year (e.g., by employment anniversary date). Unfortunately, MBO-based appraisals are unique in being logically incompatible with this solution. ■

Corporate Planning: Drafting a Blueprint for Success

Corporate planning is a formal process for defining company goals, objectives, and strategies. It guides organizational behavior, enabling businesses to concentrate their efforts on achieving results. Corporate planning improves the decision-making process at every level, providing a common strategy to follow when shaping the company's future. Finally, it allows managers to determine what needs to be done, when, and how.

One of management's most important functions, then, is planning. Yet surveys show that smaller companies generally develop such plans less often than large companies; and when they do, the results are less detailed than those of larger firms. This is because small-business owners are typically entrepreneurs; their strengths and training often lie in areas other than corporate planning. Another common reason for insufficient planning is a lack of time. The CEO in a smaller company often must fill a variety of corporate functions handled by many executives in larger companies. Also, larger companies typically have layers of management that keep the daily crises from consuming top executives' time. However, these same day-to-day activities require the majority of top management's time in smaller firms. Tight finances often compound this problem. Many businesses are inadequately capitalized, so financial restraints make it difficult to allocate company resources to formally plan for success.

A FORMAL APPROACH

Despite these shortages of time, money, and personnel, corporate planning cannot be ignored. A formal approach to planning leads to more consistent results and greater success, while helping managers maximize use of the company's available resources.

A written corporate plan provides a "statement of purpose" that can be applied to all functions within the company. The statement of purpose should explain in specific terms what the company expects to accomplish and how it intends to achieve these results.

Reprinted with permission from Small Business Reports, pp 40-44, August 1987.

Formal planning addresses both immediate and future needs, generating short-term actions that lead to long-term success. Similarly, short-range goals are derived from the company's long-range objectives. Planning should be an ongoing, evolving process that continually incorporates changing conditions. For example, market changes or government regulations may periodically force the company to alter its plan. But a comprehensive corporate strategy enables management to prepare for these challenges and to develop alternate courses of action based upon various "what if" scenarios. Corporate planning, then, requires three interrelated activities: long-range planning, operational planning, and strategic planning.

Long-Range Planning   3-5 yrs.

A long-range plan serves as the company's "road map" for success. Typically covering three to five years, it defines the company's mission and objectives for the future. The long-range plan forecasts the scope of the organization; specifies objectives to be pursued; and designates authority for carrying out activities necessary to achieve objectives. It also outlines a general course of action, and describes ways in which resources can be allocated most effectively.

When developing the plan, it is important for management to distinguish between business objectives and business goals. In most cases, business objectives will not substantially change over time, although they should be reviewed annually. Goals, on the other hand, will vary according to current conditions and needs. For example, the company's long-range objective may be to acquire a strong position in a new market. This objective remains constant, while goals for developing elements necessary to gain market share, such as new products, sales expertise, and promotional campaigns, may be subject to change.

In fine-tuning the long-range plan, management must anticipate how changes in technology and business climate may affect new product and market opportunities, material availability, and other factors important to growth. The competition's current strategies should also be appraised to prepare for future opportunities and challenges. Further, a complete assessment of the strengths and weaknesses of the company must be made in light of current and projected market conditions. Finally, the expectations of those who have a financial stake in the company, e.g., stockholders, employees, customers, creditors, and government agencies, must be considered.

To make managers aware of company objectives so they can perform their duties more effectively, a formal, long-range plan should include an introduction explaining the company's current positions; a list of company objectives for the next three to five years; and projections of required levels of cash, personnel, facilities, and space. Once a long-range plan is drafted, a series of short-term operational plans can be developed that coordinate the ongoing activities of each department with overall objectives.

Operational Planning

Department managers must establish written operational plans for daily activities based upon the long-range plan. All managers, either acting independently or as members of a team, develop short-term goals for their areas of responsibility. During this process, managers should keep in mind the flexibility required for response to changes in current conditions. Operational plans, therefore, should be reviewed on a regular basis and revised when necessary.

Long-range plans emphasize conceptual, or "soft," objectives. Operational plans focus on specific, or "hard," goals stated in terms of quantitative results and well-defined time constraints. For example, developing departmental goals, determining the tasks necessary to meet those goals, assigning each task to a responsible employee, and delineating the time frame of each task should take are all segments of operational planning.

To draft an operations plan:

1. Establish direction. The long-range plan provides the direction for each operational plan.
2. Devise preliminary plans. Once direction is established, each department manager identifies and prioritizes all those elements critical to achieving the company's overall business objectives.
3. Analyze plan strengths and weaknesses. The preliminary plans are submitted to top management for review. Then, strengths and weaknesses in each plan are evaluated and discussed with the appropriate manager.
4. Adopt final plans. Preliminary plans are revised and finalized by each manager. When these plans are assembled, the result should be a comprehensive set of operational plans that will direct daily operations companywide in accordance with objectives established by the long-range plan.

Within each phase of operational planning, three specific elements must be addressed. These are budgeting, scheduling, and monitoring.

Budgeting must be sufficiently broad to encompass overall operations while being detailed enough to address specific projects. Also, the budget should relate to a fixed time reference that takes into account both necessary work flow and cash flow.

Scheduling should be linked to the budget and production requirements specified as they relate to project expenditures. When an operational plan is properly drafted, management should be able to determine at any time whether the project is on schedule and within budget.

Monitoring is the process of comparing actual results with projections. Monitoring takes the form of monthly operating statements that compare production costs with the budget. The manager for each area of responsibility keeps daily and weekly logs of departmental performance. These are then compared with the operational plan, which typically covers a year. This short-term tracking serves as a warning system to alert managers on a timely basis when corrective action is needed.

Because goals are set in quantitative terms, top management can evaluate both the progress and validity of operational plans with respect to long-range objectives. In previewing short-term plans for the upcoming months, top management can make sure the necessary resources are available.

Once operational plans have been developed, they can be used in conjunction with long-range plans as a starting point for strategic planning. While the firm's long-range plan describes ongoing objectives, the strategic plan explains how to achieve them, using information drawn from operational plans.

Strategic Planning

The company must formulate a comprehensive set of alternative courses of action. To develop these various scenarios, corporate planners must forecast requirements for financing, personnel, and facilities. These requirements are then compared with projections regarding technology, competition, market opportunities, available material, and government regulations. This enables a company to anticipate and respond to changing conditions, thereby ensuring controlled growth.

Strategic planning is an ongoing process, not a one-time project. Plans must continually evolve as updated or revised information becomes available. Thus, top management remains aware of potential opportunities and problems and can respond with appropriate actions, such as tightening quality controls; developing new products, or seeking additional customers. An effective strategic plan can be devised using five basic steps:

1. Specify actions based on three-to-five-year objectives as established in the long-range plan. For example, when the objectives to expand operations, the strategy could be to enlarge the facility.
2. Predict requirements for capital, manpower, and other resources. For example, determine the extent of expansion, including floor space, number of additional employees, and related costs.
3. Formulate various "what-if" scenarios. For example, if additional space is required, should it be built on existing property or will more land need to be purchased or leased?
4. Establish courses of action for the most likely scenarios. Management can then implement feasible activity consistent with company resour-

ces. For example, a nearby company may be vacating a warehouse that will be available for lease.
5. Review the plan on a regular basis. This allows the company to monitor its progress and make necessary modifications.

Although based in part on current operational plans, strategic planning involves uncertainties and risks. The success of the strategy, therefore, depends on management's ability to anticipate market conditions and trends. Yet these factors are the most difficult to monitor because the consequences of decisions and plans made today may not be apparent for several years. Nevertheless, management has the responsibility to maintain the strategic plan's relevance to the company's changing situation. The best approach for meeting this challenge is periodically to reappraise long-range objectives in light of current operations, and to evaluate and revise operational plans so they remain on course. To ensure this, many companies develop a corporate planning structure.

AN EFFECTIVE PLANNING STRUCTURE

Corporate planning should be carried out by the entire management team, with responsibilities clearly established for various planning activities. Although the CEO directs the corporate planning process, without the input, judgment, participation, and endorsement of managers, the corporate plan will fall short of its desired objectives.

It is estimated that the chief executive in smaller companies contributes 60 percent of business strategy, while other senior managers contribute 30 percent. The balance comes from line management. With few exceptions, recommendations are passed directly to the chief executive for approval. Thus, the CEO assumes the responsibility for providing direction and purpose to the corporate plan, as well as for instilling enthusiasm and maintaining a positive outlook throughout the planning process. Without this direction, the planning team's energies can become unfocused and misdirected.

Still, the extent of top management's involvement usually depends upon the type of corporate plan being drafted. In most companies, long-range planning is performed largely by the CEO, with assistance from other top managers. Operational planning is best performed by department and middle managers most familiar with operational procedures. Strategic planning, while still under the direction of the CEO, is most successful when performed by the entire management team using a task-force approach.

In some companies, mangers share responsibility and promote a sense of teamwork by appointing a cross section of line personnel to participate in the corporate planning process. In addition to giving employees high visibility and prestige within the organization, this planning technique provides fresh insight and added expertise in specific professional or technical disciplines.

Staff personnel can also fill a valuable support role. For example, members of staff can assist by analyzing and presenting data, as well as providing necessary groundwork. In some companies, staff can serve as "planning assistants" to the CEO, helping to coordinate the actions of the team. (In most larger firms, staff planners head their own departments.) Duties include developing planning procedures and documents; helping managers adopt long-term and strategic outlooks; critiquing the various long-term, operational, and strategic plans; and assisting and advising the CEO in the selection of the final plans.

To facilitate team planning, a mechanism should be adopted to clarify objectives and the actions necessary to achieve them. One type of representation that graphically illustrates the team planning effort is the "planning tree."

Use Planning Trees

Planning trees visually represent important objectives the company is facing, alternative courses of action to achieve those objectives, and specific responsibilities that make up each action. Major benefits of using a planning tree are: 1) attention is focused on critical issues; and 2) communication is facilitated by clarifying ideas and terminology so that different department managers have a common understanding.

Use of the planning tree requires employee participation in developing the overall plan. Members of the planning team must contribute expertise based upon the capabilities of their particular departments. Each idea or concern can then be analyzed and broken down into its fundamental elements, evaluating the pros and cons, the methods of implementation, and areas of responsibility.

To construct a planning tree, a company objective is placed at the bottom of the chart as the "trunk." Alternative action plans for achieving the objective are written above the trunk, resembling branches. Each of these action plans can then be broken down, in turn, and illustrated as a second layer of branches.

When completed, the planning tree provides a clear illustration of the company's alternative plans for the future and how they relate to the central objective. This makes the review process easier, since new elements can be added by simply expanding the tree to accommodate changing market and corporate conditions. At the same time, the tree structure keeps central objectives in focus, allowing management to consider the impact of different variables without losing sight of the desired outcome.

Regardless of the planning technique, the planning team should be assigned the responsibility of developing contingency plans to counter possible reversals. These plans prepare management to meet the challenges presented should business setbacks occur.

THE NEED FOR CONTINGENCY PLANNING

Although corporate planning gives the company greater control, business reversals can occur. To develop contingency plans, management must assess the possible impacts of setbacks; develop plans to cover contingencies; and identify trigger points that indicate when to set plans into action.

Assess the Impact

Uncontrollable factors, such as recession, inflation, legislative changes, or new technological developments, can result in financial reversals for any business. To minimize the effects of such factors, the corporate planning team must forecast potential problems based on specific worst-case scenarios, e.g., "If sales fall 25 percent and prices drop 10 percent, what will the company's position be?" In this case, sales volume, profit and loss statements, and cash-flow requirements would be projected for the next 12 to 24 months. An emergency budget should be prepared that will reflect projected drops in revenues while striving to maintain a strong cash-flow position.

When contingency plans are being developed, positive and negative aspects of each action must be viewed in terms of maintaining operations and profits. Depending upon the severity of the setback, a plan for staying in business may be required.

Develop Contingency Plans

Specific contingency plans should be devised for downturns of varying lengths and severity, covering each function of the operation. Emergency strategies would address the following areas:

1) **Financing.** Cash flow must be maximized during emergencies. Thus, contingency plans should outline means for securing monies, e.g., through supplier credit or bank loans. One purpose of the plan is to avoid selling assets to pay off debt.

2) **Pricing.** Maintain prices unless lowering prices is the only means to gain revenue. Rather than instituting price reductions, consider alternative techniques, such as volume discounts and rebates. Also, consider what price position the competition is likely to adopt during this period.

3) **Purchasing.** To maintain cash flow, analyze alternative ways to purchase materials and supplies, such as long-term credit arrangements with

OVERVIEW OF CORPORATE PLANNING

Effective corporate planning requires a close examination of company operations and objectives. Separate plans must be developed to establish long-range expectations, guide daily operations, and create strategies to meet those objectives.

Because these three types of planning are done sequentially, they can be accomplished independently. However, when considered together, long-range, operational, and strategic plans give the company both the direction and a course of action necessary to achieve ongoing success.

Long-Range Planning

- Defines the scope and direction of the entire organization
- Establishes corporate objectives for the next three to five years
- Forecasts the levels of capital, personnel, equipment, and other resources that will be required to achieve objectives
- Outlines a general course of action to apply resources to achieve objectives
- Designates management authority and responsibility for carrying out activities.

Operational Planning

- Establishes a set of written guidelines for daily operations
- Sets specific, or "hard," goals stated in terms of quantitative results and time frames
- Drafts a budget to meet those goals
- Keeps top management apprised of departmental goals and the particular tasks necessary to meet those goals
- Assigns employees to fulfill each task and schedules the time each task should take
- Monitors progress toward objectives
- Alerts managers to the need for corrective action or additional resources.

Strategic Planning

- Establishes the necessary link between operational and long-range planning
- Develops scenarios and alternatives necessary to achieve the long-range plan
- Reviews forecasted requirements for financing and facilities
- Provides an up-to-date "early warning system" that allows management to spot potential problems and opportunities
- Once potential challenges have been identified, prioritizes appropriate actions.

vendors. Otherwise, it may be necessary to pay for goods within 10 days, on delivery, or even before an order is processed by the vendor.

4) Inventory. Attempt to maintain supplies, material, and finished goods at minimal levels. However, do not lower inventories to the point where recovery will be slowed.

5) Promotion and advertising. In cases of a general economic slump, it is sometimes possible to increase market share through advertising as competitors cut back on promotion. Still, such promotional activities must be cost-effective and ads should be designed to produce a quick return on investment.

6) Employees. An experienced workforce will be vital during this period. Layoffs should, therefore, be avoided whenever possible. As an alternative, consider other economy measures, such as reductions in hours, wages, and benefits.

In general, contingency planning spells out the means for company survival. However, contingency planning should also anticipate areas of opportunity. A major element in successful contingency planning is knowing when to take action.

Identify Trigger Points

Internal and external indicators must be monitored and trigger points established. Typically, trigger points are set for indicators such as production, cost, and sales levels, and plant-capacity utilization. Usually, emergency triggers are set for both upturns and downturns within a specific time period. For example, contingency plans could be devised based on a 20 percent increase or decrease in annual sales.

Once trigger points are set, one member of the planning team should monitor business and market conditions. When a trigger point is reached, top management is notified and then the appropriate contingency plan can be implemented.

By developing contingency plans and establishing trigger points, managers reduce the chance of making the wrong decision when a setback or opportunity exists. Emergency strategies become part of the company's effort to achieve ongoing business objectives.

CONCLUSION

Every successful business does some planning, if only on an informal basis. The most successful companies, however, make corporate planning a high priority and involve all levels of management in the process. Planning becomes the unifying force that directs company actions.

Those companies that do develop long-range, operational, and strategic plans have a definite advantage over competitors. Priorities are set and objectives are validated. This, in turn, improves productivity and creates the necessary framework for controlled growth. In addition, corporate planning promotes teamwork and heightens motivation, bringing managers and employees together not only to meet but to exceed company goals. ■

Corporate Planning: A Need to Examine Corporate Style

R. V. Emerson
Bank of America, London

In the current depressed and yet highly volatile economic situation, many companies are finding they lack the skills to tackle their problems. Corporate planning concentrated on issues of organizational structure and product and market mix does not provide the essential answer, and a radical change in corporate style is required. This involves the whole area of management/employment behaviour and the building of an integrated team dedicated to creating a new organization culture.

The great skill in any business enterprise, that which determines success or failure, is not one of being able to forecast rates of growth or decline in various markets but to predict the turning points; and, in doing so, build a business which can cope with the unprecedented volatility now fairly common in the business world.

But despite this volatility and the radical changes which have often resulted from it, there has, all too often, been a lack of radical thinking in how a corporation should be re-shaped in order to cope with these new circumstances. In general, companies have looked to the established corporate planning process to re-define strategy, and usually this tends to be in terms of changes to the traditional market and product mix. This may even be glorified by a change to the mission statement, but essentially this is an analytical process. Often this is all that happens. But this is not nearly enough.

The world in which we now find ourselves is not as amenable to rational analysis as it used to be though, even in the heady days of the 1960s and early 1970s, it was never as straightforward as many people believed. As a result we must place far more emphasis and reliance on the *individual* in an organization, both in strategy formulation and, much more important, for implementation of strategy. If someone who drives a car has his vehicle transformed into a battle tank and is then thrust into a war zone, no one should

Reprinted with permission from *Long Range Planning*, Vol. 18, pp. 29-33, December 1985. Mr. R. V. Emerson is Vice President and Manager of the London Corporate Office at Bank of America.

be surprised if neither the tank nor the individual survives. The tank may have been equal to the task, but in order to ensure survival it is necessary to address not just the *skills* of the individual but the nature and attitude of this person. An over-dramatic example perhaps, but one which serves to illustrate a point.

THE SIZE OF THE TASK

We are talking here of significant and very difficult areas to effect changes, particularly in large corporations. This in itself is part of the reason for the failure of many companies to take effective action. Another is simply the lack of adequate tried and tested methods for doing so. Usually the process only goes so far as making some management changes which reflect desired changes in style. This can be at best frustrating both for the managers concerned and the people who work for them, and certainly ineffective; at worst it is frequently dangerous for the companies future viability.

But in many corporations it is vital that these sorts of changes at grass roots level be made, otherwise the whole process of long-range planning and strategy formulation will be nothing more than a paper exercise. It has to be understood when analyzing market potential whether the organization has the right *types* of people able to exploit opportunities and seek out further potential. It is at this level that a company must build the *flexibility* which is now the essential component of any long-term plan to allow for the market volatility which calls for frequent adjustments to tactics and direction.

ROLE OF PLANNING

I would argue that changes made at this level will inevitably lead to changes in the structure of the planning process itself and, even more important, the process of internal communications within the organization, that vital ingredient which ultimately determines whether things get done properly; not least because it affects the balance of power within an organization. In this, and indeed a broader sense, it has an important impact on the concept of 'corporate governance', an area recently discussed in an essay by R. I. Tricker[1] of The Corporate Policy Group, Oxford, where he argues that:

> ". . . corporate governance, the processes by which companies are run, is in need of a fundamental rethink, and should not be confused with the management of the various business involved. The evolution of ideas about companies is shown to be rooted in out-of-date ideologies which emphasize structure. The alternative framework proposed focuses on process and power. Ideas, not organizations, change events".

In this sense, it is clear that corporate planning, as a tool of senior management, has increasingly become directed towards supporting the governance role of the board of directors, and increasingly divorced from the process of management itself.

HISTORICAL PERSPECTIVE

Before going further it is worthwhile examining some background issues which should reinforce the argument for changes and help define the areas which need attention.

William Empson once defined the obvious as 'what seldom gets said'. This might be because it often comes from 20/20 hindsight when it is all too late. Or maybe in this increasingly complex world it becomes very difficult to synthesize all the data into a simple message for action. Or is it that simple messages are difficult to sell? People expect complex messages in a complex world? Yet this must be the primary role of corporate planners: to provide management with simple pragmatic conclusions that can be acted upon: to balance entrepreneurial flair or conservatism with analysis, but not to replace or stifle those management duties.

But all too often long-range planning has become too analytical and, thereby, unwieldy. There has been too much over-dependence on management by numbers; a search for techniques to replace judgment based on experience. There never was too much wrong with the BCG growth/share matrix; people simply mis-used it; they expected too much from it. It was not intended to make the decisions for management, but simply act as a guide in skilled hands. There are other examples.

It would be futile and perhaps churlish to point the finger of blame for this particular trend, but undoubtedly the business schools must share some of it. For too long they saw and taught management as a series of modules, most of them amenable to numerate analysis. Instead, it is an integrated process calling daily for judgmental decisions, often based purely on experience. But those people who thrive on this style of management feel stifled in organizations which have become bureaucratic. There must be a balance if a business is to survive in a world where the timing of decisions is even more vital than it used to be. If planning processes are not built to be flexible and support rapid decision making then they are not fulfilling their role.

Many would argue that the real weaknesses of planning systems lie with the people who use the output rather than those who prepare it— that management gets the sort of planning it deserves; and with this style of management, planning has become a substitute for decision making and real action. There have been many cases in recent years where the need for action in some organizations was all too apparent, but none was taken until new management was brought in. Are we to believe that the lack of action stemmed from inadequate planning systems and the new men brought more competent planners with them? It seems unlikely.

NEW INSIGHTS

An important recent contribution to this topic was the book *In Search of Excellence*[2]; yet it is probably not to be found in the corporate planning section of a business library. Peters and Waterman attempted to identify factors which were common in successful companies, whatever the industry involvement. They found eight characteristics which appeared to be present, and though many may argue the degree of correlation and whether there are really only perhaps six or as many as ten, there is clearly some value in these pointers.

Perhaps the most significant observations is that they are all qualitative characteristics relating to management style and beliefs; attributes such as: a bias for action; being close to your customer; providing an environment where autonomy and entrepreneurship can flourish; simultaneous loose-tight properties of control; providing a balance between centralized and decentralized management; productivity through people; hands-on, value driven, and so on. All of this pointed to the need for management *at all levels* to understand the businesses they were in by being in touch with the sharp-end. How often, as companies grow and diversify, does senior management lose contact with the business and perhaps rely on planning departments to tell them what is going on. But planning departments staffed with analysts who themselves have no real commercial experience can do little more than translate management into a portfolio analysis exercise; they cannot transmit an understanding or a feel for the business.

Professor Christopher Bartlett of Harvard[3] has argued that much of the old planning processes simply led to a 'perpetual reorganization merry-go-round'. What is now needed, he says, is to 'retain a simple structure and concentrate instead on changing managerial behavior'. One of the eight factors identified by Peters and Waterman was 'simple form'; managerial behavior, as we have seen, is the theme which runs through all the factors.

The truth behind Bartlett's observation of the reorganization merry-go-round has been evident so often. Reorganizations are frequently dramatic and highly visible and appear to indicate real action within an organization. But how often do they fail to achieve anything? Not infrequently they are the result of work done by management consultants who wish to demonstrate that something was achieved as a result of their work. Of course the theory would say that 'structure follows strategy'. This indeed should be the case and when observers see a reorganization they tend to assume that there is a clear strategy behind it. But in many cases only cursory attention is given to a careful definition of strategy, whereas enormous amounts of effort go into establishing the new structure, during which time business activity may well suffer.

Bartlett concludes by advising that 'finding the right structure is far less important than developing broader perspectives and attitudes among executives and making use of them through more flexible management processes'. This ties in well with Tricker's view that 'process and power' is much more important than structure.

WHERE NOW?

The role of corporate planning in the process of communications within an organization is a subtle one, but extremely effective if handled properly. Again, some important changes are necessary here.

It is not sufficient to establish a grand plan at board level which is then handed down to line mangers; nor is it any more effective for line units in isolation to submit their plans to head office, which are then approved or fine tuned. If plans are to be effective *all* the people who will be responsible for making them work must understand the strategy and feel committed to its success. A major weakness in long-range planning in the past has resulted from the failure of management to understand the importance in implementing these plans of *managing employee attitudes*. Whether this is most effectively done through such vehicles as task forces, appropriately structured committees, or new vehicles such as quality circles, is not so important as to realize that providing information that explains what is going on must be done regularly, and be consistent in its content. The messages must be relatively few and simple if they are to be effective. Complex messages, even in the best-managed companies, are prone to be miscommunicated and the essential elements that relate to *direction*, lost. There have to be one or two vital characteristics of the company and what it stands for that every employee understands.

In difficult times it is often tempting for senior management to take control back to the center as they perceive risks increasing. Of course this can simply result in increased risk, because this undermines motivation at the operating level at a time it is most needed. But all of the tenets put forward by Peters and Waterman can only be realized in an essentially market led company. Clearly, in increasingly volatile markets, it would be impossible for senior management in a large corporation to be able to respond quickly enough if all decisions had to be referred. Equally, it is more than ever essential that senior management establish clearly understood and firmly managed guidelines within which the various parts of the company can operate—the 'loose-tight' characteristics.

These guidelines too must be understood by employers otherwise there can be frustration when people do not realize why certain courses of action are to be excluded. There is great value in their knowing the background issues to a chosen strategy.

A CHANGE IN ATTITUDES?

It is with these themes in mind that Bank of America is now putting in place some processes whereby it is recognized that adjustments to markets and products and changes in organization structures as responses to present changes in the financial services industry will not be enough.

There can be few industries which have seen the same degree of change in market fundamentals as financial services. Perhaps airline companies with soaring, then volatile oil prices, coupled with deregulation in some markets would argue the case. But deregulation has massive effects on banking too affecting not only the nature of competition for the future but the range of products and the cost of funds. The situation is such that in the U.S.A. it is possible for non-banks to carry out a wider range of banking services than banks. At the same time, and by way of contrast, the French government has nationalized its banking community. The problems of third world debt constantly threaten to wipe out the total capital of many large banks. Fluctuating interest rates have created far greater losses for some banks than those experienced by industrial companies. And yet, simultaneous with these pressures which have severely eroded the bottom line and threatened the balance sheet, there has been the need to invest huge sums of money in computer systems simply to maintain a competitive set of delivery systems for existing products.

The list of changes and their impact is endless, but this serves to show that fine running as a management solution is not enough. The issue in many cases is not just to restore real growth but a simple one of survival. Banks are not just repositioning their various businesses, they are making radical changes to *the way they do* business; and since banking is a service industry where the role of people in designing and delivering the services is crucial, this calls for a severe examination of those peoples attitudes, motivation, style and skills.

In the U.S.A. Bank of America has hired the management consultant, Ichak Adizes to tackle the problem of reshaping attitudes and styles at the grass roots level.

During their lifespan organizations tend to go through behavioural cycles, and it is clear that many large and successful companies can drift towards a bureaucratic style of management. This is especially true of banks where bureaucracy is often seen as a virtue, creating the image of a tightly controlled and therefore safe institution. But tight controls are not enough in volatile market conditions (although, ironically, they may be even more necessary); they do not create revenues.

A MIX OF STYLES

Adizes identifies four basic styles of management[4] which are also the necessary roles of management. Problems arise when an imbalance is created between the four, usually due to the market environment. These four styles he describes as The Producer (P); The Administrator (A); The Entrepreneur (E) and The Integrator (I). In theory, every manager should represent a balance of these styles, but in practice none ever does. The need, therefore, is to build a balance through teamwork.

Problems occur when a company has drifted towards a bias of one or two of these styles (e.g. the Administrator) throughout the organization and then, as a result of market changes, the company finds itself unequal to the new tasks facing it. But reorganization, or market/product changes will not usually resolve this imbalance.

The Producer
Someone who is results oriented; an achiever, often impatient with organizational rules and people who have less understanding of the 'technical' issues.

The Administrator
Almost self explanatory: the person who makes sure that the system works as it was designed to work; but generally does not look to change that design.

The Entrepreneur
The creative person who is prepared to take risks: a self starter who tends to set his own targets which may, of course, not coincide with those of the organization.

The Integrator
Someone who looks to merge and harmonize what may be differing goals and establish a consensus viewpoint which will unite people behind a common purpose.

The types are all familiar, but the argument is that the organization takes on these styles in varying degrees. At a very simplistic level: A company may tend to promote sales and marketing people in buoyant market conditions, but they tend to be heavily oriented towards P: In a recession, it may be the accountants that take over with a bias towards A. But management tends to recruit and encourage like minded people so over time this can establish a corporate-wide style.

The first step must be to establish the particular style of the company; then, by comparing this to the nature of the task in hand, determine the deficiency. Having done so, the process of correction used by Adizes is a long and time consuming process achieved through team building. Clearly there is a temptation to leap straight into a solution, and typical reaction would be, for example, having determined that the company needs more entrepreneurial flair, to appoint new managers, often from outside the organization, to *inject* this missing ingredient. This rarely works because both the manager and employees become very frustrated at their inability to work together: entrepreneurs are not good at solutions, putting their ideas into practice, so they need that added component. Equally, if the employees have a bias towards administrative skills they will not be able to translate the ideas into action plans: you need producers for this role.

The main function behind the Adizes team building process is to add the *integration* component in order to establish the balance of skills at various points and levels within the organization until the required mix of P, A and E necessary to meet the tasks facing the company becomes an instinctive process and part of the organization culture.

In conclusion, it must be said that a great many companies have found that in the present, highly volatile but at the same time depressed economic circumstances, they are lacking appropriate skills with which to tackle the new tasks facing them. But this is not just a matter of retraining; it is an issue involving motivation and attitudes. As a result, attempts through the corporate planning function to correct the company's problems are often doomed to failure, given that they tend to concentrate on macro-issues of organizational structure and product/market mix: a level we could describe as corporate governance. In these circumstances it is essential to address the area of management/employee behavior and style; a long and difficult task to be achieved through teambuilding; but then we are now living in a totally new era in the commercial and industrial world which calls for radical and difficult solutions. ■

BIBLIOGRAPHY

1. R. I. Trickler, Perspectives on corporate governance: intellectual influences in the exercise of corporate governance. In Perspectives on Management, edited by M. J. Earl, pp. 143-169. Oxford University Press, Oxford (1983).
2. Thomas J. Peter and Robert H. Waterman, Jr., In search of Excellence. Harper and Row (1982).
3. C. Lorenz. Dangers of the corporate merry-go-round. Financial Times 23 September (1983).
4. Ichak Adizes. How to Solve the Mismanagement Crisis, (MDOR) Managerial diagnosis and Organizational Research Institute. Los Angeles (1979).

The Strategy Concept II: Another Look at Why Organizations Need Strategies

Henry Mintzberg

In the preceding article, I proposed five definitions of strategy—as a plan, ploy, pattern, position, and perspective. Drawing on these, I wish to investigate here the question of why organizations really do need strategies. In discussing some of the conventional reasons as well as the other ones—to set direction, focus effort, define the organization, provide consistency—I will consider how these may suggest not only why organizations do need strategies, but also why they don't.

SETTING DIRECTION

Most commentators, focussing on the notions of strategy as deliberate plan and market position, argue that *organizations need strategy to set direction for themselves and to outsmart competitors, or at least enable themselves to maneuver through threatening environments.* In its boldest (and baldest) form: "the main role of strategy is to evolve a trajectory or flight path toward that bull's eye."[1] If its strategy is good, such commentators argue, then the organization can make various mistakes, indeed can sometimes even start from a weaker position, and still come out on top. Chandler quotes one of the men responsible for Sears Roebuck's great success: "Business is like war in one respect—if its grand strategy is correct . . . any number of tactical errors can be made and yet the enterprise proves successful."[2] In a similar vein, Tilles explains that:

> When Hannibal inflected the humiliating defeat on the Roman army at Cannae in 216 B.C., he led a ragged band against soldiers who were in possession of superior arms, better training, and competent 'noncoms.' His strategy, however, was so superior that all of those advantages proved to be relatively insignificant.[3]

The assumption here is that the competitor with the better strategy will win, or, as a corollary, that the competitor with a clear strategy will beat the one that has none. Strategy, it is suggested, counts for more than operations:

what really matters is *thinking* it through; *seeing* it through, while hardly incidental, is nonetheless secondary. "Doing the right thing" beats "doing things right" is the expression for such strategic thinking, or to take the favorite example of the opposite, "rearranging the deck chairs on the Titanic."

Sound strategic thinking can certainly explain a good deal of success, in fact, more success than it should, since it is always easy, after the fact, to impute a brilliant strategy (and, behind it, a brilliant strategist) to every great victory. But no shortage of failure can probably be attributed to organizations that got their strategy right while messing up their operations. Indeed, an overdose of strategic thinking can impede effectiveness in the operations, which is exactly what happened on the Titanic. The ship did not go down because they were rearranging the deck chairs at all, but for exactly the opposite reason: they were so busy glorying in the strategy of it all—that boat as a brilliant conception—that they neglected to look out for icebergs.

As for the assumption that any strategy is always better than none, consider an oil company executive in 1973, just as the price of oil went up by a factor of four. What strategy (as plan) should he have pursued when his whole world was suddenly upset. Setting oneself on a predetermined course in unknown waters is the perfect way to sail straight into an iceberg. Sometimes it is better to move slowly, a little bit at a time, looking not too far ahead but very carefully, so that behavior can be shifted on a moment's notice.

The point is not that organizations don't need direction, it is that they don't need homilies. It stands to reason that it is better to have a good strategy, all things being equal. But all things are never equal. The Titanic experience shows how a good strategy can blind an organization to the need to manage its operations. Besides, it is not always clear what a good strategy is, or indeed if it is not better at times to proceed without what amounts to the straitjacket of a clear intended strategy.

FOCUSSING EFFORT

A second major claim, looking inside the organization, is that *strategy is needed to focus effort and promote coordination of activity.* Without strategy, an organization is a collection of individuals, each going his or her own way, or else looking for something to do. The essence of organization is *collective action,* and one thing that knits individual actors together is strategy—again, through providing a sense of direction. Alfred Sloan notes in his memoirs a justification of the consolidated product line strategy developed at General Motors under his leadership: "some kind of rational policy was called for . . . it was necessary to know what one was trying to do," especially with regard to duplication across certain product lines.[4] Of course, by so focussing effort and directing the attention of each part within the integrated whole, the organization runs the risk of being unable to change its strategy when it has to.

DEFINING THE ORGANIZATION

Third, *strategy is needed to define the organization.* Strategy serves not only to direct the attention of the people working within an organization, but also to give the organization meaning for them as well as for outsiders. As plan or pattern, but especially as position or perspective, its strategy defines the organization, providing people with a shorthand way to understand it and to differentiate it from others. Christensen et al. discuss "the power of strategy as a simplifying concept" that enables certain outsiders (they are referring here to independent directors, but the point applies to any interested outsider) "to *know* the business (in a sense) without being *in* the business."[5] Of course, that "little knowledge" can be "a dangerous thing." But there is no denying that strategy does provide a convenient way to understand an organization.

In the early 1980s, the business press was very enthusiastic about General Electric. A reading of the reports of journalists and financial analysts suggests that what really impressed them was not what General Electric had done up to that point but that its new chief executive had articulated a clear, intended strategy for the firm. Thus Kidder, Peabody opened a December 21, 1983 newsletter with the statement: "General Electric is in the process of becoming a somewhat simpler company to understand," the result of the CEO's statement that it would focus on three major segments—core businesses, high technology, and services. Later they explained that "one of the main reasons we have been recommending General Electric for the past three years is the dynamic, creative, motivational leadership that the youthful Jack Welch . . . has provided. . . . His energy, enthusiasm, and ability to articulate a tight and viable corporate strategy are very impressive." No analyst can ever hope to understand much about a company so diversified and complex as General Electric, hence a clear, articulated strategy becomes a surrogate for that understanding.

The important question is whether a simplified strategy for such a complex system helps or hinders its performance—and the question is not meant to be rhetorical. On one hand, such a strategy cannot help but violate the immense complexity of the system, encouraging various dysfunctional pressures from outsiders (directors, for example, who may try to act on their "little knowledge") or even from insiders (chief executives, for example, who try to exercise control over divisions remote from their understanding by putting them into the simplistic categories of "dog" or "cash cow"). On the other hand, the enthusiasm generated by a clear strategy—a clear sense of mission—can produce a host of positive benefits. Those stock analysts not only helped to raise General Electric's stock price, they also helped to fire up the enthusiasm of the company's suppliers and customers, as well as the employees themselves, thereby promoting commitment which can improve performance. Thus, strategy may be of help, not only technically, through the coordination of work, but also emotionally, through the development of beliefs.

Imagine an organization without a name. We would not even be able to discuss it. For all purpose—practical and otherwise—it would not exist. Now imagine an organization with a name but with no strategy, in any sense—no position, no perspective, no plan (or ploy), not even any pattern consistent in its behaviors. How would we describe it or deal with it? An organization without a strategy would be like an individual without a personality—unknown, and unknowable. Of course, we cannot imagine such an organization. But some do come close. Just as we all know bland people with hardly any personality, so too do we know organizations with hardly any sense of strategy (which Rhenman labels "marginal organizations"[6]).

Most people think of such organizations as purely opportunistic, flitting from one opportunity to another[7], or else as lethargic, with little energy to do anything but allow inertia to take its course (which may suggest strategy as pattern but not as plan). But we need not be so negative about this. Sometimes, lack of strategy is temporary and even necessary. It may, for example, simply represent a stage in the transition from an outdated strategy to a new, more viable one. Or it may reflect the fact that an environment has turned so dynamic that it would be folly to settle on any consistency for a time (as in the oil companies in 1973).

In one study,[8] a film company that began with a very clear direction lost it over time. If never really had formal plans; at best there existed broad leadership intentions in the earliest years. But it did have a very clear position and a very distinct perspective, as well as rather focussed patterns, the latter at least at certain periods in its history. But over time, the position eroded. the perspective clouded, and the patterns multiplied, so that diffusion replaced definition. The insiders become increasingly frustrated, coming to treat their organization more like a shell under which they worked than a system of which they were an integral part. As for the outside influences, lacking any convenient means to define the organization, they attacked it increasingly for irrelevance. Ironically, the organization turned out a number of brilliant films throughout all this, but—contrary to General Electric yet reinforcing the same conclusion—what it did do proved less important than what it did not exhibit, namely, strategy as a clear sense of direction.

PROVIDING CONSISTENCY

A return to the notion of strategy as a "simplifying concept" may provide the clearest reason as to why organizations seem to need strategies. *Strategy is needed to reduce uncertainty and provide consistency (however arbitrary that may be), in order to aid cognition, to satisfy intrinsic needs for order, and to promote efficiency under conditions of stability (by concentrating resources and exploiting past learning).*

Psychologist William James once described the experiences of the infant as a "blooming, buzzing confusion." According to Ornstein, who so quotes him, that is due to "lack of a suitable categorizing scheme in which to sort experiences consistently."[9] An organization without a strategy experiences the same confusion; its collective cognition can become overloaded, its members having no way to deal with experiences consistently. Thus, strategy is a categorizing scheme by which incoming stimuli can be ordered and dispatched.

In this sense, a strategy is like a theory, indeed, it *is* a theory (as in Drucker's "theory of the business"[10])—a cognitive structure (and filter) to simplify and explain the world, and thereby to facilitate action. Rumelt captures the notion well with the comment that "the function of strategy is not to 'solve a problem,' but to so structure a situation that the emergent problems are solvable."[11] Or, as Spender puts it (and so specifies how ambitious is research on the process of strategy making): "Because strategy-making is a type of theory building, a theory of strategy-making is a theory of theory-building."[12]

But, like every theory, strategy is a simplification that necessarily distorts the reality. Strategies and theories are not reality themselves, only representations (that is, abstractions) of reality in the minds of people. Thus, every strategy must misrepresent and mistreat at least some stimuli; that is the price of having a strategy. Good strategies, like good theories, simply minimize the amount of distortion.

"Strategy," notes James Brian Quinn, "deals . . . with the unknowable."[13] But it might perhaps be more accurate to write that strategy assumes the unknowable can be made knowable, or at least controllable. As such, it is important to emphasize that strategy is a concept rooted in *stability.*[14] No one should be fooled by all the attention to change and flexibility. When Miller and Friesen write that "strategy is essentially a dynamic concept. It describes a modus operandi more than a posture, a process more than a state,"[15] they are not talking about strategy at all but about the process making strategy. Strategy is not about adaptability in behavior but about regularity in behavior, not about discontinuity but about consistency. Organizations have strategies to reduce uncertainty, to block out the unexpected, and, as shown here, to *set* direction, *focus* effort, *define* the organization. Strategy is a force that *resists* change, not encourages it.

Why then do organizations seem to have such an overwhelming need for consistency? In other words, why the obsession with strategy? To some extent, this is a human need per se. Consistency provides us with a sense of being in control (and nowhere is this better illustrated than in the prescriptive literature of strategic management, although those of us who feel compelled to study strategy as pattern in behavior may be accused of the same thing). That is presumably why some psychologists have found that people claim to discover patterns even in streams of random numbers.[16] Moore makes this point well: strategy is "a relief from the anxiety created by complexity, unpredictability, and incomplete knowledge. As such, it has an element of compulsion about it."[17]

But there is more to the need for consistency than that. Above all, consistency is an efficient response to an environment that is stable, or at least a niche that remains lucrative.

For one thing, strategy enables the organization to concentrate its resources and exploit its opportunities and its own existing skills and knowledge to the very fullest. Strategies reflect the results of organizational learning, the patterns that have formed around those initiatives that have worked best. They help to ensure that these remain fully exploited.

Moreover, once established, strategies reduce the need to keep learning in a broad sense.[18] In this respect, strategy works for an organization much like instinct works for an animal: it facilitates fast, almost automatic response to known stimuli. To be efficient, at least in a stable environment, means to get on with things without the need to think them through each time. As Jonsson notes about "myth," his equivalent to what we call strategy as perspective:

> The myth provides the organization with a stable basis for action. It eliminates uncertainty about what has gone wrong, and it substitutes certainty: we can do it, it is up to us . . . the riskiness disappears when you 'know' what has to be done. If there is much at stake and you are uncertain as to what is wrong, action is inhibited. If you are certain about what should be done, action is precipitated."[19]

To rethink everything all the time, as Jonsson implies, is unproductive. The person who gets up every morning and asks, "Do I really want to remain married?" or even, "I wonder if it is better today to wash before I brush my teeth," will eventually drive themselves crazy or at least work themselves into inaction. The same will be true of the organization that is constantly putting its strategies into question. That will impede its ability to get on with things. (A colleague makes this point best with his proposed epitaph: "Here lies RR: he kept his options open.")

We function best when we can take some things for granted, at least for a time. And that is a major role of strategy in organizations: it resolves the big issues so that people can get on with the little details—targeting and serving customers instead of debating which markets are best, buying and operating machines instead of wondering about different technologies, rearranging deck chairs and looking for icebergs. This applies not only at the bottom of the hierarchy, but all along it, right to the very top. Most of the time, the chief executive, too, must get on with managing the organization in a given context; he cannot continually put that context into question.

There is a tendency to picture the chief executive as a strategist, conceiving the big ideas while everyone else gets on with the little details. But his job is not like that at all. A great deal of it has to do with its own little details—reinforcing the existing perspective ("culture" is the currently popular word now) through all kinds of mundane figurehead duties, maintaining the flow of information by developing contacts and disseminating the resulting information, negotiating agreements to reinforce existing positions, and so on.[20]

The problem with all this, of course, is that eventually situations change, environments destabilize, niches disappear. Then all that is constructive and efficient about an established strategy becomes a liability. That is why even though the concept of strategy is rooted in stability, so much of the study of strategy making focusses on change. But while prescription for strategic change in the literature may come easy, management of the change itself, in practice, especially when it involves perspective, comes hard. The very encouragement of strategy to get on with it—its very role in protecting the organization against distraction[21]—impedes the organization's capacity to respond to change in the environment. As Kuhn notes, in discussing the paradigms of communities of scholars, "retooling is expensive."[22] This is especially true when it is not just machines that have to be retooled, but human minds as well. Strategy, as mental set, can blind the organization to its own outdatedness. Thus we conclude that strategies are to organizations what blinders are to horses: they keep them going in a straight line, but impede the use of peripheral vision.

And this leads to our final conclusion, which is that strategies (and the strategic management process) can be vital to organizations, both by their presence *and* by their absence. ∎

REFERENCES

1. B. Yavitz and W.H. Newman, *Strategy in Action: The Execution, Politics, and Payoff of Business Planning* (New York, NY: The Free Press, 1982), p. 7.
2. A.D. Chandler, *Strategy and Structure: Chapters in the History of the Industrial Enterprise* (Cambridge, MA: M.I.T. Press, 1962), p. 235.
3. S. Tilles, "How to Evaluate Corporate Strategy." *Harvard Business Review* (July/August 1963), p. 111.
4. A. P. Sloan, *My Years at General Motors* (New York, NY: Doubleday, 1963), p. 267.

5. C.R. Christensen, D.R. Andrews, J.L. Bower, R.G. Hamermesh, and M.E. Porter, *Business Policy: Text and Cases,* 5th Edition (Homewood, IL: Richard D. Irwin. 1982), p. 834.

6. E. Rhenman, *Organization Theory for Long-Range Planning* (New York, NY: Wiley. 1973).

7. H.I. Ansoff, *Corporate Strategy* (New York, NY: McGraw-Hill, 1965), p. 113.

8. H. Mintzberg and A. McHugh, "Strategy Formation in an Adhocracy," *Administrative Science Quarterly,* 30 (June 1985): 161–197.

9. R.F. Ornstein, *The Psychology of Consciousness* (New York, NY: Freeman, 1972), p. 74.

10. P.F. Drucker, *Management: Tasks, Responsibilities, Practices* (New York, NY: Harper and Row, 1974).

11. R.P. Rumelt, "Evaluation of Strategy: Theory and Models," in D.E. Schendel and W.C. Hofer, eds., *Strategic Management: A New View of Business Policy and Planning* (Boston, MA: Little Brown, 1979), p. 199.

12. J.C. Spender, "Commentary," in D.E. Schendel and C.W. Hofer, eds., *Strategic Management: A New View of Business Policy and Planning* (Boston, MA: Little Brown, 1979), p. 396.

13. J.B. Quinn, *Strategies for Change: Logical Incrementalism* (Homewood, IL: Richard D. Irwin, 1980), p. 163.

14. D.J. Teece, "Economic Analysis and Strategic Management," *California Management Review,* 26/3 (Spring 1984): 88; R.E. Caves, "Economic Analysis and the Quest for Competitive Advantage," *AEA Papers and Proceedings.* 74/2 (May 1984): 127–128.

15. D. Miller and P.H. Friesen, "The Longitudinal Analysis of Organizations: A Methodological Perspective," *Management Science,* 28/9 (1982): 1020.

16. R.N. Taylor, "Psychological Aspects of Planning," *Long Range Planning,* 9/2 (1976): 70.

17. D.G. Moore, *Managerial Strategies and Organization Dynamics in Sears Retailing,* Ph.D. Thesis, University of Chicago, 1954, p. 34.

18. J.S. Bruner, J.J. Goodnow, and G.A. Austin, *A Study of Thinking* (New York, NY: Wiley, 1956), p. 12.

19. S.A. Jonsson and R.A. Lundin, "Myths and Wishful Thinking as Management Tools," in P.C. Nystrom and W.H. Starbuck, eds., *Perspective Models of Organization* (New York, NY: North Holland Publishing, 1977), p. 43.

20. H. Mintzberg. *The Nature of Managerial Work* (New York, NY: Harper and Row, 1973).

21. Christensen et al., op. cit.

22. T.S. Kuhn, *The Structure of Scientific Revolutions,* 2nd Edition (Chicago, IL: University of Chicago Press, 1970), p. 76.

The Concept of Strategic Gap

E. Frank Harrison

The field of strategic management deals with the relationships between the organization and its external environment. These relationships are epitomized by the concept of *strategic gap* which focuses on the fit between the capabilities of the organization and its most significant exogenous aggregates. The terms strategic gap is not new in the literature of strategic management. However, it is seldom represented as a holistic concept that encompasses the principal factors that management should consider in crafting a multidimensional strategy for the total organization. For example, Steiner and Miner describe a 'planning gap' between the potential of the organization and the operations of management.[1] Weber advances an 'uncertainty gap' between what managers want to achieve and what they expect to achieve for the total organization.[2] Grinyer and others speak of a 'performance gap' between management's objectives and the achievements of the organization.[3] Glueck and Jauch refer to 'positive gaps' and 'negative gaps' as significant factors of strategic choice for the total enterprise.[4] And, finally Ansoff, who coined the term 'gap' with regard to strategic management, propounds a 'total gap' to measure the discrepancy between management's aspirations (objectives) and the current forecast (anticipation).[5]

The definition of strategic gap adopted in this paper was derived from some of the foregoing definitions. Actually, it is closer to the one set forth by Hofer and Schendel who define a strategic gap as 'a comparison of the organization's objectives, strategy, and resources against the opportunities and threats in its external environment. . . .'[6] More simply, the definition advanced here views the strategic gap as 'an imbalance between the current strategic position of the organization and its desired strategic position'.[7] This definition is broad enough to accommodate the principal factors internal and external to the organization that should be considered by management in formulating and selecting a strategy for the total enterprise. It is also specific enough to provide a meaningful focus for students and practitioners of strategic management who seek firmer foundations upon which to make strategic choices.

Reprinted with permission from the Journal of General Management, Vol. 15, No. 2, pp 57-72, Winter 1989.

THE PROFILE OF STRATEGIC GAP

The strategic gap is a condition of imbalance between where the management of the organization would like to be and where the organization actually is with regard to its aspirations. The strategic gap is a measure of the perennially imperfect fit between the organization and its external environment. If the capabilities of the organization were fully committed to exploiting all perceived opportunities and warding off all discerned threats, there would be no strategic gap. For reasons to be discussed later, this eventuality is highly improbable. The strategic gap is conceptualized in Figure 1.

Organizational Assessment

With reference to Figure 1, organizational assessment includes a comprehensive appraisal of the major capabilities of the total enterprise. The most effective managerial strategy is likely to result when the principal strengths of the organization are being used to further its current advantage and its weaknesses or deficiencies are being corrected or reduced to increase its future advantage. This optimal state of affairs requires a systematic analysis of the generic and unique capabilities of the organization for capitalizing on opportunities, coping with threats, complying with requirements, and fulfilling responsibilities.

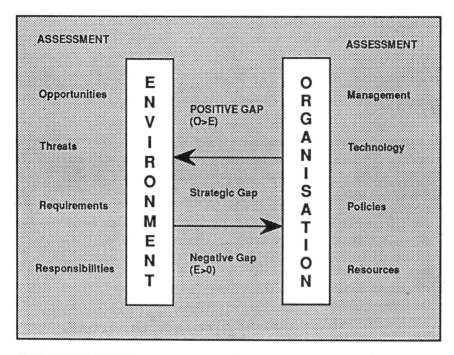

FIGURE 1. THE CONCEPT OF STRATEGIC GAP.

One rather common approach to organizational assessment involves the development of a *capability profile* that permits management to conduct an in-depth appraisal of organizational strengths and weaknesses. This appraisal should discern areas of *distinctive competence* for the total organization, i.e., its points of primary leverage where its principal strength and competitive advantage lie. These are at lest three reasons why a capability profile of strengths and weaknesses is important in measuring the strategic gap of a given organization. First, capitalizing on external opportunities usually signifies effective use of internal strengths. Second, protecting the organization from environmental threats requires knowledge of internal weaknesses as well as strengths in order to erect adequate defenses. And, third, few organizations excel in all areas.[8] 'Thus strategies ultimately are a compromise between offense and defense with the optimum balance dependent on awareness of external conditions and skillful utilization of internal resources'.[9] Therefore, 'in the process of . . . formulating strategy, the ultimate objective of the internal analysis is to draw a profile of the entity and its resources and capabilities that provides both a segmented and integrated internal picture of the strengths and weaknesses of the entire organization'.[10]

Management. The principal aggregates of organizational strengths and weaknesses are reflected in Figure 1. The first and foremost aggregate must be management itself. Management is the vital force that makes the organization go, and good management is the key factor in the successful performance of the organization. Managerial values and experience find their expression in the application of managerial judgement; and good managerial judgement is necessary for effective managerial strategy. Management uses the lessons from the past to determine what is important in the present for the progress of the organization toward the future. Managerial experience harbors the images from the past; managerial values reflect the high priorities of the present. Together the two variables act to condition, influence, and guide the judgement of management in its strategic decision making.[11] Several good studies have highlighted the significance of management as a major factor in organizational assessment leading to the formulation of managerial strategy. Examples include the study of 170 senior executives by Horovitz and Thietart in Europe and the study of 56 executives from three of the largest companies in South America by Ireland *et al.*[12,13,14] Additional studies of corporations in the United States by Halal and Dess confirm the primacy of management in formulating strategy for the total organization.[15,16]

Technology. Any assessment of the capabilities of an organization must include a review of its technology. There are many definitions of technology. Galbraith states that 'technology means the systematic application of scientific or other organized knowledge to practical tasks'.[17] Schon defines it as 'any tool or technique, any product or process, any physical equipment or method of doing or making by which human capability is extended'.[18] Or technology may be defined as 'the mechanical techniques and abstract knowledge that are employed by humans to help attain organizational objectives'.[19] In other definitions, technology is a set of principles and techniques useful to bring about change toward desired ends and 'technology is knowledge of how to do things, how to accomplish human goals'.[20,21]

Regardless of the definition adopted, it is difficult to gainsay the significance of technology as a primary aggregate of organizational capability. For by its very nature technology implies change, and it is the phenomenon of technological change that concerns management in setting strategy. Technological change may represent an opportunity or a threat. If the organization's technology is more advanced than that of its competitors, it has an opportunity to capitalize on it until the advantage is eroded. Conversely, if the organization's technology is obsolete or in danger of becoming passé, it is obviously confronted with a present or potential threat to its market position. Management must constantly scan the external environment for areas of possible technological advantage and must remain vigilant against the threat of technological obsolescence. Numerous authors including Higgins and Friar and Horwith have reaffirmed the significance of technology as a primary factor in formulating managerial strategy.[22,23]

Policies. Along with management and technology, organizational policies provide a framework within which to determine the need for strategy. The options available within prevailing policy are easily discerned. Thus the reciprocity of strategy and policy is apparent. The alternatives of strategic choice indicate the courses of action available to management. Prevailing policy indicates whether these courses can and should be pursued within the guidelines provided at the highest levels of the organization. In formulating managerial policy, it is meaningful to regard organizational policy as dynamic, for with compelling strategic inducements it can be modified by top management and the governing board. Organizational policy should provide enlightened and progressive guidance rather than restrictive and repressive controls. On balance, organizational policies provide an essential underpinning of organizational assessment.[24]

Resources. Organizational assessment has been completed when a measurement of the available resources has been taken. If management is the driving force in the organization and organizational policies provide necessary parameters for strategic guidance using the knowledge base of technology, then the final element of organizational assessment must be the resources by means of which the organization formulates its strategy and through which it accomplishes its objectives.

For our purposes, resources may be divided into four categories: (a) *institutional resources,* which include stakeholders, goodwill, image, political competence, and social responsiveness[25,26,27,28,29]; (b) *fiscal resources,* which include money and its near-equivalent, credit; (c) *physical resources* which include facilities and equipment as well as materials, supplies, and services; and (d) *human resources,* which include time, energy and intellect.[30] In formulating managerial strategy, the first step is to determine the amount and type of each resource that would be required given the selection of a particular strategy. The second step is to determine where, how and when the *additional* resources needed for strategy can be generated or acquired and at what level of risk and what opportunity cost. The third step is to simulate an allocation of the entire complement of resources among the units and programmes that are essential for the total organization to accomplish the various strategies under consideration.[31]

Environmental Assessment

Once management has completed a capability profile to ascertain the strengths and weaknesses in the principal categories of organizational capability, the next step is to assess the external environment with a view toward determining the nature and magnitude of the organization's strategic gap.

Opportunities. Doubtless the factor of greatest importance in the external environment for formulating organizational strategy is an opportunity. Opportunities are external factors and situations that will assist the organization in fulfilling its mission and achieving its objectives.[32] 'Opportunity is always a factor in determining strategy.'[33]

In a basic sense, opportunities span the entire spectrum of goods or services provided by the organization in the present and those contemplated for the future. In identifying opportunities, management must consider its competitors, unless, of course, a monopoly situation exists. By definition opportunities presume that the organization has the capability for capitalizing on them. The management, resources, and technology of the organization must be adequate for it to realize its opportunities, and there must be a willingness to accept the associated risk.

'In general terms, an organization's attempt to relate its strategy to opportunity consists of an assessment of any influence or trends in the external environment which may make a difference in what it elects to do or not do. This assessment of the external environment entails many facets: analyzing it; predicting it; attempting to change it; deciding how best to adapt to it; electing to get into or out of some parts of it'.[34] The pursuit and accomplishment of a given opportunity should make a positive contribution to the long-term health and well-being of the total organization.

Threats. Along with opportunities, information obtained from the external environment helps management to ascertain threats to the organization.

Threats are exogenous forces that may deter the organization from accomplishing its objectives and, consequently, achieving its strategy. For business enterprises, threats usually relate to the actions of competitors that seem likely to reduce opportunities, resulting in adverse effects on present or future market positions or profits. In a broader context that can accommodate most types of organizations, threats include all exogenous forces with a potential for intruding on the organization at any level and in any way so that the likely result will be competition, compromise, constraint, control or conflict with organization's mission, plans, objectives, or strategy.[35] In the words of Thompson and Strickland:

> 'Very often certain factors in (an organization's) overall environment pose threats to its strategic well-being. These externally imposed threats may stem from possible new technological developments, the advent of new substitute products, adverse economic trends, government action, changing consumer values and lifestyles, projections of natural resource depletions, unfavorable demographic shifts, new sources of strong competition, and the like'.[36]

Sociopolitical Factors. Two additional categories complete the assessment of the organization's external environment. The first category constitutes *requirements,* largely of a legal nature with appropriate recognition of the governance aspects of the political system.[37,38] Obviously the formulation of strategy is influenced by statutory requirements and legal codes which, along with legislation emerging through the governance mechanisms in the political process, can act to limit the strategic choices of management.[39]

The second category of *responsibilities* constitutes an expectation on the part of some stakeholder group or external entity that the strategy formulated by management will not work to its disadvantage. Included in this second category is the more pervasive concept of *social responsibilities*. Social responsibility is a concept that refers to the assumed obligation of a given organization to consider the social welfare or the public interest in developing and implementing its strategy.[40] With reference to business organizations, there are numerous arguments for and against more or less social responsibility.[41] Obviously management's values will influence the perception of the need to assume some degree of social responsibility in formulating and implementing strategy for the total organization.[42]

THE DYNAMICS OF STRATEGIC GAP

The dynamics of strategic gap are centered in the nature and degree of the gap reflected in Figure 1.

Positive Strategic Gap

There are two primary types of strategic gap. In the first type, if a concurrent assessment of the organization and its external environment reveals that the sum of internal capabilities are clearly greater than the aggregate of significant exogenous factors a *positive strategic gap* exists. In other words, if O > E, the strategic gap is balanced in favor of the organization. In this state, the management, technology, policies, and resources of the organization are more than adequate to exploit any opportunity, cope with any threat or meet any requirement or responsibility emanating from the external environment. The organization has a clear advantage *vis-à-vis* its external environment with a positive strategic gap. However, this advantage is one of degree, which is to say that it is curvilinear rather than linear. As the positive strategic gap tends to increase, the organization begins to incur the opportunity cost of under-utilized management, technology or resources. If not arrested, this opportunity cost can result in negative consequences for the organization. It is a paradox of the concept of strategic gap that too large a positive gap can parallel the disadvantages inherent in a negative gap. The best long-term condition is a small positive strategic gap that reflects some reserve capability within the organization to exploit unexpected opportunities or to cope with unanticipated threats.

Negative Strategic Gap

The second type within Figure 1 occurs when the significant exogenous factors are greater than the internal capabilities of the organization. This type, symbolized by E > O, means that the organization is unable to exploit available opportunities, deal with competitive or technological threats, meet its legal requirements or fulfill its expected responsibilities. It is called a *negative strategic gap*. In short, the organization is at a significant strategic disadvantage *vis-à-vis* its external environment. Obviously a negative strategic gap necessitates prompt and effective corrective action by management to redress the unacceptable imbalance. The strategies appropriate for reducing a positive or negative strategic gap are presented in the next section of this paper.

In the final analysis there will always be a strategic gap between the organization and its external environment. There will never be a perfect interface between the capabilities of a given organization and the significant exogenous factors in its environmental domain. Factors such as imperfect information, time delays in responding to externally-induced change, technological breakthroughs and managerial incompetence all contribute to the unavoidability of strategic gap. There is, in other words, a level of strategic gap, hopefully on the positive side, that is irreducible for any organization. Indeed it is not cost effective to try and create a perfect interface between the organization and its external environment. When, in the judgement of management, the strategic gap approaches an irreducible minimum, the organization has achieved a good *strategic fit*. This is a cost effective state that is both desirable and sustainable and one that should be sought by most organizations.

A TYPOLOGY OF STRATEGIC CHOICE

Figure 2 reflects a typology of strategic choice for use by managers in all types of formal organizations. The dimensions in Figure 2 tend to sharpen the focus of strategic choice by concentrating on the primary variables that characterize the concept of strategic gap depicted in Figure 1. External opportunities and internal capabilities give a two-dimensional view of strategic choice. Opportunities and capabilities are the means to the attainment of the objectives of the total organization. In the context of strategic choice, opportunities and capabilities constitute ultimate criteria that must be met over the long run if the organization is to remain viable. Moreover, the two dimensions in Figure 2 have an appreciable degree of hardness in that magnitudes of abundance and scarcity of external opportunities and degrees of internal strength and weakness are amenable to some form of measurement. Further, it is appropriate to ascribe a high degree of linearity to the two dimensions in the figure. More opportunities and capabilities are definitely better than less, as long as the benefits of a given choice clearly outweigh the costs in relation to other choices.

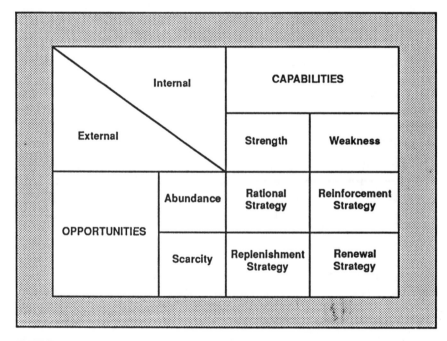

FIGURE 2. A TYPOLOGY OF STRATEGIC CHOICE.

The two dimensions in Figure 2 result in a quadratic model of strategic choice that is conceptually linked to the strategic gap set forth in Figure 1. The following sections provide explanations of general strategic possibilities for a given organization within the boundaries of Figure 2. To imbue this typology with greater credibility, each strategic choice is related to the general classification developed by Porter.[43,44]

Porter's typology of generic strategies has been evaluated and empirically tested and has been ascribed a high level of validity.[45,46] And, finally to imbue the typology in Figure 2 with greater meaningfulness for the practising manager, real-world examples of each strategic possibility will be provided.

Rational Strategy

A rational strategy is used when external opportunities are abundant and there is considerable strength in internal capabilities. This is the ideal managerial strategy for most organizations. Management is effective; technology is advanced; policies are comprehensive; and resources are productively utilized in every sense. The capabilities of the organization are fully committed (with necessary reserves in each category of capability) in pursuit of attractive external opportunities across the full spectrum of time frames. On balance, the organization has a small positive strategic gap. Idle and non-productive resources are minimized; opportunity costs are insignificant. Specific courses of action for the total organization are selected rationally with appropriate consideration for trade-off values, present values, expected values, cost effectiveness, opportunity cost, and organizational priorities. In this context, rational simply means 'objectives-oriented'.[47]

In terms of Porter's classification, a rational strategy as intended in Figure 2 suggests either a *cost leadership strategy* or a *differentiation strategy*.[48] Anheuser-Busch Co., Inc. affords an excellent example of an organization that employs both cost leadership and product differentiation to accomplish a rational strategy. Busch's low cost performance and high market segmentation contribute to its continued leadership in the US brewing industry. Many people believe that in the early years of its development, General Motors rapidly became the leader in the US automobile industry through this same type of rational strategy. As will be noted below, General Motors' strategy changed markedly in the 1980s.

Replenishment Strategy

A replenishment strategy is appropriate when there is strength in internal capabilities clearly in excess of external opportunities. In the context of Figure 1, a replenishment strategy is appropriate when the strategic gap is positive and too large to justify a rational strategy. It indicates a condition of idle resources and under-utilized capability. If allowed to persist, this condition will work to the disadvantage of the total organization. A large positive strategic gap invariably leads to negative consequences if it goes uncorrected. With a replenishment strategy, it is management's task to transform the perceived scarcity of external opportunities into an attractive abundance through various developmental activities.

Examples of replenishment strategies in the short run include: (a) attempts to diversify operations through acquisition or merger, (b) intensification of current product development efforts, or (c) marketing of various combinations of excess capabilities through arrangements such as management consulting, licensing of advanced technologies, or leasing of surplus physical resources. In the long run, examples of replenishment strategies include: (a) acceleration of research and development in existing and new product areas, (b) exploration and development of new marketing opportunities, or (c) identifying and pursuing attractive long lead-time possibilities. The emphasis in a replenishment strategy is to obtain a nearly-full commitment of internal capabilities and to reduce the positive strategic gap to proportions that will permit the use of a more desirable rational strategy.

In Porter's classification scheme, the replenishment strategy characterized in Figure 2 would be somewhat analogous to a *differentiation strategy* or a *differentiation focus strategy.* According to Porter, a differentiation strategy may be either broad or narrow in scope.[49] If it is broad in scope, it is often a differentiation in areas such as products, markets or reserve capability. For example, with its acquisition in 1985 of the Gulf Oil Co., the Chevron Corporation greatly expanded its reserves for the exploration and development of petroleum, thereby protecting its market position. If differentiation is narrow in scope, it is often focused on a particular market segment or product technology. For example, the acquisition of Crocker Bank by Wells Fargo in 1987 substantially increased the market share of Wells Fargo for banking services in the state of California and deepened its penetration of the growing market for banking services in southern California. And the acquisition of American Motors by the Chrysler Corporation in 1987 gave Chrysler a competitive advantage in the technology of increasingly popular terrain vehicles such as the jeep.

Reinforcement Strategy

A reinforcement strategy is used when external opportunities appear to be abundant and there is discernible weakness in the internal capabilities of the organization. In the context of Figure 1, a reinforcement strategy is reflective of a negative strategic gap, but one that is correctable by management with a reasonable expenditure of effort. In this condition, management should act to bolster or buttress the areas of weakness and to raise the capabilities of the organization to a level where it can begin to capitalize on attractive external opportunities. For example, a reinforcement strategy might involve: (a) a change in top management along with attendant restructuring of the organization, (b) an advancement of increasingly obsolescent technology, (c) a comprehensive revision of organizational policies, or (d) a reconfiguration and reallocation of organizational resources. If the reinforcement strategy is successful, the organization will move from a negative strategic gap to a small positive strategic gap appropriate for a rational strategy.

In the context of Porter's typology of generic strategies, the reinforcement strategy characterized in Figure 2 would suggest a *cost leadership strategy* or a *cost focus strategy*.[50] For example, General Motors has expended billions of dollars since 1980 in an attempt to regain and secure its industry cost leadership. Prior to 1980, General Motors was the exemplar of the rational strategy depicted in Figure 2. Since then, the corporation has concentrated on reinforcement. Another excellent example of a reinforcement strategy is provided by the Bank of America which since 1984 has been focusing on cost reduction and strengthening its retail banking operation in the state of California after some substantial losses occasioned by loans to third world countries in the later 1970s. Some observers believe that the recent substantial reorganization of IBM reflected a need for that industry giant to reassert its cost leadership.

Renewal Strategy

A renewal strategy results from a double negative of the dimensions depicted in Figure 2. There is a significant and usually pervasive weakness in internal capabilities accompanied by a perceived scarcity of external opportunities. The negative strategy gap is much too serious for a simple reinforcement strategy. The organization is usually in the throes of a widespread malaise with deepening symptoms of entropy. There is a very real possibility of a complete disruption of operations and concomitant failure of organizational vitality. In the private sector, bankruptcy is beckoning; in the public sector continuance of services is increasingly jeopardized. There is an immediate need for drastic corrective action to revive and renew the entire organization. Examples of renewal strategies include: (a) a complete rebuilding of the organizational structure, (b) retrenchment of all activities that do not contribute directly to the viability of the organization, and (c) substantial changes in organizational membership at all levels. Once the internal surgery has been completed and the capabilities of the organization have been substantially reconstituted, a continued perception of scarce external opportunities may permit the organization to shift to a replenishment strategy. Most likely, however, a successful renewal strategy will culminate in a rational strategy which is the most advantageous strategic choice for the long run.

Porter's typology of generic strategies also suggests that the renewal strategy characterized in Figure 2 is somewhat analogous to a *cost leadership strategy* or a *cost focus strategy*. In these types of strategy the need is extreme and compelling for the entire organization to reduce its costs in the aggregate or in specific areas. The entire savings and loan industry in the US which is currently in the throes of a massive federal bailout is reflective of a renewal strategy in the embryonic stage. The US airline industry affords numerous examples of airlines that have employed a renewal strategy. Braniff Airlines filed bankruptcy in 1981 and surfaced in 1984 as a division of the Hyatt Corporation. And Eastern Airlines is paying for its membership in the Texas air conglomerate with a bankruptcy proceeding underway at this time.

SUMMARY

This paper delineated the concept of strategic gap depicted in Figure 1 as the state of balance (or imbalance) between the capabilities of the organization and the significant factors in its external environment. An assessment of the magnitude and direction of the strategic gap begins with an assessment of organizational capabilities including management, technology, policies, and resources. This internal assessment culminates in a profile of organizational strengths and weaknesses which can serve as a composite measure of capabilities *vis-à-vis* the external environment. Gap analysis continues with an assessment of the attractive opportunities, significant threats, and important sociopolitical factors in the external environment of the organization. In the event that organizational capabilities clearly exceed the opportunities, threats, requirements, and responsibilities in the external environment, there is a positive strategic gap. If the converse relationship applies, there is a negative strategic gap. A small positive strategic gap is a natural and desirable state simply because it indicates that the organization is productively engaged in capitalizing on its attractive opportunities, protecting itself from threats such as competition and technological obsolescence while fulfilling its obligations to an insatiable group of stakeholders. In addition, the organization has some reserve capability to provide for unanticipated situations. It is also significant to note that for many reasons set forth in this paper, there will never be a perfect interface between a given organization and its external environment. If a strategic gap is indeed axiomatic, then let it be small and positive over the long run.

In Figure 2, this paper also set forth a new quadratic model of strategic choice that was related to Porter's typology of generic strategies and was bolstered by several recent real-world examples. If, for example, the organization enjoys a small positive strategic gap, it should adopt a rational strategy. This is the ideal strategic choice and one to which most organizations should aspire. If the positive strategic gap is larger than a normally sustainable level, the organization should adopt a replenishment strategy on the way to a rational strategy.

In the presence of a negative strategic gap, the organization has two strategic choices. If the negative gap is not too serious, the organization can initiate corrective action through a reinforcement strategy. If the negative gap is very serious, a renewal strategy may be required. The objective in both of these strategies is to reduce the imbalance and to convert a negative gap to a small sustainable positive gap. In short, the aim is to seek and maintain a rational strategy which is best for the organization over the long run. A rational strategy is the hallmark of effective strategic management in all kinds of formal organizations.

The concept of strategic gap depicted in Figure 1 is not without its shortcomings. Obviously it is a macro model and, as such, requires considerable further delineation of micro variables and interrelationships to render it applicable at the point of practice. Moreover, even though many of the micro variables depicted in Figure 1 have been explicated and validated through empirical research, the total model requires further validation, especially in the context of the typology of strategic choice set forth in Figure 2, before it can be considered as applicable to all types of formal organizations. Hopefully, this paper will elicit interest among researchers towards pursuing such validation. ■

NOTES

1. Steiner, G.A. and Miner, J.B., *Management Policy and Strategy*, New York, MacMillan, 1977.
2. Weber, C.E., 'Strategic Thinking—Dealing With Uncertainty', *Long Range Planning*, 17, 5, 1984, pp. 60-70.
3. Grinyer, P.H., 'The Anatomy of Business Strategic Planning Reconsidered', *Journal of Management Studies*, 8, 1971, pp. 149–212.
4. Glueck, W.F. and Jauch, L.R., *Strategic Management and Business Policy*, 2nd ed., New York, McGraw-Hill, 1984.
5. Ansoff, H.I., *Corporate Strategy*, New York, McGraw-Hill, 1965.
6. Hofer, C.W. and Schendel, D., *Strategy Formulation: Analytical Concepts*, St. Paul, Minn., West Publishing Co., 1978, p. 47.
7. Harrison, E.F., *Policy, Strategy and Managerial Action*. Boston, Houghton Mifflin Co., 1986, p. 383.
8. Leontiades, M., *Management Policy, Strategy, and Plans*, Boston, Little Brown, 1982.
9. Ibid., p. 123.
10. McCarthy, D.J., Minichiello and Curran, J.R., *Business Policy and Strategy: Concepts and Readings*, Homewood, Ill., 1975, p. 107.
11. Andrews, K.R., *The Concept of Corporate Strategy*. Rev. ed. Homewood, Ill., Richard D. Irwin, 1980.
12. Horovitz, J.H., *Top Management Control in Europe*, London, MacMillan, 1980.
13. Horovitz, J.H. and Thietart, R.A., 'Strategic Management Design and Firm Performance', *Strategic Management Journal*, 3, 1982, pp. 67–76.
14. Ireland, R.D. *et al.*, 'Strategy Formulation Processes: Differences in Perceptions of Strength and Weakness Indicators and Environmental Uncertainty by Managerial Level', *Strategic Management Journal*, 8, 1987, pp. 469–85.
15. Halal, W.E., 'Strategic Management: The State-of-the-Art and Beyond', *Technological Forecasting*, 25, 1984, pp. 239–61.
16. Dess, G.G., 'Consensus on Strategic Formulation and Organizational Performance: Competitors in a Fragmented Industry', *Strategic Management Journal*, 8, 1987, pp. 259–77.
17. Galbraith, J.K., *The New Industrial State*, Boston, Houghton Mifflin Co., 1967, p. 12.

18. Schon, D.A., *Technology and Change,* New York, Dell, 1967, p. 1.
19. Luthans, Fred, *Organizational Behavior,* New York, McGraw-Hill, 1973, p. 281.
20. Taylor, J.C., *Technology and Planned Organizational Change,* Ann Arbor, University of Michigan Institute for Social Research, 1970.
21. Simon, H.A., 'Technology and Environment', in *Emerging Concepts in Management,* 2nd ed., ed. Wortman, M.S. and Luthans, F., New York, MacMillan, 1975, p. 4.
22. Higgins, J.M., *Organizational Policy and Strategic Management: Text and Cases,* 2nd ed., Hinsdale, Ill, Dryden Press, 1983.
23. Friar, J. and Horwith, M., 'The Emergence of Technology Strategy: A New Dimension of Strategic Management', *Technology in Society,* 7, 1985, pp. 143–78.
24. Harrison, op. cit., *Policy, Strategy and Managerial Action.*
25. Freeman, R. Edward, 'Strategic Management: A Stakeholder Approach', *Advances in Strategic Management,* Vol. 1, Lamb, Robert (ed.), Greenwich, Conn., JAI Press, 1983, pp. 31–60.
26. Lyles, Marjorie A. and Mitroff, Ian I., 'The Impact of Sociopolitical Influences on Strategic Problem Formulation', *Advances in Strategic Management,* Vol. 3, Lamb, Robert and Shrivastava, Paul (eds.), Greenwich, Conn., JAI Press, 1985, pp. 69–81.
27. Summer, Charles E., *Strategic Behavior in Business and government,* Boston, Little Brown and Co., 1980, pp. 6–7.
28. Pettigrew, Andrew, 'Strategy Formulation as a Political Process', *International Studies of Management & Organization',* Vol. VII, No. 2, 1977, pp. 78–87.
29. Lyles, Marjorie A., 'Defining Strategic Problems: Subjective Criteria of Executives'. *Organization Studies,* Vol. 8, No. 3, 1987, pp. 263–79.
30. Harrison, E.F., *Management and Organizations,* Boston, Houghton Mifflin Co., 1978, p. 101.
31. Ackoff, R.L., *A Concept of Corporate Planning,* New York: Wiley-Interscience, 1970.
32. Higgins, op. cit.
33. Thompson, A.A., Jr. And Strickland, A.J., III, *Strategy Formulation and Implementation,* Rev. ed., Plano, Texas, Business Publications, 1983, p. 81.
34. Ibid., p. 83.
35. Harrison, op. cit., *Policy, Strategy and Managerial Action.*
36. Thompson and Strickland, op. cit., pp. 89–90.
37. Eells, Richard and Walton, Clarence, *Conceptual Foundations of Business,* Rev. ed., Homewood, Ill., Richard D. Irwin, 1969.
38. Monsen, R. Joseph, Jr. and Cannon, Mark W., *The Makers of Public Policy: American Power Groups and Their Ideologies,* New York, McGraw-Hill, 1965.
39. MacMillan, Ian C. and Jones, Patricia E., *Strategy Formulation: Power and Politics,* 2nd ed., St. Paul, Minn, West Publishing Co., 1986.
40. Petit, Thomas A., 'The Doctrine of Socially Responsible Management', *Emerging Concepts in Management,* Wortman, Max S. and Luthans, Fred (eds.), New York, MacMillan, 1969, pp. 44–9.
41. Davis, K., 'The Case For and Against Business Assumption of Social Responsibilities', *Academy of Management Journal* 16, 2, 1973, pp. 313–17.
42. Harrison, op. cit., *Policy, Strategy and Managerial Action,* pp. 80–1.
43. Porter, Michael E., *Competitive Strategy: Techniques for Analyzing Industries and Competitors,* New York, Free Press, 1980.
44. Porter, Michael E., *Competitive Advantage: Creating and Sustaining Superior Performance,* New York, Free Press, 1985.
45. Dess, Gregory G., 'An Empirical Examination of Porter's (1980) Generic Strategies', *Academy of Management Proceedings,* Chung, K.H. (ed.), 42nd annual meeting, New York, N.Y., 1982, pp. 7–11.
46. Wright, Peter, 'A Refinement of Porter's Strategies', *Strategic Management Journal,* Vol. 8, 1987, pp. 93–101.
47. Harrison, E.F., *The Managerial Decision-Making Process,* 3rd ed., Boston, Houghton Mifflin Co., 1987, pp. 105–43.
48. Porter, op. cit., *Competitive Advantage,* pp. 12–14.
49. Ibid., pp. 14–15.
50. Ibid., pp. 12–16.

Using Intuition to Manage Organizations in the Future

Weston H. Agor

The last major undeveloped resource may be the human brain. In the past, managers relied on their left (analytical) brains. The future offers the possibility of using our right or intuitive brains also, so that the best managers work with full, not half, power.

Organizations and managers today basically employ three broad types of management styles for making decisions. The first, often referred to as left brain, has traditionally received the most attention in management education programs. This style stresses employing analytical and quantitative techniques such as MBO (management by objectives), PERT (program evaluation review techniques), and forecasting to make management decisions. So-called rational and logical methods of reasoning are followed. Problems are solved by breaking them down into manageable parts, then approaching them sequentially, relying on logic and data as tools in the process. Computers are the primary technological assistants used. Management settings are normally highly structured and hierarchical in nature, with methods of decision making carefully planned. Examples of such organizations would be General Motors, the military, and many governmental units.

An alternative and complementary management style employs right brain skills. This approach, which has received considerably less attention and resource support in most of the leading management education and training programs until recently, stresses quite different techniques for problem solving. Reliance is placed primarily on feelings rather than on facts when making decisions. Intuitive and inductive techniques are employed. Problems are solved by first looking at the whole—often with inadequate information or data at hand. Decisions are then reached through intuitive insights or flashes of awareness. The management setting in which right brain skills are normally employed tends to be more informal and collegial. Participatory

From Business Horizons ©1984 by the Foundation for the School of Business at Indiana University. Reprinted by permission.

Weston Agor is Professor and Director of the Masters in Public Administration program at The University of Texas at El Paso and also President of ENFP Enterprises, a management consulting firm. He has served in policy-making positions in both the public and private sectors, and has consulted for such organizations as Walt Disney enterprises, Rockwell International, and Mountain Bell. His book Intuitive Management (Prentice-Hall) was published in April 1984.

and horizontal authority structures are employed, and decisions are made in a somewhat more unstructured, fluid, and spontaneous manner. Such organizations would be Apple Computers, Walt Disney Enterprises, and selected intelligence agencies.

The third style, which has often been called integrated, employs both left and right brain skills interchangeably as the management situation demands (see Table I.) Managers who rely on this approach normally feel comfortable dealing with both facts and feelings when making decisions. But, they also tend to make their major decisions guided by intuition after scanning the available facts and receiving input from the management resources and personnel available both on the left and the right of the organization. Frequently, the intuitive decisions made are in conflict with the course suggested by the available facts and forward projections based there-on. Organizations relying most on this style would be such companies as Proctor & Gamble and McDonald's, which were featured in the recent best seller, *In Search of Excellence*, as well as innovative public sector organizations such as Dade County, Florida.

TABLE 1
Brain Style in Management

Left Brain	Right Brain	Integrated
Analytical	Intuitive	Use left and right brain styles interchangeably
Deductive	Inductive	
Rely more on facts to make decisions	Rely more on feelings to make decisions	
Prefers hierarchical authority structures	Prefers collegial and participatory authority structures	
Prefers management situations that are structured and carefully planned.	Prefers management situations that are unstructured fluid, and spontaneous.	
Prefers solving problems by breaking them down into parts, then approaching the problem sequentially using logic.	Prefers solving problems by looking at the whole then approaching problem through patterns using hunches.	

USE OF INTUITION IN MANAGEMENT

The use of intuition is a critical skill in both right brain and integrative decision-making styles. Until recently, the ability to make decisions using intuition received relatively little attention, and research on the topic is still extremely limited. This situation now appears to be changing rapidly. Recently, for example, many articles have appeared stressing the importance of intuition in management decision making.[1] Such leading business schools as Stanford are also now experimenting with courses stressing the development of right brain management skills.

Why this sudden interest in intuition as a tool in management? In part, it is due to a growing dissatisfaction with the track record of the left brain style of decision making. This recent interest is also due in part to a recognition that an entirely new set of management conditions are emerging which are likely to place a greater premium on intuition in the future. As such futurists as John Naisbitt, Willis W. Harman, and Alvin Toffler have pointed out, we are entering turbulent times in which the economic and political climate will be characterized by rapid change, crises, and major structural dislocations. Technological advances will be astronomical. At the same time, as a recent study entitled *The Innovative Organization: Productivity Programs in Action* points out,[2] employees at every level in organizations will demand a greater role in decision making. As a result, bottom-up and horizontal communication in organizations is expected to increase rapidly (see Table 2.)

Under these conditions, it appears likely that individuals aspiring to top levels of management will need more right brain skills, including intuition, than ever before. This is so because the top leaders of tomorrow are going to be faced with management situations which will be extremely complex. They will need to make decisions under circumstances in which the complete data bases necessary for left brain (linear, deductive) processing will not be available, will not be adequate, or will be too costly or too slow to

TABLE 2
Trends Restructuring Skills Required to Manage Future Organizations

From Today	To the Future
a centralized society	a decentralized society
forced technology	high tech/high touch
hierarchies	networking
representative democracies	participatory democracy
machismo society	androgynous society
institutional help	self-help
vertical society	horizontal society
top-down society	bottom-up society

gather. Computer projections, which have not been very reliable predictors of the economic future even in the most stable of times, are likely to become even less so.[3] Furthermore, top managers are going to need to reach decisions in a "high touch" manner so that subordinates know and feel they have played a key role in the process.

At one time executives were reluctant to admit that they often relied on intuition rather than only on facts or computer printouts to make some of their most important decisions. Today this situation is changing. Recently, Paul Cook, founder and president of Raychem Corporation, was asked whether he used much intuition in his decision making. Cook replied that nearly all of his decisions were based on intuition, and that the only major decisions he regrets were ones not based on it.[4] Robert Bernstein, the chairman of Random House, states, "Only intuition can protect you from the most dangerous individual of all—the articulate incompetent."[5] Apparently, intuition is an integral part of Japan's recent business success as well. Shigen Okada, head of one of Japan's largest department stores, recently explained the reason for his company's success: "It is due to our adoption of the West's pragmatic management combined with the spiritual, intuitive aspects of the East.[6] William G. McGinnis, city manager of Crescent City, California, uses this formula for generating decisions in his organization:

"I believe that good intuitive decisions are directly proportional in one's years of challenging experience, plus the number of related and worthwhile years of training and education, all divided by lack of confidence, or the fear of being replaced."[7]

WHAT IS INTUITION?

If intuition is an important management tool that is likely to become more so over the next decade, what is it exactly? Psychologist Frances E. Vaughan defines intuition this way: "It is a way of knowing . . . recognizing the possibilities in any situation. Extrasensory perception, clairvoyance, and telepathy are part of the intuitive function."[8] Carl Jung defined intuition as the function that "explores the unknown, and senses possibilities and implications which may not be readily apparent.[9] Laurence R. Sprecher of Public Management Associates prefers to think of intuition as merely a subspecies of logical thinking—one in which the steps of the process are hidden in the subconscious portion of the brain.[10]

TESTING MANAGERS' ABILITY TO INTUIT

If intuition is an important management skill that can be practically used to make decisions in organizations, how do you test for it, and is the ability distributed evenly throughout management?

Over the last two years, I have tested over 2,000 managers across the country in a wide variety of organizational settings (business, government, education, military, health), at all levels of management responsibility and in various occupational specialties. The Myers-Briggs Personality Test was used because it is widely recognized in the psychology profession for its high level of reliability and validity. The findings are dramatic.

Without exception, top managers in every organization examined are significantly different from middle and lower level managers in their ability to use intuition on the job, to make decisions. Equally significant is the fact that women consistently score higher than men in their ability to use intuition, as do managers with Asian backgrounds. This suggests that both women and persons with Asian backgrounds should consider more actively marketing and developing their intuitive skills as one effective vehicle for career advancement in the organizations of tomorrow. Test results also indicate that managers with higher levels of intuitive ability are likely to be particulary effective in such key occupations as personnel, health, public affairs and relations, advertising and marketing, and intelligence or crisis management where imagination, creativity and other right brain skills are demanded.

INTUITION IN PRODUCTIVITY AND SATISFACTION

Consulting and conducting workshops on intuition for a number of major organizations has taught me that there are several practical ways that organizations can use intuition to increase both their productivity and employee satisfaction.

First, the type of brain skills required in management varies by organizational type, by level of management, by problem or issue, and by occupational specialty. Accordingly, one of the very first practical applications of testing for intuitive ability is in the overall process of selecting and placing of management personnel. Job descriptions, specifications, and exams should incorporate brain skills and style as part of the selection process. This not only will make for more precise matching of brain skills to the job requirements, but also will be more likely to lead to employee productivity and satisfaction on the job.

In my workshops, managers are tested at the outset for both inherent intuitive ability and actual use of this skill to make decisions on the job. Some of the most useful work involves not only helping managers learn about the ability they may already possess, but also assisting them in the process of actually using this skill on the job to make decisions. Both organizational productivity and personal satisfaction can be significantly increased as a result.

Second, the brain skills which are most productively useful vary by problem and issue. Accordingly, selection and placement by brain type and style in organizations of tomorrow should be situational—based primarily on the brain style appropriate for each problem or situation. Similarly, teams can be constructed to enhance maximum performance, taking into account such factors as intuitive brain skills required in a particular setting, the mix of brain types (left, right, and integrative), and personality types which will ensure a more effective team effort.

At Walt Disney Enterprises, for example, communication problems within the organization were overcome by a better understanding of the brain style each manager was accustomed to using (see Table 3.) The intuitive "imagineers" (artists, writers, craftsmen) thought quite differently about how to solve a problem from the engineers or financiers in the organization. Until each group developed a better understanding of how their colleagues thought and acted differently about problems they all faced, effective communication was difficult.

Third, it is becoming increasingly apparent that individual and organizational health is closely linked to these factors: whether a person is properly matched on the job with the brain skills he or she possesses, whether the person is fully aware of his or her dominant brain style, and whether the person is in fact using on the job his or her dominant brain style. It is also apparent that those in my national sample who indicated dissatisfaction with their present jobs were dissatisfied at least in part because they were mismatched. This is, their brain skills did not match the demands of the positions they were actually in. Obviously, both productivity and individual job satisfaction can be significantly increased within organizations through an overall human resource management program which assesses managers' different brain styles and matches them more precisely with actual position requirements. It is also apparent that an important by-product of such a program would be a reduction in overall health costs and absentee rates.

How to Develop and Use Intuition

If intuition is a skill that will become more important for future managers to possess and use, how do we develop and use it? The first rule is to *believe in it*. Recently research indicates that what we believe we can do is one of the most important factors in determining what we can in fact do. For example, one study found that CEO who believed in their ability to make decisions guided by intuition also had the highest profit record.[11]

The second rule is *practice makes perfect*. We all possess the ability to use intuition to make decisions. All too frequently, the primary reason we fail to develop our ability to the fullest is that we are simply lazy. This is analogous to the blind person who develops his or her other inherent senses to the point that color can be seen through touch. If a blind person can

TABLE 3

Management Situations Where Brain Style Is Most Appropriate

Level of Application	The Three Brain Styles in Organizations		
	Left	Integrative	Right
Type of organization where prominant	Traditional pyramid	Dynamic	Open, temporary or rapid change
Management style emphasized	deductive objective	Deductive inductive used as appropriate and interchangeably	Inductive subjective
Example settings where most effective	Quantative applications where data bases are available	Problem-solving and labor-management negotiations	Projection when new trends are emerging crises, intelligence, holistic health
Example applications	Madel building, projection	Team building, synergistics	brain-storming challenge traditional assumptions
Occupational specialty	Planning, management science, financial management, law enforcement, and the military	Top policy management and general administration intelligence	Personnel, counseling health organizational development

develop other senses to a high degree, why can't we develop our intuitive ability in the same way?

A third rule is to *create a supportive personal and organizational environment* in which intuitive skills are valued and applied in day-to-day life to make decisions. All too frequently, we reject new and different ways of solving problems because we become accustomed to a particular way of doing things. Often, it is only in crises (such as business failure or loss of health or loved ones) that we reach for alternative ways of doing things or allow our inherent intuitive skills to surface and be of assistance to us. Fortunately, however, we do not all need to experience serious traumas in life as the only means of getting in touch with and developing our intuitive ability. A series of tests, exercises, and games (for example, meditation, guided imagery, and dream analysis) can be used effectively toward this end. Primarily, they serve to focus our attention within rather than without. They enable us to create environments and settings in which our intuitive insights and understandings can more easily surface, or in which blocks to this ability (resulting from earlier life experience or habit) can more easily be removed.

The *Chronicle of Higher Education* recently reported on the successful use of one of these techniques—guided imagery—to improve the record of The University of Illinois basketball team.[12] Similarly Washoe County, Nevada, experimented with a number of such tools and techniques. Ed Everett, Assistant County Manager, points out the potential payout of such programs:

"For many organizations, the minds and creative potential of their employees represent one of the few remaining resources that can still be expanded. Not using this resource is the same as turning your back on a new revenue source."[13]

It is increasingly apparent that right brain skills such as intuition can be practically used in organizations to make decisions and that this skill is going to become more valuable in the future (see Table 4). Management education programs are beginning to create courses to develop this ability further. It also appears probable that the research findings could lead to a major restructuring of management education in the next decade appropriate to the organizational environment now emerging. By 1990, quite possibly the leading management training programs in the country (both public and private) will place just as much emphasis on the training of right brain (inductive, intuitive, and precognitive) skills as they presently do on left brain (deductive and analytical) skills to make decisions. Productivity and job satisfaction are likely to improve in future organizations if they do. ■

TABLE 4
Management Situation Where Intitution Is Most Useful

Situation	Method to use
Problem Solving	Use intution along with reason to come up with integrated solution that is both visionary and practical
Future Projections meeting crisis	Explore alternative actions with limited or inadequate information at hand, pick the option that *feels* most possible and also practical
Team building	Use test results to build the team-types that can best solve different problems at hand
Organization design and management	Use test results, work experience and own feelings to decide how to lead meetings, write memos, organize a room, communicate between departments, and pick personal staff

RESOURCES ON INTUITION

TESTS

Frances E. Vaughan, *Awakening Intuitions* (New York: Anchor Press [Doubleday, 1979]: paperback introduction to the whole subject.

Myers-Briggs Personality Test, (Palo Alto, Calif.: Consulting Psychologists, Press, 1976): intuitive portion measures ability.

Paul E. Torrance and Barbara and William Taggart, *Human Information TM Survey* (Bensonville, Ill.: Scholastic Testing Service, Inc., 1983). Surveys a persons' way of processing information according to brain style.

EXERCISES AND GAMES

Eugene Rauddsepp, *Creative Growth Games, How Creative Are You?* and *More Creative Growth Games* (Palo Alto, Calif.: Consulting Psychologists Press, 1977–1981).

Christopher Hills and Deborah Rozman, *Exploring Inner Space: Awareness Games for Ages* (Boulder Creek, Calif.: University of the Trees Press, 1978).

Alan Vaughan, "Intuition, Precognition, and the Art of Predictions," *The Futurist*, June 1982: 5–10.

Tapes produced by ARE (Virginia Beach, Vir.), Unity (Unity Village, Mo.), and Effective Learning Systems (Grand Rapids, Mich.)

Alan Vaughan, "Psychic Defender" (408 Ivy St., Glendale, Calif. 91204): test for precognitive ability for use on Apple microcomputer.

USE IN MANAGEMENT

Weston H. Agor, "Using Intuition in Public Management," *Public Management*, February 1983: 2–6.

Weston H. Agor "Brain Skills Development in Management Training," *Training and Development Journal*, April 1983: 778–83.

Weston H. Agor, "Training Public Managers to Develop and Use their Intuition for Decision Making," in Kent T. Higgins, ed., *Professional Development Handbook, 1983* (Washington, D.C.: American Society for Public Administration, 1983).

Weston H. Agor, "Using Intuition to be More Effective at Work and in Your Personal Life" (Glendale, Calif.: Walt Disney Enterprises, 1982): videotape.

NOTES

1. See, as examples, Mortimer R. Feinberg and Aaron Levenstein, "How Do You Know When to Listen to Your Intuition," *Wall Street Journal*, June 21, 1982: 16; Bennett W. Goodspeed, "Different Styles of Analysis Imperative to Business: More Often Than Not, Intuition, Not Numbers, Tells the Real Story," *American Banker*, November 9, 1981: reprint; *Harvard Business Review: On Human Relations* (New York: Harper & Row, 1979); Weston H. Agor, "Using Intuition in Public Management," *Public Management*, February 1983: 2–6; and Agor, "Brain Skills Development in Management Training," *Training and Development Journal*, April 1983: 78–83.
2. By Robert Zager and Michael P. Rosow (Elmsford, N.Y.: Pergamon Press, 1982).
3. Laurie McGinley, "Forecasters Overhaul Models of Economy in Wake of 1982 Errors," *Wall Street Journal*, February 1983: 1,20.
4. Jerry Carroll, "Over-Achievers Swarm to this Exotic Class," *San Francisco Chronicle*, February 17, 1983: 46.
5. Goodspeed.
6. Goodspeed.
7. William G. McGinnis, "Decision-Making," *Public Management*, February 1983: 17.
8. Frances E. Vaughan, *Awakening Intuition* (Garden City, N.Y.: Anchor Books, Inc., 1979).
9. M.L. Von Franz and J. Hillman, *Jung's Typology* (New York: Spring Publications, 1971).
10. Laurence R. Sprecher, "Intuition Anyone?" *Public Management*, February 1983: 18.
11. Douglas Dean and John Mihalasky, *Executive ESP* (Englewood Cliffs, N.J.: Prentice-Hall, Inc., 1974).
12. Scott Vance, "Psychologist Helps Players at U. of Illinois Use 'Imagery' to Sharpen Basketball Skills," *The Chronicle of Higher Education*, June 8, 1985: 15, 20.
13. "Editor's Note." Public Management, February 1983: back of front cover.

Decisions, Decisions: Which Approach to Take?

Herbert S. Kindler

A systematic strategy can help you select the most effective way to handle a difficult decision.

Who gets a raise? Are safety precautions adequate? Is the new budget reasonable? How shall a particular problem get solved? Organizational lore has the hero-manager—a person of decisiveness—snap out instant solutions to these complex problems, and many managers buy this image. A review of empirical studies indicates that decision makers seldom take time to develop a strategy but, rather, move quickly toward whatever solution seems best when the problem or issue first appears. Creativity and effectiveness suffer as a result.

But managerial performance depends upon good decision making. To determine whether managers tend to move too quickly or choose inappropriate decision-making processes, I conducted a study, holding open-ended interviews with 21 fourth- and fifth-level managers. They answered two questions: (1) How do you make decisions when you have a real stake in the outcome and can influence the process employed? and (2) What considerations determine whether you involve others in the decision-making process? Their answers uncovered a set of decision-making approaches and led to the development of a model that indicates when each is most effective.

THE FOUR BASIC DECISION PROCESSES

In describing how they went about making decisions, the managers interviewed often presented a series of activities; however, a focus on the activities directly producing final decisions revealed just four unique processes. Exhibit 1 summarizes the definitions and characteristics of those processes. We can gain clarity by comparing them in two sets: unilateral decision

Reprinted, by permission of the publisher from *Personnel*, January 1985, American Management Association, New York. All rights reserved.

Herbert S. Kindler is director, Center for Management Effectiveness, and professor of management at Loyola Marymount University in Los Angeles. He has 25 years of organizational experience and has published several articles on management. Dr. Kindler received his B.S. from the Massachusetts Institute of Technology, his M.P.A. from the University of Pittsburgh, and his Ph.D. from U.C.L.A.'s Graduate School of Management.

making v. collaboration, and bargaining v. the approach I have termed "decision-rule."

A unilateral process, in which an individual exercises sole decision-making responsibility, contrasts with collaboration, in which the group is decision maker. Other researchers claim that when a manager consults with others, he or she *always* retains the power to make a unilateral decision; the managers interviewed for this study, however, believe otherwise.

In a unilateral decision process, the decision maker often consults with others *individually* to collect information and perspectives. But the line is crossed into a *collaborative* process when the manager consults with others collectively.

This distinction has significant implications. If a manager gathers opinions on a one-to-one basis, he or she can usually make the final decision without insulting or offending anyone. But should a manager choose to consult with a group—even an advisory group—he or she will have trouble rejecting a strongly asserted group recommendation: Participants will most likely see contrary action as demeaning and feel their time was wasted. Such action could evoke resentment and future resistance.

Two procedures used to overcome problems in the collaborative process should be mentioned here. The "delphi" technique, developed by N. C. Dakey, encourages collaboration when participants are separated geographically. A coordinator distributes questionnaires, summarizes the returned responses, then distributes the summary, asking participants if they'd like to revise their original views in light of the others' responses. As the coordinator continues distributing summaries and asking for revisions, the participants' opinions tend to converge.

The "nominal group" technique, developed by A. L. Delbecoz and A. H. Van de Ven, is a form of collaboration used when participants lack adequate interpersonal skills. With this approach—a structured group meeting with limited verbal interaction—participants' ideas are proposed, sometimes anonymously, then clarified, and finally independently evaluated by voting.

The two remaining processes—bargaining and decision-rule—are widely discussed in the literature of negotiation. They are approaches for what social psychologists call "mixed motive" situations—that is, situations in which involved individuals have at least some opposing interests. In bargaining, two parties make demands and give concessions until a middle ground is reached, where both benefit more than if they had not agreed at all. Decision-rule involves bringing in some external criterion by which it is possible to settle differences—such as the flipping of a coin, a lottery, an arbitrator's judgement, a seniority system, or an equation that measures the long-term results of alternatives, thus indicating the best available option.

EXHIBIT 1

Definitions and Characteristics of Four Decision-Making Processes

Decision Process	Definition	Relationship between Those Involved	Dynamics	Activities That May Precede Decision	Activities That May Follow Decision	Example (in Judicial Terms)
Unilateral decision making	A person exercises sole judgment in choosing between alternative possibilities.	Hierarchical	One individual exercises sole judgment.	Consulting with others. Collecting data. Developing perspectives. Hearing adversarial debate.	Marshalling support for implementation. Appealing the decision to a higher authority.	Judge decides.
Bargaining	Each party seeks to maximize gains and minimize concessions through compromise and mutual adjustment.	Adversarial	An offer is accepted through mutual adjustment or compromise.	Forming coalitions. Negotiations-skills training.	Ratifying the agreement negotiated by representatives.	Attorneys plea bargain.
Collaboration	Participants produce an integrative decision, creating or discovering a synthesis of all informed, relevant views without violating the integrity of any.	Collegial	There is synthesis of two or more points of view.	Interpersonal skills training.	Following up on minority views not integrated in the group decision.	Jury decides.
Decision-rule	Participants accept an outside criterion to decide among predetermined alternatives.	Democratic	Participants accept outside criterion.	Necessary activity: agreement on which rule to apply and which options to consider.	Verifying the outcome (e.g., recounting the votes).	Supreme Court decides.

THE ROLE OF POWER AND ALIGNMENT

My discussions revealed two dimensions that underlie all four processes: (1) the degree to which power is used by the decision maker, and (2) the degree to which the decision maker's interests and values align with those of the others involved in or affected by decision implementation.

Consider how the power and alignment factors thread through the decision processes.

Power

In some situations, parties get what they seek by *exerting power*. Power is necessary for the person who issues a unilateral decision and experts it to be followed: The existence of a power relationship, typically involving organizational status or position, is what legitimizes sole-judgement decisions. Similarly, in bargaining—a mutual-adjustment process—participants exert power to get their offers accepted. Skilled bargainers often marshal their personal power, as well as their professional power, to maximize gains.

Other situations call for *sharing power*. Collaboration, for example, effectively synthesized a collective view only when all participants can interact as peers, openly expressing their concerns and ideas. For the decision-rule approach to work, all participants must agree to accept the final outcome.

Alignment

Alignment is the degree to which one party, in satisfying his or her own interests, also satisfies the interests of other parties involved. Such alignment may be *high*, characterized by common interests and considerable trust; or *partial*, in which convergent and divergent interests coexist.

When alignment is high, when people are all in the same boat or share common interests, the outcome of a decision will affect the manager in much the same way that it affects his or her subordinates. Consequently, this manager's unilateral decision is likely to be accepted.

In situations characterized by partial alignment, either bargaining or decision-rule is more appropriate. Bargaining allows parties to manage their differences, eventually establishing a zone of agreement. Decision-rule, which requires all parties to agree to a rule in advance, has a win-lose nature. Because it results in parties whose interests have not been advanced through its use, the rule must be perceived as fair.

THE POWER/ALIGNMENT MODEL

Depicted in Exhibit 2, the Power/Alignment model can help managers choose the appropriate decision-making process for each particular problem. It requires decision makers to assess the situation at hand and make just two judgments: (1) What degree of alignment exists? and (2) What use of power is best? The manager can infer from each situation the degree of alignment present, but may not be able to see immediately the benefits of exerting or sharing power. Fortunately, there is a systematic approach to help decision makers choose appropriately.

Responses from upper-level managers to the question, "What considerations determine whether you involve others in the decision-making process?" led to the identification of seven criteria, which can be used as a checklist:

1. Is *decision quality* likely to be improved by a joint effort, taking into account the group communication skills of those with the most to contribute?
2. Will *confidentially* permit me to share relevant information freely?
3. Whose *acceptance* is important to effective decision implementation, and would sharing power rally deeper commitment?
4. With respect to *personnel development*, would involving others in the decision-making process provide them with knowledge helpful in supporting this decision or enable them to sharpen their interpersonal skills in general?

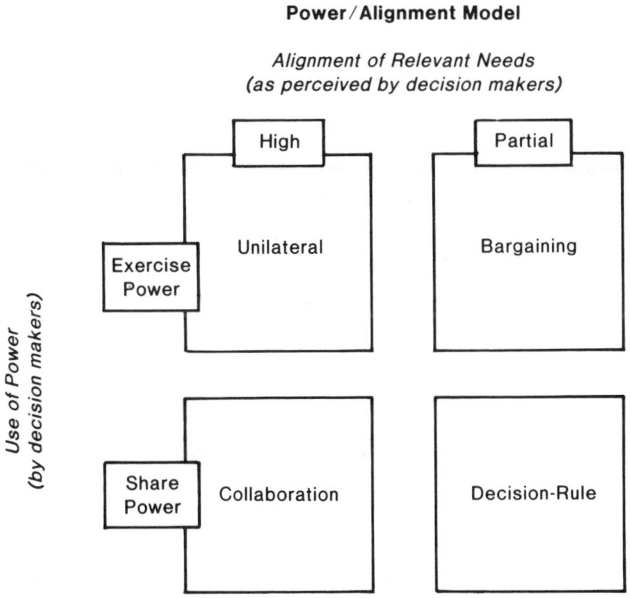

Power/Alignment Model

Alignment of Relevant Needs
(as perceived by decision makers)

EXHIBIT 2 POWER/ALIGNMENT MODEL
ALIGNMENT OF RELEVANT NEEDS (AS PERCEIVED BY DECISION MAKERS)

5. How critical is *timing*? Would extra time invested in participative decision-making save time in execution?
6. Are the *costs* of involving others—money, effort, consequences—justified by the benefits likely to result? Is the decision reversible?
7. Does *cultural propriety*—how we do things around here—indicate who should or should not be involved in this decision?

After answering these questions, managers can use the Power/Alignment model.

Applications of the Model

Described below are four situations that illustrate how the Power/Alignment model can guide your decision-process choice.

Situations #1: The Merit Increase

You have a fixed budget allocation for annual salary merit increases, one that you will distribute appropriately among your seven subordinates. Their work involves creativity and other qualities difficult to measure objectively in the framework of an annual review. Your own salary increase comes from a different budget. What decision-making process should you use to decide which subordinates are to receive merit increases and how much?

Alignment. If your subordinates believe you have no reason to play favorites, and if you are regarded as competent in making discerning performance assessments, your alignment with your subordinates is likely to be high: That is, you want to be equitable—which is most likely what your subordinates also want.

Power. Your position power is sufficient to get your judgment accepted, provided you gather performance data with reasonable diligence and conduct give-and-take interviews with each subordinates before reaching your decision. Use of your authority is appropriate to protect confidential information, and should you diffuse your power, your subordinates' interests in maximizing their individual merit increases might trigger disruptive intragroup conflict.

Process. High alignment coupled with the assessment that exerting power will work best suggests a *unilateral* decision process.

Situation #2: Management and Labor

Suppose we alter Situation #1: You are now a worker during that era in American history when sweatshop conditions prevailed and managers routinely exploited workers. You hold an important position in an organized labor union.

Alignment. The alignment of your interests and those of your manager are, at best partial. The decisions your manager makes could seriously damage your well-being.

Power. Sharing power in this situation would not be likely to encourage cooperation or foster the advancement of all interests. To meet your needs, you must exert power.

Process. Partial alignment and the decision to exert power indicate that you should use bargaining as your decision process.

Situation #3: The Interviewing Panel

You are manager of a government research agency. You invite your three engineer subordinates to help you interview applicants for a new junior position created to provide support services to all four of you. Your agency's human resources department has screened applicants and selected four who appear qualified and meet affirmative action requirements. After the panel completes its four sequential interviews, what decision-making process would be most appropriate to determine which one of the applicants should get the job?

Alignment. If you and your staff want to hire a candidate who is best able to provide the support services that all of you require, then your alignment with your engineers is high.

Power. If you assert your position power, you may diminish the enthusiasm of your engineers and reduce their motivation to help train the selected applicant. Therefore, you will probably want to interact with all panel participants as peers.

Process. Referring to Exhibit 2, you see that you have high alignment and a situation that calls for shared power. You should use collaboration.

Situation #4: Bus Assignments

You are the Metropolitan Transportation Authority (MTA) general manager. MTA recently purchased a large fleet of new buses, about half of which are air-conditioned and very comfortable. As general manager, what decision process should you use to decide which employees will drive which buses?

Alignment. This is a win-lose situation: If one driver is assigned an air-conditioned bus, someone else loses that opportunity. Drivers do not have a common interest, as they did in Situation #1. Any solution will probably result in some disappointment. This is an example of partial alignment.

Power. Since all drivers are equally qualified to drive the good buses, a process they all agree upon and perceive as fair will most likely make the ultimate decision more palatable. Therefore, you will probably want to share power with the drivers.

Process. The process drivers are likely to agree on is either a seniority system or a lottery involving driver rotation. Either would be a *decision-rule* approach, the one indicated in Exhibit 2 for partial alignment situations best served by shared power.

A Decision-Making Tool

The Power/Alignment model offers managers a vehicle to help them approach decision making strategically and proactively. They first select an appropriate process, then concentrate on finding a decision. Of course, the model doesn't automatically present the proper decision, nor does it guarantee that the proper decision will eventually be reached; it does organize important considerations managers should review before beginning a decision-making approach.

ACKNOWLEDGEMENT

The author expresses his appreciation to Robin D. Willits, University of New Hampshire, for his helpful comments of a draft of this article. ■

Managerial Ethics: Hard Decisions on Soft Criteria

Thomas J. Von der Embse,
*Professor of Management and
Medicine in Society,
Wright State University*

Robert A. Wagley,
*Assistant Professor of Business,
Wright State University*

Consider the following situations and place yourself in the role of a manager in them:

- The company decides to locate a new plant near an exclusive resort. The location is ideal for the company, but you are aware it will substantially decrease the resort's attractiveness and consequent earning power.
- An executive colleague and friend is observed by you to be in close contact with an investment broker who recently purchased a large block of your company stock. You and your colleague are on the executive committee and privy to inside confidential information concerning buy-out negotiations presently underway with a ''friendly'' corporate raider.
- A women colleague is dating a man in another department whose former male apartment-mate in another city is known to have contracted AIDS. The woman colleague is not aware of this facet of her friend's background.
- At a recent national shindig for your top sales people, you observe one of the vice presidents purchasing cocaine.
- A top candidate for your company's vacant Personnel Manager position has a background of unfaithfulness to his wife and conduct bordering on sexual harassment of women associates. You are the only member of the selection committee who knows this.

ETHICS IN MANAGEMENT DECISIONS

The above situations, and countless others like them, call for difficult and sometimes painful decisions. Often the easiest path is to ignore the situation,

Reprinted with permission, *Sam Advanced Management Journal,* Winter, 1988, Society for Advancement of Management, Vinton, VA 24179.

Dr. Von der Embse is the author of Supervision: Managerial Skills for a New Era *(MacMillan & Co.) and other books and articles; Dr. Wagley is a co-author of* Management Response to Public Issues: Concepts and Cases in Strategy Formulation *(Charles E. Merrill).*

hoping it will disappear. But the inner voice tells a manager it will not. Decision makers need criteria to guide them through the morass of facts, subtleties, conflicting thoughts and feelings. The need for guidelines is as old as management itself. While the science of management and policy-making offers a wide repertoire of analytical tools, most of these seek to optimize the rational goals of the enterprise—profit, market share, efficiency and economy. They are notably deficient, however, in assessing "soft" decision areas such as ethics. Ethical matters are largely relegated to the manger's judgment, and, in the absence of organization criteria, ethical judgments rest on some admixture of personal beliefs and whatever professional standards the manager possesses.

Significantly, neither personal beliefs nor professional standards are directly related to managing. The former usually develop in the context of personal living, while the latter relate to the manager's field of specialization, such as engineering, purchasing, accounting, personnel, law or marketing. Unless the manager is in a professional association having a code of ethics specifically for managers,[1] the decision-maker must adapt decision rules targeted for other spheres of conduct.

Another source of ethical guidelines is the organization itself. Some managers are fortunate in having organizational ethical codes which are usually statements of values centered on the product and customer mission. They often reflect the founder's beliefs and the founder's personal moral standards. Examples are Procter & Gamble, Mars, and Disney Enterprises. How useful are such codes, for the manager in the situations posed earlier? At best, they are useful as general background, but after the manager bridges the traditional value statements and the compelling logic of the present situation.

It is clear that the decision-maker needs criteria suitable for today's complex ethical dilemmas.[2] While it is not feasible or desirable to prescribe specific guidelines covering every conceivable situation, we believe that ethical guidelines can be developed to help a manager analyze the issues more clearly and apply them more consistently. The purpose of this article is to provide a framework and a direction for effectively resolving and deciding ethical matters.

MANAGERS' ETHICAL PREPARATION

In recent years, ethical concerns have become extremely important to organizations' survival. More than ever, a corporation's economic welfare is contingent on its ethical behavior. Well-known examples are Union Carbide, E.F. Hutton, Home State Bank of Ohio, and Eastman Kodak. The greatest difficulties seem to arise when the corporate standards are either non-existent or are not clear or not practiced by managers, for reasons such as personal gain, peer pressures, conflicting values and expectations, or even coercion.

Many observers lament the weak influence of colleges and universities in preparing managers for making ethical and moral judgments. The lack of exposure to values, through formal ethics courses and or other courses, is regarded as nothing short of tragic. The authors' own survey of universities and textbooks supports this observation. We found, for example, that only a handful of texts used in organizational behavior—a "core" business school course—include any chapters on ethics and, of eleven texts examined, none integrated ethics into the material. Further, of twelve samples universities accredited by the prestigious American Assembly of Collegiate Schools of Business, only one had a required course in business ethics. One observer is thus led to remark that universities are producing highly skilled barbarians in the professional and technical specialties.[3] Whether one concurs with this observation, it is true that ethics and philosophy, once mainstays of the typical university curriculum, have become tertiary, elective studies since the early 1960s, and relatively few students enroll in them except the majors in those fields.

Unlike medicine, law or other traditional professions, there is no systematic exposure to an ethical perspective in the education and development of managers. As suggested earlier, even managers having such professional background cannot easily transpose ethical decision rules to the management situation. Consider a physician who becomes a health system manager. As a physician, he employed every means possible to secure the best patient care in accordance with the ethics of his profession. Now, as administrator, he is faced with decisions where quality may have to be sacrificed in the interests of economy. Furthermore, the ethics of dealing with colleagues, suppliers, community, and employers assume greater importance and at times will overshadow matters of patient care.

In contrast with specialized professions, managerial decisions typically present more than one ethical alternative. Invariably, there are trade-offs required which befuddle the manager who cannot tolerate ambiguity. The burden of ethical judgment is heightened by this complexity. At the point of decision, managers with little or no ethical training revert to their personal moral codes and values.

MORAL JUDGMENT: ETHICAL DECISION
OR LEGAL IMPERATIVE?

Often the moral precept coincides with the ethical, as in the opening case of the woman colleague dating the man who may have exposure to AIDS. Many people would consider it a moral duty to share the information with the woman; professional ethics would also suggest that action. Legally, however, such action could involve civil liberties. Disclosure of background information might be construed as a violation of the man's privacy. Thus, the manager operating in today's legalistic environment may very well eschew his moral and ethical structures in favor of a legally-safe option. Instead of giving the woman colleague the information, he may hint that she should find out more about the man's background, or he may simply remain silent.

A useful starting point for developing a systematic approach to ethical judgments is to sort out and clarify the personal and professional issues, namely, the moral and the ethical facets. First, the issues must be distinguished, and then the substantive distinctions translated into ethical and moral behavior. Definition is an important concern for both understanding and practicing ethics.[4] The following should help to clarify.

Ethics, as suggested here, are the consensually-accepted standards of behavior for an occupation, trade, or profession. Morality denotes the precepts of personal behavior, based on religious or philosophical grounds. Such precepts might or might not be consistent with ethical practices, as implied above. When not consistent, ethics or morals prevails depending on the strength or conviction underlying the ethical principles and moral precepts.

The opening "insider information" episode is a good case in point. While disclosing confidential inside information is generally regarded as unethical, immoral, and illegal, the matter is not so clear cut from the trader's viewpoint. Some investment bankers rationalize the practice of seeking inside information as ethical because it serves their clients' interests, which they regard as their principal responsibility. They do not perceive it as immoral, either, on the premise that the client's livelihood—a morally desirable end—justifies their dealings. The inside trader is aware, however, that the activity is illegal, and this constrains their behavior more than the moral and ethical issues.

In contrast with ethics and morality, the law refers to the formal codes that permit or forbid certain behaviors. Law might or might not serve to enforce ethics or morality. For example, the sharing of research knowledge might be regarded as both ethical and moral among researchers from different companies, yet this sharing could be illegal under anti-trust laws.

Unfriendly takeovers which are closely related to insider trading, have become one of the most publicized and debated activities in this decade. Are they ethical? Moral? Legality is not an issue at present, although the law may change in the near future. The ethics involved in challenging the present directorship and extracting "greenmail" booty are questionable, but few finance professionals have declared the practice unethical. In fact, the professional ethical perspective would hold the incumbent management equally culpable for not fairly representing asset value, thereby making its firm vulnerable to a takeover.

Though they rarely invoke the term "ethics" the takeover artists underscore the plausible rationale that their activities will help the shareholders realize their full investment; indeed, their buyout attempts typically effect short-term appreciation in stock prices. Thus, from a professional standpoint, the takeover behavior is not unethical per se. But is it immoral, or at least amoral? By Judeo-Christian standards starting with the Ten commandments, one could argue that there is an aspect of theft involved in the greenmail operation that borders on blackmail. There is a semblance of avarice (thou shalt not lie). Invoking the golden rule sharpens the moral position even further: a hostile takeover is hardly doing unto others as one would have others do unto themselves (the raiders).

Another type of situation is presented in the introductory incident about locating a plant near an exclusive resort. Here the impending action is ethical by most standards and presumably legal, but of dubious morality. While the ethical viewpoint considers obligations to the company, owner, customer and employee, the moral question is more straightforward and personal: "Is it right to do this, knowing how it will affect (my) neighbor?" Though moral guidelines are not always clear when the effects are neither direct nor specific to individuals, the concerns might focus on the health and welfare of the people affected.

The situation involving the personnel manager candidate vividly reflects the ethics-morality-legal dilemma. Besides the question of revealing negative information which will probably bias the employment decision, one must also weigh the relevance of the information to the position criteria. Would the candidate's behavior outside work influence his performance as Personnel Manager? Could one predict that he would harass women associates in this organization? Since conduct "bordering on sexual harassment" is not illegal per se, what moral or ethical guidelines can be used? Many decision-makers would set aside the moral aspect and concentrate on the ethical question or what is professionally acceptable. The candidate's treatment of women associates and how to address it then becomes the central focus. Meanwhile, once the information is shared, the manager and the committee wrestle with their moral beliefs on one hand and the ethical proprieties on the other. In doing so, they are implicitly grappling with another important and complicating factor: namely, their own perspectives on ethics and morality.

GUIDES FOR MAKING HARD DECISIONS

Examining the various moral and ethical premises helps a manager understand his own basis for ethical decisions, but leaves unanswered the most important question: how should a manager decide? If a manager's moral or ethical stance on an issue is flexible, how might that flexibility be used for best results?

While we cannot provide an answer to every ethical situation, we can suggest guidelines that will help a manager find the necessary answers. The following process has been found useful for both clarifying and deciding ethical issues. The opening situations are referenced to illustrate and reinforce the prescribed actions.

1. Makes ethics an integral part of management decisions. Another author states that ethics belongs "at the core, not the periphery" of decisions.[5] This means thinking about the ethical ramifications of alternative choices, as well as in the goals themselves. The personnel manager case need not have developed into an agonizing dilemma if ethical requirements had been set previously for the position. The need for unimpeachable moral and ethical behavior would have been understood. Thus, the candidate in question would not have made the final list.

2. Distinguish the ethical and moral dimensions of the situation. Deal and Kennedy, in their work on corporate culture, underscore the significance of distinguishing moral and ethical dimensions.[6] Ideally, the moral and ethical should coincide, although they frequently do not. The manager should examine his or her moral precepts about a situation and compare them with the ethical view. Physicians often find themselves doing this in issues such as abortions which are professionally ethical but considered morally wrong by many. The axiom that one cannot legislate morality applies not only to laws but also to consensually established ethical conduct. When moral values collide with the ethical as in the plant location decision or possibly even in the AIDS situation, the manager experiences considerable dissonance and often moves to reduce it by submerging either the moral or ethical imperative. From the standpoint of reducing stress, such a resolution is better then indecision or fence-straddling compromise.

The key idea here is to first sort out the moral and ethical messages, then decide which should take precedence. Thus, disclosing the AIDS-related information may be most conscience-easing despite a possible ethical or legal conflict.

3. Seek out organizational and cultural supports. Most organizations have some kind of ethical code. This may be found in the company's policy statements and in pronouncements of top executives. In addition, many companies have formal statements on ethical behavior, as shown in Exhibit I. While most of these statements reflect moral values more than ethical standards, they nevertheless support and reinforce certain behavior in the company.

Caterpillar is a case in point. It is well known for enforcing its values, such as supplying customers with parts within 48 hours anywhere in the

A commitment to high ethical standards encompassing compliance with both the letter and spirit of the law is the heart of USG's corporate culture . . . If profitability is incompatible with ethical behavior in a business, USG will not engage in that activity. Emphasis on employee safety, product quality and equitable dealings with customers and suppliers relates to ethical considerations as much as economics.

.. 1984 *Annual Report*, p. 8

Johnson & Johnson
We believe our first responsibility is to the doctors, nurses and patients, to mothers and all others who use our products and services.

.. Pamphlet, *People Helping People*

Pitney-Bowes
. . . *Failure to properly consider the rightness of our actions clearly would be coercive to the individual integrity of Pitney Bowes people . . . Employees may not act in a manner that is legally or ethically questionable. If the employee is not sure an action is legal or ethical, the employee may not act prior to consulting with the employee's supervisor and, if necessary, with legal counsel.*

Business Practice Guidelines,
Feb. 14, 1983, pp. 2–3

Caterpillar Tractor Co.
The law is a floor. Ethical business conduct should normally exist at a level well above the minimum required by law.
The ethical performance of the enterprise is the sum of the ethics of the men and women who work here. Thus, we are all expected to adhere to high standards of personal integrity. For example, perjury or any illegal act ostensibly take to "protect" the company is wrong. A sale made because of deception is wrong. A production quota achieved through questionable means or figures is wrong. The end does not justify the means.

.. *A Code of Worldwide Business Conduct and Operating Principals*,
1982, p. 4

Goldman Sachs
Integrity and honesty are at the heart of our business. We expect our people to maintain high ethical standards in everything they do, both in their work for the firm and in their personal lives.

.. Pamphlet, *Our Business Principles* (undated)

EXHIBIT 1
EXCERPTS OF CORPORATE ETHICS STATEMENTS *USG CORPORATION*

world. So when customer service and other demands such as cost savings conflict, the manager at Caterpillar has a clear decision mandate—the customer's needs come first.[7]

In the case of the colleague and inside information, a company rule about confidentiality would help, but more useful would be a set of guidelines about every manager's obligations to all stakeholders in and outside the organization, followed by statements of values about fairness, honesty, privileged information and so forth. Of course, example is still the best teacher, particularly in the realm of ethical behavior. There is no more powerful reinforcer of ethics and values then the company culture. If culture values are weak, it behooves the executive team to strengthen them, beginning with assessing their personal mission and values. Two or three strongly-held, dominant values are far better than a creed that attempts to cover the waterfront with euphemisms people cannot identify with.

4. When several values are proclaimed, they should be consistent with the larger culture if they are to serve as beacons for everyday behavior. Japanese firms exemplify this view. The "seven spiritual" values of Matsushita are embedded in Japanese culture and tradition.[8]

1. National service through industry
2. Fairness
3. Harmony and cooperation
4. Struggle for betterment
5. Courtesy and humility
6. Adjustment and assimilation
7. Gratitude

Were these values promulgated in American companies, one could readily predict they would be met with resistance, selective compliance, puzzlement, and alienation. However, if these seven values were honesty, fair treatment, autonomy, self-respect, individual dignity, equality and neighborliness, they could be readily assimilated into everyday American business life.

5. Understand that in a complex decision situation there is always more than one ethical choice. The moral dimension must then be considered, for it provides "bottom-line" direction and perspective for weighing the various sides of the ethical dilemma. The plant location decision is a good case in point. It would be naive to frame the alternatives as build vs. no build when there are probably many choices regarding both location and plant characteristics. Once the moral direction is clear, i.e., the company will not knowingly harm the surrounding community and the rights of its people to safety, health, livelihood, and reasonable tranquility, the management team can then direct its energies to the various options. Useful guidelines are offered by Frederick in what he calls a "normative manifesto" for an ethics policy, namely, that "the claims of humanizing are equal to the claims of economizing."[9] In practical terms, this means that the net human benefits be weighed against the net economic benefits to all concerned. Naturally, this does not suggest a precise quantitative calculation, but rather a comparison of the probable outcomes with the dominant governing values. In Frederick's view, the corporate management serves best when the many interests of society are harmonized in its decisions, such as in the plant location example where manifold needs must be respected, met, and balanced.

Despite the absence of rigorous quantification, the ethical analysis must be concise and specific. Ethics is a discipline much like law, finance, engineering and management science. In fact, some will argue that the standards for ethical discourse are more exacting than in other areas. Ethical judgments are not to be made *ad hoc*. They must be rooted in substantive principles and applied consistently.[10] This is especially crucial in the important decisions where several values are at issue.

6. Decisions imply and require commitment. If an executive can, in conscience, give something less than full commitment and support, the decision is not the best one available. The manager should go back to the basic value considerations and decide again accordingly. Here the distinction among ethical viewpoints plays a key role. The manager who chooses the moralistic view usually exhibits the strongest commitment. This is because the moralist is reinforced both ethically and in principle.

For example, after the Tylenol incidents, McNeil Consumer Products, the maker, decided to remove all its capsulized products from the shelves and subsequently abolished tamper-proof capsules. The driving force in this decision was ostensibly moral. The company moved swiftly and resolutely to preserve its reputation and prevent further harm to consumers. Had McNeil adopted a consequentialist approach, it might have acted only on the inventory lots and locations in question. The greatest good for the greatest number; "consequentialism" judges the ethics by the net results. A contractarian view would have applied legal guidelines, possibly resulting in extensive litigation. "Contractarian" denotes a legal contract approach. The agreement determines what is ethical. The decision path chosen was no doubt the most immediately costly but clearly the most profitable in the long run. Consumer trust in Tylenol was maintained. Had management taken a more defensive legalistic posture, Tylenol would not exist today. Another case in point was Procter and Gamble's decision about Rely tampons. Procter and Gamble, a company long known for its strong moral values, acted consistently with its tradition to eliminate Rely, once the association with toxic shock syndrome became clear. This was done without fanfare or defensiveness. Procter and Gamble had made a rare mistake, but the remedy had reaffirmed its commitment to product quality and to its customers' needs.

CONCLUSION

Ethics should be as relevant in management decisions as economics. Important decision matters invariably have ethical ramifications. By consciously evaluating the ethical and moral dimensions, the manager enhances the quality of the final decision. And by examining his or her own ethical posture, a manager can make crisper, more appropriate ethical judgments. No one familiar with the area would suggest that the problems facing the manager are easy to decide ethically. But if ethical decision-making criteria are not developed, a firm's strategic position will be weakened. While considered soft criteria, ethics promote tough-minded assessments and produce the hard decisions that test a manager's commitment and courage. ■

FOOTNOTES

1. The National Management Association (NMA) and The Institute For Certified Professional Managers (ICPM) are examples.
2. Joseph A. Pichler, "The Liberty Principle: A Basic for Management Ethics," *Business and Professional Ethics Journal*, Winter, 1983, p. 19–29.
3. Gerald F. Cavanaugh, *American Business Values*. Englewood Cliffs, N.J.: Prentice-Hall, Inc., 1984, p. 153.
4. Randall M. Evanson, "Ethics in the Business Curriculum: How Transmissible is The Indefinable?," *Collegiate News and Views*. Fall/Winter, 1984, pp. 27–29.
5. William C. Frederick, "Toward CSR3: Why Ethical Analysis is Indispensible and Unavoidable in Corporate Affairs," *California Management Review*, Winter, 1986, p. 136.
6. Terrence E. Deal and Allan A. Kennedy, *Corporate Cultures*, Reading, Mass.: Addison-Wesley Publishing Company, 1982.
7. Thomas J. Peters and Robert H. Waterman, Jr., *In Search of Excellence*. New York: Harper and Row, 1982, p. 283.
8. Richard T. Pascale and Anthony G. Athos, *The Art of Japanese Management*. New York: Warner Books, 1981, p. 75.
9. Frederick, op. cit., p. 139.
10. David Vogel, "The Study of Social Issues in Management: A Critical Appraisal," *California Management Review*. Winter, 1986, p. 149.

PART THREE

STRUCTURE AND STAFFING

Plans must be implemented through the structure of organization if the managerial objectives are to be accomplished within inevitable time and cost constraints. The assignment of tasks, the delegation of authority, and the allocation of resources proceeds through the organizational structure in accordance with the chain of command and the lateral network of functional departments. Decision making pushed downward to the lowest levels of management results in a decentralized structure. Decision making held at the top of the organization reflects a centralized structure. Each approach has its advantages and disadvantages. Several of the writings in this part of the book deal with these significant aspects of organizational structure.

Staffing is accomplished to obtain qualified personnel to perform the duties and tasks described in the written description of each position in the organization structure. The personnel department provides functional leadership in the staffing activities of most organizations. Line managers decide how many of each type of employee to hire in a given period of time. Personnel staff officers provide critical support to meet the requirements set by the line managers. Key areas of staffing include manpower planning, recruiting, interviewing, hiring, training, compensating, and separating employees from the organization. Several of these topics are discussed in the writings in this part of the book.

Why Decentralize?

Robert E. Levinson

It's about time! We are seeing a new trend in American business schools. Everyone now wants to get on the bandwagon and begin teaching a course in entrepreneurship; it seems to be the "in thing." And our large, centralized businesses have been doing everything they can to decentralize. Centralization breeds dehumanized and "robotized" executives, they say, and this prevents them from practicing entrepreneurship.

Actually, the demand for entrepreneurship courses is resulting from a shift in the interests of the student body. Alexander W. Astin, president of the Higher Education Research Institute, said in a recent article that since the late 1960s there has been a sharp decline in the percentage of freshmen who intend to major in English, languages, history, or philosophy. The fields that have shown the largest increase in popularity since 1960 are business, computer science, engineering, and agricultural forestry.

Astin also said that there was a sharp decline in the humanities. He believes we are witnessing a sharp and continuing decline in virtually every field that has traditionally been associated with a liberal arts education. The career field showing the largest absolute increase in popularity since 1966 is business. Twenty percent of all freshmen aspire to such careers today, as compared to 10 percent earlier. In this same survey of hundreds of thousands of college freshmen, there were 15 to 20 items pertaining to personal values and life goals. The item which has increased in popularity the most is "being well off financially." The survey said that during the past ten years, student endorsement of this value has jumped from 40 percent to 70 percent of all freshmen. Most of the values that have increased in popularity in recent years have to do with money, power, or status. People are going to college because they want better-paying jobs, because they want to be authorities in their fields, because they want authority over others, because they want public recognition, and so on. Fortunately, our business schools are beginning to realize that they must deal directly with these needs. There-

Robert E. Levinson is president of REL Enterprises, Inc., of Boca Raton, Florida, a hotel management and operation firm.

fore, I believe there will be a continued surge in teaching in the general field of entrepreneurship.

Although most large American corporations have been very slow to respond, some (such as IBM, General Electric, DuPont, and American Express) are making some attempts to bring the entrepreneurial philosophy into their divisions. The book, *The 100 Best Companies to Work for in America*, by Milton Moskowitz, Robert Levering, and Michael Katz, cites 30 entrepreneurial companies as being among the 100 best. Moskowitz said the reason these companies scored so highly was that their founders continued to play an active role in management. These companies have kept the qualities of being small even though they have grown large.

There still seems to be a tendency for the CEOs of large, centralized corporations to be stuffy, aloof, and old-fashioned. Many still want to make every decision, and are poor delegators. It's becoming more in vogue to decentralize, and executives are beginning to discuss this with the "boss," but progress in this direction had been slow. Pressure is growing to unseat these CEOs, however.

THE "DINING-ROOM TABLE SYNDROME"

Over the years, many of today's students have heard their fathers and mothers complaining at the dining-room table that they feel dehumanized or "robotized" by the centralized, bureaucratic companies for which they work. Young people who have heard these horror stories from their parents are now entering college, and their attitudes are changing. These students still want to go to business schools, but they do not want to follow in their parents' footsteps by choosing the traditional corporate life.

This "dining-room table syndrome" is a very important part of any child's development. Things that are said—or not said—can have a major, subliminal impact upon a child's development. When parents talk at the table, the subjects of their jobs and what happened during the day are usually a major part of the discussion. It is a time when working fathers or mothers are able to let off steam about their frustrations and dilemmas regarding their relationships with their bosses or their feelings about the companies for which they work. How many young people who are urged to go into business would want to follow in footsteps that are so fraught with problems and frustration?

Within the next five years, a new crop of executives who have studied and seen entrepreneurship in action will enter the hallowed halls of some of our centralized corporate behemoths and make much-needed changes. One can only hope that these changes will give employees a chance to think and operate more on their own. Decentralization can give business executives more opportunities to utilize their entrepreneurial instincts and run companies and divisions creatively.

The road to developing entrepreneurs is not without problems. According to Harry Levinson, Ph.D., of the Levinson Institute, "entrepreneurs require a special kind of psychology and particular relationships to their own fathers. These are not to be found in everybody, and despite the widespread effort to stimulate entrepreneurship, I don't think a great deal is going to come of it unless there is careful selection and encouragement of certain kinds of people who are unable to tolerate supervision and organizational structures."

William Zucker of The Wharton School at the University of Pennsylvania comments, "We have observed, but again there are not data, the way the corporate entrepreneur is different from the autonomous entrepreneur. In these situations, the autonomous entrepreneur is ready and willing to take on the slings and arrows of outrageous fortune and forge ahead, because of the ego drive which fosters such a feeling. In the corporate framework, the entrepreneurial drive is somewhat sublimated, or is held in check because of the hierarchical structure of the organization and the way in which one must report and get things approved."

TALK VS. ACTION

In a recent informal survey of mine, most of the executives I interviewed said that the issue of encouraging their executives to be entrepreneurs had been the subject of many discussions. Many of these same companies have done very little, if anything, to solve the problem, however. One executive said that he had discussed the subject often with both his superiors and subordinates, and that there was intense interest from below but none whatsoever from above. In other companies, there have been only half-hearted attempts to decentralize.

I often hear executives make comments such as "we say our company is decentralized, but it is not a reality," or "we find that middle managers want to be treated with respect and receive proper recognition, and not just be another statistic." In contrast, Terrence J. Smith, an executive with American Express, says that his company recognizes the fact that executives must have a chance to express their entrepreneurial spirit, and that the company works hard at creating an environment that is conducive to the entrepreneurial spirit.

There is now a wave of executives talking about how they can express their entrepreneurial skills. Many of these same executives will leave their corporate cocoons to try running their own businesses or to find companies that will give them more freedom. This is especially true in high-technology industries, where executives are attracted by high-risk and high-reward situations. One interesting phenomenon is that of Metromedia, which had a leveraged buyout in order to become private. John W. Kluge, Metromedia's president, said at the stockholders' meeting that one key reason for taking the company private was so management could pursue long-term projects without having to face criticism for any pressure on short-term earnings, or for the lower stock price that might result.

Don Gevirtz, chief executive officer of the Foothill Group, Inc. of Los Angeles, one of the biggest independent lenders to businesses, said in his book *Business Plan for America* that entrepreneurially oriented small companies now create most of America's jobs, produce most of the innovation in the marketplace, and provide product diversity for customers and competition for old-line firms. Small companies, said Gevirtz, provide excitement, a sense of freedom, and a reaffirmation of the American free enterprise spirit.

THE SMALL BUSINESS BOOM

The Small Business Administration reported that enterprises employing fewer than 20 people increased 31 percent, from 3 million to 3.9 million, between 1976 and 1982. Women are setting up shop in record numbers. According to the Department of Labor's Office of Women Business Ownership, female-owned businesses are increasing at a rate five times that of male-owned concerns. By 1982, 28 percent of self-employed Americans were women. Some 2.7 million women were self-employed in 1983, up 72 percent from the 1.5 million recorded 10 years earlier, and up 5.5 percent over the figures of 1982.

Based on the findings of my survey, it appears as if the majority of the companies interviewed are providing various "perks" for their executives. These perquisites, however, are often somewhat of a ploy; management hopes that they will tie employees to the company sufficiently to deter their leaving the ranks. Unfortunately, I believe that, although these perks are extremely tempting to executives, they do not touch the main body of what I consider a serious problem. Executives who are true leaders need to express their skills, and cannot stand to be suppressed for long periods of time. Now, with all of the talk about entrepreneurship, many executives are able to build up enough courage to go out on their own. One of the reasons that this is happening is that venture capital is much more available today, and executives who have been dreaming about their own businesses are finding it easier to get the cash. These executives are willing to give up equity, as long as they remain in control.

Gail Gregg, in a June 1984 article in *Venture*, said that "Americans are discovering a new kind of investment vehicle—the entrepreneur. As individuals and institutions alike turn to high-risk, high-return investing, their enthusiasm fueled an estimated $30 billion investment to entrepreneurs last year, a far cry from the cottage industry that supported entrepreneurs just seven years ago. Informal venture investment by family and friends and, increasingly, by other entrepreneurs, accounts for billions more."

From 1976 to 1980, 51 percent of all new jobs were created by small businesses, and there are almost 10,000 new jobs being created each week in our country. People are leaving the ranks of big corporations, or are starting their own businesses rather than joining large corporations. This trend towards individual entrepreneurship can't be stopped; it is spurred by basic instinct. Large, centralized corporations will have to start changing their thinking to cope with this widespread entrepreneurial philosophy.

In the next few years, I believe that American corporate recruiters are going to find a very interesting situation when they visit college campuses in search of potential employees. Students will ask more questions about how companies operate, and will ask whether or not they can express their own ideas and feelings—in other words, whether they can use entrepreneurial skills as work. These recruiters will have some interesting stories to report to their bosses, and might find it hard to fill their quotas. For that extra-special person, they might even have to make some promises that will allow the student more freedom. This, of course, will help the entrepreneurial movement and help executives to start thinking differently.

In a March 1984 article in the *Wall Street Journal*, Jay Gaines of Oliver & Rozner Associates, a recruiting company, said that "within a large company, once you reach a certain level of responsibility, the funnel narrows." J. Gerald Simmons, president of Handy Associates, another recruiting firm, says that change often gives "rebirth to an individual" who has reached a plateau at a large company. Mr. Simmons also said that the number of people leaving large companies who he places in smaller concerns has more than doubled in the past five years. All of these factors just might make some of the stodgy, outdated centralized companies wake up and realize that people are not robots, but rather human beings who want to express leadership, intuition, and business acumen. The idea that people in organizations are expendable will become passé, and the feeling that people are the greatest asset to any company will spread.

One company that is outstanding in its quest to develop people, and operates in a very decentralized manner, is Johnson & Johnson. Their annual report says, "The company is organized on the principles of decentralized management, and conducts its business through operating subsidiaries which are themselves, for the most part, integral, autonomous operations." Johnson & Johnson has approximately 50 divisions that are operated in this way, and is one of our country's outstanding examples of how decentralized companies cannot only be successful and profitable, but can also develop talented people.

Although it is basically a centralized company, IBM has been moving toward decentralized management. In Europe, for example, IBM is dividing its subsidiaries into five operating groups. IBM feels that these changes will give the division managers more authority.

MAKING IT HAPPEN

I believe that American businesses will be better able to compete in world markets when companies and their various divisions are driven by a more entrepreneurial spirit that enables individuals to think independently and, therefore, be more productive, creative, and more competitive in world markets. The speed necessary for quick decisions is not available in large centralized companies, yet precisely this ability is needed in very competitive markets. The problem today is that our educators and students are thinking seriously about this entrepreneurship problem, while our industries are still giving it lip service.

The first step in allowing managers to operate entrepreneurially is to decentralize large corporations and place executives in charge of units with the authority and responsibility to make them work. The reason this is difficult, according to one executive of a decentralized company, is the fact that when the company becomes decentralized, the CEO loses a degree of authority, which can be somewhat frightening. On the other hand, a secure, intelligent, and well-rounded CEO will enjoy the excitement of developing other executives' potential management skills. The CEO who decentralizes the company and allows others to develop will be doing a real service to the stockholders and improving the future of his or her company. This new effort may arise from necessity, but will be enjoyable once it is started. Companies should take advantage of their executives' skills and let them exert some business freedom for the good of the company. They should also reward employees financially for good performance.

Here are five steps for keeping executives within the corporate family and beginning a program of operating as a company of entrepreneurs:

1. Decentralize.
2. Give actual responsibility and authority to key executives.
3. Let executives express their managerial skills, and give them a chance to make their own business mistakes on the road to excellence.
4. Monitor these executives and encourage them to make business decisions on their own, so that they can measure the results of these decisions not only in dollars and cents, but in terms of the effects on the people involved.
5. Establish a basic corporate policy that people are the biggest asset of the company, and make it clear that the development of these people will contribute greatly to the company's strength.

The desire of business people to control their own careers is immense. Companies will have to change. Those that do will be successful; others will lose out, stagnate, and merge with others to continue in a centralized manner. When these companies get too big, the government will pass legislation to limit their size, and we will start all over again with small businesses.

Wouldn't it be nice if centralized companies were to wake up now, and not go through this wasteful and unnecessary cycle? ■

Delegation, Authority, and Responsibility: The Myth and the Reality

Stephen C. Bushardt
Aubrey Fowler, Jr.
Eric P. Fuselier

A generally accepted principle of management holds that the amount of authority delegated to subordinates should equal the responsibility given them [3, 6, 8, 12, 13]. This concept is consistent with Drucker's classic definition of management as "accomplishing tasks through others" and the perceived need to delegate responsibility for task accomplishment while providing authority to utilize organizational resources for that purpose. Unfortunately, the real world frequently presents managers with situations in which their responsibility exceeds their authority. In such instances there are differences between the conceptual framework in which responsibility and authority are equalized and the real circumstances in which responsibility is delegated without sufficient authority to utilize all resources needed to carry it out.

The purpose of this article is to examine the difference between the theory and the reality of delegating. Since many managers and their employees are charged with greater responsibility than their authority allows them to fulfill, how can they meet their responsibility, and what is the potential impact on the employees and the organization? These and other questions are addressed in this article.

THEORY VERSUS REALITY

Supervisors are responsible for managing their employees, for obtaining high productivity from them, for ensuring a reasonable level of turnover and absenteeism, and for acting as the initial contact in handling employee grievances and complaints. However, most supervisors have no authority over hiring and little over dismissal. This function is performed by the personnel depart-

Reprinted with permission from Akron Business and Economic Review, Vol. 19, No. 1, Spring 1988, pp 71–78.

Stephen C. Bushardt *is Associate Professor of Management at The University of Southern Mississippi.*

Aubrey Fowler, Jr. *is Associate Professor of Management at Nicholls State University.*

Eric P. Fuselier *is in the Department of Management at Louisiana State University.*

ment and by managers above the supervisor level. Supervisors today generally have little or no authority over their subordinates' salaries or other benefits. In many organizations work assignment decisions for subordinates are defined in union contracts or policies set by someone else. The supervisor is responsible for things over which he or she has limited authority, contrary to the requirements of management theory.

The marketing manager is responsible for developing a highly effective marketing program for the company's product. The reality is that he has a limited control over product design and product quality, an insufficient advertising budget, and a time schedule dictated by others. If the product fails in the market, who will be held responsible? Rest assured that the marketing manager will be responsible even though he did not have decision-making authority over several factors that substantially influence product success.

The phenomenon of responsibility exceeding authority is not limited to supervisors and marketing managers but tends to be characteristic of most positions within an organization and of most organizations: business, non-profit, and governmental. What is particulary interesting is that the gap between the level of responsibility with which one is charged and the amount of authority one is delegated tends to increase as one moves up the organizational hierarchy. In essence, while the top-level managers have greater authority and greater responsibility than lower level employees, the amount of authority they have relative to their responsibility is frequently less.

This increased gap between responsibility and authority at higher organizational levels is a function of two factors. One is that the scope of responsibility expands as one moves up the hierarchy. This expansion in scope requires some control of or coordination with an increasing array of functional activities without any direct authority to utilize the resources allocated to them. For instance, a production supervisor's responsibilities are almost exclusively concerned with utilizing equipment, materials, and operative personnel to achieve production goals. Any problems encountered with areas outside of production are generally left to the general foreman. Therefore, the general foreman, who is also responsible for production goals, has a greater need to interact with personnel, purchasing, and maintenance—areas over which no direct authority is held. This lack of authority in these areas increases the gap between the general foreman's level of responsibility and the authority available to exercise that responsibility.

A second factor increasing this gap is that the process of delegation allows for the exchange of authority from a superior to a subordinate but not for an exchange of responsibility. When responsibility is delegated, the one receiving it becomes accountable to the delegator, while the delegator retains accountability to his or her superior. In essence, the delegation of responsibility adds to the total amount of responsibility held within the hierarchy.

This inability to delegate accountability along with responsibility is referred to as the principle of absoluteness of responsibility [8, p. 428].

On the other hand, when authority is delegated, the delegator relinquishes control over the resource involved and thereby reduces his or her total authority. Therefore, the process of delegation itself serves to diminish one's authority without allowing for a reduction in responsibility, thereby increasing the gap between authority and responsibility.

An organization's formal structure impacts on the authority-responsibility gap. The organic structure, due to the lack of role clarity, tends to lead to a greater imbalance between authority and responsibility than the mechanistic structure with its clear lines of authority and responsibility [2]. For example, in an organic matrix organization, the project manager may need a particular individual for his project but probably lacks the authority to order that individual to work on his team.

The gap between authority and responsibility is likely to be more closely associated with different organizational subunits, as identified by Lorsch and Lawrence [10]. More specifically, organizational subunits that operate in environments of high uncertainty are likely to have a greater discrepancy between responsibility and authority. For example, the discrepancy is likely to be greater in the marketing department as opposed to the accounting department.

The type of technology utilized is likely to impact on the authority-responsibility relationship, as structure is closely associated with technology. A routine technology utilizing uniform tasks leads to a clearer role definition. A nonroutine technology utilizing variable tasks leads to ambiguity [7, p. 246]. The gap between authority and responsibility is, in large part, a by-product of the lack of role clarity. The clearer the job definition, the more likely authority will equal responsibility. The central issue is how managers can meet their responsibilities with inadequate authority. The issue increases in relevance as one ascends the hierarchy and is involved in organizations tending toward an organic structure.

MEETING RESPONSIBILITY WITH LIMITED AUTHORITY

Since reality suggests that managers will not always have sufficient authority to meet their responsibilities, they must find an alternative avenue to successful performance. One such avenue is to bridge the gap between authority and responsibility with the development of personal power. Here a distinction is made between authority and personal power. Authority is the right to utilize resources given by the organization and may be referred to as legitimate or referent power. Personal power is the capability to utilize organizational resources on the basis of one's own ability to influence those who have authority over those resources. Personal power may come from expertise, charisma, persuasiveness, obligation, or membership. These forms of power are not created by the organization but by the manager's individual actions. They may benefit the organization in the furtherance of its goals and are necessary to managers having insufficient authority to meet their responsibilities. A brief discussion of each of these sources of personal power will illustrate their usefulness to the astute manager in bridging the authority-responsibility gap.

Expertise

Expertise in this context denotes the holding of knowledge relevant to the accomplishment of organizational objectives. Those who are perceived as having expertise are able to influence the decisions of others who need that expertise to meet their own responsibilities [5, 7, 9]. Therefore, having expertise involving organizational activities outside one's area of responsibility can create an opportunity to induce others to use their resources in a manner supportive of one's own needs. Furthermore, expertise within one's area of responsibility applicable to subordinate levels of authority can help to direct subordinates into using their resources in the most effective manner. Finally, expertise may serve as a basis for engaging in persuasion, obligation, or membership, thereby increasing personal power.

Charisma

Charisma may be defined as the ability to favorably influence the actions of others as a result of one's personal characteristics and the response of others to them. A variety of characteristics including personality, dress, likability, empathy, understanding, and forcefulness are involved in charisma. Charisma is useful in an organizational setting because it induces others to want to do things that please the charismatic individual [7, 9]. This increases that individual's personal power and, if properly utilized, can influence the actions of others in ways that facilitate the accomplishment of responsibilities. If one needs the resources of others and holds charismatic influence over them, the others' desires to please may cause the resources to be made available to the charismatic individual or to be used in a manner consistent with his or her needs.

Persuasion

Persuasion is the ability to use language to convince others to do what one wants them to do. It includes the content of the message delivered and the manner in which it is conveyed. The content would involve an explanation of the need of the persuader and the way in which the recipient's authority may be exercised to meet that need. The manner of the persuader is directed toward making the recipient want to exercise authority to assist the persuader [7, 9, 11]. That manner may include such factors as charisma, flattery, threat, logic, or an offer of exchange. Whatever the basis, the object of the persuasion may be induced to engage in actions beneficial to the persuader in areas for which the one providing assistance has no responsibility.

Obligation

This source of personal power is a process where one assists others in ways not required by one's own responsibility. This assistance is intended to create a debt on the part of the assisted party owed to the one providing assistance. The intention is to utilize the sense of obligation associated with the need to repay the debt to induce the assisted party to provide aid in the future that he or she would not normally provide [7, 9]. In essence, this process involves helping others to meet their responsibilities and then counting on them to assist in the future. Care is needed to ensure that the repayment never exceeds the initial assistance or a reverse obligation is created, placing one in the power of someone else rather than being in a power position.

Membership

Membership involves the joining with others into unofficial or non-hierarchical groups for the purpose of promoting mutual interests. These groups, often comprised of individuals from different levels or areas of the organization, serve to pool resources controlled by group members and to use those resources to assist group members in achieving individual responsibilities. Groups can also serve to share expertise and to influence organizational decisions affecting members [5, 7]. Furthermore, groups serve as a basis for political power within organizations as a means of influencing decisions in areas outside the area of responsibility of group members.

BENEFITS OF THE RESPONSIBILITY-AUTHORITY GAP

If one were to examine individuals within organizations, two conclusions would be readily apparent: Successful managers, those who meet the responsibility for which they are charged, tend to be more adept at creating personal power than less successful managers. The second conclusion, which follows from the first, is that individuals in higher level positions tend to be more effective at developing personal power than individuals in lower level positions. The second conclusion reflects the reality that successful managers tend to move up within the hierarchy while less successful managers either remain in lower level positions or leave the organization.

This brings us to the central point of this article: the gap between authority and responsibility is beneficial to employees and to the organization. The failure to provide subordinates with full authority needed to execute their responsibility provides subordinates with job enrichment, helps to develop subordinates' interpersonal skills, distinguishes between levels of performance, and serves to develop hierarchical integration within the organization.

Job Enrichment

Because subordinates lack the necessary authority to meet their responsibilities, they must develop personal power. This process often converts a dull, routine job into one that is challenging, leading to opportunities for subordinates to exercise their creative abilities. The individual is continuously involved in a complicated game where he or she must develop strategies for cooperation with others while building the power base needed to execute responsibilities [4].

Subordinate Development

The process of developing personal power encourages subordinates to develop their skills. The subordinates, by learning more effective communication skills as well as skills in interpersonal relations, leadership, and basic management, can avoid the consequences of failing to meet his or her responsibility and receive the benefits associated with meeting these objectives. The pressure to develop these skills stems from the failure to provide subordinates with sufficient authority to force compliance with their decisions or desires while being held accountable for results. Subordinates fulfilling their responsibilities are forced to rely on their own ability to influence others through persuasion, negotiation, and compromise. They must also know enough about the organization to recognize what is or is not important to others and to be able to offer return value for the assistance they receive.

Distinguishing Between Levels of Performance

Given the decreasing amount of authority relative to responsibility that occurs as one ascends the hierarchy, it is important to identify those subordinates at lower levels most adept in creating personal power in order to identify higher management potential. When a manager holds subordinates accountable for greater responsibility, then they have authority to execute; the manager is in a position to identify those individuals who are most successful at creating personal power. In essence, the manager is separating the milk from the cream, where the cream represents those subordinates who have potential for higher level positions.

Hierarchical Integration

By requiring subordinates to develop personal power to meet their responsibility, coordination is improved within the organization. The process fosters cooperation between individuals and among groups as the interdependency of organizational life is brought down to a personal level. In creating personal power, managers develop dependency on other organizational members as well as external sources of assistance. In order to increase their personal power, they must develop an understanding of the problems of others and be willing to assist them in return for assistance they receive. This results in a greater understanding of the organization as a whole and a greater range of knowledge from which to engage in decision making. The creation of personal power to meet responsibility is an important means by which organic organizations achieve integration.

HOW MUCH AUTHORITY TO DELEGATE?

Clearly a number of benefits can be realized by making authority less than responsibility, but the question remains, how much authority should a manager delegate to his subordinate? That depends on the subordinate's ability to develop personal power. When delegating, the manager should ensure that the authority delegated, when added to the personal power that the subordinate is capable of creating, is equal to the responsibility for which the subordinate is accountable. This suggests that, for a given level of responsibility, the more talented subordinate should be given less authority than the less talented subordinate. The imbalance between the amount of authority and responsibility should be within the subordinate's ability and opportunity to create personal power but not so great as to make effective job performance impossible. The purpose is to stretch the employee to encourage him to develop personal power. The imbalance between authority and responsibility should be large enough to create a challenge but not impossible given the employee's skills and the situation. As the employee's personal power base and skills increase, the responsibility relative to formal authority should be increased.

The myth of delegation that says responsibility should equal authority can be expressed mathematically as:

responsibility = authority.

The reality of delegation suggests that this expression should be modified so that:

responsibility = personal power + authority.

The reality of the delegating process requires more of the manager than simply assigning authority and responsibility to subordinates. The manager must assess each subordinate's ability to create and exercise personal power in order to ensure a proper balance between the responsibility given and the combination of authority and power acting to meet that responsibility. While this is certainly an art and not a science, it is an apt description of the process as it occurs in organizations [1]. It is time to reject the myth of delegation, perpetuated in management theory, and to accept the reality that effective managers have been facing for years. In essence, the organization explicitly delegates to the individual the authority to use resources in meeting organizational needs and individual responsibilities. To the extent that the authority given is insufficient to fully meet responsibility, the organization implicitly authorizes the individual to exercise his or her personal power in meeting responsibilities. This combination of implicit and explicit authority should serve to achieve organizational goals while challenging managers to stretch their abilities to achieve effective performance.

SUMMARY

The delegation process as described here differs from what most of us learned in school but only restates what we have experienced on the job. One tends to be responsible for many things over which one has no authority. It is time to drop the myths and deal with the reality of the work place as it actually is. It is unlikely that authority will ever equal responsibility in the real world, and, furthermore, it would be detrimental if it did. There are benefits to the organization and the individual from a disparate delegation of authority and responsibility that outweigh any negative effects of insufficient authority to meet responsibilities. ∎

REFERENCES

1. Brown, David S. "The Changing Role of the Manager." *Supervisory Management*, 27, 7 (July, 1982), 13–20.
2. Burns, T., and G. M. Stalker. *The Management of Innovation*. London: Tavistock Publications, 1961.
3. Caruth, Don, and Bill Middlebrook. "How to Delegate Successfully." *Supervisory Management*, 28, 2 (February, 1983), 36–42.
4. Farrant, Alan W. "Spread Your Delegating." *Supervision*, 45, 12 (December, 1983), 8–10.
5. Hamner, W. Clay, and Dennis W. Organ. *Organizational Behavior: An Applied Psychological Approach*. Dallas, Texas: Business Publications, Inc., 1978.
6. Huffmire, Donald W. "Learning to Share the Load." *Nation's Business*, 72, 9 (September, 1984), 30–32.
7. Khandwalla, Pradip N. *The Design of Organizations*. New York: Harcourt Brace Jovanovich, Inc., 1977.
8. Koontz, Harold, Cyril O'Donnell, and Heinz Weihrich. *Management*. 7th ed., New York: McGraw-Hill Books Co., Inc., 1980.
9. Kotter, John P. "Power, Dependence, and Effective Management." *Harvard Business Review*, 55, 4 (July/August, 1977), 125–36.
10. Lorsch, Jay, and Paul Lawrence, eds. *Studies in Organization Design*. Homewood, Illinois: R. D. Irwin, 1970.
11. McMurray, Robert N. "Power and the Ambitious Executive." *Harvard Business Review*, 51, 6 (November/December, 1973), 140–45.
12. Mescon, Michael H., Michael Albert, and Franklin Khedouri. *Management*. New York: Harper and Row, 1977.
13. Stoner, James A. F. *Management*. 2nd ed., Englewood Cliffs, New Jersey: Prentice-Hall, Inc., 1982.

Downsizing: How to Survive in Times of Organization Shrinkage

George S. Odiorne

One thing corporations, government agencies, and non-profit organizations have in common is a downturn in the size of the work force. Recently, at a meeting of corporate human-resource managers from 20 giant firms, over 90% reported that they are reducing their work force. For some, this will mean early retirement—which will be voluntary for many, involuntary for others. Oil companies are making reductions in employee strength in the range of 15 to 20%. Airlines, banks, and hospitals (all consumer-durable companies) are among those organizations playing this game of *Reduction in Force (RIF);* however, despite the sharp ousting of workers from payrolls, in general the level of employment seems to be almost as high as that of *new* service; industry jobs are being created as fast as older manufacturing positions decline. Mergers and acquisitions account for much of this growing phenomenon. When *WELLS FARGO* bought out *CROCKER BANK* in San Francisco recently, 60 of the 80 top officers were *RIF*fed. The federal **Gramm-Rudman Act** will no doubt impact heavily on government agencies facing RIFs. This cutting of federal budgets reaches into state and local government programs as well, since all agencies have depended on federal funding for such extras as child care, health care, and other social needs.

Everywhere we turn these days, it seems that the RIF is the theme of the hour. But unlike many previous reductions in force, today's RIF appears to have a more humanistic quality. Out-placements, generous separation allowances, accelerated pension plans and the like are part of the separation routine of most employers.

While it is no bed of roses for a worker to be laid off (which usually requires a search for another job by the worker and his having to take a reduction in income), a problem also occurs for those who are retained: "How do we run our organization with fewer people?" Often, when such a

George S. Odiorne is The Harold D. Holder Professor of Management and also Professor of Economics at Eckerd College, St. Petersburg, FL. Prior to this, Odiorne was dean of the School of Business Admin. at the U of Mass—Amherst. Odiorne's business experience includes his association with General Mills, Inc., American Management Assoc., and American Can Co. His BA is from Rutgers and his MBA and Ph.D. are from New York U. Odiorne is listed in WHO'S WHO IN AMERICA and is a member of the National Management Association's Management Hall of Fame.

reduction in employee strength happens, there isn't much expectation for increased productivity.

Two major economic effects seem to be apparent when a reduction in the size of corporate and/or government ranks occurs: First, the glamour of getting a job with a giant corporation—with all its attendant security—which once lured young people some 20 or 30 years ago, has become less attractive. After all those years, that same job security does not seem to have such a bearing on "the package" now. Though corporate sales grow steadily and profits stay on the rise, the number of people employed by large corporations is not growing; instead, it is shrinking. When this is made public, it may well be that young people fresh out of college will start casting their fishing nets in more teeming waters. The influx of new service businesses by entrepreneurial younger executives has never been greater.

The second economic effect is this: Overall salary levels in organizations are not rising. The inflationary days of the 70s, known as times of double-digit inflation, have been quashed insofar as labor costs are concerned. The arithmetic is easy: Lay off a higher-paid older worker; then hire an inexpensive one. This cuts labor costs. Too, the "give-backs" which the unions have been pressed into making to, for instance, airline employees, automobile workers, forestry products workers (who are all highly paid to begin with), add up to cost savings for the payroll budget. As a vehicle for curbing inflation, this does control labor costs.

Competition from offshore workers is getting tougher as Korea, Singapore, Taiwan, and other emerging nations produce modern consumer products. Also, foreign firms which manufacture in the United States have even been able to bring about lower labor costs through lower wage rates. And they have provided more modern and up-to-date plants.

HOW CAN A MANAGER DEAL WITH A
DOWNTURN IN THE WORKFORCE?

Say you are a manager in an organization that just announced a reduction in the size of the work force of 10% or more. How should you react? Let's take a look at how some managers did respond to just such a directive when the word came down: "Cut back." Six standard responses were characteristic of managerial behavior:

1. Cry a lot. The first stage of dealing with a downturn is to cry—copiously. As one general manager reported to me: "I sleep like a baby; I wake up every two hours and cry." Others, especially public officials whose budget has been *axed*, go public with loud cries of: ". . . It is an injustice; clients will be hurt," adding that managers who are doing the cutting are insensitive clods, if not downright mean-spirited. Usually this is not too visible inside the corporation because the new slogan is not that "the squeaky wheel gets the grease"; now, it is ". . . gets the axe." A few firm orders from above to "quit yer bellyaching" will quiet the most vociferous crier.

2. Threaten a cutback in service. Take the case of the school superintendent whose budget is cut 10%. His first move is to eliminate some services which will hurt parents most! The superintendent cuts out free school lunches, then football, and then basketball—which in the state of Indiana, for instance, is a *religion.*

In other organizations, the trick is finding what it is that customers value most. Don't dare cut out any excess fat in administration; instead, make your incisions where they will be most visible. Faced with a determined budgeter with sufficient experience and knowledge of the ropes, that just won't work. He moves in, telling the manager to cut administration as much as he cuts the visible service.

Then the time comes to turn to the next remedy.

3. Turn against other parts of the organization. "Cut *them;* not *me,* because my team is more important than theirs . . ."

In universities, the various colleges start pointing to such things as the low student/teacher ratio in such subjects as English, the classics, or the Humanities—and they declare that these should be cut the most. The School of Education is also a favorite target. In corporations, general-line managers begin to suggest that some of the fat be cut at corporate headquarters level. Divisions which have had low profits are lynched by higher-profit divisions. Everybody becomes expert on the weaknesses in other parts of the organization, and interdepartmental warfare occurs.

4. Lobbying and politics. When it appears that none of the above actions will work, and that top echelon management is really serious this time, then the organizational politicians start pursuing their connections by lobbying, calling in old debts, twisting arms, and building coalitions of two-against-one in the budget battles. Inside the corporation, the politically naive seem to suffer more than the politically adept, just as they do in government. In Washington, the farm lobbyists, bank lobbyists, labor unions, and welfare agencies start buttonholing legislators to save their programs. Power, training, persuasion, and negotiation pay off here. If you can save the organizational unit directed *by you* in making deals, it's worth trying. But even this seems to have failed in the case of Gramm-Rudman.

5. Cut evenly across the board. Confronted with the problems various bureaucratic groups have in both government and in corporate organizations, the harassed and besieged chief executive may resolve a specific problem in what is considered the worst possible way: by cutting every part of the organization by a fixed percentage.

Cut as many salesmen as personnel types—percentage for percentage. This seldom hurts during the first year when the cuts are reasonably small. Any organization can survive a 5% cut without losing anything that anybody with any sense could possibly want to keep. In fact, it may be a healthy kind of regimen and will trim the fat that builds up in any organization. Later, when 10 and 20% cuts are to be made, a more professional approach is needed, and that's when a different breed emerges.

A NEW CLASS OF ADMINISTRATORS
EMERGES IN TIMES OF DOWNTURN

Running an organization when everything is looking up is fairly easy. The excitement of hiring new staff members, of building new plants, and of creating new job descriptions calls for one kind of skill. Since it *is* exciting and innovating to expand the organization and command ever-increasing budgets, even the difficulties seem minor. When everything takes a downturn, however, managers sometimes find it hard to make the adjustment. In unfamiliar waters, these managers become *misfits*. Misfits usually live in a passionate state of mind, and this attracts unfavorable attention. Often, such managers don't survive the change. Then they are replaced by other kinds of managers—the ones who welcome the downturn because it affords them a challenge and the opportunity to move up. These leaders talk confidently about getting "more bang for the buck"; being "lean and mean"—and such jargon. Here are eleven aspects of this new breed's action strategy for getting more from less:

1. Set new goals. Many managers use **Management by Objectives (MBO)** in times of *downturn*—exactly the reverse of their management systems during *upturn* times. Both of these management methods set clear, tough, attainable goals that change the character and direction of the organization; the difference is that the upturn manager sets *growth* goals and the downturn manager sets *shrinkage* goals. Each is meeting a critical issue of the organization.

2. Use the systems approach. Using this systems approach is more than simple common sense or orderliness: It is a planned study of the relationship between "inputs" and "outputs." When inputs such as budgets, personnel, material, and supplies are cut, the goal is to continue to produce the same—or higher—levels of output, goods, and services at lower costs. While there are physical limits to this, it is possible.

Change the way things are done: Drop the lowest output services; rearrange, simplify, question every detail, and constantly monitor the relationship between inputs and outputs. This is the basis of cost accounting and industrial engineering, and it is the meaning of productivity: More output with less input. Some managers specialize in this method: they relish it and seek out places where they can work their systems. This systems approach has become a tool of the new professional manager. *(Older* "upturn" managers hate it with a passion!)

3. Avoid the activity trap. One guiding principle for the new type of downturn manager is to eliminate any activity which is not yielding anything to the organization's goals. Often, a significant part of the "fat" organization's expense is consumed in producing activity unrelated to any kind of useful result. The organization is thus ensnared in the activity trap, and what was once a goal is now activity for its own sake. The new breed of manager is aware of the pervasive effect of the activity trap and is constantly at the ready to eliminate it. Procedures, habits, traditions, and old ways are all subject to suspicious scrutiny, and when no valuable output results, these are lopped off.

4. Use of the learning curve approach. Cost accountants in major firms have known for years—as have military contractors—that the learning curve, called the "experience curve" by the *Boston Consulting Group,* works in trimming costs. Every time we double our experiences, or the cost and time for doing a job, or produce a product or task, costs drop by 15 to 30%; that is, if an airplane's original cost is $100,000, the second cost would be between $75,000 to $85,000. This is because of the "experience factor," the improved procedures, better personnel skills, and the elimination of waste. This drop in cost does not occur automatically, however; it has to be forced by management. Skilled managers press for this in time of downturn.

5. Put a freeze on all hiring unless top management approves. During a downturn, it should be a firm rule that if anyone resigns, he cannot be replaced by someone who is hired by the *local* manager; instead, approval must be obtained from the very top of the organization. This will slow things down; it will require much in the way of explanation; and it will demand review by all intermediate levels. If it is vital to replace personnel, the process *can* be speeded up, but that will shrink the organization through attrition.

6. Use the rule of 20/80. According to *Pareto's Rule,* there is a natural maldistribution between cause and effect. This equates to the fact that 80% of sales, production, inventions, etc. are produced by 20% of the workers; 20% of the sales personnel generate 80% of the sales; 20% of the workers produce 80% of the scrap; 80% of the profits are produced by 20% of the divisions. Easy, isn't it? In times of cutback, look for the most productive as well as the least productive units; then cut where the output is least—expand where the profits, costs, and quality are highest.

7. Use the portfolio approach. *The Portfolio Approach*, popularized by that same Boston Consulting Group, classifies all products, agencies, clients, etc. into four categories. These are displayed by the construction of a grid with two dimensions: *growth* and *intermediate performance*. Those high in both dimensions; for example, growth and profit, fit into the upper right hand square of the portfolio. Such a product is called a "star" and that's where exemptions are recorded for building for the future. Those high on growth but low on profit or performance are "problem children." Times of downturn call for remedying these problems or for getting rid of those products or units. A third category embraces a product whose growth in importance is not occurring, yet is a solid contributor for the immediate future. This is called a "cash cow" and doesn't deserve much funding for research, development or promotion, since it has limited prospects for the future. High output and tightly controlled inputs can be expected from products in this category.

The last category in the portfolio is the product with low potential and low contribution. What a dog this is! When times are tough, this should be the first to be eliminated. The idea is that a proposed strategy should be used for making tough decisions during a downturn.

Shine your stars; cure your problems; milk your cows; abolish the dogs.

8. Share the workload. In some organizations, the response to a required reduction in force is to share the damage equally. If the employees are in agreement, reduce the work week and pay everyone in the organization accordingly, thereby preserving more jobs for more people. If a union is actively involved, obtain its agreement and cooperation. If there is a stiff seniority clause in the union contract, however, this probably won't fly. With non-union white-collar occupations where there is a high percentage of employees who are part of dual-income families (as well as other employees who could use extra time off), sharing the workload just might work.

9. Hire outside consultants. Many organizations facing a need to cut back but are reluctant to make decisions internally—hire consultants who come onto the scene to recommend and even make cuts. These strangers to the company will, of course, be resented at first—even feared—and accordingly be very unpopular, but they do save a bit of face for management. Efficiency experts, methods engineers, and the like have never been loved (and of course they realize that this is true, but they do their jobs without compunction just the same). Since they don't have emotional ties to the organization, they can be objective. The hiring firm simply gives them target figures and authorizes them to go through the firm, making decisions on whatever needs to be eliminated.

10. Use seniority to make reduction decisions. When the organization has a union, the laying off of the *last hired workers* is probably part of the contract, and this resolves the problem of where to cut. Even if there is no union involved, seniority can still be used. This does have merit. The criteria for making such reductions are clearcut and the dates indisputable: *Last in, first out.* The disadvantage may be that you might keep some older deadwood and let some younger stars go.

11. Set up a vigorous outplacement office. No matter which personnel reduction plan is adopted, it is a smart idea to create a professionally-staffed and competently executed outplacement program. These are best if run by professionals who know how to: lead and conduct counseling sessions for RIFFed personnel; teach them how to write hard-hitting resumes; teach them interview-skills; and plan and execute hard-sell marketing programs for any and every imaginable kind of potential employer. This is not an entirely happy situation for the employee, but it is a social and moral obligation for the employer—and it can create goodwill in the long run.

It has become apparent that the skills of the downturn manager are new ones requiring our learning of how to relate to situations in a different way entirely. New personnel may even be needed. On the other hand, oldtimers who headed the upturn can learn how to be downturn innovators as well. ■

Dilemma and Decision
Roy Hill

Centralization or autonomy: which way should a company jump?

"Sometimes I wish the computer had never been invented," Heinz Gutsch complained. "It is too easy now for corporate staff in Pittsburgh to obtain information they don't really need and reach decisions they ought not to be taking."

"It started *before* they tapped into our computer," said colleague Stephan Langer. "Do you remember that memo? As from January first, it said, all new product development plans and budgets must be submitted to the appropriate staff officer, so that product policy can be coordinated on a worldwide basis."

"Yes," Gutsch agreed, "An excuse for standardization. And look where it has got us. Nowhere."

"With Pittsburgh calling all the shots."

"Our French and British companies have the same complaints," said Gutsch. "I was on the phone to Marsden, in Bristol, the other day. Browned off, was how he put it."

"His job, like mine, has been de-enriched," Langer observed. "The opposite of what ought to happen to a middle manager of proven ability."

"Helmut has left already," said Gutsch, gloomily. "He couldn't stand being second-guessed. Not by people who aren't attuned to the needs of the German consumer."

In the Dortmund beerhouse, both men had been drinking heavily. Both had worked for Fritzler Appliances before it was taken over by Swiftsure Electrical Devices Inc. and renamed Handi-Utensils AG. Their conversation

---

This fictionalized case was developed by *International Management* Senior Editor Roy Hill.

The solution to this month's dilemma is suggested by Steffen Fokdal, senior partner in Copenhagen with the biggest Danish management consultancy, T. Bak Jensen A/S, and currently president of the Danish Association of Management Consultants.

reflected a disease called demotivation that had spread through Swiftsure's foreign subsidiaries like the bubonic plague.

In fact, Swiftsure was suffering from an advanced case of corporate schizophrenia. One persona was that of a decentralized output whose chairman could say, hand on heart. "All of our subsidiaries are free to make their own tactical and operational decisions without corporate interference. Here at corporate we hold the purse strings. That is all."

The other face was of a company whose corporate staff was besotted by the welter of information available to it through data processing networks. It was a godsend to centralized decision making. But its potential for bottom-up planning and participation somehow got overlooked.

Nobody at corporate considered that Gutsch, Langer, Marsden and gang might know their own products, their own markets, better than the staffmen in Pittsburgh. Nobody, that is, except Philippe Jouvet, a young French-Canadian MBA who had been acquired along with a Montreal-based home appliances manufacturer.

BLISTERING REPORT

Jouvet had impressed chairman Harry Grayson more by his numeracy than anything else. His abilities at reading a balance sheet were undoubted. So when results from the European subsidiaries had begun to turn down, Jouvet had been sent to Bristol, Paris and Dortmund, more to look at the figures than anything else.

His brief was to discover why the competition was beating Swiftsure in the sale of cordless household appliances, mixers, can openers, electric knives and similar articles. And being an MBA, and therefore highly intelligent, he had concluded early on that the reasons lay in factors not revealed in the data that poured into Pittsburgh for collation and interpretation.

In Paris he discovered first that Parisians were unforgivably rude about his French-Canadian accent; and second that an electric knife that had been forced upon the French subsidiary against its better judgment by Pittsburgh was a sales disaster. The frugal French housewife preferred to use Swedish-steel knives, obtainable at a fraction of the price of Swiftsure's electric carver.

Jouvet also learned that the best-performing brand manager had joined the opposition. He had done so after discovering that a marketing campaign he had devised, which he thought was confidential between himself and the president of the French subsidiary, had been electronically tapped, discussed and vetoed across the Atlantic without either his participation or his knowledge.

In Dortmund, Jouvet happened to be drinking a glass of wine when he overheard, in the adjoining cubicle, what Gutsch and Langer were saying.

His German was by no means perfect, but it was more than adequate to get the gist of the middle managers' complaints. He spent the next seven days talking with people in the German subsidiary.

On his return to Pittsburgh, Jouvet presented Grayson with a blistering report. Swiftsure was decentralized, it said, only by virtue of geography and not in operational reality.

Mass marketing and centralized decision making had been allowed to go too far.

Foreign subsidiaries, while nominally autonomous, had lost not only control of their own capital spending but felt they were powerless to do any meaningful planning. Also, the speed with which Pittsburgh could react to every initiative from overseas had given staff people an irresistible yearning to interfere in detail when such interference was counterproductive or totally demotivating to the field.

As chairman Grayson studied the report, conflicting thoughts and emotions chased across his mind. He was pleased that the perception and enterprise he thought he had detected in Jouvet had been vindicated. At the same time he was annoyed by the tone of some of the report, which reflected on him as much as it did on some of the vice presidents, who were so clearly out of touch with sentiments, if not developments, in some of their operating companies.

RATIONALIZATION NEEDED

At the same time, Grayson had before him a report from his executive vice president to the effect that more, not less, product rationalization was needed. "This is an industry in which profits are often less than 5% of sales, and price-cutting is a way of life," the vice president had written. "Attached you will find my plan for closing down the British and French manufacturing facilities and concentrating production in Germany. You will also find a schedule of the local product lines that can be eliminated."

Clearly, Jouvet's report was not going to go down well with some of the senior executives. Grayson also knew something that the others did not know. He had inside information that a major rival manufacturer had been secretly buying Swiftsure shares, building up its holding. The company was undoubtedly under threat.

So was now the best time for a major rethink and possible reorganization? If so, which way should he jump—towards greater centralization or more autonomy?

Lack of consultation, and not centralization, is the real issue.

This is a situation that many companies face, although not always in such an extreme form. In fact, chairman Grayson of Swiftsure Electrical Appliances has two dilemmas on his plate. One is what to do about the corporate predator that is ready to pounce and gobble up his company. The other is how to restore the morale of the poor managers in Europe, who have been driven to the beerhouse by thoughtlessness and lack of consultation by the corporate staff back in Pittsburgh.

From a strategic point of view, the dilemma illustrates the need to turn a production-oriented corporation into a marketing and profit-oriented one. It also shows that management is not about given orders, but developing creativity—making decisions and making them work.

The people in Pittsburgh think that what is good for the American consumer is also good for the European housewife in every one of the 14 or so countries of Western Europe. In other words, they are far from being market-oriented.

It is a situation that is quite familiar in Denmark, where there are companies that have been unsuccessful in penetrating the German market because they persist in treating it as a single entity. In fact, it is five or six distinct markets, from Hamburg in the north to Munich in the south and from Cologne in the west to Berlin in the east.

But to return to Grayson's problem. . . .

First, he must conclude that the outside predator can only be repulsed, if it is not already too late, by better results from Swiftsure than 5% profit from sales. Therefore, if the rationalizations proposed by his executive vice president are essential, as one suspects they are, then closing down the British and French manufacturing facilities, and eliminating some of the local product lines, will have to be started as speedily as possible.

'JUST ANOTHER U.S. MARKET'

The need to rationalize and eliminate overlapping products should not be made an excuse for over-centralized management, however. The trouble with Swiftsure is not that it has decided, rather late in the day, to take unpleasant decisions, but that it has reached those conclusions without consulting its foreign subsidiaries. Indeed, it seems as though not one corporate executive has ever climbed aboard a trans-Atlantic plane and headed east. To them, Europe is just another U.S. market, like Texas or California.

If the vice president's plan for improving Swiftsure's results has not been discussed with the subsidiaries, Grayson should immediately convene a meeting with the managing direction of all the European companies. It should be in Europe, not America. This will both remind the people in Pittsburgh that jet transport exists and reassure the Europeans that change is on the way that will strengthen the corporation outside the United States.

The meeting should begin with a frank statement from Grayson that results are not good enough, that drastic action has to be taken and that he is presenting the vice president's plans as a basis for discussion, even though time is short and they have to reach a decision at that meeting.

He should also admit that the subsidiaries have legitimate complaints, so far as communications between themselves and Pittsburgh are concerned, and that urgent steps are being taken to improve the situation.

He should announce that future board meetings will be held in Europe regularly and that at least one head of a subsidiary will participate in management-board meetings.

He should announce, further, that since marketing is so important to the company's future, there will be a conference in Europe before the next three- or five-year marketing plan. Also, the yearly budget and action plans from each subsidiary must include a detailed assessment of local marked opportunities in the year ahead, which will be returned by Pittsburgh with comments and requests for clarifications, within a specified time.

Grayson should announce his intention of holding production and technological discussions with the subsidiaries as soon as the immediate crisis is out of the way. And he should say that he has appointed an executive to produce an action plan for improving communications generally and ensure that corporate headquarters does not take major decisions affecting the subsidiaries except after full consultation.

These steps, or a permutation of them, will at least ensure the beginning of a genuine dialogue between the company and its subsidiaries. It will not ensure that correct decisions are taken, of course. But it will greatly reduce the margin for error and ensure that no manager will be able to say: "I don't take responsibility for what happened because I wasn't consulted."

GETTING THE BALANCE RIGHT

Although Swiftsure, as presented in the Dilemma, is an extreme case, it is not, unfortunately, an isolated one—though consultants might be out of business if it were! In every country there are companies that fail in international markets because they have not got the balance between central and decentralized decision making right, and because adequate reporting systems, where they exist, are misused.

In most countries there are also big success stories. In Denmark, for example, ISS and Nova, services and manufacturing companies respectively, come to mind immediately as firms that are both international and successful.

There will always be some degree of conflict between the pull of the corporate center and subsidiaries wanting to fly off and do their own thing. The trick is to keep the subsidiaries happily revolving around the center in harmony and yet in a state of constructive tension, like the planets around the sun.

Grayson may not be much of a philosopher but at least he now has the opportunity—perhaps his last—to take determined action. ■

Rebuilding After A Restructuring

Mary Miles
New England Editor

Which will it be for you in a corporate merger, acquisition, or restructuring? Pain or gain?

A corporate restructuring can be a golden career opportunity—or you may find disaster waiting outside your office door.

During the past three years of corporate turmoil, some MIS/dp executives and managers have lost their jobs. Some have been forced to cut staff and put ambitious but costly projects on a back burner. For others, restructurings have afforded the career opportunities of a lifetime.

What determines your fate in a restructuring? There are many factors, some of which are beyond your control. Generally, the MIS/dp executive who is perceived by top-level management as a vital part of the team responsible for the bottom line has fared best.

One former manager, who prefers to remain anonymous, learned this lesson the hard way—by paying for it with his job. As director of management services in the information systems and services department of a major northeastern-based packaging manufacturer, he discovered that it's not enough to run a first-rate operation. You must aggressively seek out upper MIS management to promote and defend your staff.

The former manager accepts partial responsibility for the elimination of his department after the restructuring of his employer. "Looking back, I believe I could have convinced top management of our potential effectiveness following restructuring," he says. "The new director didn't really understand our activity," he adds, "Management services represented a bridge between ultimate users, decisions-makers, and the computer resources that could be used to help resolve their problems." The new manager's background in systems development allowed him to maintain an efficient operational flow—but he was unfamiliar with using computers for management support.

Staff changes had taken place over several months. The director had been fired and the department streamlined. Three managers, including the director

Reprinted from Computer & Communications DECISIONS, January 28, 1986, page nos. 52–54 copyright 1986, Hayden/VNV.

of management services, ran the department while an outside consulting team was called into reorganize the department, reassess the budget and the organizational structure, and find a new director. "The consultants were little more than hatchetmen," says the former manager. "They didn't try to achieve a balanced perspective of MIS or the total organization, and they really created havoc."

After his appointment, the new ISS director further thinned down the department. It was then the director of management services was told that his department would be eliminated, and that it might be "appropriate" if he applied for early retirement.

Even when managers retain their jobs, they may be left with dramatically reduced staffs. Managers in this position often face the task of rebuilding operations to conform to new priorities. Often, they say their jobs are much less interesting than before. Maybe those big, exciting projects are put on hold or scrapped entirely, or the manager is directed to fine-tune existing systems.

After a 10 percent workforce reduction at Hoffman-La Rouche Inc., Nutley, NJ, for example, Ed Sauer, MIS/dp director, cut the most costly projects. Unfortunately, these are frequently the most exciting projects. "Rather than delve into the potential of new graphics capabilities or laser printers, you may find yourself spending all your resources developing projects that have already been cost-justified," says Sauer.

For some managers, a new regime brings with it unsettling uncertainties. For example, the director of applications and technology for a big subsidiary of a recently acquired transportation-equipment manufacturer found that a new parent company may not provide the "comforts of home."

Before his employer was acquired, MIS/dp served as a support resource group for the information-systems needs of line departments, says the manager. "We received much guidance from higher-ups regarding the strategic uses of MIS," says the director. "We used the computer for such applications as market-penetration analyses. And we were always quite successful in attracting the attention of senior management. They supported the idea of using MIS/dp competitively."

The new parent organization, however, believes that strategic business decisions should be made at the local rather than the corporate level. The acquirer avoided strategic decision-making, except to evaluate the decisions made at lower levels and recommendations for specific investments. The MIS/dp executive now has autonomy, but is a little intimidated that his department must provide cost justifications before undertaking new projects.

However, with all the pain and uncertainty experienced by these managers lurks opportunity. When two huge corporations join—either willingly or not—the opportunity for MIS/dp managers to make gains can be ripe. When Chevron Corp., San Francisco, acquired Pittsburgh-based Gulf Corp. in 1984, Robert Eads, corporate database administrator for Gulf, leapt into a welcome career shift. "I've always felt free to challenge corporate concepts," says Eads, who is now manager of the database section of Chevron. "To make a merger work, we must basically challenge everything we're doing. If you just want to sit back and play it safe, you've no business being a manager in times like these."

Thomas Flack, director of corporate information systems at ITT, is another MIS/dp executive who's taken a cue from a restructuring. The big New York-based conglomerate has been divesting operations during the last two years, tightening its corporate focus.

"MIS/dp is now an integral part of the business function," says Flack. He believes MIS/dp executives must be multifaceted: although they are no longer purely technicians, they must sufficiently understand the technology to apply technical solutions to business problems. And to do that, they must be able to comprehend those problems.

Because two restructurings are rarely alike, it's difficult to prepare for every possibility. Still, managers have general advice about how to dig in for the long haul—and improve your chances of surviving.

Jim Ambrose, senior manager of worldwide computer office & telecommunications operations at Polaroid Corp. (Cambridge, MA) follows the maxim, "Knowledge is power."

"During a merger, both businesses will look for the best way to integrate systems," says Ambrose. "The more you know about both organizations, the better you will be able to provide the information they need."

If a merger or acquisition occurs but dp operations remain separate, be prepared to change direction as you receive either more or less guidance and support from top management. This may force you to alter the way you work and to better articulate your needs and concerns to top management.

If you are the corporation's chief information-resource executive, it's important to maintain, or even forge, clear lines of communication with top-level decision-makers in a restructured organization. If no shared vision exists, you may have to actively forge it.

During all the excitement and transitions, it's easy to forget that realignment affects your personal life. Take time to talk to your family, advises Eads. You're not alone in your anxieties, particularly when a major career change and/or a relocation is involved. Take care of yourself—stress can wreak havoc on your effectiveness at work and on the stability of your home life.

Although the instability caused by restructuring may indicate using caution before making hasty judgments and decisions, be ready to jump at career options. Even if you're certain your organization can't do without you, surprising upsets can occur during the tremors of restructuring. It's worthwhile to keep your options open and your resume polished.

Restructuring will also affect staff morale. "The possibility of cutbacks and major changes can make employees work harder to make their presence felt," says Flack of ITT. "But morale problems can arise if the remaining employees believe co-workers were laid off arbitrarily.

At a time when managerial creativity, flexibility, and commitment are perhaps most essential to an organization, it's vital to keep your staff's spirits up. Good lines of communication can ease the pain and anxiety of restructuring. If you and your subordinates understand the changes taking place, it's easier to anticipate and prepare for how these changes will affect your department.

If your technical knowledge and expertise need refreshing, hone your technical and managerial skills. "Dp-ers should also take advantage of the excellent informal communications networks that exist," says Eads. "We can increase our knowledge through seminars and by talking to colleagues from other organizations."

An unpleasant side effect of restructuring can be the loss of many valued personnel. Specialists become restless during troubled times, says Ambrose of Polaroid. Specialists like systems programmers and telecommunications experts, are in demand everywhere. High turnover can be emotionally draining to the loyal employees who remain and financially draining to your budget.

When valuable employees leave, the workflow is disrupted. And those employees who remain may become resentful if they are asked to assume additional responsibilities. To cut down on the attrition rate, Polaroid is offering competitive salaries to employees who receive outside job offers, says Ambrose. He also recommends promoting in-house professionals and placing a special emphasis on attracting, training, and retaining new employees.

Under the best of circumstances, restructuring is a time of upheaval and confusion. But for information-resource managers, it can also be a time to broaden skills and move up the corporate ladder This can be achieved by cultivating business skills and expanding technical aptitude, by preparing for realignment, rather than waiting for it to come barreling through your department, and by offering your staff guidance and giving top management your support. ■

Managers and Downsizing
Woodruff Imberman

A company forced to downsize must take care that its managers know how to function in the new environment. A three-step method will help ensure that they can.

Managers these days are finding that they are working harder than ever, for longer hours, and receiving less than before. Executive ranks have been reduced by mergers, acquisitions, restructuring, and downsizing. Many managers are now shouldering the burden that two, three, or four managers carried in the past. How do you motivate such a manager after having announced a second year of wage freezes or cuts and further reductions in vacations and holidays? And how does he motivate his subordinates?

Even today, few experts have addressed this urgent problem in American industry in the 1980s—how to deal successfully with the human relations problems ("psychological wreckage," Harry Levinson called it) caused when overwhelming change has shaken the security of managerial ranks. What is the morale among executives left after downsizing at American Motors or Allis Chalmers today? Or Armour, or Swift? Or Eastern Airlines, Wheeling-Pittsburgh Steel, or International Harvester? Or the giant AT&T? Or Greyhound Bus Co.? Or Firestone, Sunbeam, Crown Zellerbach, Crocker National Bank, or Connecticut Mutual Life? Or hundreds of other companies?

In the early 1980s, Ford reduced by 30 percent its salaried work force in its North American operations. The company is now embarked on an effort to cut salaried employment by another 20 percent by 1990, says Donald E. Petersen, Ford's CEO. What does this handwriting on the wall do to the morale of remaining managers and their subordinates?

"It's hard to maintain morale when you're laying off people," says J. R. Wall, a vice president at Republic Steel, which had reduced its managerial staff 20 percent and imposed pay cuts ranging from 7–10 percent on the

Reprinted from BUSINESS HORIZONS, September–October 1989. Copyright 1989 by the Foundation for the School of Business at Indiana University. Used with permission.

Woodruff Imberman is president of Imberman and DeForest, Inc., a management-consulting firm based in Chicago.

remaining salaried employees. "If you ignore the problems layoffs create, you are going to lose the key people you want to keep," adds George Gordon, a psychologist with the Hay Group *(Industry Week* 1983).

DEREGULATION

Some white-collar reductions were necessitated by deregulation that left many companies (airlines, trucking firms, telecommunications companies) with no choice but to slice costs and reduce prices to match new domestic competitors. Other upheavals were caused by vicious foreign competition that took advantage of currency maladjustments and grabbed market share from Americans, making cuts in domestic costs imperative (steel, machine tools, farm equipment, automotive industries, shoes, textiles).

On top of these changes came another phenomenon—the merger and "restructure" movements in industry. In 1986, the last full year for which we have data, mergers and acquisitions rose to $190 billion. Spurred by the passage of the new tax law, the number of mergers went up by 18.6 percent, rising to 4,022 in 1986. Thousands of middle managers were fired or have been pushed into early retirement by merged companies, their careers crippled by such actions in recent years. And thousands more middle managers' careers have been blighted by their being pushed out in the cold as a result of "restructuring" and "downsizing," which saddled their companies with gut-busted debts and interest payments. The Bureau of Labor Statistics placed unemployment among managers and administrators in nonfarm industries at its highest levels since World War II. As a result, *Business Week* reports, insecurity seems to be endemic in management ranks across the country.

Whatever the chain of causes that led to the need for their companies to "downsize," astute top managements are belatedly coming to realize that one of their key tasks today is to re-establish high morale and keen motivation among their retained managers and supervisors burdened with extra duties in an uncertain environment. But many top executives, not knowing how this task can be accomplished, ignore the long-term ramifications of this problem.

Having dealt with many companies with such dilemmas, we think there are three basic but often overlooked tasks that top executives must accomplish if their management ranks are to be recharged and revitalized. A few executives and a few companies have learned how this is done, but these are exceptions. Such executives have rebuilt pride of accomplishment among their reduced numbers of managers and designed and successfully marketed lower-cost and better products to hold or even increase market share. Among such companies are Hewlett-Packard, Ford, General Electric,

Timken, Armco, Inland Steel, Cooper Tire, Xerox, Monfort of Colorado, Corning Glass, Kodak, Swift Textiles, and 3M.

What are the three basic tasks that need to be done to revitalize a company's cadre of executives and managers?

THE FIRST STEP

First, executives must make diligent efforts to define objectively their company's current major problems and honestly ask whether these problems are new or just the debris from past years of corporate torpor. What is the nature of the competitive pressure—product quality, customer service, or price? Are some competitive pressures beyond the control of the company, due (for example) to the relative values of the dollar and foreign currencies or deregulation? Or to a drop in commodity prices that has made paupers of their customers? How can the challenges of deregulation be met? Can an entire price gap be blamed on deregulation, an overvalued dollar, or the company's own internal inefficiencies? In the past, what strategy has the company used to deal with previous reverses? How well planned was this process, or was the effort simply happenstance?

Cultural Changes Required

As the company problems are defined, "business as usual" is being abandoned at most companies. In this process, some companies have come to realize that they must change their cultures from "production driven" to "market driven." Manufacturing managers now must schedule production runs not to maximize efficiency, but to coincide with the sales department, with the goal of faster deliveries of what customers want.

"We used to sell what we made," said Malcolm Hect, Kevlar marketing specialist at DuPont, discussing his company's battle to make the artificial fiber a commercial success. "Now, we make what we can sell."

In steel, "We tested the quality of our steel by tossing a bar into Lake Michigan. If it sank, we could sell it," one steel executive explained to me. "Those days seem to be gone forever. Today, our mission is to produce quality, quality, quality."

Meat industry executives selling fresh red meat once stressed yield; now they are concentrating on the "value-added" concept—to produce processed, brand-name products of consistent quality in an effort to differentiate their products and appeal directly to consumers.

In the airline industry, deregulation meant individual carriers could no longer maintain rigid pricing and compete only on service. Deregulation forced cost-cutting efficiency—and concessionary labor contracts. As most frequent flyers know, this was done at the expense of service.

AT&T moved from the "age of telephony" into the "age of information." AT&T's tradition of benign bureaucratic management (which had stayed stable in a regulated environment for 60 years) had to change. AT&T examined its current strategies and new goals and decided that a new breed of manager was needed—more entrepreneurial, more competitive, and more attuned to the marketplace. That couldn't happen until the company re-examined its goals and procedures and concluded that its managers had to be retrained. The results today indicate that AT&T did adapt indeed. But the forthright and objective re-examination by Charles Brown, chairman and CEO, had to take place before anything else. Painful as it must have been, that examination took three years. Most companies do not have the luxury of three years of introspection.

THE SECOND STEP

Having taken the first step of rigorously defining its problems, the company must then go through the second, more difficult step: What should be done about them? This often calls for changes in what is done, who does what, and how things are to be accomplished. But unless these responsibilities are discussed and allocated, no amount of exhortation will bring the operational changes about. Simply ordering the smaller cadre of managers to work harder, be more efficient, or improve quality is not enough. Should markets be redefined? What precisely are the new goals for each surviving plant or product line? How do these new goals change the objectives and activities of individual managers? How do subordinate managers and employees believe all of this can be best accomplished? A continuous, two-way exchange of ideas on these topics is necessary to generate managers' commitment, as well as a flow of ideas on how the evolving corporate goals can be most effectively achieved. Frequently, there are many good ideas at the various levels within an organization concerning what the new goals should be and the strategies needed to accomplish the newly defined goals. Unfortunately, these ideas are often not well formulated, and they are hushed by an ineffective communications process. Often, the way to break this log-jam is by having an objective third party say, in essence, "I have helped other companies tackle this process. Buried within your organization are many good ideas and strategies, hidden because they are largely implicit in day-to-day activities, and have not yet been articulated or thought out completely. Allow us to interview a representative sample of executives and managers to obtain their unfiltered views of how to deal with today's dilemmas. We'll put their strategies down on paper, so you can decide which might work best, and help you start the two-way dialogue necessary for mid-management commitment and support."

In one steel company, executives thought the lines of communication in the newly restructured organization were working well. However, in the course of our consulting assignment, we found several managers telling us quite vehemently:

> *What the reorganization lacks is communication. There is a failure to pass along information from day to day. I mean, information on machines, people, and what needs to be followed up. There's less follow-up now than ever before. Also, the priorities now are different. But nobody has time to explain them to us, or the timetable. The managers and the links are gone. As a result, you have machinery and equipment falling apart, production going one way and marketing another.*

> *Before the reorganization, our old general manager had a quality meeting every two weeks. There, we discussed complaints, goals, etc. That was one of the best things we had. But we don't have them any more. We need that link to the top again. The managers and the link are gone. Through those meetings, we would get answers for the supervisors, when they had questions. Then, everybody had a better feeling about what was going on.*

Dreams of Love

Obviously, newly defined overall company goals must be broken down to plant and department level, or else they are about as effective as dreams of love. Frequently, the senior executives of a downsizing corporation are awash in impressive one-year, three-year and five-year plans, all of which presumably will produce great results and lead to the Promised Land. But unless the starting point of this journey is identified with great precision, and unless things are being done right today, using a five-year plan as a map to the Promised Land will lead only to limbo.

The senior executives in one life insurance company that had made a major effort to cut overhead and improve productivity were surprised to hear their subordinate managers confess ignorance of the goals that needed to be attained:

> *Our average productivity in the verification department is around 85 percent, and our goal is 97.5 percent . . . I think. That's off the top of my head. That goal has been set formally about a year and a half ago. Or maybe it was last summer. Then, our productivity was maybe 80 percent, or something.*

> *We used to have goals and standards in claims processing. But not for the last two years. We sure wouldn't make any of those goals now. I have no idea how many errors we now make. All I hear is customer complaints are big here. But why?*

The same problem was found in a southern aluminum mill that had just eliminated two layers of management in a cost-cutting move:

What am I doing right? What am I doing wrong? Nobody really knows, but everybody spends a lot of time covering up. Evidently, we no longer have the ability to detect quality problems at an earlier stage of production. When the coil comes into the stacker, all the stacker now does is check the width, and whether it is lined up properly. With fewer supervisory personnel there is no way to check for surface defects on the coil, stop them there, and take corrective action. Sometimes they do, but more often they do not because they don't have time. They let 'em go.

As the numbers of managers and executives drop through attrition or forced reductions, the roles of individual managers change. One manager is forced to do the work of two or three, or an entire level of management is eliminated in an effort to cut overhead. In either case, the surviving managers are filling the roles of their more numerous predecessors. But, as the Music Man pointed out, "You gotta know the territory." A second-level supervisor in an Eastern metal fabricator described how lost he was, following his company's reorganization:

With this reorganization, it has brought a combining of the old jobs. But there is no good definition of what is expected of you. There are some short job descriptions, but plant-wide, they are not consistent and they don't add up. For example, some of our presses designed to shape metal under pressures of 60,000 to 75,000 pounds now leak hydraulic fluid badly because we are now using the new high strength steel alloys. The presses cannot handle them, and produce piles of unacceptable, out-of-tolerance parts. Who's responsible for correcting the situation? With so many gaps in management, the responsibility now falls through the cracks.

Once the goals of the organization have been broken down to specific departments, astute executives make continued efforts to make sure that each subordinate manager or superintendent understands fully what is expected from his area and why—how it fits into the Master Plan. Quite frequently, what the individual managers understand of the company's new goals, and their parts in achieving them, tends to be minimal. Constant feedback on goal attainment is necessary not only for understanding, but for positive motivation.

THE THIRD STEP

The third step in maintaining managerial motivation is increasing the management skills of surviving supervisors and managers. "For the next generation [of managers], retraining will become as important as initial training," *Business Week* (1984) reports. Adds Columbia Business School dean

John C. Burton: "Unless companies face up to this, we will be writing off a whole generation."

Tailoring a development program means the trainer must spend considerable time investigating the way the organization has traditionally worked, where the links are, and what the typical problems have been. More important, the trainer must design the development program so the thinned-out ranks of managers can learn how to handle their increased responsibilities more effectively, with less supervision and more creativity. In the process, the trainer must educate senior executives about what training should actually accomplish.

Perhaps the reason management training has been given short shrift in many downsizing companies is that most executives do not understand the differences between training for first-level supervisors and managers, and when results may be expected.

First-level training for supervisors, for example, can be delegated to the training department and tends to be straightforward, with a fairly rapid, measurable pay-off. First-level supervisors need hard skills and step-by-step methods to handle their new responsibilities. The training consists mainly of acquiring skills and techniques for handling complaints, giving instructions, disciplining, team building, dealing with absenteeism, and solving other problems that tend to occur.

Integrate Skills

Mid-level and senior managers already have those elementary skills. What they do need is the opportunity to integrate their skills in a complex, amorphous environment. The challenges that the overburdened manager faces must be presented to him realistically—in terms of his new restructured organization, his enlarged management responsibilities, his subordinates, and his superiors, all in the new, fluid environment where painful ambiguity is temporarily king and decision making is more than a mere syllogism.

Management development deals with solving problems, making decisions within a complex context, evaluating consequences, and setting and resetting priorities in dynamic situations caused by a company's reaction to its changed external environment. For example, the job-security guarantees in 1987 Ford Motor and General Motors union contracts are changing the way other companies will manage production in response to fluctuations in demand. "We're going to have to be a lot more clever in the way we manage our factories, to find alternatives to costly worker layoffs and recalls to adapt to peaks and valleys in demand," says D. H. Stowe, a Deere & Co. vice president. This means stabilizing production schedules, holding inventories down, and working harder to predict fluctuations in demand. With fewer executives, this becomes difficult unless such new responsibilities are built into the executive training.

Responsibilities

Managers must learn how to state and restate goals and objectives, and they must clarify the direction of the organization at every opportunity. They must accept responsibility for their department's activities and coordinate them with the activities of other departments. By creating an environment within their areas of responsibility that promotes understanding and team effort, these retrained managers can help their company achieve its short-term objectives and long-term goals by obtaining the best from their subordinates.

Learning these subtle skills takes time and conscious thought about the most effective ways to relate to coworkers—subordinate, peer, and superior. Superiors in downsizing companies also participate in the process, and they cannot delegate the time-consuming task of encouraging new behavior in their subordinates, when time is a scarce commodity. In this entire developmental process, executives awaken to the fact that all organizations are fractionated; interest groups will always appear; personalities will always have the potential to clash; small-group dynamics will always be there to stir the mixture; and inevitably rules and goals will multiply and become contradictory. Managerial life will always be a hectic, diffuse, demanding (and yes, an exciting) world—but more so with a tighter managerial workforce.

It takes a rare talent for managers with added responsibilities to appreciate the difference between running a department and seeing that it is well run. For survival, the managerial style of the remaining executives must change. There no longer is time to dot every "i" and cross every "t." Details, and even entire projects, are now being delegated to subordinates who often have spent years simply following orders. Training sessions in the need for risk taking are powerful survival tools in a restructured and slimmed down organization. One manager in a large frozen-food processor made the following claims about his freedom to try new methods:

In the past, it has been difficult for a manager to implement his own ideas, without the approval of God and all His coworkers. We had to sort of sneak in and do it on our own, and hope it flew. If it did, fine, if it didn't, look out. But we kept trying, and most of the time it paid off. Top management became more tolerant of new ideas. However, with all the new duties I now have thrust upon me, I don't even have time to think of new methods.

Without someone encouraging risk taking, new methods and new ideas rarely see the light of day. "If you want people to step forward and lead the parade—especially a parade into new and uncharted territory," said John F. Akers, IBM's president and CEO, "then you can't fire everyone who leads it slightly off course. You have to believe in people, and you have to give them a chance" ("The Spirit . . ." 1985).

Even in the austerity of tightening operations, management development efforts encouraging long-term innovation and creativity are an indispensable part of an overall program to ease the ailing corporation back to health. They are also critical factors in the eventual success of the organization.

An Example

One manufacturer of steel mill equipment, seeking mid-contract concessions to cut wage and benefit costs because of German and Austrian competition, faced an adamant union at the bargaining table. The union spokesman resented the company's description of its situation as teetering on the edge of Chapter 11 and the tender mercies of a creditors' committee. He resented even more the grim sermon that cutting wage rates and benefits was the only expedient for survival. He pointed to the situation in the plant: Fork trucks hauling materials everywhere—damaging and losing parts; expediters trying to find parts and blueprints for the next operation; frustrated operators waiting for tools while they and their machines sat idle; large piles of work-in-process occupying floor space, being lost and damaged; and multiple layers of supervision trying to control such a hectic environment. Why should the union members, said their leader, pay for these wasteful and expensive shortcomings that the company executives were ignoring?

Forced to look beyond the obvious wage cuts, the company tried the suggested three-step approach. First, executives obtained objective help to explore their overall situation. After exploration, the company executives admitted that the shop floor muddle was symptomatic of a more basic, underlying problem—their company's failure to coordinate the managerial fiefdoms of sales, engineering, and manufacturing, despite the efforts of eight levels of management. Traditionally, salesmen were so pressured to produce sales that they promised a potential customer virtually anything, including impossibly tight delivery schedules. In a hurry, the engineers designed the equipment so poorly that lead times on purchased items were woefully short, and building the equipment on the shop floor was an exercise in frustration. Blueprints and work orders rushed to the shop floor often contained errors. In addition, there usually was a scramble for appropriate tooling; key components purchased from outside vendors were frequently late.

Having defined their underlying problems as well as their symptoms, the executives took effective action as a second step. The sales department was reorganized, and several mechanical engineers were transferred to its staff. The salesmen's compensation system was revised, and engineers began accompanying the salesmen on their visits to potential customers. Having realistic delivery dates, the engineering department could design "buildable" equipment. The revitalized purchasing department monitored far more closely the performance of vendors, and delivery times markedly improved. In manufacturing, managers met daily with their peers from engineering to review blueprints before they were issued to the shop floor. In the shop, a "check/out-check/in" system for all tools and dies was started.

The executives then took the third step, following closely on the heels of the second. After eliminating two levels of managers, they developed a massive training program for the survivors. The program's key goal was to help the remaining managers function effectively in an environment that emphasized teamwork, cooperation, and communication among the company's different disciplines—sales, engineering, and manufacturing.

By the expiration of their labor contract, 18 months later, productivity had improved 27 percent, sales had improved by 33 percent, and no concessions were necessary.

Many American corporations have undergone traumatic changes within the last decade—for a wide variety of reasons, as previously discussed. Despite the diversity of causes, evidence and experience indicate some common-sense steps that can be taken to revive the spirits and vitality of companies facing new domestic competition fostered by governmental changes, international competition aided by a cheap foreign labor, and the burdensome debt and interest costs that accompany many corporate reorganizations.

No one suggests that the quick fix of managerial training alone can save a company. Astute top executives realize that their reduced ranks cannot function effectively with additional complex responsibilities without the extra coaching and help that training provides. Such training has a proper role, along with a top-to-bottom re-examination of corporate strengths and weaknesses; a serious effort to clarify new roles and responsibilities as the corporation redirects itself; and a renewed commitment to an exchange of ideas at all levels within the organization on how the company can best achieve its new directions. ■

REFERENCES

Industry Week, November 1, 1983, p. 23.
Business Week, April 25, 1984, p. 50
Woodruff Imberman, "Bettering Employee Performance," *Chemical Engineering*, June 19, 1987.
"The Spirit of Independence: Part II Connections," *Inc.*, July 1985, p. 64.

Downsizing: Survivors' Assessments

Lynn A. Isabella

Corporate restructuring can be threatening to a company's employees. But it can also give some of those employees opportunities for career advancement and growth.

- General Motors is expected to reduce its work force by 25 percent in the next five years.
- AT&T will cut its payroll by 27,000.
- IBM will let go 10,000 workers.
- United Technologies will terminate 11,000 employees.
- Unisys (Burroughs/Sperry) will reduce its ranks by 10,000.

Newspapers and business publications are replete with stories and statistics, such as those above, of organizational downsizing. Although companies that downsize often successfully anticipate and prepare for the needs of employees being released (through outplacement counseling, career counseling, and job placement), they may be unprepared for the strong emotions, lengthy adjustment time, diminished morale, and lower productivity experienced by the survivors of massive restructuring. In fact, companies often have surprisingly little information about the adjustments and assessments of those ultimately responsible for revitalizing the company.

How survivors view the downsizing over time and what issues need to be confronted are critical questions for executives in downsized organizations. The survivors are too important a resource to risk alienating. Therefore, it is necessary to examine how employees interpret and react to a downsizing, the dangers of not adequately responding to their needs, and some traditional solutions as well as methods for searching out more creative answers.

Reprinted from BUSINESS HORIZONS, May–June 1989. Copyright 1989 by the Foundation for the School of Business at Indiana University. Used with permission.

Lynn A. Isabella is an assistant professor of organizational behavior and administration at the Edwin L. Cox School of Business, Southern Methodist University, Dallas.

ASSESSING A DOWNSIZING

The decision to downsize is a strategic one, undertaken to improve business development and reposition for future growth and success. In terms of immediate financial benefits, companies who have downsized can point to huge dollar savings. In a recent article, *Fortune* reported that showing legions of managers the door saved $250 million a year at Union Carbide and $230 million at Du Pont. Despite the corporate rationale and corporate savings, however, downsizing is a personal, not bottom-line, issue for many who survive it. Although some employees may eventually understand and appreciate the business ramifications of the company's failure to restructure, few escape the uncertainty created by being unsure of one's place in the new organization or by the lingering memory of what the company could very well do again. In attempting to put the event in perspective, employees question the move's impact upon them personally, the effect on their job or their ability to perform their organizational responsibilities, and the effect on their career advancement and growth. The true bottom line to most employees is their own career development.

DOWNSIZING: A HOT CAREER ISSUE

Why career development should be the basis for assessing the impact of a downsizing is obvious. When a company downsizes, that action calls into question a fundamental and long-standing assumption about work. Until recently, the implicit contract between a company and its management personnel was a simple one—work in exchange for job security. In other words, if a manager or other professional performed his or her job responsibilities, at least to a minimal agreed-upon level, continued employment was never an issue. Downsizing, as a career event, challenges that fundamental premise of employment. No longer can a manager be totally secure in a position. Job security, at least by its previous definition, could be the albatross of the 1990s.

Not only does downsizing challenge the relationship between employee and company, it also challenges the traditional models upon which successful careers are built. Getting ahead used to be a matter of turning constant performance into movement up the corporate ladder. The rapid growth of America's corporations during the 1950s and 1960s ensured that there were always ladders to climb. Today, however, the economic climate, foreign competition, rising costs, maturing industries, and an oversized Baby Boom population are among the reasons that more and more companies need to retrench. Translated into career paths, this means organizational plateauing or limited career advancement opportunities. Moving up systematically in one company or a series of companies in an industry is no longer a standard or routine career advancement pattern. As Dan Levinson, author of *Seasons of a Man's Life,* stated in a *Wall Street Journal* (1987) article, ''The business environment of today is shattering the career hopes of many promising professionals.'' Frankly, no manager wants to deal with a reality of limited or reduced opportunities. Downsizing causes individuals to confront that very reality.

In addition, downsizing often compels individuals to confront certain career issues prematurely. Consider, for example, the many organizations that routinely offer early retirement packages to employees in their fifties and sometimes late forties. Retirement traditionally has come closer to 60 than 50. But individuals in their late forties, who ordinarily would look forward to another decade of company involvement, must live with the fact that their viable organizational years might be limited. Consider a young manager, strongly focused on moving ahead and building a professional or technological niche, confronted with the task of developing substantial expertise in an area soon to be eliminated from the company. Downsizing, in this case, threatens the very building blocks upon which the survivors have been constructing their future careers.

The Building Blocks of a Career

There are three fundamental factors upon which careers are built. According to career-development scholars, these are performing competently, seeking advancement, and achieving stable growth. But people do not concentrate on the same issue at the same time. Often the emphasis varies with the individual's career stage. When a person is a novice and just beginning his or her organizational adventures, career theorists tell us, competent performance and adjustment to organization politics are critical. Once a person has demonstrated and been rewarded for competent performance, he or she becomes concerned with advancement. For those at mid-career, attention is refocused toward opportunities to continue professional or personal growth, observed or anticipated plateaus, and chances to retain and build upon past achievements.

Organizations today realize the career implications of downsizing, but they appear to be less aware of the fact that people interpret major events by examining the overall effect the events have on their individual careers. In fact, research has suggested that differences in career concerns result in very different assessments of and reactions to major corporate restructuring. Organizations are composed of people who, by virtue of their being at different career stages, will experience and respond to a downsizing differently. The key to successful organizational adjustment hinges upon first understanding the survivors' different assessments. This understanding begins with realizing what questions individuals at different stages are asking.

Can I Perform Competently?

Individuals early in their careers predominately assess downsizing in terms of opportunities to display and achieve competence—in other words, to perform. They will be concerned about the extent to which the restructuring will stifle or augment the execution of their responsibilities. Performing competently at this stage, however, is not limited to satisfactory task completion. Performance also involves the ability to maneuver within the organizational "ropes." These employees look for signals that will answer the question, "Can I still appear competent in the eyes of superiors and in the larger organizational system?"

Foremost on the minds of individuals at this stage are the availability of human and technological resources, maintenance of existing networks, changes in performance standards, and shifts in direct reporting relationships (see **Figure 1**).

An accounting manager at a downsized financial services company typifies these concerns. She is relatively new to her career and has worked hard to establish herself within the company. She is concerned about the repercussions of the downsizing. A new superior, with whom she has had little formal contact, imposes new demands. She sees this as a complete disruption in the established channels of communication and subsequently questions her own ability to perform adequately.

This manager and others at the same stage can assess downsizing as a threat or as an opportunity to perform. Reallocation of organizational resour-

When the Career Question is . . .	The Major Concerns after Downsizing are . . .
Can I perform competently?	availability of resources, personnel maintenance of existing networks new performance standards good supervisors leaving
Can I advance?	opportunities to move up internal value of expertise extra demands from work, especially relative to family commitments
Can I grow and feel secure?	new opportunities for skill advancement or broadening chances to share expertise financial security job security

FIGURE 1 KEY CONCERNS AFTER A DOWNSIZING

ces could mean, albeit in rare instances, more available dollars, personnel, and equipment, as well as improved decision making. This encourages the impression that doing the best job will still be possible, and perhaps even easier. For example, when a Southwestern food chain sold off one restaurant operation, more funds were made available for the core businesses. As a result, some survivors felt as if there were more resources than before for their side of the business. Unfortunately, new organizational arrangements could also signal more work for fewer people and fewer dollars available, thereby imposing at least perceived, if not real, barriers to successful performance. New systems, processes, and reporting relationships could also seem threatening and therefore make the adjustment to new tasks more difficult. One young manager's biggest concern after a recent downsizing was that he no longer knew how to secure necessary support and resources. In addition, because organizations often terminate on the basis of seniority, some young survivors may reach the conclusion that the best and the brightest are leaving and therefore wonder what this implies about their career competence.

Can I Advance?

Once skills are mastered and competence achieved, the individual's attention turns to moving up in the organization or industry. Advancement, in the form of increased responsibility, authority, and expertise, is the career building block in this stage. As they concentrate on developing and building an expertise, the survivors evaluate the downsizing in terms of what opportunities or barriers it creates in terms of promotions, rewards, expanded responsibility, and upward mobility. The first question they ask is whether they will still be able to advance, or whether they will be part of the next round of cuts. Will the opportunities for continued challenge and accelerated responsibility remain open?

Foremost in the minds of individuals at this stage are options for upward mobility, the value of their expertise, and the extra demands that might be imposed on already-strained family commitments. For example, one young manager at a telecommunications company expressed considerable concern about the value of his talents to the company given its current strategic direction. While his group provides integral support services to the company, he is also aware that, as a result of downsizing, his division has moved from the mainstream. In addition, he realizes that advancement would at some point entail a tour of duty in corporate headquarters, more than 1,000 miles from his present location. Strong family ties coupled with the prospect of relocation required for advancement present career choices he never thought he would have to make.

On the positive side, a restructuring may be seen as creating new and different career options, or opening up paths that were formerly blocked by deadwood or given relatively little attention. One 30-year-old sales manager remarked that the corporate reorganization had left him with the distinct impression that the sales organization was now in the limelight and that his career options were, in fact, greater than before. Another human resource professional reported actually getting the marketing job she had always wanted as a result of the downsizing.

On the negative side, individuals may confront the reality of quite limited opportunities as the organizational streamlining removes niches for which people have been training. A human resource vice president at a downsized food services company, who had always seen career opportunities in different businesses, believes that those challenges no longer exist. "With a smaller organization and a more streamlined design, there just are not the positions that there used to be." Other survivors may perceive an even further reduction in top positions. As put by one manager, "I used to think only women experienced the glass ceiling. Now I know what it feels like to see the top and not be able to get there." Employees may become acutely aware that the layer or layers of management above them are occupied by individuals who just aren't going to be moving anytime soon.

People whose central career concern is advancement experience the most difficult adjustment to a downsizing. Having finally demonstrated competence in a series of endeavors, these survivors strongly believe that they have talents to offer and wish to continue to be rewarded. If opportunities are not present, they must confront the issue of how to maintain advancement potential. Although lateral assignments offer temporary challenges for some, such moves in the long term are viewed as "holding patterns" that do not answer the very direct concerns of those who wish to move up. In the end, desires for advancement conflict with corporate loyalty, and "people . . . don't know whether to get out their resume or not."

Can I Feel Secure in and Contribute to the Organization?
At some point in mid-career, employees begin to worry less forcefully about upward advancement and concern themselves more with achieving their own internal definitions of success. Some individuals continue to value upward mobility as a benchmark of success, but many others believe achieving success and contributing to the company can be realized through expansion into completely new areas, in-depth exploration of specific new roles or abilities, or refinements of current skills and expertise. The question these individuals ask after a downsizing is whether they will be able to remain securely in and contribute to the organization.

Of primary concern are opportunities for acquiring new skills, not necessarily advancing to higher corporate levels. The need for sharing expertise can be especially strong given the plateauing that some individuals confront at this time. In addition, because of the difficulties associated with job mobility beyond age 40, the downsizing can trigger substantial uncertainty and concern for one's professional and personal future. Often people wonder what is to stop the company from laying them off next time around.

Feelings of security can be a significant concern because years spent in an organization can create a level of familiarity that is difficult to rebuild elsewhere. One high-level executive, fully cognizant that he has plateaued within his company, is committed to refining expertise and remaining a valued organizational contributor even though his organizational level will not change. Years in the company have given him a thorough knowledge of the system and an extensive network of alliances. Because these elements are critical to his job and to his feelings of self-worth, the potential of losing them is simply frightening. The prospect of staying, even in bad times, looks quite good in comparison.

Viewed as an opportunity, corporate restructuring can provide new areas in which to grow. Retraining programs, opportunities to develop new skills, openings in other departments or divisions of the firm, or simply encouragement to mentor younger subordinates all can be seen as providing changes for growth and contribution despite lack of upward mobility. Viewed as a threat, the downsizing can appear to reduce those same opportunities for growth and security as individuals witness seemingly valuable employees with years of service let go or offered the option of early retirement, which in some cases is not an option at all. Sometimes this observation is coupled with the awareness that those who left may have gotten a better deal. One executive knew he had lost some valuable colleagues and friends, but he was also beginning to believe that "they were the lucky ones, especially when you look at their severance package." At other times, employees at this stage may see trusted colleagues with years of experience moved to positions known in the company as "dead ends." One senior executive in a semiconductor manufacturing operation was awarded the title of senior executive vice president and moved to a spacious office in corporate headquarters, but he had virtually no active work responsibilities. While he was aware that his technical knowledge of recent developments was not as strong as younger individuals', he also knew he had a sense of history regarding the company's strategic decisions that few in the organization matched. In his own words, "I'd feel like I was contributing if they just asked my advice once in a while."

DANGERS

There are dangers in not dealing sufficiently with the needs of survivors (see **Figure 2**). One such danger is the risk of losing good organizational contributors. Strong performers will always have other opportunities. When employees assess a downsizing as limiting their career growth, they may be quite likely to respond to outside offers, as did one young, advancing profes-

---

Failing to adequately respond to employee assessments may increase . . .

1. Loss of the "best" people
2. Burnout/Stress-related illness
3. Dysfunctional, maladaptive, or bizarre behavior
4. Psychological withdrawal/Lack of commitment
5. Negative attitudes

FIGURE 2 FIVE DANGERS

sional. A week did not go by without this individual receiving a call inquiring about his interest in working for another company. Because of his strong commitment to his employer, he had always turned down those requests. More recently, however, the growth opportunities he was assured of had still not materialized, and he did not have access to the amount and types of resources he felt he needed. He had waited but, as he said, "There has only been talk and no action in my case." He reached the point where the telephone calls were no longer as easy to dismiss. Several months later, he was the outstanding performer with another firm.

Not addressing assessments adequately can also result in increased employee burnout and stress. Tension can arise between the need to demonstrate adequate, if not superior, performance and assessments of work given fewer resources. The potential fallout is employees who are burned out or under stress. One executive at a food service operation worked six and a half days per week, often getting to work at 4 A.M. and returning home around 10 P.M., to keep up with her revised account load. She, her family, and the company all felt the effects of work overload.

Sometimes individuals will resort to bizarre, dysfunctional, or maladaptive behavior as a result of the organization's failure to meet their needs, especially when job security is the issue. At one manufacturing operation in a downsizing mode, engineers searched the trash bins to recover the typewriter ribbon cartridge that held the list of about-to-be dismissed employees. That was their way of reaffirming that they, in fact, were not on that list. These same engineers also spent hours of company work time breaking the computer code that protected the rank ordering of employees based on performance and seniority and which was believed to be the company hit list.

Another danger is employee withdrawal and apathy. After a while, even the most organizationally committed individuals may give up and withdraw psychologically. Frequently, the most susceptible are individuals who, because of their years of expertise and experience, are valuable organizational resources but have been disillusioned once too often. The result is little investment in the organization itself. They become like independent contractors; they do their jobs as prescribed, but are no longer involved in nor necessarily committed to the general welfare of the company as a whole. One executive, involved in an educational services institution, reported that he just wanted to be left alone. "I come to my office, conduct my business and, basically, keep my nose clean. I used to be very involved and committed. I just don't see any point."

Finally, failure to address the assessments of survivors can lead to negative attitudes that spill over to customers and consumers, as well as other organizational members. "Bad-mouthing" the company can have disastrous effects. At one high-tech firm, complaints were frequently received from vendors regarding unpleasant encounters with one individual pessimistic about his opportunities for advancement. Subordinates reported being concerned about their association with this individual. When that department tried to hire some junior people, a number of employees made a point to discuss in substantial detail their assessments of the state of the company with the job candidates. As yet, there have been no new hires.

ENCOURAGING SURVIVAL: A TRADITIONAL APPROACH

Naturally a company will want to increase the probability of positive assessments and minimize the likelihood of negative ones. The fact that individuals respond differently to downsizing suggests that each individual should be handled differently, depending on his or her career concerns. Survival and productive contribution are encouraged by giving people the information and the tools they need to perform and feel secure. One way to do this is to directly address the career concerns that individuals have (see **Figure 3**).

Performance Needs

When people are concerned about the availability of human and technological resources, the company needs to furnish accurate and specific information about what employees can realistically expect in terms of people, dollars, and support services. Employees need to know budgetary constraints and restrictions so they can plan their workloads accordingly. When the concern focuses on informal networks, a company can encourage senior managers to help younger managers learn the ropes. Often, young managers are especially concerned about changes in the routine and in "the way we do things around here." To the extent that these cultural shifts can be communicated in terms of how that young person should behave or expect others to act, the concern can be ameliorated. For those who are worried about new performance standards, timely and detailed information about revised expectations and associated rewards will help provide for a smoother adjustment. Superiors need to sit down with younger managers and explicitly communicate expected and desired competencies and anticipated rewards. Finally, young managers who are

When the Career Concerns are . . .	People Need . . .
Performance-Related	
availability of resources, human and technological maintenance of existing networks	accurate and specific information about resources confirmation of new networks and assurance that they will work
new performance standards	timely and detailed information about what new expectations of performace are to be
good supervisors leaving	opportunities to learn more, about able current managers and to understand the contribution those remaining make to the company
Advancement-Related	
opportunities to move up	data about promotional opportunities and timetables as well as the value the company places on different career paths
internal value of expertise	to know the strategic direction of the company and its human resource needs now and in the future
extra demands from work	specific information about the rationale for the current work organization and signals that increased effort are noticed and appreciated
Growth- and Security-Related	
career or organizational plateauing	to learn about alternative options in which they can continue to grow and contribute in their present position
new opportunities for skill advancement	opportunities to retrain and develop themselves through in-house programs or seminars outside the company opportunities for formal career assessment and task relearning
chance to share expertise	opportunities to mentor younger individuals or serve on task forces or committees
financial security/job security	assurance from the company that they will not be abandoned, through outside services, outplacement, counseling

FIGURE 3 EMPLOYEE NEEDS AFTER DOWNSIZING

troubled by the departure of immediate supervisors need to understand the contribution that those remaining can make to the company.

Advancement Needs

When employees are concerned about advancement, information about promotional opportunities and the company's valuation of different career paths is necessary. Individuals need to know what choices they have and what career paths are open to them. When the question is the internal value of a particular expertise, management within the organization needs to communicate strategic direction and resultant human resource needs.

This line of communication presents a tough issue, since many senior people in a company may simply not know what future opportunities will be. Yet, several companies are attempting to communicate the information that they do possess. For example, a major utility company has recently scheduled quarterly management meetings during which the strategic direction or changes in direction, as well as the resultant implications for individual careers, are discussed. At the first of these meetings, managers were shown charts of employee profiles, including tenures, ages, anticipated retirements, and skill-area overloads and deficiencies. These meetings were used to communicate where and when positions or particular skills would be needed. The company felt that individuals could see for themselves if there was a viable place for them in the new organization.

For those who are concerned about the extra demands from an increased workload, the company needs to communicate the reasons for current workloads and ensure that individuals are recognized for the additional effort they are expending. In other words, employees need to feel like they are being treated fairly.

Growth and Stability Needs

When the concern is career or organizational plateauing, individuals need to learn about any alternatives through which they can continue to grow and contribute. Participation on special committees or task forces, chances for lateral or downward moves, or cross-functional assignments are all ways to provide growth without promotion. When the concern is outdated skills or the desire for increased skill development, people need opportunities to retrain and develop further competencies—or simply opportunities to learn more about their own career potential. For those who want to share expertise and wisdom, the company can encourage mentorship of younger subordinates. Finally, to address the strong financial and employment security concerns, individuals need to feel that the company will treat them at least as equitably as those who were outplaced initially.

ENCOURAGING SURVIVAL: DARING TO BE DIFFERENT

Organizations attempting to meet the challenges of managing the career needs of a downsized work force are faced with conditions for which there are no ready-made formulas. Organizational pressures to deal with these challenges quickly are very real, and many employees are unwilling to wait long while the organizational answers are found. The problem is complicated by the fact that organizations too often stop at traditional solutions.

In fact, handling the career needs of survivors of downsizing calls for creative thinking and innovative programs. It also requires that organizations go beyond the traditional solutions and guidelines to engender productivity, enthusiasm, commitment, and loyalty. Getting beyond the obvious requires that companies shift attention to some of the underlying issues brought out by downsizing.

Redefining and rewarding success. Success can no longer be defined as movement up the corporate ladder. But organizations can encourage and support another definition of success, based not exclusively on promotions and salary increases, but also on changes in authority and responsibility. This could be more meaningful work and avoidance of the "managing reports, not people" phenomenon of middle management. More importantly, redefining success means establishing broader criteria for that success. If up is not the only way, other ways can be created or reinforced that simultaneously support the organization's mission and the individual's feelings of accomplishment.

Changing the meaning of job security. No longer can companies realistically promise the security or advancement in employment that many professionals have known in the past. Statements such as "there will never be another downsizing" are likely to be met with disbelief. Most professionals realize that economic factors change rapidly and the future is most uncertain. Job security can no longer be iron-clad promises of continued organizational affiliation, but may need to be aligned with generalizable, marketable, or transferable job skills that are adaptable to different company settings.

Encouraging career self-management. In today's turbulent times, much of the responsibility for career development resides at the individual level. Equipping people with the skills to understand themselves, their values, their career needs, and their goals can help ensure that they are at the right place at the right time, or that they create the right place for themselves. Ideally, if people are to successfully take charge of their careers, they need assistance in understanding their own skills, values, and priorities. Informed career decisions come from a thorough understanding of individual skills, wants, and desires balanced against organizational needs and requirements. Individuals must know themselves and have a realistic blueprint of the organization's future direction and requirements.

Although in some respects this could mean creating what Hirsch (1987), in his book *Pack Your Own Parachute,* calls "free agents," it also acknowledges the reality that many organizations simply do not know what the future holds for them. Instead of treating people as expendable resources, they should be treated as important assets. Even if their futures in the organization are uncertain, employees can gain tremendous strength and certainty from knowing where their potential lies.

Engendering a new kind of loyalty and commitment. In the past, loyalty and commitment were the by-products of what the organization could provide—job security, promotions, and salary increases. In the future, commitment and loyalty need to become the end results of individual beliefs in what the company stands for, beliefs in the contribution the organization is making. For the company this means conducting an organizational self-assessment. A change such as this requires that people in the company recognize the organizational strengths upon which the company can build. And, in the process of locating strengths, they can often find the company's weaknesses. If a company is to establish what it believes in, that company also must understand something about its needs, problems, and opportunities. Individual self-assessment is a process of understanding "who we are" by discovering "who we are not." Downsizing, as an event, brings companies in touch with what they are and, more often, what they are not.

Initial cost savings for the organization may be reached rapidly after the downsizing; individual employee adjustment may take more time to unfold. Generally, the full repercussions of downsizing are not apparent to individuals until they have lived in the "new" organization for a time. Survivor assessments and the career needs upon which they are based are crucial factors in organizational resurgence.

Disregarding employee assessments creates dangerous negative outcomes. Responding in traditional ways addresses the immediate problems. But attacking the core issues could mean reshaping the way people view organizations and their careers. That is quite an organizational challenge for those who might succeed. ∎

REFERENCES

G. Dalton and P. Thompson, *Novations: Strategies for Career Management* (Scott Foresman, 1986).

D. Hall, *Careers in Organizations* (Goodyear, 1978).

P. Hirsch, *Pack Your Own Parachute* (Reading, Mass.: Addison-Wesley, 1987).

L. Isabella, "The Effect of Career Stage on the Meaning of Organizational Key Events," *Journal of Organizational Behavior, 9* (1988): 345–358.

D. Levinson, "Stable Cycles of Executive Careers Shattered by Upheaval in Business," *Wall Street Journal,* May 26, 1987.

E. H. Schein, *Career Dynamics* (Reading, Mass.: Addison-Wesley, 1978).

Growing Concerns
Letting Go
Timothy W. Firnstahl

If I've heard it once, I've heard it a thousand times: to overcome the stresses and strains of a fast-growing organization, the chief executive must delegate responsibility.

I've been to seminars on the subject. I've read business books that deal with it. But somehow the people talking and writing about delegating fail to deal with the most important issues. That shouldn't be surprising. After all, how many have had hundreds of people working for them? How many have had to stand by as a subordinate screwed up a task that the CEO could do better? How many have had to train dozens of new employees at a time?

Unfortunately, most of these people aren't in a position to appreciate that the obstacles to delegating successfully are essentially subjective in nature. As the head of a restaurant company with nearly $15 million in annual sales and five establishments cared for by 500 employees, I am in such a position.

It's one thing to hear or read about how the chief executive's role changes as he or she delegates, but it's another thing to experience it. I found living through it to be awful.

In trying to delegate, I've encountered four problems. These are really my problems, not ones having to do with my company. The first and most obvious problem was watching someone mess up a task I could do easily in half the time. I had to learn to keep my mouth shut since interceding would frustrate my new subordinate—not to mention use up the time I wanted to save. Handing over my company—my baby—to others and standing by as they did things their own way sorely tested my faith in humankind.

The second problem had to do with identity, specifically mine. Delegating means shifting from the role of specialist—be it in finance, marketing, or whatever—to that of generalist. It means becoming a leader, and leaders

Mr. Firnstahl is a founder and chief executive of Restaurant Services, Inc., a Seattle company operating five restaurants and a wholesale fish company. It has annual revenues of about $15 million.

don't have precise job definitions. I had to give up the particular skills for which I was known and the gratification that went with applying them. I had to surrender the greatest pleasures of my professional life.

Third was the problem of competitiveness. As an entrepreneur I am extremely competitive, and I had to watch while others reached ability levels superior to my own. I could no longer enjoy being unrivaled at various jobs—cooking, tending bar, training new workers. Delegating means letting others become the experts and hence the best.

Finally there was the problem of learning a whole new job. Now I had to decide where the organization should go, secure agreement from subordinates, and keep the company on track. Learning this new job meant leaving my comfort zone for the unknown. It meant learning the art of leadership.

Fortunately, I had no choice in the matter because the organization's size had caught up with me. Six- and seven-day weeks, numerous assistants, and ingenious organization of my life weren't enough. The demands on my time associated with serving more than one million people each year were seemingly infinite. I was swamped. I realized I had to make the transition from entrepreneur to leader. I would have to find satisfaction in coaching and planning instead of doing.

To ease this transition, I came up with a three-part approach that I'll pass on to you. It won't eliminate the trauma inherent in delegating, but it may make the change a lot less painful. It goes like this:

- Recruit the best people.
- Practice "what and why" management.
- Learn to think effectively.

RECRUIT THE BEST

With their limited financial resources, new companies usually cannot attract top-notch people at start-up. But as an enterprise grows, its managerial requirements often increase beyond the capabilities of the original cadre. The added work load moves to the CEO. He or she may simply be unable to handle all the tasks at hand. So the question becomes who is competent to take over a share of the CEO's work.

In 1983, when the three restaurants, the service company, and the fresh-fish wholesaler that made up Restaurant Services had reached $10 million in sales, I realized we could no longer afford to have me as the hero in every arena. I had to get some help. I came to realize that the sum of a company is really its human resources, and high-quality people are the base from which an organization can expand. If a company's survival and growth depend on mature judgment, then having the best possible decision makers is vital.

Recruiting was difficult for me. Headhunters are expensive, and newspaper ads unreliable. After all, what worthy prospects scan the classified ads for their jobs? High-quality people are already working, not on the street.

Fortunately, I've learned other recruiting methods. Purveyors and suppliers have proven to be an excellent recruiting source because they know the people in our business. So my key managers and I often ask them for the names of superior performers interested in moving to more challenging positions. We also use industry seminars for recruiting, selecting them according to the kind of applicant we want: finance, human resource development, marketing. At seminars, we find ambitious people interested in improving themselves. During coffee and lunch breaks, we introduce ourselves and exchange business cards.

The best approach is the one most often used by Silicon Valley recruiters. They telephone potential applicants directly. It sounds difficult but really isn't. First we describe the job and its benefits, including the salary range. The recruiter does this from a fact sheet to keep the conversation running smoothly. Then the recruiter asks the candidate if he or she is interested or knows someone who might be interested. More than 80% of the people called want to talk with us or suggest other candidates.

Interviewing is the next important step. I have learned it's best to handle this task myself. For key people I don't conduct interviews in the normal sense but have open-ended discussions over a two- or three-month period. Five meetings or more are not too many to allow both sides to examine each other and to set expectations. I should emphasize that in talking with these candidates I stress our problems as well as our strengths because I have found that people appreciate candor. Furthermore, a good candidate welcomes the prospect of a challenge. Management is, after all, largely problem solving.

It's helpful to have at least one lunch or dinner with the spouse and the candidate. A job change is a major event, and the involvement of the marriage partner is important. If the spouse supports the decision, the likelihood of the applicant's acceptance of the job offer is greater.

I've worked hard to attract top-quality people. I've done whatever I can manage in the way of enticements and more. I have made available portions of my stock, paid people out of my own pocket to keep known salaries in equilibrium, created costly, unneeded temporary positions, and ruined more budgets than I care to recall.

There is one important caveat to register here. Large companies can promote from within, while small companies, as I said, often lack the talent. Unfortunately, some people in your organization may think they have the right stuff, despite their limitations. For instance, when I recruited a product developer, two managers quit. I did the right thing, but at a cost.

'WHAT & WHY' MANAGEMENT

In start-up companies, the visions are usually the entrepreneurs'—they have the clear ideas about the product or service they plan to offer. Moreover, they often have to be in all places at all times, taking care of every detail. Unfortunately, this 100% hands-on management does not permit an entrepreneur's staff to mature. Why think, if the boss has all the answers? Inadvertently, an entrepreneur usurps employee's responsibilities. Worse, people often perform well because they know the owner is right there. What happens when the owner is away?

My hands-on approach hit the shear point with the opening of our third restaurant. I needed a simple and immediately recallable, yet effective, management system. [Honestly, who can remember Maslow's hierarchy of needs, let alone use it, during a meeting?] To this end, I developed an approach I call "what and why" management and made it the organization's leadership style.

Underlying the "what" is the notion that employees cannot do what is expected without training and without a thorough understanding of their work. The instruction is behavior oriented: we show, they practice, and we feed back. This procedure is repeated until employees reach the skill levels we are seeking. The key to success in this effort is 100% focus. Complete focus while teaching the "what" is so important that we set aside time on managers' schedules solely for instruction and observation.

As an aid in teaching "what," we have developed job requirement evaluations. These are two-page forms listing key employee behaviors. Managers use them as a reference when observing and scoring employees. We reward good performance with gift certificates to our restaurants and handle poor performance by returning to teaching of the "what" and giving a thorough explanation of the "why."

The restaurant managers are periodically evaluated in manager-employee coaching sessions by home-office staff. These scores are a big part of our managers' performance evaluations. Managers advance largely on the basis of their ability and willingness to teach. One young cocktail server who was especially proficient at teaching others our philosophy worked through the ranks to become a restaurant manager in 36 months.

The "why" part of the approach is vital because it promotes values. Employees are more likely to be motivated when they understand why they must behave a certain way than when they are simply given rules. We all want to believe in what we're doing, and we want to know the importance of our work. Knowing the "why" fulfills these needs and helps develop a successful organization.

At the end of "why" explanations we ask: "Does that make sense? Do you agree?" If the answer to these questions is no, we give the employees a chance to explain their reasoning. In this way, we open what is often a mutually educational dialogue.

In one instance, our product developer and the chef of our newest restaurant had worked hard to adapt a lovely Mexican dish, prawns Veracruzana, for the restaurant. I opposed including it on the menu because it didn't fit our American cuisine image and reminded them that a clear theme is essential to a restaurant's success.

The chef and several others pointed out that the proposed offering was colorful, cost-effective, and delicious. Besides, why shortchange the guest because of a name? Good point. We came up with an American name, prawns piquant, put it on the menu, and the item is now a best-seller.

Another time, I devised a new bar concept to counter flagging spirits sales, which had been hurt by tougher drinking laws and by society's shift away from drinking alcohol. I struggled to fashion a new concept for our bars that emphasized nonalcoholic beverages with the food. I wanted to call it the NewBar because, in my opinion, it captured society's changing view of what a bar should be. I was well along in graphic design when my partner told me the name was confusing. Years ago his objection would have caused a row. Now I ask why . . . and listen.

He pointed out that the bars wouldn't look new to guests because we weren't going to remodel them. Why remodel bars that had been painted by Leroy Nieman, immortalized in the *Guinness Book of World Records,* and featured in *Time* and the *New York Times?* He convinced me that the name NewBar would have to go.

So we devised different plans, which called for a two-by-three-foot menu featuring 25 categories with more than 350 selections. As we talked, it became clear that we were shaping an extension of our current concept, not rolling out a new bar. We settled on a name: BestBar. Management and staff alike applauded the name, so that's what we call the concept.

This redirection never would have taken place if I had still had my old hands-on management approach. It took the scrutiny inherent in what and why management to come up with a better solution. The shoot-from-the-hip directives of the past have now been replaced by more thoughtful processes.

I readily acknowledge, however, that what and why management doesn't always work. On occasion, no amount of dialogue can overcome my vision of things or bring me to the other side's viewpoint. That's when I exercise the captain's prerogative. I remind my people that sometimes the captain must steer the ship into uncharted waters. I tell them that I assume full responsibility for the course I've set and then ask for their support. I tell them that trust must be part of the voyage and that it's their responsibility to help me sail the ship into the unknown.

THINKING EFFECTIVELY

Over the past 30 months, I've hired many competent people, allowing me to give up overseeing restaurants, developing recipes, writing menus, and a variety of other cherished activities. Now I have time to think. A leader must continually ask and answer the question, "What's next?" An organization can't move ahead without a clear picture of where it's going. Once the CEO has envisioned the organization's future, he or she can share that image with others. It's this shared vision that generates the impetus for growth.

What is thinking? Maybe the place to begin is by examining what thinking is not. Thinking is not reading, meeting, routine reporting, listening, observing, or "working."

Rather, it has more to do with being quiet, apart, reflective, and focused.

Real thinking is simply permitting one's mind to call up ideas not previously considered. When allowed to, it does so with remarkable aplomb. In a sense, thinking is dreaming the organization's future. It's the ability to see tomorrow and construct the company's ideal state. It's the ability to get excited about the possibilities of the future.

This envisioning process isn't mystical, silly stuff, nor is it the fatuous pap offered up by some pop psychologists: "Imagine and it will be." Rather, it's the brain-straining toil, the demanding work of constructing the organization's ideal state and ascertaining the steps required to achieve it.

Like many entrepreneurs, I used to see work as dynamic activity—moving, doing, talking. The idea of sitting quietly and thinking seemed alien, especially when a full free day loomed ahead. Yet it's essential to discipline yourself to use your time to build the organization's vision.

Faced with 10 to 15 meetings a week, I relish my thinking time and guard it jealously. I set aside time to work out answers to "What's next?" What is the next generation of products? What will the organization's future management structure look like? What remaining cherished roles can I hand over? How is society changing, and how does that affect the company? How will the company's future vision be financed? The questions go on and on. That's what thinking is about. If you don't think about where the company is going, who will?

Here are four rules that have helped me think better.

1. View Thinking as a Strategy. Thinking is the best way to resolve difficulties. Maintain faith in your ability to think your way out of problems. Recognize the difference between worrying and thinking. The former is repeated, needless problem analysis while the latter is solution generation.

Sometimes I can't sleep because of business concerns, so I convert worrying to thinking by getting up and listing troubling problems and possible solutions. After a few minutes of jotting notes, I invariably go back to bed and sleep soundly.

2. Schedule Large Blocks of Uninterrupted Time. Because thinking takes time, it must be scheduled. Carve out large blocks of uninterrupted time during periods when you are at your best. I have found that the beginning of the week is my prime time, so I schedule Monday as my thinking day. If I have much to think about, I even schedule an entire week just for that purpose.

3. Stay Focused on Relevant Topics. Pummel your mind until it produces the quality thinking you seek. The ideas are there; you ferret them out.

4. Record, Sort, and Save Your Thoughts. Ideas are the product of your work; they must be recorded, sorted, and saved. Try writing them on 3 x 5 cards, one idea per card, so that they remain "mobile." Use a handheld recorder to capture thoughts while driving. Maintain topic files as repositories for your observations. Files of ideas about the organization's future are your most important store of information.

I have learned to delegate effectively in large measure by accepting the fact that it's an emotionally wrenching process. But I have eased the way by recruiting superior performers, using what and why management, and increasing my available thinking time. The rules are simple, and they foster company growth. They are doing that for our company. ■

Will Someone Please Tell Me Exactly What Personnel Executives Do?

Margaret Magnus

1. **Give first chances.** Robert W. Brocksbank, while manager of college relations and recruiting at Mobil Oil Corporation, created a minority recruitment program that invites 20 college sophomores to New York for a one-week orientation to the business community.

2. **Give second chances.** New York state's Department of Motor Vehicles hires women at the Bayview prison to answer phone inquiries, and a California Youth Authority program offers jobs to inmates as reservations agents for TransWorld Airlines.

3. **Give employees time off for good behavior.** New York Life Insurance Company cut absenteeism 21% through a lottery incentive program that gives bonds or paid days off to employees with perfect attendance.

4. **Give employees time off for bad behavior.** Some 200 companies are experimenting with an approach to give employees—who are late, do a sloppy job or mistreat a colleague—a day off with pay to decide if they want to keep their jobs.

5. **Send employees home.** When the number of employees at Union-Mutual Life Insurance doubled, the Portland, ME, company ran out of office space. It sent some of its employees to work at home and commute by telephone.

6. **Send employees hiking.** Open year 'round, Steelcase's Camp Swampy in northern Michigan offers employees 1,178 acres of wilderness, skiing, hunting and organized sports.

7. **Send employees packing.** To attract and keep its employees, the Detroit-based Kelly Services is providing its 450,000 temporary employees and 3,000 full-time employees with a travel club.

8. **Send employees picking.** 42,000 employees at Ex-Cell-O Corporation's 41 locations now have a flexible benefits program thanks to compensation manager Kenneth H. Loeffler.

Reprinted with permission from *Personnel Journal*, pp. 40–47, January 1987.

References available on request.

Also contributing to this story were Allan Halcrow, managing editor, and Bob Martin, assistant editor.

9. **Pick employees' minds.** When individual employees at 3M develop a new product that produces a minimum of $2 million in US sales a year, they receive 3M's equivalent of the Nobel Prize: the "Golden Step Award."
10. **Keep customers in mind.** To personalize service and keep a "family feeling" at the Miami Lakes Inn, Athletic Club, Golf Resort in Florida, the company hired a memory expert to teach employees to recognize the names and faces of guests.
11. **Mind the shop.** At General Motors Corp.'s Lordstown, OH, assembly plant, 20 hourly employees were taken off assembly-line jobs and instructed to walk around the plant inquiring about quality problems. Their mission: solicit worker suggestions.
12. **Shop for employees.** When the City of Los Angeles was faced with a shortage of qualified data processing employees, it hired an executive search firm to find the workers and lease them to the city with an option to hire.
13. **Shop for child care.** James C. Soule, vice president of human resources at Steelcase, Inc. in Grand Rapids, MI, helped parents find day care for 356 children through the company's employee child-care referral program.
14. **Send employees shopping.** Marriott's Great America amusement park in Santa Clara, CA, cut turnover 80% after hiring an advertising agency to develop a $10,000 shopping spree as an incentive to keep seasonal employees on the job.
15. **Send employees house-hunting.** When employees must relocate, it's the personnel manager who organizes house-hunting trips, helps employees sell their old homes and hires brokers to find new homes.
16. **Shorten the mileage from home.** Lockheed Missiles & Space Co. in the San Francisco area put employees in the fast lane when it computerized an employee carpool system.
17. **Get extra mileage from training programs.** United Van Lines opened its van driving class to the other 800 employees at the company's St. Louis headquarters.
18. **Train to retain.** Westinghouse's College Station, TX facility completely overhauled its training program and became more selective in hiring when it added two robots to the production line and reorganized production into work teams.
19. **Retain to train.** Jeffrey A. Cantor, director of training at DDL-OMNI Engineering in Silver Springs, MD, and the Maritime Training Institute in Norfolk, VA, created a three-month program under the Job Training Partnership Act to train entry-level shipyard workers.
20. **Train to be fit.** The Southern California Rapid Transit District and the Los Angeles Police Department hire exercise specialists to keep employees in shape (and keep worker's compensation claims down).

21. **Train to be fat.** When businesses needed Santa Claus to come to town 3,000 times before Christmas, Western Temporary Services showed temporary Santas how to add girth for mirth.

22. **Cut corporate fat.** Jack F. Gow, former senior vice president of human resources at GAF Corp., says the personnel department's job is to help contain costs, increase sales and improve profits.

23. **Count calories.** Employees at the Sunnyvale, CA, plant of Lockheed Missiles and Space Co. shed a whopping 14,378 pounds in 90 days as part of an overall wellness program to reduce absenteeism and combat rising health care costs.

24. **Trim excess spending.** George L. Morawski, section manager for compensation, classification and employee relations for the State of Arizona, installed a cost containment program that reduced health-care cost increases from 25–30% per year to a more manageable 16%.

25. **Spend money to earn money.** The vice president of personnel at a retail chain anticipates doubling his training budget to more than $1 million a year to train an anticipated 20,000 retail salespeople.

26. **Spend to hire.** Corporate recruiters pay a median $15,017 to hire a new employee and can pay as much as $27,030 per hire, reports The Saratoga Institute.

27. **Spend millions.** Expenditures for the personnel function range from a low of $30,991 in smaller firms to a high of $65 million, with a median of $500,000, reports the Bureau of National Affairs.

28. **Hire millions.** There were 111,832,000 people working in the US civilian labor force as of Nov. 1986.

29. **Hire thousands.** Every summer Six Flags faces the roller coaster of seasonal employment when it has to hire and retain 35,000 employees to staff its amusement parks.

30. **Tempt new hires.** Starting salaries for college graduates jumped 12.6% in the 1984/85 college recruiting season, according to Abbott, Langer & Associates.

31. **Hire temps.** Corporations spend close to $16.3 billion to hire five million temporary workers ranging from file clerks to lawyers, chief financial officers, high-tech specialists, engineers and even doctors.

32. **Reward hire standards.** At First National Bank of Chicago, some 40 top executives can lose as much as 10% of their incentive compensation if their departments fail to meet hiring, retention and promotion goals for minorities and women.

33. **Enforce safety standards.** Air Products & Chemicals Inc. of Allentown, PA, is just one of 320,000 manufacturing businesses affected by OSHA's right-to-know requirements covering 575,000 hazardous chemicals and an estimated 14 million workers.

34. **Play it safe.** M. Michael Markowich, director of human resources, and Jo Anna Farber Bartello, special assistant in human resources, at

United Hospitals, Philadelphia, created a file audit system to make sure the hospitals' personnel records could stand up in court, if needed.

35. **Pay it safe.** An accident-free year and 100% attendance help get employees of Diamond Fiber Products in Thorndike, MA, into the 100 Club—Daniel C. Boyle's innovated way to reward employee achievements. Members show off by wearing jackets emblazoned with the company's logo.

36. **Pay employees for the time of day.** When Stuart J. Mahlin was vice president/director of personnel at The Provident Bank in Cincinnati, he didn't pay all employees equally: those who worked during the bank's peak hours got more.

37. **Pay employees for what they know.** Jack J. Phillips, manager of human resources for the Southern Division of Vulcan Materials, spearheaded the development of a skill-based wage classification system that increased employee morale, reduced turnover and improved productivity.

38. **Pay employees for what they do.** The personnel department at Highview Stores earned an extra $184,599 for the company when it put in a performance-based pay program that increased sales by 5.3% and dropped inventory shrinkage by 80.7%.

39. **Lend employees.** Mary Kay Cosmetics hired an executive search firm to locate other Dallas-based organizations to "borrow" its employees during a slow period, saving the company $165,000.

40. **Bank on employee performance.** Kathy K. Blackburn, personnel director at the First-Knox National Bank in Mount Vernon, OH, ties the bank's employee recognition program to the bottom line and recognizes outstanding teller service, branch loan collections and branch deposits.

41. **Monitor profit and laws.** At two Boise Cascade plants in International Falls, MN, assistant human resources manager Jerry Wennstrom cut worker compensation costs from $13 million to about $2.5 million by monitoring claims, redesigning jobs, transferring disabled employees to Social Security and forcing able but unwilling employees to accept jobs.

42. **Lay down the law.** Companies are giving employee training in business ethics. 208 top US corporations have written codes of conduct, 99 have formal training programs, 40 have high-level ethics committees, and 17 have ombudsmen to handle employees' ethical problems.

43. **Lay down plans for the future.** John D. Gridley, manager of human resource planning at Ebasco Services, Inc. in New York, developed a computer program to help managers determine who would be where (and when).

44. **Plan for retirement.** Control Data Corp. spends between $300–$350 per retiring employee for a three-day LifePath seminar. Director of Human Resources Robert Jones believes the benefit helps attract good people and adds to the company's public image.

45. **Keep retirees happy.** "Once a Champion always a Champion," is the motto of the Connecticut-based Champion International Corp. which created Paper Mates, a retirement club designed to help alleviate some of the stress of retirement.

46. **Keep retirees healthy.** Personnel departments are responsible for medical benefits even after employees retire. Hewitt Associates reports 91% of the 812 firms it surveyed provide medical coverage to retirees before age 65, and 85% provide coverage after age 65 when Medicare begins.

47. **Rehire retirees.** Faced with a shortage of skilled workers, Donald De-Ward, director of personnel administration at The Travelers in Hartford, CT, urged former employees to "Un-Retire" and to come back to work part time.

48. **Work tirelessly.** Listed in "Who's Who in American Women," Kathryn D. McKee is also president of the Personnel Accreditation Institute (PAI), former member of the State of California Industrial Welfare Commission Motion Picture Industry Wage Board, past president of the International Association of Personnel Women (IAPW), founding member of the Western International Personnel Group, and recipient of the IAPW 1986 member of the year. She's accredited by both PAI and the American Compensation Association and is senior vice president, compensation and benefits, at First Interstate Bancorp in Los Angeles.

49. **Take time out.** Enriching employees' lives and corporate support of the arts go hand in hand for ARCO. The oil company hosted "A Night at the Opera" for 1,400 ARCO employees and their families who attended a dress rehearsal of The Dallas Opera.

50. **Make time pay.** Employees at Albert Steiger, Inc., a retail firm based in Springfield, MA, and at Blue Bell, Inc., a clothing manufacturer, in Greensboro, NC, receive diamonds, sapphires and gemstones as a reward for their time with the company.

51. **Make time flexible.** To combat the Silicon Valley's 60% annual turnover, ALZA's human resources director Harold Fethe offers flextime for employees of the pharmaceutical research firm.

52. **Make time fly.** Joseph H. Tancrell, assistant vice president of human resources at State Mutual Life Assurance Company in Worcester, MA, teaches kids of working parents what to do between the time they come home from school and when their parents come home from work.

53. **Make advertising fly.** Lenore Willoughby, employment manager at McDonnell Douglas Astronautics Corporation in Huntington Beach, CA, spent $24,831 for a one-page newspaper ad to attract 20 engineers.

54. **Advertise a move.** When Citibank relocated 1,200 employees from Park Avenue to a renovated warehouse on the seedy, desolate West Side of New York, it developed a fantasy video to explain the new neighborhood's benefits. The move was phased in with no employee defections and a minimum of grumbling.

55. **Make a lateral move.** Michael G. Gorys, vice president of human resources at Oak Industries, Inc. in Rancho San Bernado, CA, spent three and one half years in a senior operating assignment to better understand the personnel requests of line management and operations.

56. **Move employees . . . move jobs.** Walton E. Burdick, IBM vice president for personnel, balances resources: He moves work to the people and people to the work. In 1985, he transferred 7,300 employees at a cost of almost $60,000 each.

57. **Move employees up the corporate ladder.** At the Minneapolis, MN-based Honeywell, Inc., vice president for human resources Foss Boyle, and corporate vice president of human resource planning and development David Dotlich, created the Lund Awards to recognize managers who develop the talents and careers of the people reporting to them.

58. **Move themselves up the corporate ladder.** Janice Stoney invested several years in Northwestern Bell's recruiting and personnel department before she was promoted to chief operating officer.

59. **Move personnel agents into the field.** When employee questions and problems arise in any one of the 150 locations of Vulcan Materials, the divisional human resources managers dispatch personnel representatives to field the problems.

60. **Report from the field.** TRW, Inc. standardized its automated personnel system to meet the needs of 100-plus operating units around the world and to provide for uniform, corporate-wide reporting.

61. **Field problems.** Seven San Francisco-area corporations—Levi Strauss & Co., the Pacific Telesis Foundation, Mervyn's, the BankAmerica Foundation, the Wells Fargo Foundation, AT&T and Chevron Corporation—developed an employee educational program on AIDS.

62. **Listen to problems.** Linda A. Schumacher, director of human resources at La Guardia Marriott Hotel in East Elmhurst, NY, says "for employees who experience domestic violence, the workplace is often the only respite," and feels victims of domestic violence should be included in employee assistance programs.

63. **Listen to answers.** Pitney Bowes has been listening to employee suggestions for 42 years. It does a 50/50 split with employees of any savings from the suggestions.

64. **Listen to experience.** Assistant Training and Development Director Robert Blomberg at RMH Health Services in Rochester, MN, asked CEOs from AT&T, Munsingwear, Blue Cross and Blue Shield of Iowa, and George A. Hormel & Co. to teach what they practice at the company's management development forum.

65. **Experience temporaries' success.** Why do personnel managers hire temporary employees? Work overload, cover for vacationing employees, cover for employees on leaves of absence, assist with special projects, cover for sick employees, fill vacancies of departing employees, and fill positions when permanent employees aren't financially justified, according to the Administrative Management Society.

66. **Experience adversity.** Within the next five years, both the husband and wife in 75% of all marriages will be employed. Personnel managers are responding by offering dual-career relocation programs.

67. **Overcome adversity.** Faced with downsizing the organization from 600 to 200 employees in New Jersey, New York and Houston, Haclon SD Group, Inc. provided career continuation assistance and hired outplacement consultants for the laid-off employees.

68. **Overcome distances.** Private firms in Kansas City anted up more than $106,000 to transport 200–300 city teenagers to their jobs in the suburbs.

69. **Overcome differences.** For 70% of the engineering work force at RacalVadic, English is a second language. To reduce cultural and language differences, the Sunnyvale, CA, modern manufacturer instituted an English language course and intercultural training.

70. **Make the difference.** At the Honda plant in Marysville, OH, 2,423 workers produce 875 cars per day. At the AMC Jeep plant in Toledo, OH, 5,400 workers produce 705 cars per day. What accounts for the differences in productivity? Personnel management.

71. **Make the team.** Joan Lefkowitz, director of human resources at Burger King, introduced the "Varsity Crew" concept to build team spirit, improve on-the-job skills and provide a sense of belonging to its employees. Some of the rewards: team sweaters and jackets.

72. **Make it happen.** When Frank Dooher, vice president, human resources at Boston Financial Data Services, Boston, sees "an individual who's trying like hell . . . but it just isn't happening for him," he refers the employee to an outside firm for attitude testing and career recommendations.

73. **Make it happy.** The personnel department at Odetics, Inc in Anaheim, CA, is part of a Fun Committee that sponsors sock hops, an employee repertory theater, a company swimming pool, carrot-grams,

flying dog houses and a roaming six-foot alligator—all to build employee morale.

74. **Make it clear.** Metropolitan Life Insurance Company developed an interactive computer system—housed in kiosks accessible to employees—to provide convenient information about benefit programs.

75. **Clear employees.** At Lockheed-California Co., Manager, Personnel Security Neil J. Adkins requires all prospective employees, including former employees being rehired, to participate in a drug screening program.

76. **Clear the way.** Richard K. Broszeit, regional personnel manager for Dow Jones & Company, Inc. started the Druthers Program (as in, "I'd druther do that than this") to help employees explore new career options without leaving the company.

77. **Weigh the options.** The Lotus Development Corporation in Cambridge, MA, sponsors a nutrition education program for employees during the lunch hour.

78. **Offer options.** ESOPs—employee stock options plans—are growing. The National Center for Employee Ownership reports 7,400 employee ownership plans covering 7.4 million employees.

79. **Option the rights.** At Stratford, CT-based Sikorksy Aircraft, 163 employees earned patents assigned to the company. To recognize these innovators, Sikorksy gave them a special badge marked with a symbol to indicate their achievements.

80. **Write contracts.** The personnel director at an entertainment company successfully negotiated a two-tier wage contract for its 900 unionized clerical employees. Existing employees keep their wage rates; new employees begin at a lesser rate.

81. **Write programs.** Joel Lapointe, director of administrative systems at W. R. Grace in New York, is installing a human resources information system—including PCs and mainframes—to cover more than 40,000 employees in 100 locations.

82. **Do right by employees.** Harry Petrie, vice president of personnel services at Revlon, was honored by the EEOC for his principle that "talent and hard work should be the only rule in evaluating job performance."

83. **Help employees do right.** The 200 employees at the Moultrie Container plant of Miller Brewing Company reached two million employee hours without a lost-time injury. Posters, monthly supervisors meetings, training, newsletters, safety recognition programs, regular inspections and one-to-one safety talks were all key elements of the program, says Industrial Relations Manager Steve Cates.

84. **Help employees help themselves.** Roger Good's employee assistance program at Bechtel Power Corp. in San Francisco refers employees with alcohol, drug or other problems to appropriate community agencies.

85. **Help employees help others.** Karen Ingraham, manager of employee activities at GenCorp in Akron, OH, uses a computer program to match employees with community volunteer programs.

86. **Help employees find jobs.** The merger between Gulf Oil and Chevron squeezed many employees out of a job. J. F. Stright Jr., Gulf's director of professional recruiting and placement, set up a 24-hour job referral hotline to find employment for out-of-work employees.

87. **Find employees for jobs.** At General Dynamics Electronics Division in San Diego, CA, Pery Myers, manager of employment, posts Dick Tracy posters and cartoons to remind employees to help detect talent for the organization.

88. **Try new ideas on the job.** Gould Defense Systems, Inc. in Cleveland tried an on-site medical clinic and saved $210,000 in the first year. It cut average back-injury work absence from two weeks to less than three days and boosted productivity by $114,376 a year.

89. **Respect employees' ideas.** The National Suggestion Systems reports 900 companies representing 13 million employees paid nearly $128 million last year in awards for employee suggestions. Companies saved more than $1.25 billion from these suggestions.

90. **Respect employees.** Herman Miller celebrated its employee ownership plan (in which full-time employees with one year of service or more earn stock in the company) by picturing all 3,265 owners in its 1985 annual report.

91. **Teach employees respect.** "If looks could kill . . ." is required viewing for employees at Sheraton Hotels. Corporate Training Coordinator Tim Driscoll is using the murder-mystery film to improve customer relations and service.

92. **Earn respect.** General Electric's Aircraft Engine Business Group in Evendale, OH, won the "company of the year" honor from the National Alliance of Business for its national pilot program to train and retrain disadvantaged people in industrial machining and fabrication.

93. **Earn thousands.** The highest paid personnel professionals work in companies with 10,000 or more employees, have 25 or more years of experience, have a graduate degree and supervise a staff of 25 or more people. These professionals average $59,919 a year, but can make more than $300,000 depending upon the company, says Abbott, Langer & Associates.

94. **Share earnings.** The Quill Corporation in Lincolnshire, IL, designed a program to give employees a share in any health savings. The result? A 35% reduction in health care costs for two years.

95. **Share responsibility.** James H. Brockman, vice president of corporate relations at Rushmore Health Systems, Inc. in Rapid City, SD, put employees in charge of scheduling their own time off through his Paid Personal Leave program.

96. **Exercise responsibility.** "Many of the most forward-looking CEOs are looking for top HR managers who can report directly to them and help them solve the key issues on staffing, compensation and productivity," says Alan F. Lafley, a managing director at Korn/Ferry International and former HR advisor to David Rockefeller at Chase Manhattan Bank.

97. **Be responsive.** The company cafeteria is more than a lunch-time convenience. One food service company kept employees happy by making the holidays merrier with bulk sales of ingredients for baked goods, party catering, sale of holiday desserts, and food demonstrations, such as cookie decorating.

98. **Respond to information.** More than 81% of the employees at the Reprographic Business Group at Xerox Corporation in Webster, NY, better understand their work group objectives thanks to a new performance appraisal system created by Norman R. Deets, manager of human resources management, and D. Timothy Tyler, manager of personnel planning and programs.

99. **Inform employees.** Prevention is often the safest route. That's why Mary Lou Arey, manager of development in Du Pont Company's employee relations department, spent two years and more than a half million dollars to develop a four-part personal safety and rape prevention program.

100. **Stay informed.** Robert H. Bohan, director of personnel at Kentucky Finance Company in Lexington, KY, has been reading *PERSONNEL JOURNAL* since 1957. He says, "the magazine helps me keep up on different things going on in personnel management." ■

The Costs and Strategies of Hiring

Eric Rolfe Greenberg

Senior Financial Officer, responsible for financing, budgeting, and related activities; master's degree in accounting or business administration; minimum ten years' experience. Salary range: $60–65,000.

This classified ad did not run in any newspaper. Instead, it was one of 12 position descriptions presented to nearly 500 human resources managers by the Membership Briefings and Surveys staff of the American Management Association. For each of those positions, the respondent managers were asked what recruiting strategies they would employ—and how much they would expect to spend to fill the position. AMA then analyzed the data to establish national and regional benchmarks, and examined how companies of different size and scope would go about hiring the needed personnel.

The survey confirmed what professionals in the field have long known: that newspaper and magazine advertising are by far the most widely employed recruiting strategies, and the favored place to spend the budgeted recruiting dollar. The primacy of advertising holds across geographic lines and regardless of corporate size or function.

Yet while advertising is everyone's favorite way to recruit, there are important differences among human resources professionals as to how much should be spent and where the advertising dollar should go. Local newspapers or national? Trade journals or regional magazines? The answers

Reprinted, by permission of the publisher, from *Management Review,* February 1986 © 1986 American Management Association, New York. All rights reserved.

Eric Rolfe Greenberg is associate editor for research on AMA's Membership Briefings and Surveys staff, and was project director for *Hiring Costs and Strategies: The AMA Report.*

This article is based on material gathered for *Hiring Costs and Strategies: The AMA Report.* Its findings are based on 450 responses to questionnaires mailed in August 1985 to a nationwide selection of human resource managers. Two basic questionnaires were employed, each offering six position descriptions and requesting the respondent to give information on three positions of choice. Advertising costs were but one of 12 discreet areas of inquiry; others included recruitment strategies, recruiter salaries and assignments, travel, lodging and entertainment expenses, testing policies, and relocation budgets.

Prepared by the AMA Membership Publications Division, *Hiring Costs and Strategies: The AMA Report* has been mailed to AMA members in the Human Resources Division. AMA members may purchase additional copies at $85, nonmembers at $100.

differ with the size, location and economic activity of the advertiser. Budgeted dollars also vary with the position to be filled, and while it is generally true that more ad dollars are spent in pursuit of the high-salaried executive, that rule is by no means hard and fast.

To fill the position of senior financial officer briefly described above, 90 percent of survey respondents would spend advertising dollars. In comparison, only half would pursue the next most favored strategies, checking previous job applicant files (52 percent) and hiring an executive search firm (51 percent); only a third would use a private employment agency. In the choice of advertising as the primary recruitment method, corporate size makes no difference. Whether small (less than $50 million in annual sales), medium ($50 to $500 million), or large (more than $500 million), nine out of ten survey respondents would advertise for the position.

They would not, however, spend their dollars identically. Small companies put the greater share of their ad dollars into local advertising, while large organizations buy more regional and national classified ad space. Small companies also budget fewer dollars, whatever the medium. While 82 percent of small company respondents would advertise for the chosen post in local newspapers, only 23 percent would budget $1,000 or more for such space; comparatively, just over half of the large company respondents would target local newspapers for job advertising, but they'd budget twice as much, and half the advertisers would spend more than $1,000 on the space.

Conversely, three-quarters of large-company respondents would advertise for the position in the national press, and would budget an average of nearly $2,500 to do it; less than a third of our small-company respondents would go national with their advertising, and most would spend no more than $1,000 on the space. Mid-sized organizations are indeed in the middle: half of them would buy national advertising, though, budgeting $2,500 for the space.

With such a huge difference in the use of national advertising, it is surprising to note the similarities in the choice of trade and professional journals as advertising media. For all of the 12 positions featured in the AMA survey, 36 percent of the large-company respondents would allocate ad dollars to such journals; 38 percent of mid-sized companies would do so; and 33 percent of small firms. Again, the difference is in the dollar amounts. Large companies allocate an average of $1,750 for trade journal classified advertising; mid-sized companies budget $1,000 on the average, and small companies $750. For the specific position of senior financial officer, the large companies would spend freely in trade journals, budgeting an average of more than $3,000; both mid-sized and small companies would average just over $800 for such space.

The survey found that companies with high turnover rates spend much more freely on job advertising than companies with low turnover. "High" turnover, for purposes of this study, means an annual rate of 15 percent or more; "low" turnover indicates a turnover rate below 5 percent annually. Two hundred and twenty survey respondents fit into the "high turnover" category; 63 into the "low." Though the type of advertising each group chose did not differ dramatically, the dollar allocations did. For all positions given in the survey, 87 percent of the "high turnover" group would advertise locally, as would 82 percent of the "low turnover" group; but the former would budget an average of $972 for local ad space, while the latter would spend an average of $630. The contrast holds for regional advertising ($1,420 for the "high" group, $1,150 for the "low"). The sample for low turnover companies advertising nationally is too small to be statistically valid.

A company's location affects both advertising strategies and dollars expended, the AMA survey revealed. In the less populated areas of the West, recruiters sensibly spend more on national advertising than do their metropolitan brethren on either coast. Forty-one percent of survey respondents from the Mountain States would allocate national advertising dollars for any of the 12 positions outlined in the survey; the average elsewhere is 28 percent. Fully half the Rocky Mountain respondents would advertise in trade and professional journals; the figures shrink to 37 percent of West Coast firms, 33 percent in the North Atlantic region, and only 26 percent of the survey's New England respondents.

The greater expense of national and trade advertising is offset somewhat by the lower costs of local advertising. Among respondents, the typical ad budget for local advertising in the Mountain states was under $250; in the Midwest it was between $500 and $1750, and in New England the mode leaped to over $1,000. Indeed, 26 percent of New England-based respondents would spend over $2,000, and an additional 7 percent over $3,000, on local ad space; none of the survey's Mountain State respondents would spend more than $1,000 locally.

What would be the shape of the typical advertising budget for a senior financial officer? The greater share of survey respondents would spend between $500 and $1750 for local classified advertising, a like amount for regional ad space, and an additional $2,000 to $3,000 on both the national, trade and professional press. The probable cost: $6,250.

But the survey sample offers wide variations. Ten percent would do no advertising at all for the post, trusting an executive search firm or employment agency with the task of rounding up candidates. Fewer than half would go beyond the local press if they were to advertise at all. The "typical" budget offered above represents the survey's *mode*, the most frequently reported responses; the *average,* or *mean,* expenditure is far less. Including in the sample those who would spend no ad dollars at all, the averages work out to $650 in local advertising, $540 regionally, $720 nationally and $345 in trade and professional journals: a total of $2,255.

The cost of advertising generally lessens with the salary and responsibilities of the job to be filled. Among the hypothetical positions described in the survey questionnaire was one for a plant personnel manager, with an annual salary of $40–42,000; respondents reported an average advertising budget of $1,210. For an entry-level computer programmer salaried at $26–28,000, the average was $950, with more than half that amount dedicated to local advertising.

Clearly, the decision to advertise, and the allocation of advertising dollars, has a huge impact on the overall cost of hiring. A closer look at the figures for the plant personnel manager mentioned above gives ample proof. Just under 60 percent of our respondents would advertise locally for that position; the decision to do so would cost an average of $635. Only a third of our sample would advertise for the job regionally; they'd spend an average of $1,110 to do it. Only 18 percent of our respondents would advertise in national media or trade journals; once committed, they'd spend an average of $1,655 in the national press, and $975 in the professional journals. Thus, depending on the degree of exposure the advertiser sought, the average cost of ad space could go as high as $4,375—and the sample turned up respondents willing to spend twice as much to find the plant personnel manager they desired.

Of all the recruiting strategies reported in the AMA survey, none were so variable as advertising practices, and none showed anywhere near the same range in costs. The fees for executive search firms and private employment agencies varied by perhaps 15 percent from the mean (25 percent for the former, 18 percent for the latter), and such items as referral awards showed a nationwide similarity. But advertising costs are very much a mixed bag, and the calculations made by individual human resource managers affect the cost-per-hire as no other single decision. ■

	High Turnover (+15% ann.)		Low Turnover (−5% ann.)	
	Would Advertise	Average Budget	Would Advertise	Average Budget
Senior Financial Officer, $60–65K				
Local	85.9%	$1,240	37.3%	$ 600
Regional	48.4%	$1,430	36.4%	$ 890
National	40.6%	$2,050	31.8%	$ 1,415
Trade/Professional Journals	46.9%	$1,770	36.4%	$ 350
MIS Director $55–60K				
Local	80.3%	$1,090	85.7%	$ 570
Regional	40.9%	$1,915	42.9%	$ 1,100
National	43.9%	$1,490	35.7%	$ ***
Trade/Professional Journals	54.5%	$1,094	35.7%	$ 950
Plant Personnel Manager, $40–42K				
Local	87.0%	$ 720	85.7%	$ 575
Regional	48.1%	$1,280	50.0%	$ 775
National	25.9%	$1,900	33.3%	$ ***
Trade/Professional Journals	37.0%	$1,380	16.7%	$ ***
Product Manager, $32–85K				
Local	92.7%	$1,040	66.7%	$ ***
Regional	43.9%	$1,370	55.6%	$ 700
National	17.1%	$1,225	27.8%	$ 1,360
Trade/Professional Journals	43.9%	$ 740	44.4%	$ 700
Computer Programmer, $126–28K				
Local	95.3%	$ 890	90.9%	$ 315
Regional	38.8%	$1,105	22.7%	$ 600
National	9.4%	$1,540	4.5%	$ 0
Trade/Professional Journals	20.0%	$1,325	31.8%	$ 300

***insufficient sample

How to Interview Job Applicants

Alice Gore King

Ridgefield, Connecticut

Recently a corporate vice-president told me, "I have difficulty inter-viewing job applicants. My training is not in human resources, and I often make mistakes in hiring."

This executive is not in a minority. Many managers find themselves out of their depth when called upon to interview. How about you? Do you come away from an interview without the necessary information you need to make a successful hiring decision? If so, then you're not reaping the benefits of the interview. After all, the purpose of an interview is to get information about a person.

To get the most from an interview, it's important to remember that a job interview is essentially a social situation in a business setting. The rules of give-and-take and small talk apply. But the process involves more than the talk itself and falls into three stages: before, during, and after. Let's look at each in depth to see how you can get the maximum worth from the interviews you conduct.

BEFORE THE INTERVIEW

Before meeting with any job candidates, you should define your goals. This will help you to see what you need in the person you are planning to hire. For example, you might be aiming to double your sales, improve the quality of your services, facilitate communication between the company and the stockholders, attract more clients, or expand your publications department. Based on your goal, decide what qualities the person you hire should have. Include *everything.* Don't eliminate yet qualities you'd like but are afraid you won't be able to get. You can pare down later if you find your sights are too high.

You might set up your requirements in categories, such as education, training, skills, experience, and personality.

Review the characteristics of the last people who held the job in your company. What were their backgrounds, abilities, and strengths? Which do

---

you still require? What other ones do you now need? Interestingly, the job may not be at all like the one the previous person was hired for—because it has developed and expanded since.

Write down the results of this thinking. Include the person's hoped-for background, the functions of the job, and the salary and benefits.

To find the person to fill the job, look at a number of sources.

Start with your own company. You may know employees in other departments who would like to work in yours. You may have an eye on someone you think has good potential. Other employees may have friends or relatives they would like to suggest. Your human resources department will have the names of employees who would like to be transferred. It can also help you identify outside sources like employment agencies, school and guidance counselors, and college career placement offices. It may also have résumés of unsolicited applicants.

Actually, some of the best placements are made in this way, often surpassing the well-screened applicants referred by personnel services. One reason is that these applicants are conducting a job campaign. They have analyzed their backgrounds, studied job opportunities, and otherwise have done their own screening.

Another source of applicants is classified ads. If you place an ad, word it carefully to reflect the job description you wrote. Also, be selective in your choice of media to reach the audience you want—for example, a trade publication for a person with a specialized background.

If you have difficulty finding the right person, you might want to consider using a "temp" service if that's appropriate to the job. There are two reasons for this. First, it will tide you over. Second, through the service you may find the permanent person you want. Granted, it is not the perfect arrangement. You want someone who will stay. But it might help you mark time.

Be specific and detailed when you list the job specifications with your human resources department and with employment agencies and placement offices, or when you write a classified ad. If the information you give out is incomplete or inaccurate, you'll only waste your time interviewing unqualified applicants.

Also, be honest about the job. Some employers mislead applicants in an attempt to play down the less attractive features of the job. Equally important, during the interview process, stick to your specifications. Some employers change their minds as they go along—when they see applicants with qualifications they hadn't expected to find, they tighten their requirements and neglect to notify the placement offices. If you do change your specifications, let your personnel department know. If you specify a B.A.

and then decide that you want an M.B.A., for example, be sure to tell everyone who's working on the job placement.

During this phase, you should naturally be getting ready for the interview itself by lining up the questions you want to ask. There will be ones relating to the work itself and others dealing with the way it will be done. Since the answers are apt to be always in the affirmative, ask for examples when the time comes.

List the things you want to tell applicants about the work and the company—for instance, the title and mission of the job, the duties involved, how much supervision there will be, the relation of the job to others in the organization, the working conditions, the amount of travel involved, and the opportunities for advancement for someone in the position.

Arrange to give your full attention to the applicant. Get someone to hold your phone calls and not let people come in to your office and interrupt you. If this is impossible, take advantage of it. Tell the applicants that such interruptions are a part of the job and that they will have to accept them.

Be ready to take notes. Also, before the interview starts, review any résumés and correspondence about the person that you may have on file.

If you have asked for an application to be filled out, notice its appearance: legibility, accuracy, and completeness. These reflect the way the person works.

DURING THE INTERVIEW

You can learn a lot about people if you go out to the waiting room to get them. They may be staring off into space. They may be reading the house magazines on the table. They may be arguing with the receptionist because they don't want to fill out an application or don't like to be kept waiting. All are clues.

The interview itself has four parts: putting the person (and perhaps yourself) at ease, getting the information you need, allowing the applicant to get further information from you, and winding up.

Start the interview by breaking the ice. Experienced as you are, there is still a hurdle of strangeness that must be jumped. A real estate broker once said to me, "I do a lot of hiring, and when I start an interview I feel as though I were on display myself—as if *I* were being interviewed." And as experienced as some of the applicants are, and many of them are not, they need reassurance.

A polite remark will do, something like, "You have an interesting background." (Notice the word "interesting." It's safer to say that than "You have a good background,'' which can paint you into a corner if in the end you have to say it's not the right background.)

If you and the applicant share a common sport, hobby, or alma mater, you might begin the conversation by commenting on that.

They not to start by asking, "Tell me about yourself." It's a convenient beginning for you but a terrible one for the applicant—like being asked to tell a funny story. You can start things rolling by asking about something in the résumé. For instance, you might ask, "Talk about your work as fulfillment manager. How did you handle discounts? Was the warehouse location a problem?" These questions are not as threatening as, "Why do you want this job?" or "Why do you think you are qualified?"

There are a number of questions that some employers often ask, and that career counselors give job applicants to prime them for interviews. Some are aimed at uncovering information. Some are what job hunters call "trick questions" to see *how* a person answers. They include: "What do you think of your college?" "What do you do best?" "What are your weaknesses?" Applicants are taught to give the so-called "right" answers like, "My greatest weakness is that I drive myself too hard and am apt to "overwork," which are self-compliments and no help at all.

Here are a few questions you may find useful, depending on your business and the job to be filled.

For beginners: What are your special abilities? What were some of your extracurricular activities in school? What have you learned from your summer jobs? What have you done that shows initiative (or the ability to get along with others, meet the unexpected, or be persuasive)? What would you expect to do on your first day?

For the experienced: What evidence can you give of your success in selling (research, establishing a new department, administering budgets, or whatever)? What difficulties did you have to overcome when you took over as production manager? How did you do it?

Notice that all of these questions require full answers: they are not "yes or no" questions.

Always—with neophytes or experienced job holders—ask a personal question when you see an opportunity. It can be on any subject—sports, a TV program, trip to Europe, or family. It's a change of pace. The candidates may not realize they're still on view, and the way they field the question can be revealing.

As an applicant talks, try to read some of the signals he or she is unconsciously giving out. There are small signs that betray emotion—clicking a pen, playing with a paper clip, talking nonstop, not looking you in the eye. These indications of tension may be temporary and wear off as the interview goes on, or they may represent a permanent trait.

See what the applicants know about your company as a result of homework they did, not to impress you but rather to get a better idea of how they would fit in. A magazine publisher once said at a career conference, "Show us that you know our magazine, but don't come in with a copy under your arm."

And *listen.* Let people finish what they're saying (unless they're so longwinded that you have to put a stop to them). Giving them a chance to make their point gives *you* a chance to see what idea they're developing, and also means they'll be fully attentive to your next question. When you interrupt, people are so anxious to get back to what they were saying that they don't hear what *you* are saying.

Also, watch for what they *don't* say. That may be just as important as what they *do.* When they give you information that you didn't ask for, it can mean that they didn't know the answer to your question.

You may want to see samples of their work if it is appropriate to the job. Or you may want to see them perform. Editors sometimes give copyediting or proofreading tests. Office managers give typing and shorthand tests. One marketing manager thrusts a broken stapler at sales reps and says, "Sell me this!"

You will have to draw out some people who are not good at interviews—who don't know how to present their qualifications—although they may be fully capable of filling the job. On the other hand, you may have to guard against those who are so eager to be hired that they talk very convincingly. One employer hired a public relations assistant because of a well-designed kit of promotional materials only to find the person couldn't write, a vital skill that was never uncovered in the interview.

Allowing applicants to get information from you can be a test in itself. Take them on a tour of the officers or plant, and have them meet others with whom they might be working. Notice their comments and questions. Some will ask about things related to the work: hours, sick leave, vacations, benefits. (Don't worry about a question about salary as long as it's not the first question—that's being practical). Some will want to know the company's attitude on matters like consumerism, pollution, and community involvement.

Winding up entails letting the person know the interview is over. Some candidates seem to want to keep the conversation going, and you may have to help them. Some of the recognizable tips are: your pushing your chair back, gathering up the résumé and your notes, and thanking them for coming in. At this point, you should make it clear how things stand. Perhaps you are considering others and will be in touch. Then, again, you may want the candidate to call you next week. Or you have already seen others who are suited to the job. If the last is the case, you may want to soften the blow by promising to pass the person's résumé along to someone else in the company who has a job opening. But if you so promise, do it. In such an event, you may also want to suggest other companies for the individual to try.

In choosing your words, remember that people hear what they want to hear, not necessarily what is said. One person told a friend, "I'm being considered for the job." Actually, the recruiter had said, "We'll keep you in mind." This sounds like an innocuous remark but to the job applicant it seemed to hold promise.

Now comes the third and final stage.

AFTER THE INTERVIEW

You will want to review your notes, the résumé, and any samples left with you. As you go over a person's background, be careful to give weight to his or her *skills,* not just knowledge or experience in your field. Such experience can be much overrated. It may not be necessary and can always be acquired, whereas skills are essential and transferable.

You might make a rating scale and rank the applicants on such counts as training, ability, experience, attitude, personality, evidence of leadership, and ability to make decisions. Check to see if there was something that came out during the interview that didn't jibe with the written record. Was a candidate evasive about a question? Was one fulsome? A long explanation about why someone was fired, for instance, may be a cover-up.

If you can't make up your mind about a person, it might help to get another opinion from someone in the company or from those who referred the applicant. Or you might arrange a second interview, which is a good idea anyway. Sometimes people come across quite differently on second viewing.

You may want to check references when you get down to the wire. But don't depend on these. Former employees are cagey about giving out too much. Job title and dates of employment are the bare bones of what you can expect. If you want more substantial material, your best bet is to talk to someone you know who knows them.

When you have made your decision and have filled the job, notify those who have been referring candidates to you and the other applicants as well. If you don't have time to call the other applicants, put the burden on them to call you to learn the outcome. There are painless ways to say "no"—an example, "We found someone who has more qualifications than you." Honest and kind. ■

How Companies Avoid Mistakes in Hiring

Harry Bacas

Sophisticated tests are joining other methods of screening job applicants.

We're going to invest $20,000 to $40,000 in a new employee in the first year, so we're pretty careful how we pick them,'' says Roy A. Smith, vice president of Associated Packaging, Inc., in Goodlettsville, Tenn.

Smith's company sells and services machinery that manufacturers use to encase their products in plastic blister packs, gift wraps and other kinds of packaging. The company employs clerical workers, salesmen and customer service technicians.

For service people, the company asks area technical schools to send it students with electronics skills as job applicants. First screening is done by telephone, and the likeliest candidates are invited in for an interview conducted by the service manager with Roy Smith or his brother Joe, the company president, sitting in.

"The service manager evaluates their skills," says Smith. "I try to evaluate what kind of employee they will make—their attitudes, how they answer, whether they have long-range plans that would fit our business or are just looking for a job. Remember, these people will deal directly with our customers.

"Finally, when we find the person we want to hire, we will look at his grades, talk to his instructors and check his background."

For clerical employees, the company runs an ad, contacts the local employment office and then follows the same procedure, with the office manager doing the interviewing and one of the partners sitting in. Of 50 applicants, 10 may be screened by phone and perhaps three will be invited in for an interview and typing test.

Such procedures for evaluating job applicants are probably typical of most small businesses. But many businesses also are turning to written tests, psychological evaluation, lie detectors, handwriting analysis and use of outside consultants as part of their employment screening and selection process.

Robert J. Solomon, associate professor of business administration at the College of William and Mary and a management consultant, believes businesses are increasingly interested in using quantitative selection procedures to hire the most effective people.

He says many companies gave up tests and measurements in the 1960s and '70s because they were afraid of incurring antidiscrimination suits. But he says that such fears are often misplaced and that it is the job of consultants like himself to educate companies in how to use tests legally. (See related story, page 45.)

Solomon says companies must analyze a job to identify the performance issues they want to test for. Next they should choose selection procedures that are objective and as nearly as possible simulate the actual job.

The Commonwealth Edison Company in Chicago, for example, has used an ''honesty'' test for nine years as part of job application procedures at some divisions.

Robert Bassett, industrial relations manager at the company's general office, says ''discharges for theft and forgeries and malingering (which we consider to be theft of a day's pay) have dropped by a factor of 10 to 1'' since the company started using the test.

Produced by P.O.S. Corporation of Chicago and sold nationally to about 2,000 clients, the test is a set of 40 statements that the applicant is asked to mark as true or false. The statements are sentences like ''every normal person is sometimes tempted to steal'' and ''if a person steals once he is likely to steal again'' and ''I get mad easily and then get over it soon.''

The test, administered in the employer's personnel office, takes 15 minutes or less to complete (Bassett says most people can do it in 5 minutes.) then the personnel officer phones P.O.S. on a toll-free line, reads the answers, and in about 2 minutes is given a score.

Scores are assigned five possible ''risk'' ratings—excellent, good, average, poor or serious. P.O.S. suggests that applicants rated as poor or serious risks may not be hired unless there are other considerations.

There are no right or wrong answers, explains P.O.S. Vice President Mark C. Dunne, and the rating method, considered proprietary, was developed 10 years ago in conjunction with extensive polygraph testing. Dunne says the questionnaire ''came out with 98 percent accuracy in finding the poor risks compared with the results of polygraph testing.''

"We only claim to evaluate honesty," Dunne says, "but honesty includes many things, like faithful attendance, giving an honest job of work, not being late. All we want to do is identify those who are *not* honest. The test is just a tool, to be used along with all other screening and selection methods."

P.O.S. charges from $8 to $12.50 per test, depending on the quantity bought. The scoring phone call is free.

Another company that produces a test for honesty as part of a wide range of psychological tests for policemen, clerks, transit operators, managers and others is London House, Inc., of Park Ridge, Ill.

London House had sales of $5.6 million last year for nine different sets of tests for business, "but 80 percent of our queries are about honesty," says spokesman Karla Kizzort. She says the honesty queries are greatest from food service companies, banks, and jewelry stores, supermarkets and other retailers.

Such concern about honesty is not surprising. The American Management Association has found that in one year in the 1970s employee pilferage amounted to $17.5 billion. Its study showed that in 20 percent of the companies that went out of business that year, employee theft contributed to the failure. The Bank Administration Institute says 83.5 percent of bank losses are due to internal fraud.

London House employs several industrial and research psychologists on its staff of more than 100, but most of its tests were developed and validated over a period of years at the University of Chicago Human Resource Center.

Scoring of its tests can be done by telephones, with written confirmation sent by mail, or by the employer, using guidelines for hand scoring. In some cases London House provides software to enable the client to produce evaluations on the client's own computer.

"Any test has to have two things," says Kizzort. "It has to be legal, meeting all the nondiscrimination guidelines of the Equal Employment Opportunity Commission. And it has to be thoroughly validated. That means it has to be shown to measure or predict what it says it measures or predicts."

Even the best test is only one tool to reveal a job applicant's aptitude, personality and potential.

"You really need a combination of testing and face-to-face interviews, because you have to see the live person to get your intuition and judgment to work," says William Terris, director of industrial psychology at DePaul University and head of London House's psychological services.

London House publishes a 60-minute test called Transit Operators Selection Inventory, which has been used by more than 100 transportation authorities to select new bus or train operators. It measures an applicant's experience and background, skills and abilities, and emotional health. The test also measures an applicant's potential for drug abuse and violent behavior.

The Washington Metropolitan Area Transit Authority began using the test after postaccident medical examinations showed a correlation between accidents and substance abuse by operators. It later made the test a regular part of screening for prospective bus operators, along with a check of employment, driving and court records.

More extensive—and more expensive procedures are involved in a London House battery of tests called STEP (System for Testing and Evaluation of Potential). It is used to evaluate potential managers. The tests contain from 790 to 1,000 questions.

The tests are scored by hand and cost up to $250. The battery may take several days to administer. But it is still less time-consuming than evaluation by peer review and less expensive than sending people to the special personnel assessment centers maintained by some large corporations.

The STEP system begins with a job analysis to make sure the tests to be given measure the functions important to the jobs under review. Tests for bank officers will emphasize different characteristics than those for manufacturing supervisors.

After testing, an analyst draws a personality profile of each candidate and compares his skills and abilities with those required at different levels of a company's hierarchy. Sixteen performance dimensions from judgment and decision making to communications and coping with emergencies are scored.

The objective is to help an employer find the best match between a candidate's abilities and a job's important functions.

Says Kizzort; "The better a person fits a job, the longer he or she is likely to stay in it, and the more productive he or she will be during that time. In addition, employees who know that their company takes this kind of care in fitting people to jobs are more likely to feel loyalty toward their employer.

An entirely different kind of "testing" with the same aim—evaluating a certain person's suitability for a certain job—analyzes handwriting as an expression of personality. Sometimes called graphology or graphoanalysis, it has been used by an estimated 4,000 to 5,000 U.S. companies.

"Graphoanalysis is a science, not a gimmick like palmistry or astrology," says one practitioner, Sheila Kurtz, president of A New Slant, Inc., of New

York. "Since handwriting is a direct projection of mental activities, it is next to impossible, no matter how hard the writer may try, to conceal or disguise his or her mental traits by intentionally altering the writing. Handwriting is just as personal and distinctive as fingerprints."

Although handwriting analysis has a long history and is more widely practiced in Europe than here, there is little agreement on standards. Margaret Manna, who runs Mannagraphix in Irvington, N.Y., and studied at the International Graphoanalysis Society, tells clients to write 200 words or more on unruled paper. But Accu-Scan, a system developed by AEA Resources for Business in Wayne, PA., supplies questionnaire forms that contain ruled lines. The system bases part of its analysis on whether the candidate writes on, above or below the lines.

A fourth company, Handwriting Research Corporation in Phoenix, is the first to computerize handwriting analysis. Formed 2 1/2 years ago by three university-trained counselors and psychologists and a computer systems expert, HRC uses a data base drawn from more than 2,000 handwriting research studies, the bulk of them European, published from 1922 to 1984.

With a candidate's writing sample in front of him, an HRC analyst answers 204 questions about it—the slant of the letters in degrees, for example, and to what extent the slant is consistent. The computer takes the answers and compares them with 249,000 combinations of answers in the data base, performing more than half a million calculations on each sample.

HRC's basic report, priced at $50, plots candidates' personality traits on a matrix, showing each applicant's strengths and weaknesses in areas previously determined to be important for the job in question.

For $70, the report also includes a telephoned verbal assessment by an HRC analyst of the candidate's intellect, social skills, integrity, emotional stability or behavior under stress.

For $125, the report includes a 175-trait personality graph and a written summary of what it shows.

Soul S. Khalsa, one of HRC's principals, says the company's business has been largely in California and the Southwest but is widening. Clients have ranged from entertainment companies to security agencies and construction and development firms. He says companies' needs differ.

"In construction," he says, "energy level is important as well as drug or alcohol abuse tendencies and team-building skills. In hotel work, it's social skills, graciousness, warmth, rather than mental abilities. We evaluate the pros and cons and let the employer make the decision."

Khalsa says recent studies calling the validity of the polygraph into question have boosted the use of handwriting analysis.

One client, Xerox Corporation's computer services division in Los Angeles, used HRC analysis to rate telemarketing personnel. It found, says Ron Bell, a Xerox sales manager, that "the accuracy rate was 100 percent; the high scorers were our superstars, and the low scorers are no longer with us."

But many employers still hire without tests of any kind. William M. Hein, president of Creative Resources, Oklahoma City, which does retail catalog design and photography, says "we have been terribly happy with the people we've got. I have let only two people go for lack of ability."

He says his staff artists or photographers judge an applicant's portfolio of pictures for technical competence and he himself evaluates attitude and checks references.

Checking references is more important than some employers think. A study by Opinion Research Corporation for Ward Howell International, an executive search firm, says 26 percent of companies it surveyed had hired people in the past year whose resumes turned out to be inflated or inaccurate. Gilbert Dwyer, president of Ward Howell, says employers should check "not just those references the applicant tells you to call, but should dig, as we do, into places he has worked, his peers, friends, banks, lawyers."

Ronald Pilenzo, president of the American Society for Personnel Administration, is leery of tests unless they are thoroughly validated and have been proved relevant to a firm's job situation.

"If you're smart enough to interview a candidate properly, to ask the right questions, to check the person's track record," he says, "you shouldn't need a test to tell you whom to hire." ■

AS EASY AS PIE

Because hiring any new employee is important to a company's success, the process of selection should be methodical, say two experts.

Carol Schneider-Jenkins, manager of human resources at Oximetrix, Inc., Mountain View, Calif., and Norma Carr-Ruffino, management professor at San Francisco State University, suggest using the PIE method.

PIE (prepare, interview, evaluate) was developed by the American Electronics Association. Using a separate PIE form at each step, you first prepare for an interview by developing a profile of the qualities of a successful performer in the job.

Next, you conduct the interview, drawing information from the candidate about his qualifications and then telling him about the job.

Finally, you evaluate each candidate by comparing your rational and intuitive impressions with the profile of the successful performer.

Copies of the three PIE forms are available by sending a self-addressed stamped envelope to PIE Forms, Administrative Management Society, 2360 Maryland Road, Willow Grove, Pa. 19090

How, When To Tell Employees They Don't Have A Job For Life

George E. L. Barbee
Executive Director
Price Waterhouse
Waltham, Mass.

Recent mergers, plant closings and downsizings have forced a new definition of the social contract between employer and employee.

About twice a year, I'll have lunch with Greg, a generally gregarious vice president of human resources at a Fortune 500 chemical and energy company. Last month's lunch revealed a particularly somber side of this man, and it didn't take long to get his concerns on the table.

"Back in the 1950s, we hired a whole bunch of chemists" he explained, "and I, personally, told many of those guys that, if they did a decent job, they'd have a job as long as they wanted one. I even implied the assurance of a very comfortable retirement." He continued, "Now, there are extreme pressures to trim the ranks and, frankly, we haven't conditioned our employees for this change."

Sadly, Greg is not alone. The recent spate of mergers, plant closings and downsizings has forced companies—and employees—to develop a new definition of the traditional social contract between employer and employee. It's now time for financial self-reliance among all employees.

Salary increases are no longer automatic. Additionally, liberal benefit packages, wholly funded by the company, are a thing of the past. And a smooth, predictable career path is no longer guaranteed. The days of "cradle to grave" provisions have given way to an era where employees must insulate themselves from the volatility of today's economy. Innovative companies, therefore, are encouraging employees to take a more active role in their financial futures, while considering their company benefits more as a foundation of benefits upon which government programs and the employee's own personal resources should be added.

Reprinted with permission from PENSION WORLD, OCTOBER 1989. Copyright © by Communication Channels, Inc., Atlanta, GA, USA.

George E. L. Barbee is executive director of the Personal Financial Services Group at Price Waterhouse in Waltham, Mass.

Altering that "cradle to grave" mindset is no small task. It requires artful communication—to employees, to the community, to investors, and to the industry.

The closing of a plant or division—or a drastic reduction in staff—can be analogous to radical surgery. The cutting off of a limb to save the body.

In a crisis environment, one doesn't have the luxury of softening the bad news with some good news. In a major downsizing, human resource executives are faced with some wrenching decisions, including "Who should say what?" "When?" "And to whom?"

In such circumstances, intelligent, well-planned communication is crucial—to preserve a positive relationship, not only with those leaving, but also with those staying. Unfortunately, this awkward situation often causes management to couch their communications, saying too little, too late. This allows the "rumor mill" to perpetuate some very wrong messages, not the least of which is that the company is ruthlessly firing its local employees—without concern for their well-being.

Effective communications mean delivering substantive information quickly and talking with employees until they completely understand the situation. It's important to stay ahead of the "rumor mill" and to show genuine concern for employees. However, effective communication implies that you have something relevant to say—other than "goodbye."

The most efficient "radical surgery" occurs when a company shares the reasons for terminations, as well as some useful benefits designed to help departing (and remaining) employees. Increasingly, financial outplacement assistance is being provided, along with the more traditional career outplacement services.

Departing employees very often find themselves with sudden money via separation bonuses, early retirement incentives or pension fund distributions. Those people become ripe targets for the hundreds of salespeople offering investments, real estate or insurance.

Therefore, it is becoming common for downsizing companies to arrange for independent organizations to provide financial advice to help departing employees deal with their investment options—not to mention the potentially precarious period of time between jobs.

Hopefully, many benefit administrators will never have to endure the trauma of the "radical surgery" inherent in a major downsizing. It's likely, however, that most human resource executives will consider some "elective surgery" to reduce the need for the most drastic measures. Examples of "elective surgery" are: the revision of hiring, welfare and pension policies;

short-term incentive programs for early retirement; voluntary separation offerings; and relocation opportunities as an option to termination.

For example, a major oil company, beset by tumbling prices, hoped to eliminate 5,000 jobs within a few months. It announced an early retirement incentive plan to cover 15,000 pension-eligible and vested employees. Pension eligibility was liberalized for targeted personnel, and other incentives were offered based on age and length of service.

Consequently, the company engaged a financial planning and communications organization. With the assistance of the company's human resources department, personal information was assembled on each of the targeted employees—age, length of service, marital status, and number of children.

The outside organization then prepared and distributed a 15-page personalized workbook to every employee. Each workbook contained a financial analysis of an employee's individual circumstances to facilitate the decision-making process. Also, the outside organization conducted seminars at 75 locations across the country to supplement the information provided in the workbooks. All workbooks were received and all seminars were conducted within a six-week period.

Voluntary terminations far exceeded the company's estimates, reducing the need for layoffs considerably. Since withdrawals were voluntary, the negativity was significantly lessened and the morale of the departing and remaining personnel was left intact.

The employees who elected to take early retirement indicated that they had done so because of the personalized communication of the plan. The company achieved its cost-cutting goal (while maintaining its good name in the marketplace) and the goodwill of its departing and remaining employees, despite a trying situation.

To continue the "medical" analogy, now consider preventive medicine— that is, telling employees that they must become more involved in their overall financial futures.

In essence, the key is to communicate to employees their new financial responsibilities and to do so earlier in life. New techniques called personalized employee communications are effective for two reasons, the first being the integration of company and employee's personal resources. By presenting company benefits and compensation information as the foundation, and encouraging the integration of personal (outside the company) financial resources, companies are subtly elevating the role of the individual as the key provider.

The second reason personalized employee communications are effective is the selection of benefits information provided. Rather than communicate all benefits in full detail to all employees, companies are increasingly using expert systems technology to selectively match employee needs with only the relevant details of the total benefits program. For example, younger employees can be provided only summary retirement financial information, without all the complex details of tax-advantaged withdrawal options, Medicare elections, and Social Security phase-ins.

For an overall healthy corporation, then, relevant and personal communication to employees is prescribed. Employees should be cared about as people, and not just numbers. This is accomplished by what is said, how it is said, and when it is said. An employer's relationship with each employee is bound by a social contract, and there is much that can be done to reframe that social contract without tearing the fabric of employee loyalty. ■

Early Retirement or Forced Resignation: Policy Issues for Downsizing Human Resources

Frank E. Kuzmits
Lyle Sussman
Associate Professors of Management
University of Louisville

We live in an era where downsizing, also known as "demassing" and "streamlining," is a familiar concept to industry analysts and others who follow human resource trends in the corporate world. In the past few years, the corporate axe has fallen on the heads of managers, executives, and professionals in such well-known firms as Apple Computers, AT&T, CBS, DuPont, Eastman Kodak, Exxon, General Electric, Atari, Polaroid, and Union Carbide. It is estimated that over 300 companies have trimmed their staffs in the past two years, resulting in a net reduction of about a half a million white collar employees.[1]

There was a time in corporate America when a reduction in force affected the blue-collar manufacturing worker almost exclusively. More often than not, these workers represented the steel, rubber, automobile, chemical, or textile industries—those labor-intensive, smoke-stack industries that traditionally treated labor as an expendable resource to be hired and fired in concert with the ebb and flow of the company's economic fortunes. Most managers and professionals—particularly those in the upper echelons of the corporate hierarchy—felt relatively secure in their jobs even though the company may have been struggling through difficult times. While a company reorganization or streamlining effort occasionally resulted in the loss of a few white-collar jobs, most of the cuts affected the men and women on the lower rungs of the organization.

Reprinted by permission, *SAM Advanced Management Journal,* Winter, 1988, Society for Advancement of Management, Vinton, VA 24179.

A consultant for banks and industry, Dr. Sussman has also co-authored three books on management and communication; Dr. Kuzmits has published two texts on human resource management. The authors collaborate on the weekly column "Managing People" for the Louisville Courier-Journal.

Today, it's a different ball game. "Streamlining" is likely to include white collar groups along with their blue-collar brethren. And in many cases, the personnel cuts are directed specifically toward the upper-level groups.

Why the recent trend toward white-collar downsizing?

The primary motive, of course, is economics. Even a relatively small downsizing effort can result in enormous labor cost savings. For example, the DuPont Company's voluntary retirement program in 1985 resulted in a staff reduction of 11,200 employees, enabling the chemical giant to achieve annual after-tax labor savings of $230 million. Chevron and Union Carbide estimate their annual savings resulting from early retirement plans at $200 million and $250 million, respectively. Xerox's recently announced plan, in which 1,000 salaried employees will take early retirement is expected to result in "substantial" savings, although the company has provided no figures.[2]

There's also little doubt that the current popularity of "merger-mania" has in part fueled the growing trend toward downsizing. Superimposing one corporate structure on another often results in surplus labor through a duplication of responsibilities—a situation which is more likely to exist among the managerial and professional staff than among the employees who run the assembly lines and perform routine clerical functions.

An argument can also be made that the increasing use of downsizing stems in part from the growing demise of corporate loyalty. In years past, the corporate culture of many firms included an unwritten rule that the jobs of upper-level employees were secure as long as the company made money and the staff did their jobs. In turn, employees felt an attachment to the corporation that translated into hard work and staying put.

The corporate environment is radically different now. Bottom-line results overrule considerations of job security and the once-heralded concept of corporate loyalty. Cost-cutting programs have dealt a severe blow to managerial and professional job security, and there's little doubt that managers are beginning to feel the heat.

A recent survey of middle managers from 600 companies conducted by Lou Harris & Associates for *Business Week* supports this contention. The survey showed that only 44% of the respondents believed they could stay with their employers for as long as they wished as long as they did a good job. Forty-four percent believed they may not be able to, and 12% were not sure. Sixty-five percent of the managers believed that salaried employees today are less loyal than they were 10 years ago; 29%, about as loyal; 5%, more loyal, and 2%, were not sure.[3]

The increasing use of downsizing as a technique for boosting productivity, profits, and efficiency has won the favor of stockholders and Wall Street analysts. Downsizing sends the message that a firm is truly serious about strengthening its competitive posture, even to the point of taking the knife to what many companies have historically considered their most important resource—their people.

IMPLICATIONS FOR MANAGING HUMAN RESOURCES

There's little doubt that the financial impact of downsizing can be positive. Nevertheless, downsizing raises a number of critical human resource issues that deserve serious attention from top management. A firm's approach to the downsizing issue will not only have an impact upon its current and future economic health, it could well increase the risk of employee litigation because of alleged age discrimination. It may have other effects—on the morale of employees who survive a downsizing effort, on the success of present and future company programs and projects, and on the public's perception of the firm as a socially responsible employer.

Once the need to trim the labor force has been established, management has two basic options for accomplishing the task: early retirement or forced resignation. Let's look more closely at the characteristics of each option.

EARLY RETIREMENT

When early retirement programs vary somewhat from firm to firm, all have one element in common: a financial inducement to retire before the "normal" age of 62 or 65. Such plans have become increasingly popular. According to Hay/Huggings & Company, a benefits consulting firm, about 11% of all companies offer senior employees a bonus for retiring early.[4]

Most early retirement packages—particularly the generous ones—are labeled "5-5-4" packages. Such plans add five years to the employee's age and five years to the employee's length of service when calculating early retirement benefits. The plan also provides for a lump-sum payment of four weeks of pay for each year the employee has worked. Less attractive plans include "3-3-2" or "2-2-1" packages.

The extent to which the early retirement pot is "sweetened" is dictated by two factors: the company's ability to fund the initial cash outlays, and the amount of personnel trimming needed. Lucrative early retirement packages, such as the "5-5-4" plan, are usually undertaken by large firms with sufficient cash reserves who review overstaffing as a serious obstacle to organizational productivity.

If the primary goal of early retirement programs is to trim the ranks of senior employees, incentives to leave early almost always accomplish this objective. As an example the DuPont Chemical Company expected its recent early retirement program to eliminate 12,000 to 15,000 employees over a three-year period. In fact, their goal was reached in little more than a year.[5]

FORCED RESIGNATION

Early retirement and forced resignation share one common objective: to reduce operating costs by trimming the labor force of excessive or expendable human resources. But that is where the similarities end.

To retire early is the employee's choice. It is voluntary, and presumably done after seriously weighing the advantages and disadvantages of working versus retiring.

But forced resignation, regardless of its euphemistic label, is the company's decision—a decision which may result in considerable economic and emotional trauma to the affected employees.

Obviously, the selection of early retirement as a downsizing strategy is the option most favored by employees. But is it the most beneficial strategy for the company? Which downsizing option is the most costly? Which is likely to result in a loss of critical talent? Which runs the greatest risk of litigation? Such questions underscore the need for management to select a downsizing strategy only after careful consideration of the particular issues, circumstances, and constraints it faces. A discussion of these issues follows.

CASH OUTLAYS

The primary objective of downsizing is to pare labor overhead and bolster profits and productivity. But the method chosen to trim the labor force can itself be costly, particularly early retirement.

For an early retirement program to succeed, employees must see a clear economic benefit to retiring early. The financial incentives that firms must offer to motivate large numbers of people to take early retirement can amount to huge cash outlays. For example, Chevron's program is expected to cost the company $90 million in severance pay and benefits; Union Carbide's effort cost the firm $70 million in up-front charges.[6] Kodak's buyout in 1986 reduced the company's net income by $140 million that year.[7]

Of course, the formidable front-end charges can usually be justified as an investment: the long-term savings that result from a shrunken payroll are expected to far exceed the initial cash outlays. Annual savings are estimated at $200 and $250 million for Chevron and Union Carbide, respectively.

Nonetheless, early retirement is likely to be a far more expensive downsizing strategy than forced resignation, where severance packages—if any—are often meager. For example, employees included in American Motor

Company's series of forced layoffs in 1985 were offered nothing more than the standard severance package. AMC's plan enabled a fired employee to receive his salary for up to 6 months, depending on length of service.[8] It's probably safe to suggest that a firm selecting the forced resignation option cannot, in most cases, afford the generosity of its better heeled counterparts.

LEGAL ISSUES

Today, any action involving human resources also involves legal considerations, and downsizing is no exception. The principle law pertaining to the downsizing issues is the Age Discrimination in Employment Act of 1978 (ADEA). The Act prohibits discrimination against an employee age 40 or older in regard to any term or condition of employment. (President Reagan signed a bill eliminating the 70-year age cap on October 31, 1986. The bill, which took effect January 1, 1987, covers private employers, state and local governments, employment agencies, and labor unions with 25 or more employees).

It would seem obvious that corporate decision-makers should exercise extreme caution to ensure that a downsizing strategy does not run afoul of the ADEA, regardless of the method chosen. But statistics show that ADEA violations are on the upswing, and forced resignations are high on the list of ADEA complaints.

In 1985, a total of 16,784 job-related age discrimination charges were filed with the Equal Employment Opportunity Commission, a 52% increase over the 11,063 complaints filed in 1982. The leading cause of complaints in 1985 was wrongful discharge, alleged in 9,188 cases. Charges of wrongful layoffs also were high on the list.[9]

Because EEOC statistics show that forced resignations and layoffs are likely to be the most problematic from a legal standpoint, the early retirement option becomes increasingly attractive as management places a premium on staying out of court. The risk of litigation is considerably higher with a strategy of forced resignations.

RISK OF LOSING VALUED EMPLOYEES

For decades, the goals of personnel and human resource management have been to attract high quality people and to foster a sense of mutual loyalty between the employer and employee. These goals are consistent with contemporary human resource philosophies which stress that organizational success is directly linked to success in attracting, developing, and retaining a competent, motivated workforce.

Downsizing may be an obstacle to these goals. The sword of downsizing contains two edges—one that slashes labor overhead and one that has the potential to carve a chunk of competent and skilled employees from the labor force. When significant numbers of valued employees accept a firm's early retirement offer, the success of current and future programs and activities can be jeopardized. Clearly, the risk of losing critical talents and skills is much greater through an early retirement strategy.

As the early retirement window opens, management has no control over who jumps out. Without fail, some of the employees who bail out will be those who management would much prefer to stay—perhaps as many as 10% to 30%.[10] DuPont expected about 6,500 employees to take the company's offer of early retirement, but over 11,000 decided to leave early. As a result, DuPont was forced to hire many back as consultants to work on critical projects.[11] "A general buyout has risks to it. Some of the people you're absolutely counting on to stay may opt to take it, warns Richard Calmes, Vice President of Human Resources for American Motors."[12]

A petroleum company's experience with early retirement clearly underscores the risk of this strategy in losing people who were needed for critical operations. The company was forced to temporarily close a refinery because almost every worker at one of its power plants accepted the company's offer of early retirement. According to D. Quinn Mills, a Harvard professor who observed the blunder, "the corporate officers had simply issued orders to get rid of people, but had no sense of the people they wanted to leave."[13]

The risk of losing critical skills is greatly reduced through a strategy of forced resignations. With the option, management can downsize with minimum disruption to the organization's strategic plans and purposes. By choosing who goes and who stays, the most effective employees and employees with the most essential skills may be retained, and the threat of endangering current and future plans, programs and activities is lessened.

THREAT TO ORGANIZATION CLIMATE AND CULTURE

Carving a sizeable chunk from the ranks of human resources will not only alter the formal organization structure, it will also influence and reshape the informal organization. Those who leave will have an effect on those who stay—the "survivors." And the culture will be more adversely affected when the decision to leave is **involuntary rather than voluntary.** While an early retirement program is often accompanied by retirement parties and luncheons, a wave of forced resignations is often met with shock and bitterness by those who leave, and with hostility, fear, and insecurity by those who survive.

To an extent, the emotional impact on those who are forced to resign and those who survive can be minimized by well designed programs and activities. Attractive severance packages coupled with outplacement counseling and support services can lessen the anxiety and emotional trauma that normally accompanies an involuntary job loss. And for those fortunate enough to escape the path of the downsizing scythe, efforts should be made to minimize the guilt, anxiety, and anger often felt by survivors. This can be accomplished by allowing survivors to discuss their feelings with each other and with management, encouraging employees to avoid dwelling on the past and focusing instead on the future, assigning meaningful tasks to get survivors' minds off the layoffs, and encouraging employee ideas to create a sense of employee ownership in the restructured company.[14]

Although mechanisms exist to allay the trauma that results from layoffs, there is some question whether companies seriously consider the feelings of employees when creating and implementing layoff strategies. According to Richard Holan, Director of the Center for Management Development at Duquesne University, "Corporations try to do what's right in the legal and actuarial sense. Period. Do they also show consideration and sensitivity? Not a lot."[15]

IMPACT UPON PUBLIC IMAGE

Few downsizing plans escape the scrutiny of the media. In the past few years, the business press has detailed the strategies of many large firms to reduce their staffs. When these strategies are published, the public image of the firm in question is often affected.

Whether the public's perception of the firm is enhanced or tainted depends to a large degree on the downsizing method chosen and the way in which the plan is implemented. Because early retirement plans are voluntary, this method rarely meets with the public's disapproval.

Involuntary layoffs or forced resignations, however, are quite another matter and run a great risk of public alienation. Published accounts of long-tenured managers and professionals receiving terse notes of quick dismissal, and interviews with bitter employees whose jobs were cut with little or no severance pay or outplacement assistance, could well damage the image of the firm in question. This is particularly true when the details of the account, replete with accusatory quotes from the victims, are chronicled in a national business publication.

To summarize, the impact of downsizing goes well beyond mere economic considerations. Trimming the labor force—more particularly—the specific method chosen to cut staff—will affect not only the firm's economic status, but also the overall competency of the human resource group, the success of current and future business strategies, and the organization's culture and image. The issues we have discussed are summarized in Figure 1.

Faced with a need to trim the labor force, which option—early retirement or forced resignation—should an organization select?

There is no "right" answer. Each firm must critically and thoroughly examine its financial condition, human resources, business strategies, legal environment, and corporate culture. The strategy selected should result in a balance between the economic advantages of downsizing and the risk of impairing the firm's human resources. ▪

Methods of Downsizing

Variable	Early Retirement	Forced Resignations
Cash Outlays	Relatively High	Relatively Low
Legal Issues	Relatively Low Risk of LItigation	Relatively Higher Risk of Litigation
Risk of Losing Valued Employees	Relatively High Risk	Relatively Low Risk
Impact Upon Organization Climate and Culture	Minimal Impact	Relatively High Likelihood of Negative Impact
Impact Upon Public Image	Relatively Low Negative Impact	Relatively High Risk of Negative Impact

FIGURE 1   COMPARISON OF TWO METHODS OF DOWNSIZING AND THEIR IMPACT UPON CRITICAL ORGANIZATION VARIABLES

REFERENCES

See A. Beam, "When the Grass Isn't Greener," *Business Week,* August 4, 1986, p. 45–49; M. Lynch, "As Recession Deepens, White Collar Workers Join the Jobless Ranks," *The Wall Street Journal,* December 7, 1981, p. 1; and P. Pascarella, "When Change Means Saying You're Fired," *Industry Week,* July 7, 1986, p. 47–51.

J. Nielsen, "Management Layoffs Won't Quit," *Fortune,* October 28, 1985, p. 49; A. Bennett and D. Sease, "To Reduce Their Costs, Big Companies Layoff White-Collar Workers," *The Wall Street Journal,* May 22, 1986, p. 11; "Xerox Says 1,000 Workers Chose Plan for Early Retirement," *The Wall Street Journal,* January 22, 1986, p. 6.

"When the Grass Isn't Greener," p. 49.

R. E. Winter, "Ready to Quit?" This Might be the Year To Do It," *The Wall Street Journal,* January 16, 1985, p. 23.

"Management Layoffs Won't Quit," p. 49.

Ibid.

"To Reduce Their Costs, Big Companies Layoff White-Collar Workers," p. 1.

Ibid.

"Age Bias Cases Rose in 1985," *Resource,* December 1986, p. 2.

A. Beam, "When the Grass Isn't Greener," *Business Week,* August 4, 1986, p. 45.

Ibid.

A. Bennett and D. Sease, "To Reduce Their Costs, Big Companies Lay Off White-Collar Workers," *The Wall Street Journal,* May 22, 1986, p. 1.

Ibid., p. 23.

L. Reibstein, "Survivors of Layoffs Receive Help to Lift Morale and Reinstill Trust," *The Wall Street Journal,* December 5, 1985, p. 31.

F. Kessler, "Managers Without A Company," *Fortune,* October 28, 1985, p. 52.

PART FOUR

ORGANIZATIONAL LEADERSHIP

The doing parts of the manager's job involve the motivation of people through the exercise of leadership and communication. Motivation deals with the creation of a desire on the part of subordinates to perform above some minimally acceptable level. To elicit motivated performance from its employees, management should appeal to individual needs that require satisfaction for a continuation of exemplary results. To the extent that effort is translated into performance with a reward that meets the expectations of the individual, reinforcement of the desire to perform at an above average level will be sustained and the individual will strive to meet management's expectations for even higher levels of output. The writings in this part of the book describe some of the established approaches to motivated performance by employees in organizations of all types.

Leadership refers to the actions taken by managers to obtain motivated performance from followers. There are many theories of leadership. Indeed there seems to be an inordinate fascination with this part of the manager's job. Leadership is the managerial function that involves working with and through people to get the job done in the best possible way. Leadership includes an optimal combination of the key variables in the leadership situation. These variables are (1) the leader, (2) the followers, (3) the nature of the work to be accomplished, and (4) the nature of the work environment. The writings here discuss various aspects of leadership.

Communication involves the specific means and techniques through which followers are exhorted by leaders to perform in pursuit of managerial objectives. Communication problems including deflection, delays, and distortions of critical messages constitute a source of endless difficulty for managers in organizations of all types. The articles in this part of the book deal with some of the means to improve communication in organizations along with the benefits likely to result from such improvement.

Motivation Theories: An Integrated Operational Model

Harry E. Wilkinson
President, University Affiliates, Inc.

Charles D. Orth
Senior Associate,
University Affiliates, Inc.

Robert C. Benfari
Senior Lecturer
Harvard Graduate School of
Arts and Sciences

A manager's job is to influence the people in the organization to achieve the goals and objectives with optimal efficiency and effectiveness. One of the most critical and vexing concerns of management and supervisory personnel in any organization is understanding motivation and its role in performance. Many managers are frustrated because there are so many concepts or theories of motivation, each of which seems to work in some situations and not in others. In this article, we attempt to minimize this frustration. We modify a number of motivational concepts and theories in order to unify them in an integrated model that will help managers see the interrelationships among them. Next we show how the model can guide managers to effective action, leading to improved performance.

THE EVOLUTION OF MOTIVATION THEORIES

Motivation theories attempt to identify the factors that influence behavior, particularly the ways in which people respond to the actions of those around them and to other stimuli in their environment. Our social and work environment has been evolving rapidly since the industrial revolution. Kotter[1] observes, "Today, we no longer have a socially simple world. And powerful forces are making it more, rather than less, complex all the time." He goes on to point out the increasing "dependencies" among people and between

Reprinted by permission, *SAM Advanced Management Journal,* Autumn 1986. Society for Advancement of Management.

Dr. Wilkinson was formerly Dean of Business Administration at Northeastern University: Charles Orth was assistant dean at the Harvard Business School; Dr. Benfari publishes and consults in the fields of psychology and behavioral science.

workers and managers, as well as the increasing "diversities" among people. Zaleznik and Kets de Vries[2] observed, "People are products of experiences they have never relinquished. Personal history will always make its claim even though it operates silently, and paradoxically, usually beyond the individuals' awareness." Although motivation theories began with simple approaches to the relatively simple work environments of the time, in the complex organizations and society of today it seems apparent that people are motivated by multiple influences[3] including their perceptions of the expectations others have of them and their own expectations (Kotter op. cit.), self images and self concepts[4] [yielding proactive behavior], and their personalities and life experiences (Zaleznik and Kets de Vries op. cit.) [yielding reactive behavior].

In the less complex era of the early 1900s, motivation theory assumed that the employer essentially bought or exchanged the purchasing power of his wage dollars for the worker's time, interest, effort and contribution. This kind of reward/exchange theory was probably the first widely accepted motivation theory. It was the foundation on which Taylor[5] built his concepts of scientific management, efficiency and work simplification. At that time, it seemed to accurately describe workers' responses to existing environments.

As time passed it became clear that monetary rewards, including the plethora of incentive wage and bonus plans, did not by themselves buy interest, commitment and motivation. In the post World War II era, new motivation theories were evolved by the behavioral sciences in response to the changing environment of the time. Especially noteworthy were the conceptual contributions of Douglas McGregor[6], Abraham Maslow[7], Frederick Herzberg[8], David McClelland[9], and John Morse and Jay Lorsch[10].

MCGREGOR'S THEORY X AND THEORY Y

The "Taylor" (or classical) school of management is a straightforward one emphasizing the need for formal, well established lines of authority, clearly defined jobs and sufficient authority to meet responsibilities. It remains more dominant in the less skilled, blue collar, labor intensive organizations such as assembly line manufacturing of simple products. (Some of these products are now made in the less complex environments of developing countries.) McGregor (op. cit.) postulated that there was a second approach more suited to some organizations. This second approach is often called the "participative" school of management. Its focus is on involving organizational members in the decision making process to increase motivation, to give them a clearer picture of the factors involved, and to make them potentially capable of performing more effectively in their jobs. This approach appears to be more dominant in professional or creative organizations such as research and developmental laboratories, high-tech manufacturing and sales, hospitals, advertising agencies or consulting firms. It also appears to be the approach used by the companies identified in "In Search of Excellence"[11] and by the Japanese.[12]

McGregor (op. cit.) identifies the psychological assumptions, generalizations and hypotheses about human nature and behavior that underlie these two approaches. He names them Theory X (classical) and Theory Y (participative). While Theories X and Y are the underlying beliefs and are not themselves managerial strategies, they have become synonymous with styles of management. They represent the two ends of a spectrum; most organizations function near the center of the spectrum, slightly to one side or the other.

Theory X

The assumptions that characterize the Theory X view of human behavior include the following:

1. The average human being has an inherent dislike of work and will avoid it if possible. Because of this, most people must be coerced, controlled, directed and threatened with punishment before they put forth adequate effort to achieve organizational objectives.
2. The average human being prefers to be directed, wishes to avoid responsibility, has relatively little ambition and wants security above all.

To some degree these assumptions characterize organizations that specify rigid standards of work behavior, that have stringent rules and regulations which are rigorously enforced, and that tend to follow Taylor's concepts of "scientific management". Historically, there has been some evidence of at least limited confirmation of these underlying assumptions in the day-to-day affairs of industry, or else these notions would no longer be around. McGregor, however, believes that many aspects of human behavior are incompatible with the Theory X assumptions.

Theory Y

The other end of the spectrum proposed by McGregor is predicated upon the following assumptions:

1. The expenditure of physical and mental effort in work is as natural as in play or rest and the average human being learns, under proper conditions, not only to accept responsibility but to seek it.
2. People will exercise self direction and self control in the service of objectives to which they are committed and this commitment is a function of the rewards associated with their achievement.
3. The intellectual potential of the average person is only partly used in organizational settings and the capacity to exercise a relatively high

degree of imagination, ingenuity and creativity in the solution of organizational problems is widely, not narrowly, distributed in the population.

McGregor concluded that his Theory Y approach to behavior is the best one for managers to follow. Many managers have observed that in some companies and situations, a management style leaning toward the "Taylor" approach (Theory X) works while in others it fails miserably, and conversely, a management style leaning toward Theory Y, while having successful application in some situations, does not always work well in others.

In trying to resolve this difficulty, Morse and Lorsch (op. cit.) developed a contingency theory based on the nature of the task or work. They propose that managers "must design and develop organizations so that the organizational characteristics fit the nature of the task to be done." They further state:

"Enterprises with highly predictable tasks perform better with organizations characterized by the highly formalized procedures and management hierarchies of the classical approach. With highly uncertain tasks that require more extensive problem solving, on the other hand, organizations that are less formal and emphasize self-control and member participation in decision making are more effective."

To test their contingency theory, Morse and Lorsch conducted a study involving four plants or organizational units. Two of these performed relatively certain tasks: manufacturing standardized containers on high-speed, automated production lines (Akron plant and Hartford plant). The other two (Stockton labs and Camel labs) performed the relatively uncertain work of research and development in communications technology. One of each pair was evaluated by that company's management as highly effective (Akron and Stockton) and one as less effective (Hartford and Camel).

In brief, they found that the more effective manufacturing plant (Akron) tended toward a more formalized and controlling organization (Theory X) while the less effective plant tended toward a less formalized and controlling organization (Theory Y). In the research and development organizations, however, the opposite was true. The more effective research and development organization (Stockton Labs) tended toward a less formalized and controlling organization (Theory Y) while the less effective (Camel Labs) tended toward a more formalized and controlling organization (Theory X). Thus, the successful organizations were different in character (one tended toward Theory X the other Theory Y) but in each the management style in the organization apparently fit the requirements of its task very well.

Morse and Lorsch concluded that the task-organization fit is simultaneously linked to both individual motivation and effective unit performance. The implications for managers is the selection of an appropriate set of actions that will move them toward a task-organization fit. The proper question is not "Theory X or Y?" but "What organizational approach is most appropriate, given the task and the people?" (See Exhibit I.)

MASLOW'S NEED HIERARCHY

The Taylor theory of motivation presented a view of people as motivated to restore equilibrium. Satisfaction and inactivity were regarded as normal states (McGregor's Theory X). But for Maslow (op. cit.), the satisfaction of a need did not imply satiation and quiescence. Maslow postulated that

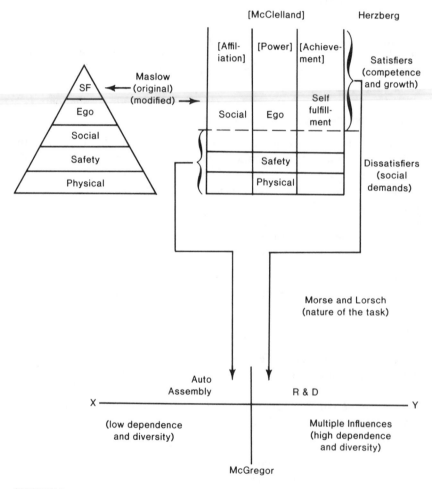

EXHIBIT 1

people are continuously in a motivated state but that the nature of the motivation is fluctuating and complex. Further, Maslow theorized that human beings rarely reach a state of complete satisfaction except for brief moments. He regarded activity to satisfy ever changing needs as the normal state. He put it this way:

"Gratification of one need and its consequent removal from the center of the stage brings about not a state of rest, but rather the emergence into consciousness of another, higher need."

As one desire becomes satisfied, another takes its place, and as this desire becomes satisfied, still another replaces it. This sequence of emerging needs formed the basis of Maslow's *hierarchy of needs.* The basic human needs that Maslow defined are:

1. Physiological needs (food, air, water)
2. Safety needs (order, stability, rules)
3. Social needs (affiliation, love)
4. Ego needs (status, respect of peers)
5. Self-fulfillment needs (self-actualization)

Maslow hypothesized that these sets of needs are arranged in a hierarchy starting with the physiological needs at the bottom, progressing through safety needs and so on, to the need for self-fulfillment which stands at the top. According to Maslow, the lower needs in the hierarchy must be satisfied before the higher needs can emerge. In other words, one will experience the ego needs only after physiological, safety and social needs are met.

Nevertheless, in highly professional organizations such as R & D groups, many people seem to be motivated by social, ego and self-fulfillment simultaneously. Some people appear to have these needs to a degree that can never be fully satisfied. Thus, it seems reasonable to modify Maslow's concepts so that the three highest needs operate in parallel and are open ended. Both the original and modified Maslow concepts are shown as part of Exhibit I.

HERZBERG'S TWO FACTOR THEORY

Herzberg (op. cit.) postulated that "the factors involved in producing job satisfaction (which produces motivation) are separate and distinct from the factors that lead to job dissatisfaction (which produces hostility)." The two feelings of satisfaction are not opposites of each other but separate and distinct:

"The opposite of job satisfaction is not job dissatisfaction, but rather NO job satisfaction; and similarly, the opposite of job dissatisfaction is not job satisfaction but NO job dissatisfaction."

Contemporary society is seen to guarantee satisfaction of the lower needs (Maslow's physiological and safety needs, and at least a small increment of satisfaction in the higher needs). Thus, the purpose of work behavior is not to satisfy these lower needs: "The best types of feelings that such (lower) need fulfillment can lead to is job attitude neutrality." However, if management should interfere with the otherwise assumed fulfillment of these lower needs, such as might be the case under arbitrary layoff and firing procedures, then not having these "hygiene" needs fulfilled leads to dissatisfaction as expressed by hostility, conflict and/or crisis.

The other set of needs, "satisfiers," relates to higher human nature: Maslow's social, ego or self-esteem and self-fulfillment needs. Since contemporary society does not guarantee fulfillment of these needs, the purpose of work behavior is to do so. Thus, Herzberg postulates that when a job presents the worker with opportunities to satisfy these higher needs, he or she will be motivated to better work performance. Here again, Herzberg postulates, if the jobs does not offer opportunities to satisfy these higher order needs, it will not lead to job dissatisfaction but rather to job attitude neutrality and to motivation.

Herzberg argues that satisfiers are the motivators by which to obtain commitment and drive; therefore, management should provide jobs that offer opportunities for achievement, recognition, challenge, growth, responsibility and accomplishment. At the same time, management must prevent what Herzberg calls the "hygiene" factors (Maslow's lower level needs)—company policy and administration, supervision, interpersonal relationships, working conditions, salary, status and security—from becoming sources of dissatisfaction, leading to hostility.

To the question "How do you motivate employees?", Herzberg has but one answer: "The only way to motivate the capable employee is to give him challenging work for which he can assume responsibility" (and thus derive at least partial satisfaction of his higher needs). The best of all possible job *contexts* or job environments can only remove any dissatisfiers. To promote job satisfaction and motivation, one needs to provide a good job *content*. Herzberg's concept can be viewed as a special application of Maslow in a highly complex industrialized society, in organizations having tasks and people more appropriate to McGregor's Theory Y.

MCCLELLAND'S NEEDS FOR ACHIEVEMENT, AFFILIATION AND POWER

David McClelland (op. cit.) developed a theory of motivation based on the relative strengths of the needs for achievement, affiliation and power. Originally most concerned with his belief that the need for achievement was central to effective managerial behavior, McClelland later became convinced that the need for power was equally important and that, in fact, the relative strengths of all three needs (in effect, a motivational profile) had to be analyzed in the context of the kind of organization the individual was managing.

The need for achievement governs an individual's orientation to tasks he faces in the organization. Is the person motivated by the rewards for a job well done? The needs for affiliation and power govern an individual's interpersonal relationships. Does the person seek friends, strive for leadership, is he or she warm and friendly? By examining Maslow's upper three levels in a totally different way and redefining them, they can approximate McClelland's power, achievement and affiliation needs. McClelland's affiliation needs are analogous to Maslow's social needs and his achievement needs appear related to Maslow's needs for self-fulfillment. Power needs appear to embrace some social and self-fulfillment needs, but seem more related to ego needs since power puts us "above" others and gives us status. (See Exhibit I.)

MULTIPLE INFLUENCES

In our current increasingly complex society, Kotter (op. cit.) notes increasing "dependencies" and "diversities" among people in organizations. Our own observations are consistent with this view and we further postulate that people's actions derive from multiple, not singular, influences. At least three interdependent sets of influences are operating: expectations, self image or self concept, and intrinsic factors. The last of these multiple influences leads people to be reactive, while the first two lead people to be proactive (controlled) in their responses in any given situation. Personality, subconscious biases and even long forgotten experiences (Zaleznik and Kets de Vries op. cit.) are among the intrinsic influences leading to reactive behavior. Thus, the response depends on which set of influences is dominant at the time. The resulting behavior of an associate may be quite different from what the manager anticipates or what it would have been if a different set of influences had been dominant. Thus, the motivations of an individual will be different depending on which set of influences are dominant.

By negotiating expectations and understanding the "diversities's' and backgrounds of those upon whom the manager is "dependent," he or she can predict reactive and proactive responses of individuals or groups. By selecting the time and method of interaction with others the manager can enhance the probability of the desired reactive or proactive response to further organizational goals and objectives.

The degree to which these sets of influences are different appears to be related to 1) the amount of dependencies and diversities inherent in the organization as suggested by the level of ambiguity, uncertainty, and complexity; and 2) the number of different experiences that have occurred in the individual's past as suggested by a) cultural background, b) education, c) professional achievements and status, and d) organizational achievements or position in the hierarchy of the organization. The greater the dependencies, diversity and number of experiences, the greater the apparent degree of difference. The first of these seems to correspond with the Morse and Lorsch task-organization fit and both fit with Kotter's "dependencies" and "diversities." This suggests that in complex organizations where a Theory Y style is effective, the multiple influence model will have greater application than in less complex organizations where a Theory X style is more effective.

INTEGRATION

The results of integrating and summarizing these various theories of motivation as revised and reformed can be expressed diagrammatically (Exhibit I). Note that Maslow's lower level needs are allied to Herzberg's hygiene factors or "dissatisfiers" and that these, in turn, are the motivational factors most often observed operating in McGregor's Theory X type organizations. Conversely, Maslow's higher level needs, analogous to Herzberg's "satisfiers," are the dominant motivational factors observed in organizations treading toward a Theory Y style of work and management. McClelland's affiliation, power and achievement needs are a somewhat different amalgam of Maslow's three higher level needs.

Industrial societies as a whole are becoming more ambiguous, uncertain and complex, levels of education and diversity of backgrounds are increasing, and larger numbers of people view themselves as professionals who must depend on each other for the achievement of organizational goals and objectives. This suggests that in these complex societies the midpoint on the Theory X-Theory Y spectrum is shifting to the right while the dotted line between satisfiers and dissatisfiers in the Herzberg scheme is moving upward.

We conclude the following:

1. Herzberg's dissatisfiers are similar to Maslow's first two levels of need plus some small increment in each of the top three needs in his hierarchy.
2. These dissatisfiers tend to be related to the autocratic structured management style of Taylor or McGregor's Theory X.
3. Morse and Lorsch have identified this autocratic style as more effective for routine tasks.
4. Herzberg's satisfiers are similar to Maslow's top three levels of need.
5. McClelland's achievement, power and affiliation needs are a different mix of Maslow's top three levels of need.
6. These satisfiers are related to the participative management style described by McGregor as theory Y.

7. This style, according to Morse and Lorsch, appears more effective for tasks with high levels of complexity.
8. The nature of the people and of the tasks being performed causes higher and higher levels of dependency, diversity, uncertainty, complexity, education and professionalism. Therefore, the greater the observed difference between reactive and proactive behavior, and the greater the applicability of Multiple Influences.

As a result of modifying these motivational concepts in order to tie them together in an integrated model, the manager is able to see relationships among them. This integrated model provides an analytical framework for any supervisor or manager trying to improve the performance of individuals, groups or the entire organization.

USING THE INTEGRATED MOTIVATIONAL MODELS

Many, if not most, managers believe that they should study motivation to better understand what influences or motivates their employees. While this focus can be helpful in understanding the behavior of individuals or groups, no simple theory or model addresses the two most important tasks of the manager: first, building and using relationships to achieve organizational goals and objectives, and second, designing work systems and developing an organizational climate that motivate most employees toward higher levels of performance.

Human Resources Management

The integrated motivation model is an important contributor to decisions on fundamental policies affecting the management of the organization's human resources. It simplifies the manager's task by demonstrating that, while each of the theories embraced by the model have made specific contributions, there is no essential disagreement between them but rather a different application, depending on the people and environment in each situation.

It seems clear, for instance, that the assumptions about human behavior associated with McGregor's Theory Y and supported by the higher level motivational needs of Maslow, McClelland and Herzberg all point toward design of work systems emphasizing responsibility, participation and commitment of workers at all organizational levels. This approach is most appropriate in our highly complex society in organizations with high levels of interdependence and diversity (Kotter op. cit.).

In "Managing Human Assets"[13] the authors present two alternate work systems. Model A (the traditional work system) and Model B (the high-commitment work system). Model A is based on Theory X assumptions and lower level needs of the theorists (effective in organizations with low levels of interdependence and diversity or in less complex societies). Model B is based on theory Y and higher level needs. While acknowledging that the traditional work systems have been applicable to blue-collar and clerical workers while high-commitment work systems have been reserved for professional and managerial systems, the authors note that successful experiments have been conducted recently, especially in new organizations, applying Model B to all levels, including blue collar and clerical. They project increasing reliance on Model B to achieve optimum performance in our increasingly high-tech society.

Examples

Two specific examples, both involving clerical personnel, demonstrate the use of the integrated model. In most organizations in our highly complex society, a manager has a high dependency on his or her secretary and there is often a high level of diversity between their backgrounds and experience. Thus, the relationship between them can be strengthened by a Theory Y, multiple influence approach in behavior. Beyond this, the manager can use a Model B approach (high commitment work system) in modifying the secretary's job to include greater responsibility, participation, and opportunities for increased contribution and personal competence. This will lead to greater mutual respect, less status differentiation, high level of mutual affiliation and referent power (reciprocity)[14] and therefore higher levels of performance.

On the other hand, if the manager does not see or accept the high dependency and diversity and approaches the secretary in a Theory X manner—as an extension of a typewriter or word processor—and uses a Model A (the traditional work system) approach to define the secretary's job, the integrated model tells us that the secretary's motivation, performance and job satisfaction will be minimal.

Another example of the utility of the integrated model is the typing or work processing pool. In a Theory X approach by managers who assume low levels of dependence and diversity and use the traditional model A to design the work of the pool, people will be placed in single skill, simple positions for which they are already qualified or can be easily trained. The usual result of this approach is low motivation, low performance and low job satisfaction leading to low morale, high turnover and excessive training costs. What does the integrated model tell us about this situation? It tells us that the plus values of the traditional highly structured and supervised pool organization are not really plus values in our complex society.

If we shift our assumptions in the theory Y direction, we can see that the integrated model gives us a different orientation. We see the need for relatively small, self directed teams of word processors highly interactive with a small group of managers. In this way, strong cooperative relationships are built and the word processor teams gain status and job satisfaction; they accept tasks as a team and gain acceptance and rewards as an effective self-governing and evaluating team, possibly in competition with other teams. Using the integrated model in organizations with high levels of dependency or diversity tells us that the high commitment work system (model B) reinforced with a positive Theory Y management style, leads to high motivation, productivity and the real cost-effectiveness of a secretarial or word processing pool.

The integrated model tells the manager how to adjust managerial style to the realities of human motivation in the workplace and how to proceed in developing work systems, given the social and organizational environment and the nature of the people.

NOTES

1. John P. Kotter, *Power and Influence,* The Free Press, a division of Macmillan Co., New York, NY 1985, p. 22 (diversity p. 17, expectations pp. 108/109).
2. Abraham Zaleznik and Manfred F. R. Kets de Vries, *Power and the Corporate Mind.* Bonus Books, Chicago, IL, 1985 (2nd Ed.) p. xii.
3. Harry E. Wilkinson, Robert Benfari and Charles D. Orth, "Influencing People in Organizations", UAI, Potomac, MD 1986.
4. Arthur W. Combs and Donald Snygg, *Individual Behavior: A Perceptual Approach to Behavior,* Harper & Row, New York, NY, 1959, pp. 126–144.
5. Frederick W. Taylor, *Scientific Management,* Dartmouth College, Hanover, NH, 1912.
6. Douglas McGregor, *The Human Side of Enterprise,* McGraw-Hill, New York, 1960.
7. Abraham H. Maslow, *Motivation and Personality,* Harper, New York, 1964.
8. Frederick Herzberg, *Work and the Nature or Man.* World Publishing Co., New York, 1966.
9. David C. McClelland, *The Achieving Society,* D. Van Nostrand Co., New York, NY, 1961.
10. John J. Morse and Jay W. Lorsch, "Beyond Theory Y", Harvard Business Review, May/June 1970, pp. 61–68.
11. Thomas J. Peters and Robert H. Waterman, Jr., *In Search of Excellence,* Harper & Row, New York, 1982.
12. Richard T. Pascale and Anthony G. Athos, *The Art of Japanese Management,* Warner Books, New York, 1981.
13. Michael Beer, Bert Spector, Paul R. Lawrence, D. Quinn Mills and Richard E. Walton *Managing Human Assets.* The Free Press, A division of Macmillan Inc., New York, N.Y. 1984, pp. 164–175.
14. Robert C. Benfari, Harry E. Wilkinson, Charles D. Orth, "The Effective use of Power", *Business Horizons,* May/June 1986, pp. 12–16.

Try to Understand the Forces of Motivation

Bob Williams

You don't need to delve deeply into human behavior but it helps to understand how people and companies behave

When we form a limited company we form a new legal entity, a corporate 'person', and the key to understanding even for most complicated organization is to consider corporate behavior in the same way that we would consider the behavior of a person and the behavior of small groups or families. The patterns of behavior, although more complex in the larger organization, will be subject to similar pressures.

The purpose of this article is to consider why and how companies, partnerships and entrepreneurs, are motivated to behave in certain ways: particularly, why some are content with following and being controlled by the market, while others strive to lead, innovate or control.

While not wishing to delve too deeply into the psychological theories we cannot escape the fact that the motivation of entrepreneurs and companies is inextricably linked with and bounded by the precepts of human behavior. Companies are, after all, groups of people interacting with other groups. We can express and explain these behavioral patterns by considering some simple models which have remained consistently useful and provide a summary of the types of group behavior that affect motivation.

The first and most important types are described by Warren Bennis and Herbert Shepard in the following terms: *dependence; counterdependence; interdependence.* Dr. Bion of the Tavistock Institute of Human Relations refers to: *forming, norming, storming, performing.*

We can easily relate the Bennis and Shepard model to our own childhood and to the childhood of those close to us.

Dependence. The stage of childhood where we are dependant on our parents for protection, ideas etc. and from which we grow.

Reprinted with permission from *Accountancy,* Vol. 97, pp. 90 ff, May 1986.
Bob Williams FCMA Minsht MICM is managing director of Cleveland Davis, Business and Management Consultants, who specialize in company strategy.

Counterdependence. As we grow, much as the teenager, we become dissatisfied with projecting the image and wishes of our parents. We react against those images, rejecting 'their' values and attempting to develop our own in an adolescent phase, seeking to stamp our own mark on the world.

Interdependence. With greater maturity we realize that we need the help of others and develop an interdependent attitude.

So it is with new companies, businesses and partnerships. First, in a dependency phase, the group 'forms' and group behavior is 'normalizing'—the group identity and purpose is far more important than the needs of the individuals in the group. As the group develops the members express a desire to make their own mark, impose their own character and exhibit trends of deviance and counterdependence. Eventually, as these deviant trends are seen to be counterproductive in isolation, although sometimes useful, a stage of interdependence is reached where the values and desires of the individuals are recognized by each other but are pooled to strengthen the collective contribution.

In this scenario leaders develop. Initially as counterdependents, they are often isolated for their deviance and either rejected from the group, or they dominate the group. Eventually, either of these states is found to be unacceptable by both parties who realize the advantages of the contribution of the others in an interdependent role. These patterns of behavior are common to all groups, whether the local scout troop, a company board, or the Cabinet.

In a small start-up situation between two or three entrepreneurs, these stages of development—in which the three needs of the 'group', the 'task' and the 'individual' combine towards effective purpose, or diverge away from effectiveness—can be clearly seen. Initially the team members are very task-oriented and will subserve their needs to that of achieving the task. Once the task becomes routine, the team members are liable to start to give precedence to their own needs (why can he get away with doing X when I have to do Y: why does he earn more than me? etc.).

Group leadership may change and the style of group decision-making will change. Eventually the group members accept that the contribution of each is different, that the group is stronger together than apart, and that it must satisfy the needs of the group as well as looking to the needs of the task if it is to function effectively. Further, it must also satisfy the needs of its members.

But we need to be careful about simplistic models, for even in a one-man scenario, the analogy to human stages of development is somewhat of an oversimplification. In different scenarios, and at different times, we all tend to choose to adopt, or are pushed into different roles. The same person will in one situation be leader, the 'counterdependent' on the verge of interdependence, and in another the pacifist interdependent or the 'childlike' accepter and follower.

HIERARCHY OF NEEDS

To be successful a group needs a blend of leaders, followers, activists, rationalists and pacifists. Groups full of entrepreneurs are likely to be more stormy: groups of administrators more passive. However, each will develop its own leaders and work through the same phases. Over and above these stages of development and group needs we have an overlay of individual needs. Tabled by the behavioral scientist Maslow as a 'hierarchy of needs', these related to our physical requirements at any point in time.

At the foot of the pyramid we have the needs for food and shelter, the physical needs. When these are satisfied we move up the pyramid to consider our safety. Not just physical safety but also reassurance that we are not operating in a malign environment. When these needs are satisfied we next consider our social needs, to be an accepted part of society, and then the needs of our own ego—the ability to respect ourselves and have respect for others. Only when we have satisfied ourselves in these respects can we consider the luxury of self-fulfillment, the need to make the most of and develop our own capabilities.

By combining these three models described—stages of growth, the group/task/individual relationship and the hierarchy of needs—we can intelligently reflect on the behavior of most individuals and groups.

What is it, then, that motivates a business? Why do some succeed while others fail? How can we identify the team most likely to succeed?

First we need to understand that in business there is not an order of progression as simple as that implied by looking at a traditional organization chart. Second, we need to remember that different people have different abilities, skills and limitations.

Traditionally, the young cadre of an organization are exposed to different environments of increasing responsibility until the most able are identified and promoted. However, life is not as simple as this implies, and the group in which any particularly aspiring manager will have to compete will be comprised of people who are all different stages of their personal development. Nor is it as simple as progressive development, for external events push us up and down the hierarchy of needs, and roles chosen or forced on us push us into behavioral patterns that then trap us into responding in certain ways. (For example, the most experienced person in a group will normally be pushed into a 'father' figure role; a team member under attack will be pressured to react, not in the way he wants to, but in accordance with the behavior that the other team members expect.)

QUESTIONS TO ASK

To understand how a group is working and to maximize the chances of being able to influence that group, it is therefore necessary to take a step back and first consider the motivations of its individual members. Having done this, one can then apply the same analysis to the group. Is its survival threatened or is it well-established and likely to be more altruistic, less dominant and perhaps divisive? What is currently going on in the group? Who is adopting which roles? Is leadership or direction being challenged? If so, by whom and why? Is the real problem being talked about, or is some issue a front for some greater problem that is being avoided?

Groups under threat and those that are dealing most with security needs tend to be very cohesive and task-oriented while that threat is present. The nature of work-life in a society with almost four million unemployed will therefore be more task-oriented, subserving the needs of the individual to that of the group or task. However, a consequence of this is that the group does not service its needs properly and is therefore weaker. Dominance by individuals (leaders) is more pronounced, as is inequality. By complete contrast however, in areas of high unemployment considerable apathy can develop in respect of the task (which is seen to be likely to fail in any event), but group cohesiveness can still develop. The risk of this sociocohesiveness is that the group will then create its own tasks which may be considered delinquent (e.g., vandalism), antisocial (law-breaking) or even revolutionary or anarchistic.

Within the larger organization, the more remote the threat of survival of the business, the more the social demands of the group will enforce themselves. The further up the hierarchy one moves, the more complex the group dynamics become. By definition, these groups will be dominated by those who retain enough counterdependency to wish to succeed/dominate. The internal politics will become more complex and the stakes of the game higher until the competition between individuals—the 'power game'—threatens the business survival of the key figures and sometimes the business itself. Indeed, in businesses that operate outside of the law, actual survival may also be at risk. (The analysis, comprehension and management of the power game is a specialized subject beyond the scope of this article.)

Most readers will either be familiar with, or have heard of McGregor's studies of Theory X (controlling, checking and inspecting) and Theory Y (self-actualizing, self-propelling, self-developing) management styles, and it is important to recognize that the style of management will affect the behavior of the company.

HERZBERG ON MOTIVATION

But how can we explain motivation? The clearest work here has been carried out by Herzberg. Although much of his work oversimplifies, it is very easy to understand. He was dissatisfied with the absence of positive suggestions and strategies that sociologists had produced and so he studied the task aspects of the driving forces of the business. He recognized that reward and motivation were not simply 'carrot and stick' measures and could be divided into those that truly motivated—the potential 'satisfiers'—and those that were potential dissatisfiers—the 'hygiene' factors.

The importance of this separation is the realization that some alleged motivators did not truly motivate, but they needed to be satisfied so that the jobholder could forget about them and concentrate on work. If dissatisfied by these 'demotivators', he/she would be diverted from the task or motivation, but these factors did not, by themselves, motivate. These potential dissatisfiers were identified as company policy and administration, interpersonal relationships, technical supervision, pay, security and status.

It has to be understood that Herzberg's studies were largely carried out in a period of high employment, labor unrest, and natural pay growth over and above inflation. His work remains, however, the most comprehensible and simple explanation as to why some organizations find it difficult to motivate. Obviously the current environment is somewhat different and I have attempted to update the model for the 1980s. Herzberg derided the bonus and piece-rate systems because they were invariably 'adjusted' so that a bonus could always be earned and, as such, simply became part of the expected level of pay, which was a dissatisfier if reduced in real terms. The motivator thus ceased to motivate and became just a cause for complaint.

Experience since this date has lead me to conclude that, while this is true in many situations and particularly true in respect of company-wide profit sharing bonuses, the 'reality' of the 1980s has lead not only to an acceptance that reward should be linked to sales achievement, but that this is eminently desirable as an alternative to the 'cost of wages' being seen as an overhead cost that must be contained and reduced. For the 1980s at least, and in respect of situations or teams which can identify their output and relate it to their efforts, this way out of the overhead syndrome can be a direct motivator.

In my own company, the rewards of the consultants are linked to their own income-generation and the rewards of the administrators are related to a simple-to-manage system. Each person is provided with a bonus potential of 10% of salary. The 'natural' level is 0%. Monthly each person advises his/her manager of how much bonus he/she should receive and is asked to justify it. Particular achievements and contributions over and above the norm can thus be justified. Managers may not pay the staff they manage more than an additional 5% overall. I have therefore changed Herzberg's hygiene factor and introduced a new motivation, 'individual profit sharing'. The revision must be correct. If it were not, entrepreneurs would not seek their fortunes by leaving secure jobs and venturing out.

WHAT MOTIVATES?

What, then, motivates one man to set up and develop his own business? I have mentioned fortune seeking but this is not the complete answer, for it is partly due to his need to be in control—and the successful businessman will often find it difficult to share that control as his company expands—partly it is a need to compete and win, and partly it may reflect a stage where membership of a group is not important. He will not obtain sufficient motivation within the confines and income discipline of the larger company and will seek direct control over the motivating factors.

Thus the successful small businessman is more likely to be a loner, or one who sees little threat in failure (where loss of business, wealth or face does not significantly threaten his faith in himself). Here we have an important separation: those who need to succeed and to prove their success, and those who just wish to tread their own path. The former are more likely to gain business growth, the latter to tread their own path purely for self-actualization rather than financial reward.

To gain a useful understanding of the behavioral forces motivating your own work situation, or that of a client—who may be an individual or a group of companies—it is necessary to take a step back from the task and to ask yourself some simple questions: how far has the client developed in person at this point in time? What is the client seeking to achieve? The answer may not always be the obvious one, especially if the client is behaving defensively. If you can relate to a client in terms that equate with his own goals—and whether you agree or disagree is almost irrelevant—then the chances of his accepting your advice will be greatly improved, and the advice that you are offering is likely to be more relevant to his needs. This does not mean saying just 'yes' or giving the answer he wants to hear, but giving an answer that he sees as relevant, not just 'more useless advice from yet another accountant who doesn't understand.'

In your own work environment, an improved knowledge of why colleagues (and you) are acting in certain ways will help you to develop your work relationships and not be trapped into reacting in ways that will be detrimental to the achievement of all of your goals. Sensibly used, this understanding can help to create a situation where you can motivate yourself more constructively. ■

How to Build Employee Commitment

William L. Ginnodo

Commitment: The state of being bound emotionally or intellectually to some course of action.

—American Heritage Dictionary

Faced by increasing costs, competition, budget cuts and work pressures, managers are searching for ways to get more from their employees. In that search, it is important that they understand that building commitment is not the same thing as motivating employees. The two approaches are philosophically different, and they get quite different results.

Most North American managers have been taught that the way to get work done through people is to *motivate* them—that is, find a way to drive them, sometimes through the use of incentives. This approach is based on the assumption that managers should make the decisions and employees should follow orders.

If you're supervising only Depression-era or World War II-era employees, that may work reasonably well because they tend to value security, money, stability, and company loyalty. They may have doubts about your orders, but they will usually comply with them to avoid jeopardizing their situations.

Today's younger workers have a different outlook: They most highly value meaningful work, autonomy, inner growth, and recognition. If they don't like your orders, they will probably do only the minimum needed to get by—and apply their primary energies outside the workplace.

It is very difficult to *motivate* this new breed of employee, because money is less important to them than their central values, and they can easi-

Reprinted with permission from NATIONAL PRODUCTIVITY REVIEW, V8N3, Summer 1989. Copyright 1989 by Executive Enterprises, Inc., 22 West 21st Street, New York, NY 10010-6904. All Rights Reserved.

William L. Ginnodo is president of PRIDE Publications, Inc. and publisher of Commitment-Plus newsletter in Arlington Heights, Illinois. Previously, he was associate director of the American Productivity Management Association, productivity coordinator for a division of Westinghouse Electric Corporation, and division chief for the U.S. Office of Personnel Management. This article is based on is visits to more than fifty North American organizations during the past four years.

ly find other jobs. But, as high-performance managers in many organizations have demonstrated, it is possible to take nonmanipulative actions that turn on employees and move them to high levels of commitment and performance (see **Figure 1**).

DISCRETIONARY EFFORT: WHERE THE ACTION IS

The key to obtaining higher levels of commitment and performance is to create an environment for *self-motivation.* In such an environment, employees voluntarily apply more discretionary effort on their jobs.

What is *discretionary effort?* In *Putting the Work Ethic to Work,* a 1983 research report for the Public Agenda Foundation, Daniel Yankelovich and

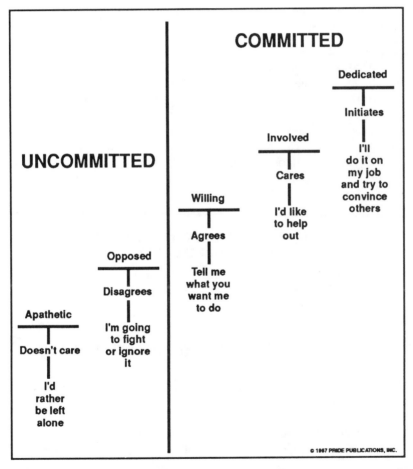

FIGURE 1 LEVELS OF COMMITMENT IN THE WORKPLACE

John Immerwahr liken it to discretionary income—the money that's available to spend after expenses and taxes have been paid—noting that it is "the difference between the maximum amount of effort and care an individual could bring to his or her job, and the minimum amount of effort required to avoid being fired or penalized; in short, the portion of one's effort over which a jobholder has the greatest control. Put another way, discretionary effort focuses our attention on that portion of effort that is controlled by the jobholder, rather than by the employer or the inherent nature of the work."

During their in-depth interviews of a random sample of American workers, Yankelovich and Immerwahr learned that "fewer than one out of four (23%) say they are currently working at their full potential, while nearly half (44%) say they do not put any more effort into their jobs than is required to hold on to them. The overwhelming majority (75%) say that they could be significantly more effective on their jobs than they are now."

Referring to this mental outlook as a "commitment gap," the authors present persuasive evidence that:

- the gap is widening.
- the United States is unlikely to revive its competitive vitality without addressing the commitment gap.
- managerial training and skill have not kept pace with the changes that have affected the workplace; as a result, the actions of managers blunt rather than stimulate and reinforce the work ethic.
- because managers can no longer stimulate effort through the existing reward system and through traditional methods of supervision, they must rely on jobholders' internal motivations to guarantee high levels of effort and good quality work.

THE HIGH-PERFORMANCE MANAGER: WORTH WORKING FOR

There are, of course, managers who effectively tap the internal motivations of people and thereby stimulate and reinforce the work ethic. They can be called *high-performance managers,* because they get high performance from their employees.

In more than six hundred interviews with managers and employees, I have learned that high-performance managers:

- Have a sense of mission, are results-oriented and clear on priorities, lead the way, and communicate expectations;
- Are proactive regarding issues, know when to ask "Why?", and are unafraid to tackle problems;
- Are approachable, open to new ideas, willing to listen, and respectful of others;

- Delegate, coach, trust, allow others to fail, and provide needed resources;
- Share information, are consistent and flexible, and have integrity and a sense of humor; and
- Recognize good performance, show appreciation, and promote teamwork.

Interestingly, the people who identified these characteristics also acknowledged that high-performance managers are hard to find. Many said that they would like to work for one themselves! Why? Because such managers make work psychologically rewarding. As one manager noted, "If work is psychologically rewarding, it turns us on and causes us to be proud of what we do."

THE ACTION LEVERS: SIX CRITICAL SUCCESS FACTORS

But how do high-performance managers make work psychologically rewarding? The answer: They pull the right *action levers*. The Public Agenda Foundation report noted, "Managers hold the 'action levers' that have a significant effect on how much commitment people will invest in their jobs, or, to put it another way, how much discretionary effort people will invest in their work."

Based on my observations of high-performance managers in fifty-three companies and public sector organizations throughout North America, I believe these are the action levers that cause people to apply more discretionary effort on their jobs:

1. Focus on Mission and Values

To help speed and solidify the Ford Motor Company's recovery in the mid-1980s, its management developed a statement designed to tell everyone what the company stands for. Called the "Mission, Values and Guiding Principles," or MVGP, it is framed and hung on walls throughout the corporation. The MVGP is a constant reminder that:

- Ford is involved in several dynamic industries: automotive, aerospace, communications, and financial services.
- success depends on people, products and profits.
- quality, customer service, continuous improvement, employee involvement, partnership with dealers and suppliers, and integrity are everybody's business.

But developing and distributing the MVGP was just the beginning. An explanatory booklet was mailed to the homes of Ford's 185,000 employees, along with a letter signed by Chairman Donald E. Petersen. And meetings were held—starting with top management and cascading to all levels—to discuss the meaning and application of the MVGP.

Why go to such lengths? "We want everyone to use the MVGP in their day-to-day activities," said Paul Banas, Ford's manager of employee development strategy. Is it making a difference? "At this facility, we live by the Mission, Values and Guiding Principles," responded Bill Smith, manager of Ford's Maumee, Ohio, Stamping Plant. "Both the union and management support the concepts, totally. It's a way of life here; we know people and quality are number one, and every decision is based on that."

Many organizations—whether at the corporate, divisional, or unit level—have developed mission and value statements. They underline the uniqueness of the organization, give work special meaning, mobilize people, and unify them around common causes. In short, they *inspire* people. And the managers who use them in a positive, nonmanipulative way are winning their people's minds and hearts.

2. Emphasize Continuous Improvement

Why is continuous improvement a turn-on for employees? Sometimes it isn't. Unless they see something in it for themselves, people generally don't respond to posters, pep talks, or threats exhorting them to work harder, faster, or smarter. Employees often regard productivity and technological improvements and cost reductions as benefiting only the company, management, or shareholders.

But improving quality or service is quite a different matter. That's done for a *good cause:* to satisfy the customer. Everyone can get behind that. And doing it is psychologically rewarding, a source of pride. The Public Agenda Foundation report was very explicit on this point. "Nothing corrodes the work ethic more than the perception that employers and managers are indifferent to quality," it noted. "Conversely, a strict, even harsh emphasis on the highest standards of quality reinforces the conviction that work has an intrinsic worth and meaning."

That's why the adage, "If it ain't broke, don't fix it", is so out of tune with modern employee perceptions. Behind it is often a management mindset that says, "The status quo is OK, let's not change things." Employees know that *everything* can be improved, if only in small ways. Just ask them and they will tell you how.

3. Involve Employees

TRW's chairman and chief executive officer, Joseph Gorman, provided the high-performance manager's rationale for involving employees when he observed, "We're in a crisis situation, and we're steadily losing ground. We need an ongoing minor labor-management miracle, not just for this year but for next and the year after, knowing that our competitors will be trying equally hard. Business-as-usual must be totally unacceptable. The change must be fundamental and pervasive. And it must involve *all* in the organization—from top management to production workers, both line and staff. No one and no function can be immune; all must contribute. Nothing can be sacred!''

Managers at TRW use a range of employee involvement techniques, tailored to fit their situations. These techniques include quality circles, adhoc improvement teams, self-contained work cells, self-managing work teams, and suggestion systems. Managers also take the time to walk around and ask individuals for their ideas. The goal, said Gorman, is to "end up with a work force that cares more, knows more, and does more.''

4. Remove Barriers

In the work environment, a barrier is anything that keeps people from performing at their best. And since, as the Public Agenda Foundation study found, 75 percent of workers could be significantly more effective on their jobs than they are now, there must be a lot of barriers in the workplace. **Figure 2** shows the areas in which barriers that affect commitment, self-motivation, and performance, lie.

If you ask a cross section of white-collar employees whether they and their supervisors are clear on work expectations, they will answer "Yes" only 25 percent of the time. Ask blue-collar employees how much time they spend each day searching for tools or materials, and chances are many will say something like, "Two hours." Finally, if you ask workers if they think they have had enough training to do their jobs in an exceptional manner, most will answer with a resounding "No." Yet, managers often allow these problems to persist for years. And not surprisingly, the typical employee reaction is, "If management doesn't care, why should I?"

When managers do care, and begin using employee involvement techniques to start a dialogue, people respond willingly and appreciatively with ideas that make their managers and organizations look good. The fact is, most individuals want to produce products or services that they can be proud of.

5. Measure and Share Results

Both employees and managers have an aversion to measurements that are used to drive or manipulate them. But they do like to know what the group score is—how they are doing compared to the competition, the prior period, or customer expectations. Here is what four managers have told me about the importance of score-keeping in their organizations:

- "We've exploded the myth of low productivity in the public sector," said Ron Contino, deputy commissioner in New York City's Department of Sanitation. "All it takes is a willingness on the part of management to involve labor in the decision-making process, and some degree of im-

FIGURE 2 THE MAJOR BARRIERS

agination in devising ways to accurately—but in a nonthreatening way—measure operational efficiency.''

- "Everyone felt a responsibility to work together, solve problems, and meet the schedule,'' said Jim Davis, product manager of Xerox's 1020 copier line, after he installed three large charts in the production area, which were updated daily, showing the number of copiers produced, the percentage of direct-free machines, and the percentage of employees on the job.
- "We're administering a client survey that asks questions about five factors that are important to customer service in financial institutions,'' said Bob Aylward, manager of customer service and operations at the Royal Bank of Canada in the Toronto area "The survey information is consolidated on a bar graph and presented to the staff in the branch so they

gain a clear understanding of the client's perception of our service. Then, the staff zeros in on weak or priority areas."

- "Our system of performance indicators isn't perfect yet," said Walt Doughton, assistant vice president of new member sales at USAA insurance company. "But we can now tell how individuals, units, and the department are doing on quantity and quality . . . We can get to problems right away, and there's a new spirit of cooperation. We've come to use this data not as a control device, but as a way to encourage improvement."

6. Recognize Achievements

Ron Contino, Jim Davis, Bob Aylward, Walt Doughton and many other high-performance managers stress the critical importance of recognizing employee achievements.

If there's no appreciation expressed for a job well done, or no celebration of major accomplishments, it follows that there is no affirmation or reinforcement of desirable performance. And without that, why should employees repeat what they have done, or strive to do better?

Recognition can come in many forms. Financial forms of recognition include cash suggestion awards, profit sharing, employee stock ownership plans, and productivity gainsharing. But recognition can also be given in the form of a simple thank you or through letters of appreciation, certificates, plaques, coffee-and-doughnut celebrations, and special recognition dinners. Whatever form it takes, recognition should be both deserved and appropriate for the occasion; otherwise, it will be perceived as insincere and manipulative. Whenever possible, managers should personally present the awards before a group of the honored employee's peers.

A response . . . A higher level of commitment . . . Self-motivation . . . More discretionary effort . . . Improved productivity, quality, and service. That's what the six action levers should produce over time. If you're not convinced that's so, think about each of the six actions and ask yourself: "What will happen if I *don't* take these steps?" And consider this: Increased commitment is a prerequisite for all improvement; if you don't get the former, you can forget the latter. **Figure 3** shows how improvement takes place. Simply put, the way to close the gap between current performance and potential performance is to build employee commitment.

OVERCOMING OBJECTIONS: FOUR STEPS TO SUCCESS

"If you decide to build employee commitment in your organization, you are likely to encounter skepticism and resistance—from your boss, your peers, your employees, and maybe even yourself. Therefore, it is important that you be "loaded for success." Here's a four-step breakthrough strategy that will help get you on your way:

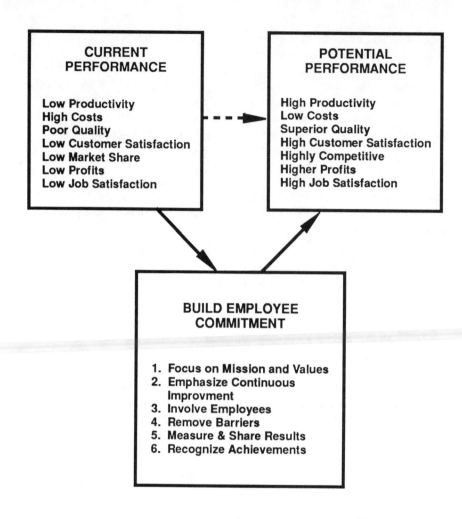

CURRENT
PERFORMANCE

Low Productivity
High Costs
Poor Quality
Low Customer Satisfaction
Low Market Share
Low Profits
Low Job Satisfaction

POTENTIAL
PERFORMANCE

High Productivity
Low Costs
Superior Quality
High Customer Satisfaction
Highly Competitive
Higher Profits
High Job Satisfaction

BUILD EMPLOYEE
COMMITMENT

1. Focus on Mission and Values
2. Emphasize Continuous
   Improvment
3. Involve Employees
4. Remove Barriers
5. Measure & Share Results
6. Recognize Achievements

© 1987 PRIDE Publications, Inc.

FIGURE 3 MANAGING FOR HIGH-PERFORMANCE

1. *Identify the Issues:* Which operational problems are most nagging your organization? What long-range concerns or goals need to be addressed? What is on your boss's agenda? In short, what business needs can you help satisfy by focusing on employee commitment?

2. *Champion a Cause:* What major improvement would you and your people be most enthusiastic about: Quality? Customer satisfaction? What are you willing to spend your own time on and "talk up" with others?

3. *Start Small:* Is there a part of your organization that is ripe for change? Is there a manager or supervisor who is frustrated or ready to take on a challenge?

4. *Begin with Barriers:* Have employees in that ripe department been asked what might be done to help them improve productivity, quality, or service? Are you willing to invest in your cause and your people— that is, spend a few hours and dollars resolving problems now, to get a significant payback later?

To illustrate this breakthrough strategy, let us assume that product defects is an issue you would like to address (step 1) as a way of better satisfying customers (your cause, step 2), and that an operations supervisor is willing to tackle the problem in his or her area (step 3). With your encouragement and support—and some training in group brainstorming or problem-solving—the supervisor should be able to identify and remove some of the barriers to higher quality (step 4). Using that experience as a precedent, you can then involve other supervisors and employees in the cause, thereby building commitment from the bottom up.

If, on the other hand, you want to take a faster, top-down approach, you can identify the issues, champion a cause, and develop a comprehensive personal action plan similar to the one shown in **Figure 4.** Such an approach will help you organize your thinking and simultaneously focus your efforts on the six action levers that build employee commitment.

In so doing, you will be creating in environment for self-motivation, which will encourage employees to apply more discretionary effort and boost their performance. Such an environment is a worthwhile goal for every forward-thinking manager. With it, organizations will prosper. Without such an environment, it is unlikely that an organization's full potential will be reached. ■

ADDITIONAL RESOURCES

Daniel Yankelovich and John Immerwahr, *Putting the Work Ethic to Work,* The Public Agenda Foundation, 6 East 39th Street, New York, NY 10016, 212/686–6610.

Thomas Peters, *Thriving on Chaos,* Alfred A. Knopf, New York, 1988.

Edward E. Lawler III, *High-Involvement Management,* Jossey-Bass Publishers, San Francisco, 1986.

Robert H. Waterman, Jr., *The Renewal Factor,* Bantam Books, New York, Toronto, 1987.

Robert H. Schaffer, *The Breakthrough Strategy,* Ballinger Publishing Co., Cambridge, MA, 1988.

Videotapes

"The Leadership Alliance," "A Passion For Customers," and "A Passion For Excellence," with Tom Peters, Video Publishing House, Des Plaines, IL.

"Customer Service," "Innovation" and "Productivity Through People," with Robert H. Waterman. Jr., AMA Film/Video, Watertown, MA.

"The Change Masters" and "Change Master Companies," with Rosabeth Moss Kanler, Britannica Films, Lake Orion, MI.

PERSONAL ACTION PLAN

Name_____ Date_____

For The Period: _____ (Months)_____ (Year)

Success Factors	Results Wanted — Long Term Goal:	Next Steps — Subgoal(s):
1. Focus on Mission and Values		
2. Emphasize Continuous Improvement		
3. Involve Employees		
4. Remove Barriers		
5. Measure and Share Results		
6. Recognize Achievements		

© 1987 PRIDE Publications, Inc.

FIGURE 4 PERSONAL ACTION PLAN

Leadership: The Essential Quality for Transforming United States Businesses

Neil H. Snyder

Associate Professor, McIntire School of Commerce University of Virginia

INTRODUCTION

In 1983, President Reagan sponsored a White House Conference on Productivity to explore the reasons for our nation's productivity problem. After increasing at a rate of 3 percent per year between 1948 and 1968, productivity in the United States actually began to decline. Among the reasons identified by conference participants were:

- the poor quality of American management;
- high interest rates;
- high structural inflation;
- huge deficits;
- a convoluted tax system:
- federal regulations that discourage creativity and innovation; and
- an educational system that, after more than three decades of massive federal support, was under fire for turning out 23 million functionally illiterate adults.

The productivity of U.S. firms has improved dramatically in recent years, but their competitiveness in world markets has not. The federal budget deficit, the U.S. trade deficit, and tax inequities have hampered their progress. All of these problems are complex, and they warrant the attention of government officials. Currently, Congress is considering no fewer than two hundred pieces of legislation designed to impose trade sanctions on countries engaging in what are believed to be unfair trade practices or to provide protection for industries believed to be particularly vulnerable to unfair competition. Additionally, United States officials are negotiating with officials from our major trading partners to reduce

Reprinted by permission, *SAM Advanced Management Journal*, Vol 51, Spring 1986, Society for Advancement of Management.

Dr. Snyder, a frequent author, was Policy Advisor for Regulatory Reform for Virginia's former Governor Charles Robb.

the value of the dollar, so American made goods will be less expensive overseas. Furthermore, tax reform and budget restraint are items that are clearly at the top of the agendas of the president and Congress.

FUNDAMENTAL PROBLEM

It is widely recognized by business people, politicians, journalists, and academicians that our nation's future prosperity depends on our ability to come to grips with these and other complex problems and to find long-term solutions. However, the real, underlying difficulty tends to be ignored because it is so basic and so obvious. It is a lack of leadership in business and government. This is the most important problem that organizations in our nation face today. It is not poor management as participants in the White House Conference on Productivity suggest, although they make a convincing case that the quality of management in the United States does need to be improved. This lack of leadership has been illustrated graphically by the authors of several best-selling books, including *In Search of Excellence, A Passion for Excellence,* and *The Change Masters.*[1]

Ironically, despite these problems and their potentially crippling effect, the 1980s have witnessed a revival of the entrepreneurial vitality that made this nation the world's economic leader and a military superpower in less than two hundred years. More individuals today are taking initiatives and formulating innovative responses to existing needs and problems than they have in this country for many years.

Also, this trend is reflected in changing attitudes about the role of the federal government in the life or our nation. We have come to realize that the federal government cannot provide the standard of living and the way of life so many people believed it could a few short years ago. This rethinking of the government's role in our society has resulted in a shift of economic power from the public sector to the private sector. For example, deregulation and reform of regulatory processes at the federal level and in several states has led to a reduction in government interference in competitive markets and has injected new life in the banking, insurance, trucking, oil, telecommunications, and airline industries.

The effects of these changes on individual attitudes are far-reaching and can be seen clearly in business organizations, as well. The rapid increase in entrepreneurial and intrapreneurial activity and the willingness of corporate giants like AT&T, IBM, and Chrysler to reassess their basic product-market orientations is a signal that businesses are reevaluating their fundamental assumptions and traditions. Now is the appropriate time, therefore, to re-examine the essential quality needed to transform United States businesses: Leadership.

WHAT IS LEADERSHIP?

Leadership is not administration or management. Contrary to traditional wisdom, leaders may or may not possess administrative or management ability. Likewise, administrators may or may not be leaders, and position in the management hierarchy is not necessarily a good indicator of leadership skills. There are three qualities that distinguish true leaders from good managers. First, leaders are men and women with vision. Second, they are able to identify and articulate the fundamental values and beliefs that will translate their vision into operational terms, and they are able to inspire others to adopt those values as their own. Finally, they are action-oriented people; they possess confidence in their vision and are willing to take risks to make it a reality.

Each of these qualities is essential. A person with vision who cannot articulate fundamental values or inspire others is a dreamer—not a leader. A person who possesses the first two qualities may have the best intentions, but if he or she is unwilling to take action, those good intentions have little value.

VISION

Vision is the beginning of leadership. While it is difficult to describe precisely, vision is a depth and breadth of understanding that enables leaders to detect patterns or trends in events as they unfold and to predict future events. It is believed by many that education, experience, access to critical information, and luck all contribute to the development of this quality in an individual.

However, the people at General Motors prefer to think about vision in a slightly different way. They say "you cannot forecast the future, but you can create it."[2] This view incorporates both the notion of vision, or the process of determining what the future ought to be, and the notion of action, or the process of creating a reality. There is a flavor of self-fulfilling prophecy in both of these approaches—one first imagines what the future should be and then proceeds to make it happen.

Henry Kissinger explains the role vision plays in leadership this way:

". . . the task of the leader is to get his people from where they are to where they have not been. The public does not fully understand the world into which it is going. Leaders must invoke an alchemy of great vision. Those leaders who do not are ultimately judged failures, even though they may be popular at the moment."[3]

Irving Kristol has a similar opinion. He says most of all the American people want to be governed by a "resolute, self-confident, articulate leadership—a leadership that knows where it is headed and can explain in a forthright way just how it proposes to get there."[4] According to Noel Tichy and David Ulrich, vision must "create within employees a deep sense of what the organization is trying to accomplish . . . and communicate to each department that what it offers is crucial to the organization's overall success."[5] Additionally, they suggest that "the vision needs to be logical, deductive, and plausible. It needs to help each employee see what the future holds as a rational extension of the present. On the other hand, the vision . . . must be mind-stretching and creative, and capture the imagination of employees."[6] It seems clear that leaders must possess vision and that they must impart an understanding about the value of their vision to those around them, thus inspiring their confidence.

VALUES AND BELIEFS

Individuals who possess vision may not be leaders, however, because they lack conviction. True leaders know what they value most, or what they believe, and they are willing to take risks and make sacrifices to achieve their objectives. The importance of values and beliefs in business firms was pointed out by Philip Selznick. He suggested that

> "the formation of an institution is marked by the making of value commitment, that is choices which fix the assumptions of policy makers as to the nature of the enterprise, its distinctive aims, methods, and roles. These character defining choices are often not made verbally, they might not even be made consciously. . . . The institutional leader is primarily an expert in the promotion and protection of values."[7]

Thomas Watson, Jr., the genius behind IBM, offered a similar view. After completing his business career, he explained what made his business such a success by saying,

> "I firmly believe that any organization, in order to survive and achieve success, must have a sound set of beliefs on which it premises all its policies and actions. Next I believe the most important single factor in corporate success is faithful adherence to those beliefs. And, finally, I believe if an organization is to meet the challenge of a changing world, it must be prepared to change everything about itself except those beliefs as it moves through corporate life."[8]

Watson goes on to say that adherence to those character defining beliefs is more important than technology, economic resources, organizational structure, innovation, or timing.

Values and beliefs also play an important role in maintaining the strength of our nation's resolve. In 1776, one of our founding fathers, George Mason, said, "No free government, nor the blessings of liberty, can be preserved to any people, but by . . . a frequent recurrence to fundamental principles."[9] That admonition is valid today. Because the world in which we live is so complex, James Reston suggests that presidents of the United States who are effective leaders must "have the capacity to reduce the diversity of world politics . . . to a single identity, so that the people can understand the transformation that is taking place in their lives and in the lives of their children."[10] Along the same line, Walter Lippman says that the president "is more than an administrator. He is the custodian of our nation's ideals, of the beliefs it cherishes, of the faith which makes a nation out of a mere aggregation of individuals."[11]

In their book, *In Search of Excellence,* Peters and Waterman describe seven basic beliefs adhered to by the excellent companies they studied:

- "A belief in the 'best';
- a belief in the importance of the details of execution, the nuts and bolts of doing the job well;
- a belief in the importance of people as individuals;
- a belief in superior quality and service;
- a belief that most members of the organization should be innovators, and its corollary, the willingness to support failure;
- a belief in the importance of informality to enhance communication; and
- an explicit belief in and recognition of the importance of economic growth and profits."[12]

The ideas of Peters and Waterman presented in their book have been criticized recently by some individuals,[13] although they have been received warmly by executives who are responsible for finding ways to solve the problems currently facing American business. An article in *Business Week,*[14] for example, criticized their findings because some of the companies Peters and Waterman called excellent are experiencing difficulty at the present time. Interestingly, the authors found this short-sighted view in abundance in not-so-excellent companies. As Peters and Waterman state very clearly, all organizations must deal with short-run problems. In this regard, excellent organizations are no different from the rest. But leaders in excellent companies have demonstrated over time that they are able to live through set backs in the short-run and achieve success in the long-run.

The literature suggests that identifying, shaping, and communicating character defining beliefs is a vital role played by the leader. It also suggests that the firm's top managers are the ones who play this role in excellent companies.

ACTION

The adage that actions speak louder than words is especially true for leaders. They must possess more than vision and beliefs. They must have discipline, energy, determination, persistence, and zeal to carry them through the difficult periods and, interestingly, to keep them moving forward during the good times. Teddy Roosevelt may have captured the essence of this leadership quality when he said,

. . . The credit belongs to the man who is actually in the arena, whose face is marred by dust and sweat and blood . . . who knows the great enthusiasms, the great devotions; who spends himself in a worthy cause; who at the best knows in the end the triumph of high achievement, and . . . if he fails, at least he fails while daring greatly, so that his place shall never be with those cold and timid souls who know neither victory nor defeat.[15]

SUMMARY AND CONCLUSION

True leaders share three basic characteristics: vision, strongly held values and beliefs, and the willingness and ability to take action. Possessing one or two of these qualities is not enough, because they form a gestalt—an integrated whole. Most of the problems businesses face today result from a lack of leadership. However, we are witnessing a resurgence of creativity and innovation in this nation as entrepreneurs and intrapreneurs in large numbers have begun exercising their leadership abilities. These people are demonstrating by their actions that leaders do make a difference. Additionally, they are showing executives, how important it is for them to perform their leadership roles if they want their organizations to be competitive in world and domestic markets. These independent-minded individuals have risked business and personal failure to achieve success and, in the process, have created better goods and services, more jobs, and a higher standard of living for the rest of us. ■

NOTES

1. Thomas Peters and Robert Waterman. *In Search of Excellence,* Harper & Row, 1982. Thomas Peters and Nancy Austin. *A Passion for Excellence,* Random House, 1985. Rosabeth Moss Kanter. *The Change Master,* Simon and Schuster, 1983.
2. Quote obtained during the annual meeting of the Academy of Management, August 1985. San Diego, California. Source: Michael E. Naylor, General Director, Corporate Strategic Planning. General Motors Corporation.
3. Quoted in Hugh Sidey "Majesty, Poetry, and Power," *Time,* October 20, 1980, p. 39.
4. Irving Kristol. "Running Like a Dry Creek?," *Wall Street Journal,* October 6, 1983, Editorial Page.
5. Noel Tichy and David Ulrich. "The Challenge of Revitalization," *New Management,* vol. 2, no. 3, Winter 1985, pp. 53–59.
6. *ibid.* Tichy and Ulrich, pp. 53–59.
7. Philip Selznick. *Leadership in Administration,* Harper & Row, 1957, p. 28.
8. Thomas Watson, Jr. *A Business and Its Beliefs,* McGraw-Hill, 1963, pp. 4–6.
9. George Mason. *Declaration of Rights for Virginia,* 1776.
10. James Reston. "Political Leaders: Do They Matter?" *Richmond Times-Dispatch,* August 31, 1983, Editorial Page.
11. *ibid.* Walter Lippman. Quoted in Reston, Editorial Page.
12. *ibid.* Peters and Waterman, p. 285.
13. "Who's Excellent Now?," *Business Week,* November 5, 1984, p. 76. Daniel Carroll. "A Disappointing Search for Excellence," *Harvard Business Review,* November–December 1983, p. 78.
14. *ibid, Business Week,* p. 76.
15. Theodore Roosevelt. Paraphrased from a speech before the Hamilton Club, Chicago, Ill., April 10, 1899.

Reassessing the "Divine Rights" of Managers

Edgar H. Schein
MIT Sloan School of Management

The Computer Revolution will necessitate a comparable revolution in how we structure organizations, according to the author, but we have a collective blind spot that makes it difficult to embrace this challenge: we are virtually incapable of imagining a nonhierarchical workplace. The concept of hierarchy colors our most basic assumptions and beliefs about work. Soon we will need to develop a new picture of what a manager should be. Hierarchical authority will probably play a much smaller role in that picture, while coordination skills will play a much larger role. Ed.

We are at the beginning of a major organizational revolution, one being fueled by several forces:

- The competitive need to revive our industrial strength.
- The probability that information technology will eventually produce major changes in the nature of work and in the forms that organizations and management will take.
- The globalization of our economy, which is creating interdependencies that we are only now becoming dimly aware of.
- The increasing technological complexity of all areas of work.
- The changing social and cultural values surrounding the roles of work, career, family, and lifestyle at all levels of society.
- Demographic trends that are changing the composition of the workforce; it is becoming older and more multicultural, and there are more women.

Reprinted from Reassessing the "Divine Rights" by Edgar H. Schein, *Sloan Management Review,* Winter 1989, pp. 63–68, by permission of the publisher. Copyright 1989 by the Sloan Management Review Association. All rights reserved.

Edgar H. Schein is Sloan Fellows Professor of Management at the MIT Sloan School of Management. Dr. Schein holds the B.A. degree from the University of Chicago, the B.A. and M.A. degrees from Stanford University, and the Ph.D. degree from Harvard University. His research interests include organizational culture, human resource planning and career development, and planned change. He recently edited The Art of Managing Human Resources, *a collection of articles from the* Sloan Management Review.

BEYOND HIERARCHY

Some of these forces have already been analyzed effectively by others, so I will focus particularly on *technological complexity* and the probable impact of *information technology*. We have heard from many sources, most recently Peter Drucker, that organizations will be more information based, flatter, more task oriented, driven more by professional specialists, and more dependent upon clearly focused missions.[1]

Some scholars have gone beyond our present concepts and talk of *heterarchies* or *multigons*.[2] These point toward models of organization that are more like holograms, in which each part of the organization contains enough information to recreate the whole. Common cultural assumptions in an organization could be thought of as equivalent to genetic codes that permit reconstruction of the whole from any one part. Other metaphors for the evolving workplace include "harmonies of dissimilar elements" or "controlled diversity."[3]

Our thinking about these matters is hampered by one major, deeply embedded cultural assumption so taken for granted that it is difficult even to articulate. This is the assumption that all organizations are fundamentally *hierarchical* in nature, and that the management process is fundamentally hierarchical. We need new models, but we may have difficulty inventing them because of the automatic tendency to think hierarchically.

Two concrete examples will illustrate the kinds of dilemmas that arise when hierarchy is taken for granted. The first involves some consulting work I did recently with a multinational financial services institution. One group was trying to replace various specialists in tasks such as money transfer and letters of credit with highly sophisticated workstations that would permit an operator to do a range of tasks for a range of customers; most of the tasks' technical aspects could be built into the workstation in the form of expert systems.

What was now an army of specialists would be replaced ultimately with a small number of sophisticated professionals who would work at these "smart machines," thereby increasing productivity, reducing costs, and improving customer service.

In the midst of designing an organization to fulfill this vision, we came upon an unexpected problem. Who would supervise such people? How should the supervisory job be designed? What title should the job be given, and what kind of career path would lead into and out of it? Would operators spend their whole careers at the terminals, or would they become "supervisors" and ultimately "higher level" managers?

Many ideas were proposed—they could be "team leaders," or "consultants," or "service managers." But as I listened to the discussion I reached a terrifying conclusion—neither my clients nor I had the faintest idea of what this job would *really* be like, what kind of people should occupy it, or how such people should be selected, trained, and managed in terms of rewards, controls, and career paths. Even more striking, it did not occur to any of us that such professionals might not need *any* kind of supervisor. We had automatically fallen into the trap of hierarchical thinking.

A second example comes from the seminal research of Shoshana Zuboff at Harvard and Larry Hirschhorn at the University of Pennsylvania.[4] Both are interested in the nature of "postindustrial work": what will really happen in the age of the "smart machine"?

Zuboff shows convincingly that, as information technology not only automates but *informates,* operators at all levels learn how things really work and consequently no longer need their supervisors. Coordinating can be done by them and by the information system. In the short run, this will lead to all sorts of transition problems; management will try to protect its position and reassert its prerogative to "run the place." But it seems clear that, in the long run, competitive pressures will force more and more layers of management into roles other than the traditional supervisory ones. Layers of management will either disappear altogether, or else smaller numbers of managers will do different tasks at "headquarters."

This scenario sounds reasonable until one examines the implications of Hirschhorn's findings. He observes that "informated" operators in the new, networked organizations are subjected to new kinds and levels of anxiety, for the following reasons:

- they have much higher levels of responsibility;
- they work in organizations such as nuclear plants, automated refineries, or chemical plants that often have much greater danger associated with them; and
- the boundaries of their roles are much more ambiguous and fluid.

Under the old system, line supervisors provided support when crises arose. The hierarchy functioned not only as a coordination mechanism, but also as a psychological defense against anxiety. In this capacity, it served workers and managers alike, which may account for the difficulty of imagining work systems without hierarchy.

If such managerial roles disappear, the informated worker must find other sources of support or develop other psychological defenses against anxiety. Such defenses, as Hirschhorn shows, may paradoxically undermine the very efficiencies the technology is designed to create. The worker will routinize and bureaucratize the job, undermining the flexibility designed into the system. Or, worse, he or she will misread dials that indicate dangerous conditions, because of a need to deny the reality that things really could go wrong. In some cases workers will display a puzzling degree of boredom, failing to be alert when danger arises, because it is not possible to remain highly alert indefinitely during periods when things are routine.

Perhaps some hypothetical worker of the future will be adjusted to the anxiety levels of modern, technologically sophisticated workplaces, but in the meantime, how do we manage the anxious worker of today? Do we give them new authority figures and thereby reinforce the hierarchy?

Let me begin to answer that question by describing another consulting experience. I recently visited the large auto manufacturing plant at Trollhat-tan, Sweden, run by SAAB Scania, and I was impressed by the large number of fully functioning robots and autonomous work groups. The group members were all highly trained technicians who could run the robots, fix them, or replace them if they broke down. If these groups had managers, nothing was ever said about them. Group members controlled entry and exit into the group, job assignments, and working style. The overall technological design and strategy of the plant controlled the speed of the line, the product mix, and even the quality with automated checking stations that ensured correct assembly.

I was reminded of a theme that surfaced strongly during a visit to Nor-way in the 1970s. I was told when preparing for a lecture series that I should stress the role of "management," because Norwegians assumed that if you had enough good engineers and planners, you did not really need managers. This seemed like an absurd position at the time, but now I wonder if the Norwegians were not simply way ahead of their time.

Their vision becomes more explicit if we extrapolate from the work of some of my colleagues at MIT. Tom Malone, a social psychologist, informa-tion technologist, computer scientist, and organization theorist all rolled into one, speculates that future organizations may well be networks in which hierarchy either disappears altogether or plays a far less important role than other forms of coordination and integration.

Malone is developing a "coordination theory," which he distinguishes from traditional organization and management theory because he regards those as too mired in traditional hierarchical models.[5] Perhaps the organiza-tion of the future will be more like a giant, complex seesaw in which everyone must contribute to effective coordination; management as it exists today will be either invisible or nonexistent, according to this theory.

What I am trying to bring out is that we are on the brink of an organiza-tional revolution that will not simply cut out layers of management or reduce costs or force greater levels of worker participation. Something far more profound may happen that has not yet been fully grasped because, like Hirschhorn's workers, we are probably too anxious to fully grasp its im-plications.

What may well happen is that *management as a traditionally conceived, hierarchical function will disappear altogether,* to be replaced with concepts that we have not yet developed. If that happens, of course, our traditional concepts of educating and developing managers will disappear as well, to be replaced with models that do not yet exist.

Our challenge in the next few decades will be to develop these new concepts and educational strategies, but I see some severe difficulties; these stem from the implicit assumption that organizations are fundamentally hierarchical. I hypothesize that we have great difficulty even imagining, much less designing, nonhierarchical or even less hierarchical systems.

THE DIVINE RIGHTS OF MANAGERS

The clearest evidence for this hypothesis comes from managers' belief in their divine right to manage. One observes this phenomenon in labor-management negotiations, when a manager argues that union proposals infringe on "managerial prerogatives." The basis of these alleged prerogatives is seldom spelled out—and there is an assumption that it need not be.

To illustrate what I mean, I must first make a theoretical point. Organization theory has always stressed that power, authority, influence, and leadership are complex psychological concepts that cannot be understood without analyzing the relationship between superior and subordinate.[6] Employees in an organization do what they are supposed to do for one of several reasons.

- **Nonlegitimate Authority.** The person is coerced into doing something because someone with the capacity to reward or punish orders it. This form of organization, symbolized by prisons or slave labor camps, has drawbacks too obvious to dwell on.
- **Charismatic Authority.** One person is so prominent and emotionally powerful that others go along because of complete faith in and admiration for the person. This kind of authority is wonderful if such a person exists and if what that person wants to do happens to fit the needs of the group. It is not a form of authority that can be planned for, and charismatic leaders are not easy to find.
- **Tradition-based Authority.** The person does what he or she is told to do by those who have acquired a traditional *right* to give orders. This model underlies monarchies and empires once they have evolved away from coerciveness and acquired legitimacy through some claim such as the divine right of kings. This kind of claim works in a society where there is religious consensus.
- **Rational-Legal Authority.** As society evolved toward more democratic forms, organizations developed a new principle of authority, the consent of the governed. Competent people are to be promoted into positions of authority; authority resides in those positions; if the authority of the posi-

tion is abused, the subordinate has legal recourse through some form of due process. Subordinates give the boss the "right" to give orders, because they accept the *system* by which supervisory positions are filled.

This form of authority is presumed to underlie the modern, bureaucratic organization and is the principle on which corporations are supposed to operate. The rights and prerogatives of managers at each level are supposed to be spelled out and to reside in the offices. The system is supposed to be "rational" to the extent that the most competent people get promoted or appointed to the managerial positions. As we all know, the system does not usually work as designed because of power politics, intergroup conflicts, and various other emotional factors.

• **Purely Rational Authority.** The only reason for following someone's orders, within this model, is that the person is more *expert* at whatever work needs to be done. Authority is defined by task requirements and individual expertise. It no longer resides in the position but in the person, and only in the person to the extent that he or she has specific areas of competence. Thus we obey the pilot while the plane in the air, but we obey the survival expert if the plane crashes in the jungle.

As we contemplate the future of organizations, it seems reasonable to suppose that authority should be based on the purely rational model, but most organizations and schools appear to operate as if the only principles of authority that exist are the coercive, charismatic, traditional, and rational-legal ones.

Clearly, we support hierarchy as a primary legitimation of authority. We may also unwittingly be supporting the divine right of managers to define for themselves what their prerogatives are, and to defend those prerogatives solely on the basis that "it has always been this way" or that "it" is somehow intrinsic to the free market system.

What is my evidence for this conclusion? Let us look at some examples.

• **The Management-Labor Metaphor.** When proposals are made to share *ownership* with employees, we treat that request seriously and rationally as a legitimate economic issue to be examined. But when it is proposed that workers be put on the board of directors, there is immediately a level of resistance in senior management that has a moral overtone: "It is not their right to have a say in the running of the company; that is management's prerogative."

A particularly pernicious form of this assumption is expressed metaphorically. When Eastern Airlines first experimented with employee ownership, giving workers stock increased productivity and reduced costs. Some years later, when a new financial crisis hit the company, president Frank Borman suggested cutting labor costs, which led to a union counterproposal that would guarantee productivity gains if management would both increase the employee ownership share and let employees have a voice in management. Borman was quoted as responding to this proposal with the remark, "Oh, so now the monkeys want to run the zoo."[7]

We have allowed ourselves to think of organizations as two-tiered systems—management and labor—and we have allowed a metaphor to illustrate this system: labor is the animal and management is the keeper. Or, laborers are children and managers are parents. Typically, a company's early years are dominated by paternalistic thinking; possibly such thinking leads quite naturally to the idea that it is the right and even the obligation of management to take care of the "corporate family." The notion of laborers and managers being adults on a par with each other is undermined not only by rank and status but by the socioeconomic class distinctions that are frequently correlated with rank.

And I see nothing in our university industrial relations curricula that serves to undo these terrible stereotypes. By arguing for *improvements* in the labor-management negotiation system, we are reinforcing the system rather than looking for ways to reconceptualize what organizations need to be in the twenty-first century.

• **Hierarchical Teams.** We glorify teamwork, but our most popular sports analogy is football—a sport in which there is a hierarchy of coaches and positions on the field, with special attention and status attached to the quarterback. In fact, when we select managers we often look for people who have been quarterbacks or team captains. We say we are looking for leadership capabilities, but in fact we are looking for people who have experience working within a hierarchical structure. Yet, it may be that the complex, differentiated, interdependent work of future organizations will require the skills more associated with basketball, hockey, and soccer, where team performance is dependent on the players' ability to coordinate their own moves with the moves of others, and to make reliable autonomous decisions within a broad strategic framework.

The degree to which we are caught up in the unconscious assumptions of hierarchy is further illustrated by Peter Drucker's recent call for flatter organizations; he used the analogy of the orchestra. Orchestras are actually an example of *extreme* hierarchy in the service of a high degree of coordination. Typically, conductors are highly autocratic; under them are principal soloists, lead players, and sections. Orchestra members are highly conscious—and often resentful—of their positions in the hierarchy; it is only their extraordinary skill, plus the conductor's ear and precise feedback, that produces the perfection we attribute to teamwork. A first rate orchestra can in fact perform without a conductor because its members are so competent, but it is interesting to note that few orchestras are ever given that license. We seem to believe that the conductor is necessary, and we exaggerate the degree to which this powerful position is the source of the team's greatness.

• **Performance Appraisal and Reward Systems.** My colleague Lotte Bailyn notes that the seemingly egalitarian and "fair" concept of *merit pay,* or pay for performance, actually forces the organization to rank people into a hierarchy that may damage morale and performance.

Even as a concept, merit pay is difficult to defend. There is growing evidence that interdependence in most organizational situations is so high that one can only measure output reliably across organizational units that have clearly defined and relatively autonomous tasks. Yet note how obsessed organizations and managers are with ranking people and differentiating performance, on the incorrect assumption that people's performance can be improved if they are told that they are not as good as someone else. In fact, the only reliable way to improve performance is to give performance feedback whenever possible; giving feedback has nothing to do with ranking or merit pay or other systems of differentiating people. Let me offer a simple analogy. My tennis game will not improve because I am told that I am not as good as someone else. It will only improve if a coach, or a videotape, or my own self-observation shows me what I am doing wrong and how I could do it better.

The degree to which our performance appraisal systems emphasize differentiating people illustrates how deeply embedded our hierarchical assumptions are. Some systems even require rank ordering everyone in a given position category.

Senior managers believe such systems are needed because they are the only way to guarantee that the best performers will be rewarded and that poor performers will be terminated. But embedded in that notion is the idea that people are in fact doing similar things. In reality, each employee can be judged based on performance or nonperformance of a given task, and nonperformers can be appraised, trained, or fired. Nothing requires that they be compared to others or differentially rewarded. In fact, there is a growing trend to pay production workers for the number of skills they possess, not for their performance relative to other workers.

• **Job Classification and Grading.** Why do we have such difficulty instituting a "dual ladder" for individual technical and professional contributors? Why is there an almost automatic assumption that it is more important to identify managerial potential early in the career? Why do we think in terms of moving potential managers up the ladder rapidly, when professional careers are seen as more "level"? Why are managers typically paid more than individual contributors? Why do job grading systems almost automatically give higher grades to jobs that involve supervision, and measure job level by the number of people supervised?

Why do we have difficulty conceiving of organizations as networks in which "higher" or "lower" makes no sense? After all, we know that in many kinds of work situations—in project teams, in professional offices and partnerships, and in university departments, to name a few—there is a constant, active effort to reduce the hierarchy to the absolute minimum required.

- **The Culture of Management.** I recently asked a group of high-potential middle managers to identify the critical underlying assumptions of the occupation of management. Several assumptions emerged: management means working extremely hard to achieve results; management means supervising others; and management means occupying a position in an organizational hierarchy. In fact, the managers' response was that management means hierarchy.

- **Management and Business Curricula.** I have not done a detailed analysis, so I may be unfair in this area, but it seems to me that our business-management textbooks and courses emphasize the traditional, hierarchical form of organization. We teach our students how to "wield authority," and we make it clear that career success is "making it to the top."

We may not say this out loud, but it is implied even in the concept of higher education; with a degree one can enter the system at a "higher" level and aspire more immediately to a position of authority. Alumni often complain that they did not get a position of responsibility soon enough; usually they mean they did not get enough authority. "Calling the shots" is good, something to be aspired to. Invisible contribution to a team effort does not count. Reality is hierarchy, so to get as high as possible is the obvious, valid goal.

We encourage comparative performance rather than individual competence by noting how much our alumni make in their first jobs. We are obsessed with ranking our schools on a hierarchy of overall excellence that has prestige value but little meaning in terms of the actual content of the education; the ratings are not based on a detailed analysis of what actually goes on in the various management schools.

In summary, I believe we take hierarchy for granted and that we have failed to realize how the assumptions underlying hierarchy pervade our thinking both in schools and in the workplace. If it is true that organizations will be flat networks in the future, then we must give serious thought to the following questions.

- What do we mean when we say "management"?
- Will management reside in individual managers, or will it be distributed as a function in networks and working teams?
- Can managers as such be selected, trained, and developed?
- Will our models for educating managers continue to have relevance? Will we have to invent wholly new concepts of what individuals must learn how to do in order to coordinate work?
- Most important, will we have to abandon hierarchy as an organizing principle and invent new concepts of coordination and control that will generate new kinds of developmental requirements? ■

REFERENCES

1. P. F. Drucker, "The Coming of the New Organization," *Harvard Business Review,* January–February 1988, pp. 45–53.
2. B. L. T. Hedberg et al., "Camping on Seesaws: Prescriptions for a Self-Designing Organization," *Administrative Science Quarterly* 21 (March 1976): 41–65; I. Borwick, *The Truncated Pyramid* (Boston: Management Executive Center, 1980).
3. E. H. Schein, "International Human Resource Management: New Directions, Perpetual Issues, and Missing Themes," *Human Resource Management* 25 (1986): 169–176.
4. S. Zuboff, *In the Age of the Smart Machine* (New York: Basic Books, 1988); L. Hirschhorn, *The Workplace Within* (Cambridge, MA: MIT Press, 1988).
5. T. Malone et al., "Electronic Markets and Electronic Hierarchies," *Communications of the ACM* 30 (1987): 484–497.
6. E. H. Schein, *Organizational Psychology,* 3d. ed. (Englewood Cliffs, NJ: Prentice-Hall, 1980).
7. A. Gibney, *Collision Course* (San Francisco: California Newsreel/Jigsaw Productions, 1987).

The Value of Androgynous Management

Gary N. Powell

Professor of Management
University of Connecticut, Storrs, CT.

There has literally been a change in the "face" of management. That face is now female more than one-third of the time. The proportion of women managers, executives, and administrators has more than doubled since 1974 and now stands at 39%. However, most of the existing theories of management were developed with male managers in mind. Should these theories be revised now that more women are in management?

Most management theories have been blind to issues regarding the socialization of managers. They have not recognized that men, who still constitute the majority of managers, are also judged according to how well they adhere to the masculine sex role stereotype. Despite all the changes that have taken place in our society, men are still expected to be forceful, dominant, aggressive, decisive, and the like. Thus it is not surprising that masculinity remains prevalent in the ranks of management and is widely regarded as the key to managerial success. However, the fact that managers tend to be masculine does not necessarily mean that *better* managers are masculine.

In *The Androgynous Manager,* Alice Sargent argued that management theories should expand their definition of what makes a good manager beyond traditional masculine behaviors to include feminine behaviors as well—nurturance, warmth, understanding, and so on. She proposed that better managers are *androgynous,* defined as a style that blends the masculine and feminine behaviors previously seen as belonging exclusively to men or women. Sargent and Ken Blanchard, co-author of *The One-Minute Manager,* further proclaimed that "the one-minute manager is an androgynous manager."[1]

Sargent offered two primary reasons why managers should be androgynous. First, she assumed that female managers tend to bring different qualities to the job than male managers, with women being more feminine

Reprinted by permission, *SAM Advanced Management Journal,* Spring 1989, Society for Advancement of Management, Vinton, VA 24179.

Dr. Powell is author of the book, Women and Men In Management *and is a nationally recognized scholar and educator on the subject.*

and men more masculine. However, according to an extensive review of the literature in my book, *Women and Men in Management,* male and female managers actually are quite similar in personal characteristics. The sex differences that have been found are few and tend to cancel each other out.[2] Second, she argued that androgyny is the best route to fulfillment in managers' personal lives and one that makes them happier people. This was the early view of androgyny among psychologists. Nevertheless, others have argued that the masculine component of androgyny benefits people more than the feminine component. Before androgyny is accepted as the ideal state of being, we need to be sure that androgynous individuals are truly better off in life.[3]

In this article, we shall consider the value of the androgyny concept for managers. First, we shall evaluate its compatibility with existing concepts and theories of management. Second, we shall consider how to implement androgynous management.

ANDROGYNY AND MANAGEMENT THEORY

Management theories have varied over the years, and no universal agreement has been reached on which theory is best. Most theories, however, have made reference to feminine as well as masculine characteristics. Before we can determine how androgynous management fits into existing theories of management, we need to review the major types of theories.

Great-man theories were among the earliest management theories. They were developed in the belief that knowledge about the personalities of individuals who have influenced the course of Western civilization provides insight into what makes a great leader. The leaders typically examined were such men as Winston Churchill, Thomas Jefferson, and Alexander the Great. The bias of these theories is captured by their label. Women, such as Joan of Arc, Queen Elizabeth I, and Catherine the Great, who also have strongly influenced Western civilization, were ignored in the development of these theories. These theories receive little serious attention today.[4]

Trait theories assume that effective managers are endowed with personal qualities that differentiate them from their followers and can be applied to any situation. Given that all individuals do not have these qualities, only those who actually possess them are presumed fit to be leaders. These qualities are associated with the masculine sex role stereotype, such as initiative, decisiveness, and self-confidence, or with the feminine stereotype, such as sociability, tactfulness, and nurturance, and with neither stereotype, such as intelligence, physical energy, and fluency of speech. Studies that have attempted to identify the traits best suited for managers, however, have yielded few consistent findings. As a result, theories stressing universal traits of leadership have been deemphasized in recent years.[5]

Behavioral theories, which focus on the specific behaviors used by managers to influence their subordinates' actions, currently receive the greatest amount of attention. Most behavioral theories propose two types of managerial behavior: *task-oriented behavior* and *people-oriented behavior* (although labels vary, e.g., initiating structure and consideration, autocratic and democratic leadership, boss-centered and subordinate-centered leadership, concern for production and concern for people). Behavioral theories differ on whether these types of behavior are independent dimensions, with an individual being able to be strong or weak in each, or are opposite poles along the same dimension of behavior. Some behavioral theories regard one type of combination of behaviors as best in all situations. Other behavioral theories, also called *situational theories,* regard different types of behavior as appropriate for different situations. Task-oriented and people-oriented types of behavior, however, form the basis for most behavioral theories.

The linkage between sex role stereotypes and behavioral theories of leadership is apparent. Task-oriented behaviors by the leader, including initiating structure, setting goals, and making decisions, are those most associated with the masculine stereotype. People-oriented behaviors by the leader, such as showing consideration toward subordinates, soliciting subordinates' ideas, and demonstrating concern for subordinates' satisfaction, are most associated with the feminine stereotype. Androgynous management can then be defined as a combination of task-oriented and people-oriented behavior.

No behavioral theory suggests that better managers are masculine (i.e., mostly task-oriented) or feminine (i.e., mostly people-oriented), except in special situations. Some behavioral theories, such as the Managerial Grid Theory, suggest that better managers are androgynous by advocating a combination of task-oriented and people-oriented behavior. Although they did not offer their own theory, Susan Donnell and Jay Hall reached the same conclusion in a study of nearly 2,000 managers. High managerial achievers successfully integrated their concerns for task and people; average achievers concentrated on the task at the expense of the people performing it; and low achievers showed little concern for either task or people. Donnell and Hall provided a possible explanation for why the ranks of management are filled with individuals who exhibit predominantly masculine behaviors, even though such behaviors are seldom exclusively recommended. These individuals may be the organization's average managers, who perform well enough to retain their positions but not well enough to be considered excellent performers.[6]

IMPLEMENTING ANDROGYNOUS MANAGEMENT

How should an organization that wants to promote the use of androgynous management proceed? Sargent said that such an organization faces three tasks:[7]

1. Developing a climate that creates the opportunity for value shifts, behavioral change, and skill development.
2. Developing strategies that require and encourage androgynous management skills.
3. Developing reward systems that reinforce the use of these skills.

For a shift towards androgynous management to take place, the organizational climate needs to support learning, growth, personal change, and a concern for the interaction between task and people. It needs to demonstrate a high concern for the individual and the work group as well as the organization itself. Human resource managers can play an important role in encouraging this type of climate. However, the support of top management is essential.

The human resource management strategies available to organizations include changing policies and practices, restructuring jobs to increase teamwork, and giving employees the opportunity to get involved in goal setting and work scheduling. According to Sargent, the challenge is to establish programs that promote meaningful interactions between people, positive feedback, recognition, and participation. Androgynous management is best fostered when programs emphasize collaboration and interdependence rather than competition and independence.

Androgynous management also needs to be appropriately rewarded, both formally and informally. Performance appraisals of managers should recognize and praise listening skills, expression of feelings, and sensitivity to employee needs and problems as well as the ability to develop and implement organizational initiatives. Criteria for effectiveness should include both masculine and feminine dimensions appropriate for the particular managerial job.

Individuals who wish to be more androgynous should start by assessing their strengths and weaknesses to determine whether they should increase or decrease their masculine or feminine behaviors. For example, you may have no trouble in getting across your own ideas and positions on issues (masculine quality), but you want to develop your ability to express your personal feelings better (feminine quality). First, you will need your boss's support. Then you will need to take some risks in expressing your feelings and see how your efforts work out. Feedback from your coworkers and boss about how you are doing will be helpful. Having people with whom you can candidly discuss your efforts at change will also be beneficial. Finally, you will need organizational support for trying to change. Unless the organization is receptive to or is actively promoting androgynous management, you will seem very strange to others who are used to the "old you." This is why it is difficult for already-successful individuals to make major changes in their behavior on their own.

Training programs can be useful for introducing the concept of androgynous management to employees and helping them with their struggles to change. These programs typically include self-assessment, feedback from others, and discussion of how to respond to hypothetical and real situations in an androgynous manner. The emphasis in such programs should be on the creation of a safe environment in which people can explore their feelings about change and develop plans for change. As others have argued, it makes little sense to separate women and men in such programs. Support of the opposite sex can be very helpful in making personal change, particularly if the direction of change is towards acquiring skills typically associated with the opposite sex. Also, separation assumes that men and women bring different needs and abilities to the managerial job, an assumption that is not warranted.[8]

CONCLUSION

Androgynous management *does not* represent the inevitable wave of the future as more women enter management or the secret to happiness in life. It *does* represent a simultaneous concern for task and people that is compatible with the advice many have given to managers but in different terms. However, in many settings individual managers cannot become more androgynous on their own without taking considerable personal risk. They need organizational support to make the change successfully. Despite management traditions, neither women nor men ought to be expected to live up to the masculine stereotype in their managerial roles. Organizations will be far better off if, instead, they encourage their managers to be androgynous. ■

FOOTNOTES

1. Alice G. Sargent, *The Androgynous Manager* (New York: AMACOM, 1981); Kenneth H. Blanchard and Alice G. Sargent, "The One Minute Manager Is an Androgynous Manager," *Training and Development Journal*, May 1984, Vol. 38, No. 5, 83–85.
2. Gary N. Powell, *Women and Men in Management* (Newbury Park, CA: Sage, 1988).
3. Sandra L. Bem, "The Measurement of Psychological Androgyny," *Journal of Consulting and Clinical Psychology*, 1974, Vol. 42, 155–162; Ellen P. Cook, "Androgyny: A Goal for Counseling?" *Journal of Consulting and Development*, May 1985, Vol. 63, 567–571.
4. Bernard M. Bass, Chapter 3, "An Introduction to Theories and Models of Leadership," in *Stogdill's Handbook of Leadership* New York: Free Press, 1981).
5. Bass, Chapter 5, "Traits of Leadership: A Follow-up to 1970."
6. Robert R. Blake and Jan S. Mouton, *The Managerial Grid* (Houston: Gulf, 1964); Susan M. Donnell and Jay Hall, "Men and Women as Managers: A Significant Case of No Significant Difference," *Organizational Dynamics*, Spring 1980, Vol. 8, No. 4, 60–77.
7. Sargent, Chapter 15, "Toward an Androgynous Organization."
8. Elizabeth B. Bolton and Luther Wade Humphreys, "A Training Program for Women: An Androgynous Approach," *Personnel Journal*, May 1977, Vol. 56, 130–234.

The 1990s: From Managing to Leading

Dana Gaines Robinson

Training isn't just necessary for today's employees if companies are to be ready for the job demands of the 1990s. Supervisors, too, need to make sure they have the skills and knowledge to be successful in the every-demanding years ahead. What will the future portend for managers? What can they do to be prepared for the new style of management the future will require?

Managers in America today share similar dilemmas. The labor force is changing, organizational structures are different, social and economic forces are new and constantly evolving, and the marketplace is now global. Certainly, many of the "tried-and-true" management techniques developed and used through the 1970s and 1980s are yielding unacceptable results as America moves into the 1990s. Why is that the case? What exactly is changing?

PRIMARY CHANGES EXPECTED IN THE 1990S

In the 1990s, the following changes are expected:

- The workforce will be diverse, with 50 percent of it female and 43 percent minority; 20 percent will be "guest" workers from foreign countries.
- The average worker will be 40.
- Illiteracy will be a problem, with 18 percent of adults reading at or below the fifth-grade level.
- There will be insufficient numbers of people for entry-level positions; at the same time, this shrinking labor force's "mind-set" will reflect that of baby busters who value jobs with variety, flexibility, choice, emphasis on autonomy, and "psychological ownership."
- Half the workforce will be working on a permanent part-time status, others will be job-sharing, and still others on some type of flexitime; thus, there will be a variety of job structures in the workplace.

Reprinted, by permission of publisher, from SUPERVISORY MANAGEMENT, June/1989 ©1989. American Management Association, New York. All rights reserved.

Dana Gaines Robinson is president of Partners in Change, a management consulting firm located in Pittsburgh, PA.

- Management span of control will continue to increase as organizations delayer; some managers will have 50 or more people directly reporting to them.
- The use of teams and task forces to accomplish work will increase; emphasis will be on collaboration, not competition.
- Workers will continually learn and prepare for their next job; people entering the workforce today can expect up to six career changes in their working life.

MANAGEMENT STYLE FOR THE 1990s

What is required of managers to be successful in such a dynamic and changing environment? The key is to move away from a style of "management" and toward a style of "leadership." As the leadership transition model below illustrates, there is a clear difference between these two approaches. The more traditional management style found in typical bureaucratic organizations stresses using a slow, chain-of-command decision-making process. Here, managers control and "tell" their employees what to do, and both managers and employees must ask permission before acting.

What style needs to replace this approach? There are six points to consider:

LEADERSHIP TRANSITION MODEL

From a Style of MANAGING Others:		To A Style of LEADING Others:
Directing others	⇨	Guiding/Developing
Competing	⇨	Collaborating
Using Hierarchy	⇨	Using Network
Consistency/Sameness	⇨	Diversity/Flexibility
"Slow" Decision Making requiring permission	⇨	"Fast" Decision Making using judgment
Risk-Averse	⇨	Risk Taking
Individual Contributor	⇨	Team Player
Being Managed	⇨	Self Management
People as Expense	⇨	People as Asset

The author wishes to acknowledge Julie O'Mara and David Jamieson for their work in development of this model.

---

1. The leader's primary role will be to coach and develop people. Often, managers, especially at the first level, are doers more than managers. Typically, they have as much, or more, technical expertise than their employees. This will no longer work in the 1990s, when managers may have dozens of direct reports who work in the highly skilled, fast-paced niches of today's marketplace. The leaders of the future will be chartered with selecting employees and developing them so they can take on wider and wider responsibilities with less and less supervision. The reward for leading in the 1990s will be found not in doing but in developing people.

2. Leaders in the 1990s must provide wide parameters to help employees become "self-managed." With the ever-increasing spans of control managers are acquiring, it is no longer possible to "manage" others. There simply isn't time to make assignments, monitor, and control each employee's contribution. And employees of the future will want to be "left alone," to work with a high degree of autonomy. This is where psychological ownership of the job develops. So leaders of the future must develop people to perform without close supervision, and they must learn to be comfortable with less control.

3. Leaders in the 1990s will both participate in and encourage teams and teamwork. The traditional management model encourages individual contributions and rewards. Often, organizations encourage internal competition—departments working in a race where one department "wins" while other "lose." In the information age, such dynamics will not be successful. What will be required is the synergy that results when several people, focused on a common goal, work in a collaborative manner. When employees work this way, more is accomplished than could ever be done by them working independently. Leaders must model and coach for this collaborative approach to work.

4. Leaders in the 1990s will encourage speed in all facets of the job. Fast, faster, and fastest will be the words that drive business in the 1990s. To meet this challenge, leaders must adopt practices that encourage rapid and speedy response from workers. Decision making must be pushed down to the lowest level possible; employees must be "empowered" to act rather than have to seek permission to do so. For this to happen, they will require development in decision making and judgment as well as access to all information. In some organizations, the present norm is "when in doubt, *don't* tell." In the future, however, managers must be biased toward communicating any and all available information. Only with current information can employees make proper decisions. Additionally, employees must be encouraged to go directly to a needed resource rather than work through the traditional chain-of-command; therefore, networking will be important.

5. Leaders must encourage innovation and risk taking to meet the ever-changing challenges facing organizations. Traditional management models discourage taking action unless it is almost certain to be effective. Because of this, many employees learn that the punishment for failure outweighs the reward for success; so they try nothing new. For innovation and risk taking to thrive organizationally, leaders must allow for failure. Those risks that do not succeed should be turned into learning experiences.

6. Leaders of the future know that the competitive edge they have in today's marketplace is their people. In the traditional model, people are seen as expenses that must be minimized and controlled. In the leadership model, people are viewed as assets that require investment.

MANAGERS TODAY, LEADERS TOMORROW?

To become leaders, managers first need to determine where they are currently demonstrating the leadership qualities illustrated in the leadership transition model, and where there is need for change. For example, are they coaching and developing their employees and spending substantial time in that effort? Have they indicated to their employees the parameters within which they can act without asking for "permission?" And are those parameters wide? Do they make a concerted effort to pass on to them all the information they have?

To fully prepare for the upcoming changes, which will only magnify in time, it is important that managers invest in their personal development. They should seek out training programs that teach the basics of leadership, and they should encourage their own mangers to provide on-the-job experiences that will produce growth in areas like team management.

Managers should also analyze the jobs they have reporting to them, as well as the people who hold those jobs. Does the job structure encourage employees to manage themselves and take actions when required? Are employees developed so they can successfully work in a fast-paced, independent working structure? If not, managers must begin making the necessary changes.

Certainly, there will be major challenges impacting upon managers in the 1990s. Managers can either allow those changes to come upon them like a wave crashing at their feet or prepare for the changes and ride the wave in. The challenge is theirs—and so is the choice.

SUMMING UP

To be successful in the 1990s, managers will have to develop a "leadership" style of management. What does this leadership style entail?

First, a manager's primary role will be to coach and develop people. Second, managers will need to provide wide parameters to employees so that employees are "self-managed." Third, managers will both participate in and encourage teams and teamwork. Fourth, managers will encourage speed in all facets of the job. Fifth, managers will encourage innovation and risk taking to meet the ever-changing challenges facing organizations. Finally, managers will treat employees as assets, not expenses, and they will need to invest more time and resources in training and development.

What Good Leaders Do

Larry B. Meares

What are the personal qualities of a true leader? The author details 50 leadership recommendations for HR professionals.

What makes a good business leader? The 50 recommendations in this article represent my personal list of leadership qualities—a list that I have built over the years with the help of many business scholars, researchers, associates, and managers. If you have read much about the art of leadership, you will undoubtedly recognize the influence of many distinguished people on my list. In some ways I agree with all of them; in others I do not. My approach was to evaluate their own recommendations based on their logic and practicality, try these recommendations out, and then store them away for future reference.

As I've gained insight and knowledge over the years, I have found that by liberally redefining the work of others, I could fit it together in new ways that worked best for me. I could then weave this information into a personally useful theme that includes the points on the list of recommendations. The list is intentionally not organized or prioritized in any particular fashion, as every person must reach his or her own conclusions on this score. In adapting the list to your own needs, or in passing it along to other managers in your company, please feel free to discard or add whatever you want and use what you feel works best for you.

Reprinted by permission of publisher, from Personnel, September 1988©1988. American Management Association, NY. All rights reserved.

Larry B. Meares is an internal consultant with Leaseway Transportation Corporation in Cleveland. He is responsible for the support mission of assisting in the creation and maintenance of positive and productive work environments for the company's nonunion operations. Before his affiliation with Leaseway, Meares was founder and president of LBM Associates, Inc., a management consulting firm specializing in organization development and personnel resources. During his career, Meares has created and led corporate, group, and division human resources and industrial relations functions in both union and nonunion service and industrial environments. As a production manager, he has also had firsthand manufacturing and supervisory management experience. He received his B.S.B.A. degree in industrial relations from the University of Florida and his M.B.A. in organizational behavior through an employer-sponsored postgraduate program.

Before you read on, let me offer you one admonition: You may have found, or will likely find at some point, that it is quite difficult to live according to all the recommendations on the list. Please don't let this deter you—attempting to fulfill your potential as a leader is, I have found, a lifelong endeavor.

THE CONSEQUENCES OF LEADERSHIP

This list of recommendations, if applied reasonably well, will probably have consequences with which you may or may not be comfortable. For this reason, you should review the following list of consequences before you totally commit yourself. You will experience the consequences through the following effects:

- Higher and sustained productivity.
- Lower turnover.
- Increased adaptability to change.
- Greater creativity.
- Higher trust levels.
- Mutual interdependence.
- Committed, "turned-on" people.
- Absence of visible positional power and/or status symbols.
- Elimination of top-down control.
- More consistent, constant, noncapricious leadership.
- Better customer satisfaction and quality.
- Different leadership role.

Neither this list nor the list that will follow is intended to be an all-inclusive list of consequential changes. However, I hope that the examples given in each will illustrate the importance of their respective points.

FIFTY RECOMMENDATIONS FOR LEADERSHIP

Here are the 50 recommendations, presented as a result of my research and experience, and not arranged in any particular order of importance:

1. Flatten the hierarchy. (Stay in touch with what is going on below you in the organization's structure.)
2. Widen the span of control one step more than you are comfortable with. (This promotes personal organization, delegation, and participation.)
3. Increase the frequency and quality of two-way communication. (Search for ways to inform and gather information.)
4. Cross-train everywhere—up, down, and laterally. (This creates competence.)

5. Involve everyone possible in planning and evaluation, and provide feedback as immediately as possible. (This creates the opportunity for participation and elicits greater commitment and creativity.)
6. Avoid tops-down direction; create bottoms-up self-direction. (This promotes motivation vis-a-vis self-management.)
7. Listen, ask questions, act, and be timely. (This is the adhesive of leadership that holds everything else together.)
8. Be visible and remain accessible. (This keeps you aware and others comfortable.)
9. Avoid tops-down rules and regulations that attempt to control from outside-in; install mature guidelines that promote self-control from within. (This promotes mature reactions and attitudes as opposed to immature reactions.)
10. Help job performers to establish clear, quantifiable performance and behavior standards for themselves; reward on the basis of these standards; successful completion. (This promotes self-sufficiency and the ability to evaluate objectively.)
11. Eliminate status symbols for the few; give status to the broad spectrum of employees. (This makes everyone a potential participant and co-opts organizational synergy.)
12. Avoid installing programs that make some people psychologically "taller" than others, thereby creating an organization of "haves" and "have nots." (This creates organizational energy and provides the foundation for people to work "with" one another.)
13. Hold everyone to his or her commitments. (This maintains crispness of execution and assures that commitments are respected.)
14. Insist on intellectual honesty from everyone. (This will help everyone deal with the proper level of specificity and be open with one another.)
15. Insist on openness and integrity, but do so with sensitivity. (This helps assure that hidden agendas and communication channels are properly dealt with.)
16. Hire and retain only those people who have a work ethic that matches your own; facilitate participation and involvement from others in the selection process. (This helps the organization to share the value of productivity demonstrated by its leadership.)
17. Stress value-added thinking rather than quantity of output or activity thinking. (This makes effort count and encourages quality.)
18. Don't let up when things are going well; keep the organization lean and stretching, plan for change, and look for new ways to improve. (This will assure constancy of purpose and a leading edge.)
19. Watch costs and staff additions closely. (This prevents too much bureaucratization and promotes evaluation and analysis.)

20. Provide many ways to recognize, compliment, and "build up" people. (This promotes personal ego satisfaction and job enrichment.)

21. Don't make promises you can't keep. (This promotes your credibility and establishes a role model for others to emulate.)

22. Admit when you are wrong. (This promotes your credibility and generates an organizational value that integrity is "in," along with a value that tolerates risk taking.)

23. Apologize when you have erred. (This promotes both your personal esteem and the message that sensitivity and openness are valued.)

24. Thank people who have helped you. (This expresses gratitude, expands your ability to recognize others, and encourages others to do likewise.)

25. Value and communicate to others the fact that the enterprise's success is the ultimate foundation of everyone's security. (This maintains the focus on personal effort, competition, productivity, quality, and customer satisfaction as opposed to artificial methods of sustaining security.)

26. Keep your "power club" in your back pocket, and use it only when you have to. (This lets you deal interpersonally and persuasively; it promotes two-way communication and trust.)

27. Try to care genuinely about yourself and others; believe in the assumption that most people will want to do their best if given the right environment, especially if you have been careful with Item 16. (This maintains openness, supports trust, and promotes participation and delegation.)

28. Realize that your most productive internal focus is the removal of obstacles that prevent others from performing as well as they should. (This encourages internal self-control and increases productivity.)

29. Provide opportunities for others to grow in terms of knowledge, performance, and contribution. (This aids organizational competency and personal job satisfaction.)

30. Train people to manage their commitments and their time through some commonly used system. (This promotes self-organization and fulfillment of organizational objectives.)

31. Develop—and live by—a super-ordinate goal that focuses on your organization's reason for existence. (This helps everyone to remember his or her purpose and the reason for his or her security.)

32. Be aware of the state of the marketplace, and make sure that everyone else is aware of it. (This awareness promotes concern, involvement, competency, and commitment.)

33. Stress flexibility as a valued asset. (This helps lessen the resistance to constant change.)

34. Promote creativity through employee participation and promotion. (This involvement generates personal ownership, growth, and commitment.)

35. Be assertive rather than aggressive with people. (This encourages and establishes the role model for openness as opposed to abuse.)

36. Have the courage to step forward, to lead the way, to say what you need to say. (This gives testimony to your leadership and encourages others to follow.)

37. Promote risk taking by accepting mistakes made by others through their caring and effort. (This helps others to experiment and try things that improve the organization and its objectives.)

38. Squelch backbiting by facilitating confrontation. (This allows others to be open and deal candidly with each other.)

39. Uncover and explain rumors. (This will encourage people to ask for clarification and verification rather than to pass the rumor on.)

40. Counsel problem performers through a focus on behavior rather than on the individual; be sensitive to the self-esteem of others. (This permits the person's focus to be on self-improvement rather than on hurt feelings or damaged self-esteem.)

41. Celebrate appropriately both large and small successes, including the achievements and accomplishments both of the organization and its individuals. (This shows that success and recognition are valued and encourages positive attitudes and efforts.)

42. Train people to question the status quo and to search for new and better ways of doing things. (This encourages creativity and helps prevent "maintenance thinking"—that is, thinking that defends and sponsors only the status quo—from developing.)

43. Perform in the same ways that you want others to perform. (This promotes your leadership stature and a congruent connection between word and deed.)

44. Spend time reflecting on the "what-ifs" of the future. (This enhances vision and planning an encourages you to examine alternatives to current thoughts and ideas.)

45. Keep the focus of the organization and its people on the superordinate goal. (This creates specificity and value-added thought and action.)

46. Remember when you are trying to motivate others that the carrot motivates others to perform through a process of external seduction, while meaningful participation motivates them to perform from within. (This lets you decide whether you want mere "movement" or true motivation.)

47. Remember that we all have our ups and downs, our bad times and good times—and be sure to take both into account. (This serves as a reminder that everyone is human.)

48. Be aware that change is often uncomfortable, and that with large groups of people it may take a long time to accomplish, depending on the degree and complexity of the change. (This cautions against expecting too much too soon and promotes careful planning of both the content and process of change.)
49. Once you know for certain that you have made an error in your staffing, have counseled for improvement, and have failed to achieve it, do not avoid sensitively confronting the person and resolving your error. (This keeps the organization and its performance standards at optimum levels.)
50. Promote and practice patience, not malingering and apathy. (This will give the organization and its people an attitude of reasonableness and reality.)

I offer one final thought, which seems to best fall within the category of "enlightened self-interest": If you want your own needs to be met, take care to satisfy the needs of those upon whom you depend to satisfy your needs. In giving of ourselves, we expect to have our own needs satisfied in return. When we get, we give to satisfy the needs of others. ∎

Helping Young Managers Bridge The Generation Gap

Benson Rosen
Thomas H. Jerdee

There are a lot of differences between the 'Me' generation and the one that lived through the Great Depression. But they can learn to work together.

In response to an aging work force and new retirement and pension laws, many organizations are paying more attention to older employees. Workshops and counseling programs aimed at helping people plan and prepare for retirement have become almost commonplace. But another problem bubbling up from the same demographic stew is largely ignored: the difficulties that arise between senior employees—those who still have a way to go before retirement—and the younger managers who have become their bosses.

For young managers, communicating performance problems across the generation gap is particularly difficult. Only the dullest can be unaware that some older, more experienced employees view them with skepticism or resentment. Young managers may fear that attempts to help older employees will meet with hostility and resistance. As a result, young manager are likely to avoid communication with older employees, or to fumble when they do try.

The long-term effects of poor communication across the generation gap are threefold. For the older employee, it may lead to low motivation and, in some instances, to visible rebellion and retaliation. For the young manager, the result can be frustration, ineffectiveness and, in some instances, a decision to leave the organization. For the organization, the effects are increased conflict, lack of commitment, and declining productivity and quality.

Reprinted with permission from the March 1985 issue of Training, The Magazine of Human Resources Development. Copyright 1985, Lakewood Publications Inc., Minneapolis, MN (612) 333–0471. All rights reserved.

Benson Rosen and *Thomas H. Jerdee* are both professors at the Graduate School of Business Administration at the University of North Carolina at Chapel Hill. This article was adapted from their book, *Older Employees: New Roles for Valued Resources* (Dow-Jones/Irwin, Chicago, 1984).

Organizations that improve the intergenerational communication skills of young managers can heighten the performance and job satisfaction of young and old alike. One way to do so is to design a workshop aimed at young managers who manage older workers.

The first order of business in this kind of workshop is to sensitize these managers to the value differences between younger and older employees. Next, they need to be alerted to the pervasive influence of age stereotypes on managerial decisions. Finally, workshop participants need to fine-tune their own problem-solving and communication skills to help them deal with performance problems across the generation gap.

VALUE DIFFERENCES

The same kinds of conflicts, misunderstandings and resulting problems that develop between parents and children can develop between younger and older workers.

Consider the values held by senior employees who are products of the post-depression generation. Many of these people share a strong work ethic and place a premium on job and financial security. Some were first- or second-generation immigrants who retained many customs from their homelands. They had their own standards of dress, listened to music from a different era and accepted as given such principles as family solidarity, respect for authority figures and patriotism.

Contrast these values with those of workers who entered the labor force during the past decade. Younger workers may have grown up under more permissive child-rearing practices. As part of the "Me" generation, they tend to place a high premium on self-actualizing work. Some of them reject their parents' aspirations to upward mobility and dedication to work in favor of a lifestyle that leaves them ample time to pursue leisure activities. Some are suspicious of big business and big government. Some demonstrated in the streets during the '60s and '70s. Many have experimented with drugs. This generation dressed in blue jeans, listened to hard rock and adhered to the motto, "Don't trust anyone over 30."

Given these differences in attitudes, values and lifestyles, is it any wonder that communication between younger and older workers—let alone young managers and older subordinates—occasionally breaks down? Older managers scratch their heads and puzzle over why younger workers seem to believe that the world owes them a living. Middle-aged workers battle mid-life crises and worry about the meaning of life. Younger workers vow to avoid burnout and search for jobs that will let them do their own thing. Yet, to work effectively together, these employees must learn to appreciate each other's perspectives on work and life.

Where does training come in? After a frank discussion of value differences and how they influence supervisory styles and expectations, workshop participants might examine several specific problems that may arise between younger and older workers. Cases, incidents, roles plays and simulated decision exercises can help participants of all ages realize how quickly and easily supervisors tend to fall back on age stereotypes in day-to-day decision-making.

SPECIAL PROBLEMS

According to sociologists, the way we interact with another person depends on whether we have defined that person's status as higher than, the same as or lower than our own. If all of the status cues are consistent, the appropriate behavior becomes obvious. For example, when a young management trainee meets an older, distinguished-looking man at a cocktail party and determines early in the conversation that his new acquaintance is president of a major international bank, the management trainee adjusts his behavior accordingly. He listens attentively, defers to the banker's opinions and works hard to create a favorable impression of himself.

What would happen if this older gentleman turned out to be a janitor? He would be accorded higher status based on his age and experience, but lower status based on the prestige level of his occupation. And the management trainee might find himself in an awkward situation because the status cues are inconsistent.

Young managers find it awkward to supervise older employees because of comparable status inconsistencies. Their jobs require that they plan, supervise and evaluate the work of older employees yet providing feedback—particularly negative feedback—to a veteran subordinate can make a young manager uncomfortable. The problem becomes more complex if the older employee has many years of experience in the organization. And what if the manager is a young woman?

The kinds of problems that often develop in status-inconsistent relationships between younger and older employees, illustrated in the following incident, should be considered in a management awareness workshop.

Case 1: The Hart Bypass

At age 35, Joanna Hart's star was on the rise at Niagra Investments. She was the first female chief economist and the highest-ranked woman in the company. She realized that her behavior would be closely watched. However, she felt that the insights about power and politics she had gained in her previous positions would serve her well.

One of Hart's many responsibilities was Niagra's advanced management training program. The company placed a great deal of emphasis on in-house training for analysts and brokers. All new analysts and brokers spent five months in training, attending short courses on various aspects of economics, finance and investment. Experienced brokers and outside experts taught these courses. It was considered an honor to be assigned to the training faculty, and brokers selected to teach a course received a $7,500 bonus.

Frank Crandall, a 22-year veteran with Niagra, taught the advanced investments course. His course had been well received in the past, but complaints about his teaching effectiveness had recently come to Hart's attention. In the end-of-course evaluation, students commented that Crandall had failed to cover the newer econometric forecasting models. Other unfavorable comments focused on his use of dated examples to illustrate economic principles.

Hart knew that the complaints against Crandall could be political dynamite. She learned that Crandall took great pride in his teaching. She also was aware that several other brokers wanted a chance to teach the advanced investments course. Hart guessed that Crandall would become defensive if she confronted him directly about his poor teaching ratings. He had made many friends at Niagra over the years, and the last thing Hart needed was a coalition of angry old-timers bucking her every decision, Yet she felt that it would be unconscionable to jeopardize the quality of the training to spare Crandall's feelings.

Rather than risk an argument, Hart reassigned Crandall to an investor-relations position. She stretched the truth a bit and told him that the recent proliferation of complex investment instruments had led to a deluge of calls and letters, creating an overload for the investor-relations staff. She also hinted that this would be a temporary assignment.

Crandall accepted the reassignment at face value and moved into his new role. He found the work repetitive and unchallenging. His memos requesting a reappointment to the training faculty went unanswered for months. When a reply finally came through, it explained vaguely that his services were still needed in investor relations. Over time, he grew discouraged. He took an unusually large number of sick days. The head of the investor relations section reported that Crandall had developed an apathetic attitude to customer inquiries.

Hart again puzzled over how to handle Crandall's deteriorating performance. She wanted very much to spare his feelings and to avoid an unpleasant discussion. And after all, she reasoned, how could a young woman and relative newcomer to the firm convince a 22-year veteran to change his ways?

About 10 months later, Hart reassigned Crandall. This time, she sent him to a small satellite office in the suburbs. She felt that nothing positive would come out of a confrontation, so she again explained the reassignment as a temporary measure until the office manager could properly train a new analyst.

Crandall grudgingly accepted the change. As time passed, colleagues in the office noticed that he seemed to withdraw; he seldom spoke with others in the office. The office manager characterized him as a case of "borderline depression." Three months after his second reassignment, Frank Crandall called the corporate personnel office and requested immediate early retirement.

Analysis

In management-awareness workshops, participants' reactions to the Hart Bypass case typically vary. Some of the younger participants agree with Hart's decision to avoid openly confronting Crandall with his negative teaching evaluations and his poor performance in the investment-relations department. In fact, they are likely to argue that the case reached a satisfactory conclusion with Crandall's voluntary early retirement.

Other participants point out that Hart's unwillingness to confront Crandall set off a chain reaction of misunderstandings. They argue that by circumventing Crandall rather than confronting him, Hart escalated a minor performance problem to a point beyond reconciliation. As a result, the organization lost a valued senior employee unnecessarily.

No formula resolves all of the misunderstandings that develop between young supervisors and older employees. But young managers can learn confrontation and problem-solving skills that will help them deal with the performance problems of older employees—or any other employee for that matter. Honest confrontations give employees the opportunity to improve their performance and open up the possibilities for creative problem-solving by both the manager and the employee.

Confronting Poor Performers

Real risks *do* exist in open confrontations. At Niagra Investments, Hart felt that Crandall would react defensively to criticism from a young manager and that others in the company would resent her pulling rank on an experienced senior employee. Whether her concerns were justified depends largely upon her skills in communication, confrontation and problem-solving.

Effective confrontations clearly and unambiguously communicate the nature of the poor performance, spell out the organizational consequences of unacceptable behavior and give the poor performer flexibility in choosing how to improve.

Specific examples of unsatisfactory performance communicate much more effectively than vague characterizations of the employee's motivation or personality. Telling Frank Crandall that his students want exposure to sophisticated econometric-forecasting models gives him a clear message; telling him that his teaching is deficient or incompetent does not. Similarly, telling Crandall that he handled too few investor inquiries is preferable to labeling him apathetic.

Effective confrontation requires managers to spell out the impact of substandard performance on the department or unit. In confronting Crandall with his low productivity in dealing with investor inquiries, for example, Hart could have said, "When you handle only a few investor problems, the burden of answering the remaining calls falls unfairly on other brokers and drives up costs for maintaining good investor relations."

Effective confrontation gives the poor performer an opportunity to save face and to make a commitment to improve. Open-ended statements that identify specific areas that need improvement are better than directives about future behavior. For example, Hart might have used this open-ended statement. "I'm concerned that you aren't covering econometric-forecasting models in your investment courses. This deprives our new brokers of information about important tools necessary for carrying out their jobs."

An open-ended confrontation shifts the burden for improvement directly to the ineffective performer. The supervisor is sending a message that she trusts the subordinate to take the initiative and work toward improvement. It allows the subordinate to select the course of action that seems personally compatible.

Consider how Frank Crandall *might* have reacted to a direct, open confrontation on the missing econometric-forecasting models. He might have agreed immediately to include them in his next course. He might have volunteered to change teaching assignments. He might have requested a one-year leave of absence from teaching in order to brush up on econometric models.

If Crandall were the one who selected a strategy for solving the performance problem, he probably would be highly committed to it. And naturally, Crandall's boss retains final approval over his course of action. Hart has no obligation to go along with a plan that would create problems elsewhere in the organization.

Note that the philosophy underlying open confrontation differs markedly from the basic assumption with which Hart approached her problem—the assumption that Crandall would react in anger. The confrontational strategy assumes that when senior employees learn of their substandard performance, they will make a good-faith effort to improve. Management decisions that circumvent senior workers assume that they will be unwilling or unable to improve.

The pessimistic view of the reactions of older workers comes from age stereotypes. It sets the stage for self-fulfilling prophecies: Older workers who are seen as resistant to change are unlikely to change.

Case 2: Pressure in Personnel

Joanna Hart was not the only young executive at Niagra Investments with problems in supervising a senior employee. Barry Alderman, who was in charge of Niagra's college recruiting program, could not remember a more hectic time in his life. During the past two months, Alderman had visited 24 universities and had interviewed more than 200 MBA students for entry-level investment -adviser positions. The experience had been exhausting. Because of his road schedule, Alderman had been forced to rely heavily on his administrative assistant, Betty Aluise, to handle many of the duties he usually attended to personally.

Since returning to the office, Alderman had become increasingly aware of Aluise's aloofness. He sensed that she was purposely avoiding him. He also noticed that she became evasive when he questioned her about a late travel voucher or a missing applicant file. A little investigating revealed that she was behind in her routine responsibilities and was now more than a week late with an important EEO/AA report. Aluise's failure to attend a monthly staff meeting was the last straw for Alderman. He was determined to get her back on track or to find someone else who was capable of managing the work load. He left her a note requesting an 8:45 meeting in his office Monday morning.

Aluise had been having her own doubts about her ability to manage the growing work load and about her future at Niagra Investments. Returning to full-time work four years ago at age 53 represented quite a change for her. Although she had worked as an executive secretary before her marriage, her previous positions had been much less demanding than her present one.

At home, she had become tense and short-tempered. Finally, she confided to her husband that she thought her boss was subtly pressuring her to quit. She explained that Alderman had told her to complete several complex monthly EEO/AA reports without lessening her regular work load. The reports required many statistical calculations, some of which were beyond anything she had ever encountered before. Completing the reports accurately seemed to take forever.

As a result, she worked through lunch hours two or three times a week and ended up skipping staff meetings just to catch up on her regular paperwork. She felt both overwhelmed and incompetent. With six years to go before her retirement, she wondered why her boss wanted to force her out.

Analysis

The way that Alderman handles the Monday morning meeting with his administrative assistant will have a lasting effect on their ability to work together in the future. Betty Aluise could easily become increasingly frustrated, feel unfairly treated and resign. On the other hand, if Alderman uses effective problem-solving skills, his working relationship with Aluise will improve and she will be more productive.

Alderman needs to use an approach that will minimize her defensiveness, capitalize on her experience and insights, and build commitment to resolve the problem. The problem-solving process outlined in the accompanying box is one that is effective in solving work-related problems. It requires managers and employees to work through a sequence of steps from problem identification through evaluation of implemented solutions.

Alderman might begin the meeting by explaining that he wants to follow this problem-solving sequence. His goal is to reduce the threat and defensiveness inherent in the situation and assure his employee that the two of them will be working toward mutually acceptable solutions to their work problems. Accordingly, he might begin with a statement along these lines; "Betty, I'm concerned about several problems, and I hope the two of us can work together to solve them." Note that Alderman's approach focuses on the need to solve problems, not on assumptions about who is to blame.

Problem identification begins with the kind of open-ended confrontation described earlier. Alderman might say, "I'm worried about missing the EEO/AA report deadlines. Without those reports, I can't complete my monthly recruiting reports on time. I'm also concerned that some of the routine paperwork has fallen behind. If we delay in scheduling applicants for second interviews we risk losing some excellent prospects."

Alderman now must attempt to see the situation from his employee's perspective. Aluise would likely tell him that she had worked extra hours in order to catch up. Perhaps she also would reveal that the complex statistical calculations are a problem for her and have slowed her down. Alderman may be surprised to learn that his assistant feels very insecure about her future. As the meeting continues, we might expect the following dialogue:

Manager: "I think I have a better understanding of the problem. The report deadlines are fixed. We can be a little more flexible about your other assignments, but they can't be postponed very long either. Let's take a few minutes and consider our options. Can you see any way that we can meet our schedules without making your work load impossible?" (Alderman has set the stage for brainstorming alternative solutions, step 2 in the problem-solving sequence.)

Assistant: "Maybe we could hire a 'temp' to handle some of the paperwork during your heavy travel period."

Manager: "Let me note that. I'll write down each possibility we come up with. Then we can go back and see which alternative seems most practical. Your idea made me think that we could look into reorganizing some of the work among our present staff. Perhaps someone from another department could come over here and lend a hand."

Assistant: "Maybe a computer program could calculate our EEO-statistics. I don't know much about computes, but maybe someone could write a program that we could use each month. Over time, the cost of creating the program would be recovered by the efficiency."

Manager: "We should look into that. I didn't realize how much trouble the calculations were causing. Would you be interested in enrolling in a statistical refresher course? The company would take care of your tuition expense."

Assistant: "I don't have much statistical aptitude. Given how far behind I am now, taking time to attend a refresher course would create more problems."

Manager: "Well, we have to come up with several good ideas for catching up. I suggest we meet again on Wednesday morning to decide how to handle the problem. In the meantime, we can gather more information about our proposed solutions. I'll check on the availability of existing computer software and how much it would cost to have a program tailor-made for our EEO reports. Would you look into the costs of hiring a temporary employee for two months and find out whether we can borrow someone from another department?"

Betty Aluise probably leaves this meeting feeling enormously better than she has for months.

At their Wednesday meeting, Alderman and Aluise should have at hand the information necessary to evaluate alternative solutions to the work overload problems. They will be at step 3: choosing a mutually acceptable solution.

Let's say they were able to rule out two alternatives quickly. Aluise reaffirmed her decision not to attend a refresher course in statistics. The personnel budget for the year could not be stretched far enough to hire a temporary employee. Accordingly, Alderman and Aluise focused their discussion on the remaining alternatives.

They agreed on a two-part plan of action. Beginning immediately, Alderman would redistribute the assignments so that an employee with strong statistical skills would work on the quantitative portion of the EEO/AA reports. In return, Aluise was to write the narrative section of several new reports in addition to performing her other duties. They also agreed to purchase several computer software packages on approval, the goal being to find a program that could handle the EEO monthly statistics.

Before the meeting ended, Alderman and Aluise agreed to meet again in two months to evaluate the success of their plan. In the meantime, Alderman made a mental note to check informally with Aluise and other members of the personnel staff to ensure that the work load was fairly distributed.

In workshops on managing older workers, young managers like Joanna Hart and Barry Alderman can develop the skills to confront their senior employees about performance problems and to use effective problem-solving skills to resolve the conflicts. By practicing these skills, young managers gain the courage to deal openly and directly with senior workers. The payoffs: reduced misunderstandings, better decisions, strong commitment to mutually agreed-upon decisions and more trusting work relationships with senior employees. ■

THE PROBLEM-SOLVING SEQUENCE

1. *Problem identification*

   Manager confronts senior employee with performance problem.
   Manager attempts to see situation from employee's perspective.
   Manager and employee agree on problem definition.

2. *Brainstorming alternative solutions*

   Manager and employee contribute ideas for solving problem.
   Evaluation of ideas is temporarily suspended to foster creativity.

3. *Choice of mutually acceptable solution*

   Manager and employee evaluate each alternative.
   Alternative that most effectively responds to problem definition is selected.

4. *Solution implementation*

   Manager and employee agree on how solution will be implemented.
   Timetable for implementation is set.

5. *Evaluation of solution*

   Manager and employee assess effectiveness of solution implementation.
   Ineffective solution stimulates redefinition of problem
   (begin sequence at step 1).
   Ineffective solution stimulates need for new alternative solutions
   (begin sequence at step 3).

Benefit from Creative Communication

Bob Martin
Assistant Editor

Four benefits communications programs effectively and creatively respond to employees' unparalleled need for information.

RAZOR SHARP CLARITY WITH THE EDGE

Born from the merger of Mercantile Texas and Southwest Bancshares companies, MCorp, a Texas-based bank holding company, embraced its reorganization as an opportune time to implement a new employee benefits program.

Finalized in October 1984, the merger meant more than a realignment of capital and assets. It carried with it a new identity and the chance to build a new image, both publicly and internally.

Exercising the unique opportunity to establish new loyalties and rebuild those eroded, one of the first programs implemented by the new management team was a flexible benefits program for the company's 12,500 full- and part-time employees.

Christened *The Edge*, the new plan was introduced in 1984 and received mixed reviews: The flexible benefits plan was a welcome alternative to traditional benefits packages, but the communication vehicle and execution left a lot to be desired.

"The first year the program had a fairy tale theme," says Jane Voisard, manager, employee communications at MCorp.

"Talking to employees we found a current of dissatisfaction—they didn't relate to the theme and didn't think it fit reality," she says.

Reprinted with permission from *Personnel Journal,* pp. 66–72, November 1986.

Each of these programs is a "1986 Gold Quill" winner, an award presented annually by the International Association of Business Communicators for outstanding efforts in business communications.

Personnel Journal thanks the IABC for its contribution to this supplement.

All "Gold Quill" programs are summarized in the IABC's publication, "No Secrets, Gold Quill Winners Tell All." IABC, 870 Market St., Ste. #940, San Francisco, CA 94102, $30.

"The merger was friendly, and was a perfect opportunity for change. And as it turns out the new benefits were seen as one of the most positive aspects of the change, but something had to be done about the plan's image," Voisard adds.

The first place Voisard and her staff turned to determine a course of action was the company's employees.

The employee communications department, a division of human resources, surveyed the employees and found:

- 67% of the employees were female
- 72% were between the ages of 20 and 39, with the 20–29-year-old bracket the largest segment
- The plan components that rated most favorably were the ability to buy vacation time, a broad range of life insurance options, and medical coverage opportunities
- The least desired were the pension plan and MoneyMax, a package of long-term savings plans combining employee and company contributions
- Pension, MoneyMax, supplemental health and dependent care reimbursement plans were not understood by a large segment of the employees
- 93% of the employees favored the freedom of choice the new plan afforded them, but many found it to be an intimidating decision-making responsibility.

Because there was an apparent correlation between the demographics of the employee population, the lack of understanding of complicated options, specifically pension funds and MoneyMax, and their enrollment rates, Voisard deduced that the communication vehicle needed to be an easy-to-understand but comprehensive document—spelling out the positive aspects of those plans that had distant effects, i.e., retirement benefits.

In addition, she set out to create a positive, friendly tone in the primary media, which was to remain *The Edge* magazine. This, she reasoned, would overcome the intimidation inherent in the benefits selection process.

She also sought to relate the magazine more closely to the employees than the previous year's publication.

With a budget of $165,000, she set plans for a four-color, 72-page publication with a print run of 21,000 copies.

Once the approach had been framed, content was determined by human resources staff members with guidance from the San Diego office of The Wyatt Co., a benefits consulting firm.

Voisard used several vehicles to meet her specific goals.

Incorporating employees in the publication increased its relevancy. Employees were used in all the published photographs illustrating various benefits options.

Employees also wrote short testimonials that were interspersed throughout the magazine, along with each employee's signature, giving each quote a sense of authenticity and, therefore, credibility.

According to Voisard, the use of employees did more than just increase interest in the benefits plans: It was a terrific morale builder, too.

A conversational, friendly writing tone overcame the intimidation of benefits-related decisions.

"The first thing we did was simplify the approach, which in turn reduced many enrollment errors," Voisard says.

"But the easy-to-read writing enabled employees to understand and relate to the material and brought it down to earth for them.

"The conversational tone didn't make the employees feel like they needed a translator to understand it—something that usually increases anxiety over making such decisions.

"That's where most benefits communication gets into trouble," she adds, "It gets bogged down in facts and in the legal parameters."

Additionally, the use of humor—accomplished through employee photos plating people in exaggerated situations with accompanying humorous cutlines—reinforced the essence of the illustrated benefit.

An open format underscored the uniqueness of the program while enhancing the message.

The use of employees in humorous photos not only reinforced the essence of the illustrated benefit, it was a terrific morale builder, too.

The use of bright colors, white space, and the corporate typeface set in a 13-point, easily read size guided the reader through the book and provided a clean, uncluttered atmosphere that complemented the tone of the writing.

The use of colors and screens on charts and forms gave them added excitement and focused attention on these examples.

The photographs were randomly dispersed throughout the book for comic relief and also as a cost-containing measure: By keeping them limited to one form on a printing signature, the expense of using four-color printing was minimized. The effect, however, was of a high-quality product—an impression not lost on the employees.

Enrollment increased following the production and circulation of the new magazine, but review of its success is an on-going process, Voisard says.

In fact, the magazine was changed in its second year as a result of informal and formal employee feedback.

This year, personal data were computer posted so each employee got an individualized summarization of benefits allowances and how much the various options would cost each month.

Much of the introductory information has been reduced in this upgraded personalized approach, Voisard says, with introduction to the overall program now offered during an initial employee orientation period.

In addition, newsletters, published on an as-needed basis, are dedicated to the program, its changes, and related factors.

The program also occupies regular space in the company's quarterly and bimonthly employee publications.

"As a single enrollment piece, and with the new personal fact sheet, the publication is relevant to each individual and has been the reason for an increased understanding of options and gradual enrollment changes," she says.

Additionally, regional personnel representatives have reacted favorably and have been able to better respond to employee inquiries, she adds.

And not only has the benefits program received increased support, but according to Voisard, during a time of change and its accompanying inclination for resistance, *The Edge* provided just that in cementing management-employee relations.

"I'm constantly receiving requests from employees to be included in the next year's issue," Voisard sums.

THE SWEET ROLE OF IMPROVEMENTS

The MINT theme, common in all communications materials, worked to coordinate disparate media so employees recognized each piece as part of the campaign.

The Public Service of New Hampshire (PSNH) was recovering from fiscal hard times when it introduced a new benefits plan to its nonunion employees in 1985.

Implementing a campaign built on the theme *MINT* (More Income Not Taxes), and using the candies as its central symbol, the company offered a new 401(k) plan to encourage retirement savings.

Following a period of hard times, accentuated by near bankruptcy in 1983, the utility had cut back on expenses, including employee communications.

Such fiscal sacrifices put the utility back on firmer footing in business terms, but left it with ground to make up in employee relations.

In addition to soothing scars of the leaner operating years, management strove to announce the program before an upcoming negotiating session commenced.

"Management wanted to ensure that employees perceived the new benefit coming from it, as opposed to the common perception that all benefits were union driven," says Lea Peterson, a communications specialist with William M. Mercer-Meidinger's Boston office, the consultant that developed the campaign for the utility.

"It isn't that management has a poor relationship with the union," Peterson says, "it just wanted to show that *it* was responsible for making positive changes, not just the union.

"Too frequently in the past, the union was recognized as the initiator of change and management got no mileage from the programs it introduced," she says.

Management's goal to announce the program before the upcoming negotiating sessions gave Peterson and her PSNH counterparts only three months to conceive, develop and implement a campaign.

Because management was pushing the project, it wasted no time approving or making recommendations.

This cooperation, coupled with accelerated production schedules, increased staffing at the Mercer-Meidinger office, and contracting with vendors in close proximity to the utility to expedite final production, enabled the program to be completed within the prescribed deadline.

The following information blitz was executed:

- **Week One**—Announcement letters were distributed to the pertinent employees
- **Week Three**—Posters reinforced the initial announcement with an on-the-job introduction to the new program
- **Week Four**—Highlights flyers were mailed to the target group
- **Week Five**—Meeting leaders' training sessions were conducted
- **Week Six**—Employee meeting invitations—containing two mints emblematic of immediate and future tax breaks—were distributed
- **Week Eight**—Advance management briefings were conducted
- **Week Nine and Ten**—Employee meetings were conducted in which enrollment kit materials and more mints were distributed
- **Week Eleven**—Enrollment reminders were posted.

During contract bargaining and subsequent membership ratification, the 401(k) plan was accepted by union employees, too.

This occurred during the middle four weeks of the program so communications materials were extended to this additional audience.

Initial monitoring of employee reaction indicated acceptance, but showed employees wanted more options for investing their savings.

In response to these findings, the company announced a new enrollment period to commence January 1986.

A follow-up campaign was initiated entitled *ImproveMINTS,* and a color change, from green to gold, communicated a differentiation in the updated materials.

Summary flyers were sent to employee households in October 1985 and employee meetings, conducted in November 1985, were used to disseminate new information kits.

Employees received meeting invitations with three gold-wrapped mints symbolic of the new investment opportunities.

Both campaigns elicited a composite 35% enrollment rate, 10% above PSNH's goal for total enrollment.

Since the initial enrollment period, Linda Heaney, human resources systems and planning supervisor, says the program has offered two re-enrollment periods, offering an upgrade from 6% employee salary contributions to 8% and then again to 10%.

"The upcoming changes in tax laws will mean more communication with employees, too," Heaney says.

"Obviously, an important aspect of all employee communications is that it be done continuously."

She says participants in the plan are given updated information on a quarterly basis; before enrollment periods, participants and eligible nonparticipants are provided new information.

Formal and informal employee feedback is one of the most crucial steps in the communication process.

Monitored by human resources staff members, department heads and district managers, employees reported the campaign was the most professional and creative campaign the company had undertaken, according to Peterson.

The $45,000 program reinforced the importance of good employee communications with a noticeable improvement in employee morale—the type of supportive momentum the company needed in the wake of its financial storms.

Peterson says the keys to the campaign were its attention-getting mechanisms.

"When conducting this type of campaign, I recommend our clients view it as if they're advertising a product to a consumer—in this case the employees being the consumer," she says.

"Coordinate disparate periodic media with one theme so employees recognize each piece as part of the overall product.

"The other key is to keep each aspect as simple as possible with a specific focus. Nobody wants to sit through a long-winded video or read anymore than they absolutely have to," she says. If information is too cumbersome, no one will absorb it.

"As with any ad campaign, do market research, understand your audience and anticipate it responses.

"Include in your overall plan a follow-up mechanism. Too many executives discount surveys because they think they're too elaborate, but a followup is your only means of evaluating a program and defending the dollars spent on production," she says.

AT&T'S SOFT SELL: THE RIGHT CHOICE

In the most significant break-up in America's industrial age, the 1984 AT&T divestiture left its customers confused, its employees dismayed and skeptical, and management at each of the newly formed communication units scrambling for answers to new problems.

Following the restructuring of AT&Ts former divisions, Bell Atlantic—the company formed from the union of Bell of Pennsylvania, Diamond State Telephone, Chesapeake and Potomac Telephone Cos., New Jersey Bell, its Network Services Inc. and corporate headquarters—decided one area in which it would change would be its employee benefits.

Because the business climate was more competitive, Bell Atlantic management projected that 25% of its previous customers would be using alternative technology. In dollar terms this projection meant an estimated $1–2 million loss of revenue.

Although the general market was more competitive, Bell Atlantic continued to be a regulated utility, and was feeling the heat as consumer groups petitioned utility commissions to retrain rate hikes.

Management dedicated itself to tight fiscal management. Obviously, employee benefits with their related expenditures, were targeted.

Subsequent, a personalized benefits program was developed for Bell Atlantic's nonunion management personnel—first-level supervisors up to top management.

According to the Wyatt Co., many employees were reeling from the divestiture and management employees were anxious. They feared the unknown and felt change was bound to be for the worst.

These fears, combined with tangential concerns, led the management team responsible for implementing and communicating the new benefits program through a careful, methodical course.

"We started with focus groups to get a sense of how people would respond to change and to find out how best to communicate the change and the benefits package itself," says Judy Bryant, a Bell Atlantic district staff manager, benefits planning.

"Our primary goal was to make sure people understood why we were changing," she says, "Then we had to make sure the employees knew how to make the decisions affecting their benefits."

The focus group approach revealed a skepticism toward the program and the demand for a soft sell.

"The focus groups pointed out they didn't want glitz, just the facts," Bryant says, "Anything else would be viewed suspiciously."

Management weighed these concerns accordingly and combined them with its own goals, including:

- Create employee awareness of the need for cost reductions
- Develop employee acceptance of the personalized flexible benefits plan
- Demonstrate to employees that although the new program enhanced cost reductions, it had relatively little impact, in dollars-and-sense terms, on employee benefits, and in some instances offered advantages
- Assuage employee anxiety, skepticism and fear of change
- Unify the separate operating units to a single identity with Bell Atlantic.

With these goals and objectives in mind, and the feedback from the focus groups incorporated, Bell Atlantic and its consultant, the Washington DC office of the Wyatt Co., developed a five-month multi-media campaign.

The communication efforts began with a round-up, and appraisal, of the findings of the focus groups.

Once the goals and objectives were solidified and a design concept accepted, a newsletter was distributed to the pertinent work groups.

Designed in six editions, the first newsletter provided an overview of the program and its rationale.

Each subsequent issue was devoted to a specific benefit.

In addition, 10 weeks before the July 1, 1985, enrollment date, an information hotline was established.

In May 1985 mandatory employee meetings, averaging two to four hours in length, were conducted.

At these meetings a videotape was aired showing group discussions similar to the focus groups used to initially identify employee attitudes.

The videotape also worked as a question-and-answer vehicle to get employees thinking about their benefits.

During these meetings employees were also given personalized benefits workbooks that gave them their company-provided personal benefits allowances and costs for the various options.

The workbook explained each benefit and how the plans could be mixed and matched.

After the meetings, personal computers were available to provide information on how the various package mixes would affect each employee's income and benefits expenditures.

"After the workbook and its tie to the newsletters, employee surveys showed that the PCs were the most favorably rated aspect of the program," Bryant says.

During the period of introduction, management expected three traditional phases of employee response, she says.

An employee newsletter was designed to provide an overview of the program, with subsequent editions used to explain specific benefits.

"There is an initial fear of the unknown, then as more information is provided, employees realize it's not so bad.

"But when they add up price tags for their selections and compare them to their allowance, their reaction may not be enthusiastic."

The third stage was when the personal computers helped.

"Employees were able to add up several different combinations of options, using pre-tax plans and tax-deferred options and see the actual effect on their take-home pay. The net results allayed the second down-turn in employee reactions," she adds.

Following the enrollment period, each employee received a benefit confirmation statement ensuring that the company received and recorded the enrollment plan as the employee had wanted.

An employee survey was then conducted by Bryant's staff and the Wyatt Co.

The results indicated general satisfaction with the plans, specifically with the PC component—74% said they would enroll by PC if that option were available.

Following the feedback period, the second year's communications efforts were tailored.

"One of the things our survey turned up was that employees didn't have enough information about their price tags and allowance soon enough to determine their benefits package," Bryant says.

Consequently a price tag calculation kit was developed to help employees determine their allowance before their workbooks arrived.

Diskettes were sent to each department throughout the company and host personal computers were set up in Arlington, Virginia.

Employees called the host computers and transferred information from a data base there to their own computers.

The information could then be manipulated by employees just the way they were able to do the first year at the introductory meetings.

"Of the 22,000 employees in this group, we processed 19,000 calls to the host computers," Bryant says, explaining that some employees called more than once.

In addition to the price tag calculation kit, a new personalized employee benefits workbook was distributed this year as well as a comparison chart that illustrated the difference costs and coverages of the several HMOs and Blue Cross/Blue Shield, the group insurance carrier.

"With so many truly different corporate cultures in one company, adopting a unified approach was more complicated than we anticipated," Bryant says.

"The key to making any type of communications effort work, and particularly benefits, is to not skip over what the employees think.

"Right up to the production stage, we ran materials by employees to get their feedback."

A UNIFORM APPROACH AT HYATT

At the Chicago-based Hyatt Co., decentralization makes the personnel director at each hotel the primary person responsible for employee communications.

Providing the tools to make personnel directors better-than-good communicators was the goal of top management.

This was no easy task. The directors had no formal training in employee communication and focused more on traditional personnel responsibilities. As a result, the quality of publications produced on local levels was generally low.

In a continuing effort to upgrade the personnel director position and the personnel department's communications, the corporation, with the help of the Chicago consulting firm, Multivision International Inc., designed a guide to print communications.

According to Multivision, Hyatt's pride in decentralization made creating prototype "corporate-approved" newsletters, handbooks and so on, an unacceptable solution to the problem.

Instead, "A Common Sense Guide: Employee Print Communications," a three-ring bound handbook was produced.

It offers personnel directors at Hyatt's more than 90 locations an overview to print communications, a model of a personnel handbook, guidelines and suggestions for publishing a local newsletter and an appendix/glossary that includes reproducible logos and other artwork.

"By providing local directors with as much information as possible they don't have to reinvent the wheel every year and a half," Harold Morgan, Hyatt director of personnel, says, "and it also helps them react to immediate changes."

For example, Morgan cites Hyatt's recent acquisition of a hotel in Texas.

"I called the new personnel director and told her we had two weeks to make the change.

"With the information in the communications handbook, she'll be able to put together employee handbooks and have them to the printer in a week," he says.

"When we open a new Hyatt, we can't take three months to make a new employee handbook. We've got to get the new employees transferred over right away."

Each of the first three sections of the handbook begins with a purpose statement and the goals of each publication.

Following the purpose and objectives statement, each chapter delves into design elements of the particular piece and appropriate production guidelines.

The handbook closes with a glossary covering design and printing terminology.

"Our goal was to get personnel directors through the (mechanics) of print communications and to get them doing what they wanted to be doing," Morgan says.

"The handbook meets minimum standards for those who need to get the information out, but for the more creative types, it provides the tools to make a nice package," he says.

The handbook not only introduces publishing theory and goals, but it provides camera-ready art to elevate communication tools beyond functional to creative.

The concept, therefore, met several goals, including:

- Introduced design and production concepts
- Set minimal production and design standards
- Suggested acceptable designs with examples.

The $60,000 project has enhanced not just benefits communications, but employee communications of all types, Morgan says.

"People are socialized in Hyatt to do everything possible for customers," he says, "but you must start by doing everything possible for employees."

To make its employees feel like they're getting the same instant feedback from superiors that they get from guests, Morgan says local personnel directors must be autonomous.

The communications handbook, however, is only one part of the communications package.

Initially, employees are introduced to many of the corporate programs during an orientation period.

Although benefits, for example, are recommended for frequent publication in the local newsletters, new employees are provided corporate-generated brochures on each aspect of its benefits package during orientation.

But the information flow doesn't stop there.

Orientation is supported by small group meetings to discuss benefits.

"When 45 housekeepers get together, it's easier for one to ask how does this affect me, than if they're in a meeting of 500 people—then you've lost them.

"When you've got similar people, with similar lives, meeting together, they're much more comfortable and the effort is more productive and more worthwhile," Morgan says.

In addition, traditional aspects of the industry afford other opportunities for verbal give and take as well.

"In the restaurants and various departments within the hotels, a line-up gives the department managers a chance to go over such items as specials for the day, hotel promotions, and benefits," Morgan says.

"Occasionally, a hotel will have bad morale . . . and tons of factors can affect its employees.

"That's why communication is so important," Morgan says.

"Whether transferring to a new company or a change in benefits, every employee, right down to each custodian, is affected. And they all care about change. We've got to show we care—that's how communication gets started." ■

Communication Barriers in the Workplace

Cheryl L. McKenzie
Carol J. Qazi

Employers with non-native employees cannot be reminded too often that various problems in understanding language and gesture can hamper the employees' work. This article outlines the areas of difficulty and suggests some solutions.

Communication breakdowns between native English-speaking supervisors and their non-native speaking co-workers cause a loss in productivity that can be computed directly into dollars and cents for many American firms. In the San Francisco Bay area's Silicon Valley, for example, foreign employees comprise as much as 60 to 90 percent of the workforce in some companies. If a spoken or unspoken message between American and foreign co-workers assumes too much, lost time will result, impeding productivity. Consider this example: "A lot of times, I'll assign him a project," a manager of a San Jose, California, area company said of one of his co-workers. "He'll act like it's okay, but when I've already gone back to my desk, he's still standing there!"

The real question is, did the employee, who has a masters degree from an American university, really understand the parameters of the assignment or, automatic deference to a superior (which is a custom in some cultures), was he politely agreeing to a request he didn't quite understand?

Although many companies are providing instruction in English as a second language for their foreign workers, both employees and their supervisors continue to express frustration over frequent misunderstandings that cause performance errors and confusion on the job. Risk of error may be too high in business and industry; therefore, workers may choose to do nothing, when a message is unclear rather than to do something wrong. In the classroom, teachers are trained to expect errors as part of the learning process

From *Business Horizons* © 1983 by the Foundation for the School of Business at Indiana University. Reprinted by permission.

Cheryl L. McKenzie is the academic coordinator for Studies in American Language at San Jose State University. *Carol J. Qazi* is a lecturer in the same program. Both authors have worked with industry in designing programs to teach English as a second language and workshops to increase cultural awareness.

and to reduce penalties for these errors so that students will take risks. However, industry raises the penalties for errors (loss of jobs, promotion, and so on) and thus restricts risk taking. The nature of American business and industry may never allow the penalties to be lowered; therefore, efficiency in communication must be increased.

Because of the sharp increase in the number of foreign employees in American companies, an awareness of potential cross-cultural verbal and non-verbal communication breakdowns is increasingly important. When we hear an idiom used incorrectly or a word mispronounced so badly that even in context we can't decipher the meaning, we are able to point to the misunderstanding immediately and ask for or give clarification. However, since cultural perceptions are not always possible to verbalize and therefore identify, neither the American nor the foreigner can explain why he feels negatively about the conversations or actions of the other person. In short, linguistic, or speaking, competence doesn't necessarily result in cultural competence for the foreign-born worker. The result may be a mutual uneasiness or distrust with no basis that either person is able to identify. People often unconsciously assume that non-verbal communication is universal, and it is not.

POINTS OF BREAKDOWN

The following hypothetical situation will illustrate three important points often inherent in cross-cultural communication breakdowns: A foreign-born computer programmer asks her manager for a report she needs. "It's in my middle drawer," responds the busy manager who glances momentarily over the rim of his glasses. He points quickly to the employee, then toward his desk drawer. Fifteen seconds later, however, the manager is surprised when he looks up and sees the programmer still standing in the same place waiting patiently for the report.

This incident dramatizes a typical example of communication failure which occurs daily. By stating "It's in my drawer," the manager felt he was granting permission to the programmer to help herself to the report. The programmer, on the other hand, was still waiting for the explicit words of permission from the manager for her to enter his desk or for him to get it for her. Secondly, unbeknown to the manager, he had just insulted the programmer by pointing at her with his index finger; the extended index finger, which Americans use so routinely to point to objects or to summon, is an impolite gesture in the programmer's culture. Finally, the programmer's culture has a rule of "saving face" which requires that one should not reveal emotions at any cost. In this case, showing her discomfort about the pointing incident would probably cause embarrassment to herself and her superior.

Ambiguous or misinterpreted verbal communication can add to communication slowdowns or breakdowns. Americans are often unaware of the extent to which they use idiomatic words and phrases in their speech. Expressions like, "He's burned out," or "Poor Mary, she's frazzled by the end of the day," are just two examples of everyday phrases that nearly everybody uses. One Chinese employee, on hearing that some co-workers had had a "ball" over the weekend, asked whether they had played football. Many foreign workers report feeling uneasy when jokes are told in the office and they are unable to laugh at the punchlines. Jokes are often very culture-bound, and while the foreign employee wants to share in the humor, he or she simply can't. Lacking the idiomatic vocabulary on which the joke depends.

Idioms, coupled with the American tendency to pronounce words incompletely (consider "bread 'n budder" for "bread and butter"), can result in the foreigner's frustration and the American's misunderstanding of that frustration.

TWO SOLUTIONS

First, Americans can keep in mind that two factors can contribute to misunderstandings: verbal and non-verbal misinformation, and, often, the accidental confusion over the two. When an American makes a request or remark and the foreign worker seems not to understand, it may be that the foreign employee heard the English words clearly, but the underlying assumptions were not there. It is also possible that some employees will not indicate that they have failed to understand either the spoken or unspoken message for fear of embarrassing one of the participants.

One time-effective and pleasant way of dealing with communication problems in the workplace is to "feed back" the information that was received. And workers, as well as their manager, should be encouraged to do this. For example, you say, "So, you'll order those typewriter ribbons from Tom's Office Supply?" to which the foreign employee might reply, "Oh, I'm sorry! *"Tom's!* Yes!"

Secondly, Americans can keep in mind that such important parts of the communication process like hand gestures are not universal, so a certain gesture used in the work environment might not always produce the expected results. The same can be said for directives or simple exchanges. A message may have implications for Americans that people from other countries might not grasp. For example, an American reported asking a foreign co-worker, "Could we have lunch today?" (implying, "I'd like to discuss business with you over lunch"), and was surprised to receive the response, "Oh, no, thank you. I brought my sandwich." It is important for Americans to remember that most new Americans have in many cases learned written, formal

English from outdated textbooks and from teachers whose first language was not English. Foreign workers often don't know informal, spoken phrases such as, "They fought and made up" instead of "They fought and reconciled." An American should realized that a message might have been idiomatic, and take an extra minute to explain the idiom to save more precious minutes in the future.

When it becomes evident that something has gone wrong in a conversation, some steps can be taken to reestablish communication and get the job done:

- Try to recall the gestures that accompanied the verbal message. Restate the message without the gestures.
- Remember what was actually stated and what other directions or requests were implied in that statement. State all messages verbally.
- Recall what words and phrases were used in making the request or giving the directions. If they were idiomatic, restate using more formal language.
- Recall the manner in which the message was delivered. Repeat the message more slowly. ■

PART FIVE

ORGANIZATIONAL PERFORMANCE

All organizations have a culture of their own which reflects acceptable patterns of behavior and established ways of accomplishing the work of the organization. In a formal sense, culture manifests itself as organizational policy. In a context of lesser formality, culture simply reflects the actual and symbolic social norms of the workplace.

Organizations are also characterized by the potential for conflict which lurks just beneath the overt organizational culture. Conflict has several sources among which is a disregard for the culture. To avoid unacceptable interruptions in the work flow of the organization, managers should expand their knowledge of the causes and indicators of conflict thereby increasing their ability to reduce the incidence of disruptive conflict. The basic idea here is that the more you know about conflict, the more you can make it work for the organization rather than against it.

Control refers to the actions of management in guiding the organization toward the attainment of its objectives by ensuring that actual outcomes occur in conformity with planned outcomes. More specifically, once management implements the plans of the organization through the organizational structure and the budgetary process, control involves: (1) setting standards derived from the managerial objectives, (2) measuring operating results against the standards to evaluate variances from the plans, and (3) initiating and consummating timely and appropriate corrective action to minimize unacceptable variances from the standards.

These three sensitive and significant organizational phenomena—i.e., culture, conflict, and control—are treated in the writings in this part of the book.

Corporate Culture
Dr. Larry Senn

*Does your corporate culture stimulate innovation or foster apathy?
Here's how to gauge your company's climate for success*

The chief executive officer (CEO) of a successful major oil company decided he wanted to diversify out of oil due to serious political threats and questionable long-term growth. He established elaborate plans to implement his new strategy and announced the plans to employees and the public. Following several years of floundering at his attempts to build new businesses, the CEO was replaced and the company is now firmly back in oil.

Why is it that highly successful organizations, with long histories of prosperity, can fail miserably when attempting to change their direction or strategy? Why is it that identical programs succeed in one firm while failing abysmally in another?

One of the answers lies in the phenomenon of corporate culture, a subject that has been ignored for many years as a "soft" topic. It is also a topic that has recently become part of daily conversation in corporate board rooms, thanks to books like *In Search of Excellence* and *Megatrends*.

Corporate culture consists of the norms, values and unwritten rules of conduct of an organization, as well as the management style, priorities, beliefs and interpersonal behaviors that prevail. Together, they create a climate that influences how well people communicate, plan and make decisions.

Managers moving to a new company often encounter culture shock when they find that the new firm does not respond as the old one did to their directives. Likewise, the failure of mergers and acquisitions is often due to cultural incompatibilities. It is somewhat like two people who decide to marry based on financial statements, only to discover serious personality conflicts once joined.

Reprinted from *Management World*, with permission from AMS, Willow Grove, PA 19090. Copyright 1986 AMS.

Dr. Larry Senn is chairman of Senn Daleney Associates, Long Beach, California.

Regarding the oil executive, part of the reason he was unable to succeed with his strategy was that he didn't understand his company's culture. Typically, oil operations require long-term investments for long-term rewards, contributing to a culture entrenched in history and tradition.

New businesses need a short-term view with an emphasis on current returns. Using this strategy violated employees' basic beliefs about their roles in the company and the traditions which were underlying the culture. As such, it had no chance to succeed. The question is, what could he have done differently? What is the significance of the concept of corporate culture?

Strong corporate values let people know what's expected of them. They clearly spell out how people are to behave most of the time, allowing employees more time and energy to be innovative. Furthermore, if employees understand what the firm stands for and what standards they are to uphold, they are more likely to make decisions that will support those standards and reinforce corporate values.

Even more important than culture's ability to guide employees' behavior is that culture can make or break a firm's efforts to adapt to a changing economic and social environment. Few managers consciously recognize what their company's culture is and how it manifests itself because it is a difficult concept to understand. As one manager said, "it's like putting your hand in a cloud."

When an organization is in touch with its culture, its chances of success in changing strategy increase dramatically.

NEW IDEAS

An example of this is Charles Chips a family-owned snack foods firm based in Montvale, Pennsylvania. The company went through a cultural adjustment a few years back when Steve Musser, son of the company's founder, took over the firm. Musser found top management slow to react to new developments, unwilling to experiment with new marketing approaches and out of touch with its own inventory, production problems and employee morale. He began placing greater value on rapid response to the marketplace and to innovation and professional management skills.

He also brought in consultants to help systematically reshape culture norms and devise new policies supporting the new values. This included training managers to help them adapt and giving promotions and raises as rewards for innovation and other entrepreneurial efforts. Since blending these new ideas into the company fabric, management has acquired a brisk attitude and Charles Chips has posted numerous improvements, including a 38 percent gain in productivity.

How does a manager uncover the current culture in an organization and what does he or she study in order to start the process of understanding? The place to start is a study of the firm's dominant leaders, past and present.

What were their general philosophies, objectives, preferences, biases and priorities? What were their styles of leadership and management techniques? What was their understanding of the firm's similarities and differences with others in the same industry? What was their understanding of the broader industry setting and how they fit in (for example, community values and norms, competition and location)?

In addition, look at how the dominant leaders dress, what their outside interests are and what gets talked about in meetings. Discover what themes dominate their on-site visits, their memos and their social chit-chat. Look at what matters receive extraordinary attention and what gets attended to post-haste.

Besides the dominant leaders other areas within the organization should be included in the analysis. Important clues as to a company's character can be found in the charter or statement of an organization's mission (what it wants to do): goals and objectives; history and tradition; and finances.

In addition, the company's organizational structure, financial reporting methods, management information systems, criteria for hiring, new hire manuals and orientation processes should be studied.

Look at how money is spent. What gets rewarded, particularly with fanfare? Why are people fired? Analyze performance review forms at all levels.

CHANGING VALUES

Once an organization thoroughly understands its culture, how does it go about shifting direction? Over time, an organization's culture becomes a shadow of its leader and leadership team. Their values, methods and styles filter down and influence much of what goes on in their organization. Therefore, efforts to reshape a culture must begin at the very top, with long-term, solid commitment. Lip service to the new values has almost no impact.

The leader and his or her team must cast different shadows if the culture is to change. When senior managers serve as role models of action, accountability and teamwork, people within the organization are encouraged to pull strongly in the same direction.

James E. Burke, chairman of Johnson & Johnson, has been painstakingly clear in his efforts to redirect his division presidents from their former independent posture into a more cooperative, team approach. He has redefined the company's previous concept of winning.

Placing greater emphasis on cooperation between divisions, he now asks people to compete with other companies instead of with each other. He speaks enthusiastically about the new values and has allocated resources to develop and install new multidivision marketing and product groups. He also supports training and marketing programs which cut across division lines.

Consistency in every aspect of a culture is another essential element of a successful shift in direction. Employees can't be fooled. They understand the real priorities in a corporation. At the first inconsistency, they become confused to "buy in."

AN EXAMPLE

Chase Manhattan Bank in the mid-1970s was jolted by a sharp skid in earnings and a plunging return on assets. The top executives decided the fault lay with a culture which rewarded people more for appearance than performance. In order to shift the emphasis from style to performance, managers beat the performance drum through a series of changes: new, stepped-up communications between top management and the rest of the staff, new role models, overhauling salaries and incentives, providing greater rewards for top performers and an advanced management course.

All aspects of an organization, from the strategic plan, to the structure, to the reward system, must convey the same message and support the new values.

In addition, when changing direction or strategy, managers must also noticeably shift much of their time and attention to the new values in order to convert employees' typical reaction of skepticism to one of belief.

A major department store chain in the Midwest wanted to create a more customer service-oriented environment in their stores, one where the salespeople were friendly, attentive and took a personalized approach to meeting customer needs.

The president began discussing customer service at management meetings. His memos included customer service as a topic. Besides applauding people for sales results, they were also publicly acknowledged for improved service. When visiting stores, senior management discussed customer service and sales with store managers. When in the stores, they greeted customers. When they stopped to talk to salespeople, they also talked about customer service.

The result? Employees began to realize the importance of customer service and there was a significant shift in the level of service in the stores, verified by customer surveys. A sizable increase in sales accompanied the new focus.

Another important element in shifting culture is making corresponding changes in organizational design, including structure, reward systems, job descriptions, performance review, training programs, the strategic plan and the mission statement to support the new values. If not done, the changes will be short-lived.

A final aspect of reshaping a culture is telling "hero" stories. Heroes are people in the culture who personify its values and provide tangible role models for employees to follow. The stories are those that describe what the heroes have done and get told and retold at meetings, social gatherings, in the office, in newsletters and at banquets.

For example, Chase Manhattan would select outstanding performances, reflecting increased earnings or return on assets, and spread those stories throughout the organization. Burke at Johnson & Johnson would spread dramatic tales of teamwork between divisions. These examples of teamwork would be highlighted in print, announced at meetings, rewarded publicly at banquets or discussed over lunch.

Understanding an organization's corporate culture and knowing how to manage it can be management's major leadership strength. Case studies have verified that reshaping culture is a critical part of management's ability to guide an organization through an ever-changing environment. The good news is, given our dynamic, competitive economy, it is possible to reshape a company's personality. However, a thorough understanding of the phenomenon, knowledge of the "how-to's" and the commitment to make it work is essential. ∎

Are You Corporate Cultured?

Edgar H. Schein

Sloan Fellows
Professor of Management
Massachusetts Institute of Technology,
Cambridge, MA

Most of us live in organizations and must deal with them, but we continue to find it difficult to understand and justify much of what we observe and experience in our organizational life. Too much seems to be "bureaucratic" or "political" or simply "irrational." The concept of organizational culture holds promise for illuminating this confusing area. It is particularly relevant in understanding the mysterious and seemingly irrational things that go on in human systems.

The word "culture" has many meanings and connotations. When combined with "organization," the result will almost certainly be conceptual and semantic confusion.

The term "culture" should be reserved for the deeper level of basic assumptions and beliefs that are shared by members of an organization, that operated subconsciously, and that define in a basic "taken-for-granted" fashion an organization's view of itself and its environment.

These assumptions and beliefs are learned responses to a group's problems of survival in its external environment and its problems of internal integration.

The assumptions come to be taken for granted because they solve those problems repeatedly and reliably.

Thus, what is meant by "culture" is a pattern of basic assumptions that have worked well enough to be considered valid and, therefore, taught to new members as the correct way to perceive, think and feel in relation to those problems.

These assumptions may be invented, discovered, or developed by a given group as it learns to cope with its problems of external adaptation and internal integration.

Reprinted with permission from *Personnel Journal,* pp. 83–96, November 1986.

Excerpted, with permission, from *Organization Culture and Leadership* by Edgar H. Schein. Jossey-Bass Publishers, 433 California St., San Francisco, CA 94104, $22.95.

Unless we learn to analyze organizational culture accurately, we cannot really understand why organizations do some of the things they do and why leaders have some of the difficulties they have.

An examination of cultural issues at the organizational level is essential to a basic understanding of what goes on in organizations, how to run them, and how to improve them.

Effects of culture on strategy. Many companies have found they can devise new strategies that make sense from a financial, product or marketing point of view, yet they cannot implement those strategies because they require assumptions, values and ways of working that differ from the organization's prior assumptions.

Action, for example, is a company that grew up and became successful by marketing a complex product to sophisticated customers.

When the company later developed smaller simpler and less expensive versions of this product for a less sophisticated market, its product designers and marketing and sales divisions could not deal with the new customer type.

The sales and marketing people could not imagine what the concerns of the new, less knowledgeable customer might be; the product designers continued to assume they could judge product attractiveness themselves.

Neither group was motivated to understand the new customer type because, subconsciously, they tended to look down on such customers.

Failures of mergers, acquisitions and diversifications. When the management of a company decides to merge with or acquire another company, it usually carefully checks the financial strength, market position, management strength, and various other aspects of corporate health.

Rarely checked, however, are those aspects that might be considered "cultural": the philosophy or style of the company; its technological origins, which might provide clues as to its basic assumptions; and its beliefs bout its mission and future.

Yet if culture determines and limits strategy, a cultural mismatch in an acquisition or merger is as great a risk as a financial, product or market mis-match.

Some years ago, for example, a large package-foods company purchased a successful chain of hamburger restaurants but, despite 10 years of concerted effort, could not make the acquisition profitable.

First, the company did not anticipate that many of the best managers of the acquired company would leave because they did not like the philosophy of the new parent company.

Instead of hiring new managers with experience in the fast-food business, the parent company assigned some of its own managers to run the new business.

These managers did not understand the technology of the fast-food business and hence were unable to use many of the marketing techniques that had proved effective in the parent company.

Finally, the parent company imposed many of the control systems and procedures that had historically proved useful for it—and consequently drove the operating costs of the chain too high.

The parent company's managers found that they could never completely understand franchise operations and hence could not get a "feel" for what it would take to run that kind of business profitably.

Failure to integrate new technologies. The introduction of any new technology into an occupation, organization or society can be seen as a culture change problem.

Occupations typically build their practices, values and basic self-image around their underlying technology.

Similarly, an organization that is successful because of its mastery of a given technology develops its self-image around that technology.

If the technology substantially changes, the organization or occupation not only must learn new practices but must redefine itself in ways that involve deep culture assumptions.

For example, with the introduction of sophisticated computerized information systems and automation, it becomes painfully obvious that in many crucial areas the subordinate knows more than the boss, or that groups who previously had no power now have a great deal.

People who are in power often anticipate such changes and realize the best way to avoid the loss of their own power is to resist the new technology altogether.

Even when such power issues are dealt with, the new technology carries its own occupational culture.

Only when change has begun do managers realize that the new technology is accompanied by a whole new set of assumptions, values and behavior patterns.

The realignment of status, power and working habits is clearly a major cultural change.

Intergroup conflicts within the organization. Groups form on the basis of physical proximity, shared fate, common occupations, common work experience, similar ethnic background or similar rank level.

Once a group acquires a history, it also acquires a culture.

If groups get into conflict with each other, that conflict is difficult to reduce—mainly because a group needs to maintain its identity, and one of the best ways of maintaining that identity is to compare and contrast it with other groups.

In other words, intergroup comparison, competition and/or conflict helps build and maintain intragroup culture.

If we view labor-management negotiations from this perspective, we can ask whether each group in the negotiation has developed a culture its own, whether those cultures overlap enough to make mutual understanding possible, and, if not, how enough common culture could be established to make genuine negotiation or problem solving possible.

Negotiations in US companies seen to go faster and produce mutually more satisfactory solutions when there is shared set of assumptions about the validity of the capitalist system, the legal basis of authority, the openness of mass structure, the Horatio Alger myth, and the value of the product or service being created by organization.

Ineffective meetings and communication break-down in face-to-face relationships. Even the familiar daily problems of organizational life—the unproductive meeting, the difficulty of getting of getting a point across to a subordinate during performance appraisal, the difficulty of communicating instructions clearly enough to ensure correct implementation, and so on— may be productively analyzed from the cultural perspective.

Instead of seeing communication breakdowns as the result of lack of clarity, defensiveness or semantics, we might recognize that such breakdowns often result from real differences in how people perceive and understand things because of their different cultural memberships.

Socialization failures. Every organization is concerned about the degree to which people at all levels "fit" into its structure.

Organizations will expend considerable effort in training, indoctrinating, socializing and otherwise attempting to ensure that the "fitting in" is not let to chance.

When the socialization process does not work optimally because the new member does not learn the culture of the host group, there are usually severe consequences.

At one extreme, if the new employee does not learn the pivotal or central assumptions of the organization, that employee usually feels alienated, uncomfortable and possibly unproductive.

Such feelings may even cause valued employees to leave the organization.

At the other extreme, if the employee is "oversocialized" in the sense of learning ever detail of the culture, the result is total conformity, leading to an inability on the part of the organization to be innovative and responsive to new environmental demands.

Because an organization tends to be a conglomeration of subcultures but also has a total organizational culture if it has had enough of a history, the process of cultural learning for the newcomer is complicated and perpetual.

On first entering the organization, and subsequently with each major functional, geographical or hierarchical move, the person must learn new subcultural elements and fit them into a broader total view.

Productivity. As numerous studies of industrial work have shown, work groups from strong cultures.

Often such subcultures develop the assumption that work should be limited not by what one is able to do but by what is appropriate to do.

Productivity is a cultural phenomenon par excellence, both at the same-work-group level and at the level of the total organization.

CULTURE HELPS PEOPLE COPE WITH THE EXTERNAL ENVIRONMENT

To understand the dynamics of culture, we must understand why basic assumptions arise and why they persist.

We must develop answers to such questions as:

- What does culture do?
- What functions does it serve?
- How does it originate, evolve and change?
- Why is it so difficult to change culture?

What culture does is to solve the group's basic problems of survival in, and adaptation to the external environment and integration of its internal process to ensure the capacity to continue to survive and adapt.

There are four primary external issues.

Consensus on core mission, primary tasks, manifest and latent functions. Every new group or organization must develop a shared concept of its ultimate survival problem, from which is usually derived its most basic sense of core mission, or "reason to be."

In most business organizations, this hard definition revolves around the issue of economic survival and growth, which, in turn, involves the delivery of a necessary product or service to customers.

At the same time, society defines as part of the core mission the provision of jobs, so that members of the society have a way to make a living.

Every organization must define and fulfill its core mission or it will not survive. The mission typically also involves a deeper sense of how to survive in a given environment, where the answer to this question defines more discretely what the group ultimately views its identity to be.

At one company, for example, there was a debate around the question of whether to purchase a company in a different industry.

It was not only the economic consideration that were crucial, but deeper questions of "Who are we?" "What are we capable of?" and "What do we want to be?"

Consensus on means. The group cannot perform its primary task unless there is clear consensus on the means by which goals will be met.

How to design, finance, build and sell the product must be clearly agreed on.

From the particular pattern of these agreements, not only the style of the organization but also the basic design of tasks, division of labor, organization structure, reward and incentive systems control systems and information systems emerge.

The skills, technology and knowledge that a group acquires in its effort to cope with its environment also become part of its culture if there is consensus on their use.

Collectively, all these skills, structure and processes define what can be thought of as the means for accomplishing the organization's goals and, as can be seen, these means constitute a large part of the culture if the group or organization has a long history.

The accomplishment of the organization's goals, even though they are directed toward the outside, requires the creation of a structure inside the group to make that accomplishment possible.

Consensus on criteria for measuring results. Once the group is performing, there must be consensus on how to judge its own performance in order to know what kind of remedial action to take when things do not go as expected.

If members of the group hold widely divergent concepts of what to look for and how to evaluate results, they cannot develop coordinated remedial action.

The potential complexity of achieving consensus of criteria was illustrated in an international refugee organization.

Field workers measured themselves by the number of refugees processed. Senior management paid more attention to the favorable attitudes of host governments because those governments financed the organization.

Senior management, therefore, checked every decision that was to be made about refugees with virtually every other department and several layers of management, to ensure the decision would not offend one of the supporting governments.

This, in turn, irritated the field workers, who felt they were usually dealing with crisis situations in which slowdowns might mean death for significant numbers of refugees.

Consensus on remedial and repair strategies. The final area of consensus crucial for external adaptation concerns what to do if a change in course is required and how to do it.

If information surfaces that the group is not on target—sales are off, profits are down, product introductions are late or the like—what is the process by which the problem is diagnoses and remedied?

These processes are not limited to problem areas. If a company is getting signals of success, does it decide to grow as fast as possible, does it develop a careful strategy of controlled growth, or does it take a quick profit and risk staying small?

Of particular importance, however, is the organization's response to "bad news" or information that threatens survival.

Responses to crisis provide opportunities for culture building and reveal aspects of the culture that have already been built.

What we ultimately end up calling the culture of that group will be influenced both by its external adaptation processes and by its mode of building and maintaining itself: its processes of internal integration.

The internal integration systems are influenced by, and in turn influence, external adaptation.

Developing a common language and conceptual categories. To function as a group, the individuals who come together must establish a system of communication and a language.

The human organism cannot stand too much uncertainty or stimulus overload.

Categories of meaning that organize perceptions and thought, thereby filtering out what is unimportant while focusing on what is important, become not only a major means of reducing overload anxiety but also a necessary precondition for coordinated action.

In one organization, for example, the chairman often got angry with a member who was not contributing in group meetings and began to draw conclusions about the competency of that person.

The chairman assumed the silence meant ignorance, incompetence or lack of motivation.

The silent person, it turned out, was ready to make a presentation and was very frustrated because he was never called on to give it. He assumed he was not supposed to volunteer, and he began to believe his boss did not value him.

The danger was that both were setting up self-fulfilling prophecies. In this group, the absence of a common communication system undermined effective action.

Consensus on group boundaries; criteria for inclusion. If a group is to function and develop, one the most important areas for clear consensus is the perception of who is "in" the new group and who is "out" or "not in" and by what criteria those decisions are made.

New members cannot really function and concentrate on their primary task if they are insecure about their membership, and the group cannot really maintain a good sense of itself if it does not have a way of defining itself and its boundaries.

As organizations age and become more complex, the problem of defining clear boundaries also becomes more complex. More people come to occupy boundary-spanning roles.

In a complex society, individual employees belong to many organizations, so that their identity is not tied up exclusively with any one organization.

Locating a "cultural unit" becomes more difficult since a given organization may really be a complex set of overlapping subcultures.

But consensus on criteria for membership is always one means of determining whether a cultural unit exists in any give group.

For instance, in the Action Company every new member of the technical or managerial staff must be interviewed by between five and 10 people, and only if that member is acceptable to the entire set is he or she offered a job.

If one asks what the interviewers look for, they often say, "We want someone who will fit in."

Once a person has been hired, if he fails in an initial job assignment the assumption is made that he is a competent person but was put in the wrong job.

In the Multi Company, education is a key criterion. Most of the young technical and managerial staff come from a scientific background, highlighting the assumption that, if one is to succeed in the company, one must understand the scientific base on which it was built.

Having an advanced degree, such as a doctorate, is a distinct advantage even if one is being hired into a marketing or managerial job.

Stratifications: consensus on criteria for differentiation of influence and power. A critical issue in any new group is how influence, power and authority will be allocated.

The process of stratification in human systems is typically not as blatant as the dominance-establishing rituals of animal societies, but is functionally equivalent in that it concerns the evolution of workable rules for managing aggression and mastery needs. Human societies develop pecking orders.

The easiest way to observe this process is to watch a new group, such as a committee or training group, in the early hours of its life.

Each person comes into the situation with very different prior or assumed status, and has varying degrees of power and authority attributed to him or her.

The process of group formation then involves a complex mutual testing around who will grant how much influence to whom, and who will seek how much influence from whom.

Peer relationships: consensus on criteria for intimacy, friendship and love. Every new group must decide simultaneously how to deal with authority problems and how to establish workable peer relationships.

Whereas authority issues derive ultimately from the necessity to deal with feelings of aggression, peer relationships, intimacy problems derive ultimately from the necessity to deal with feelings of affection love and sexuality.

The leaders of Action, for example, strongly believed good decisions could be made only if everyone was encouraged to challenge authority and if peers was encouraged to debate every issue.

Needless to say, a climate of high conflict, intense competition among peers, and relatively low levels of intimacy developed.

Consensus on criteria for allocation of rewards and punishments. I n order to function, every group must develop a system of sanctions for obeying or disobeying the rules.

The specific rewards and punishments, and the manner in which they are administered, constitute one of the most important cultural characteristics of a new organization.

In one market-oriented food company, for example, the norm developed that a manager who did his job competently could expect to be moved to another, generally bigger, project within approximately 18 months.

Managers who did not move every 18 months began to feel that they were failing.

In contrast, in the Action Company the norm was established that the designer of a product saw it through from beginning to end.

Therefore, a reward was defined as being allowed to stay with one's product through manufacturing and marketing to sales.

When studying the culture of an organization, one must investigate the reward system because it reveals fairly quickly some of the important rules and underlying assumptions in that culture.

Once one has identified what kinds of behavior are "heroic" and what kinds of behavior are "sinful" one can begin to infer the beliefs and assumptions that lie behind those valuations.

CORPORATE LEADERS HELP EMBED
CORPORATE CULTURE

The most powerful mechanisms for embedding and reinforcing culture are:

What leaders pay attention to, measure and control. One of the best mechanisms that founders, leaders, managers or even colleagues have available for communicating what they believe in or care about is what they systematically pay attention to.

Even casual remarks and questions that are *consistently* geared to a certain area can be potent as formal control mechanisms and measurements.

To illustrate, a consultant was told of a company that wanted him to help install a management development program. The consultant suggested to the president that he communicate his concern by paying attention to what was being done and by reinforcing it through the reward system.

The president announced that henceforth 50% of each senior manager's annual bonus would be contingent on what he or she had done to develop his or her own immediate subordinates during the past year.

He added that he himself had no specific program in mind but that each quarter he would ask each senior manager what had been done.

As it turned out, the subordinates launched a series of different activities, many of them pulled together from work that was already going on piecemeal in the organization; a coherent program was forged over a two-year period and has continued.

Other powerful signals that subordinates interpret for evidence of the leader's assumptions are what they observe does not get reacted to.

Leader reactions to critical incidents and organization crisis. When an organization faces a crisis, the manner in which leaders and others deal with it creates new norms, Values and working procedures and reveals important underlying assumptions.

Crisis also are significant in culture creation and transmission partly because the heightened emotional involvement during such periods increases the intensity of learning.

The assumption in Action that "we are a family who will take care of each other" comes out most clearly during periods of crisis.

When the company was in difficulty, the president became the strong and supportive father figure, pointing out to both the external world and the employees that things were not as bad as they seemed, that the company had great strengths that would ensure future success, and that people should not worry about layoffs.

Deliberate role modeling, teaching and coaching. Founders and new leaders of organizations generally seem to know that their own visible behavior has great value for communicating assumptions and values to other members, especially newcomers.

There is one organization in which the president has made several videotapes outlining his explicit philosophy, and these tapes are shown to new members of the organization as part of their initial training.

However, there is a difference between the messages delivered from staged settings, such as when a president gives a welcoming speech to new comers, and the messages received when a president is observed "informally." The informal messages are the more powerful teaching and coaching mechanism.

In the Action Company, the president made an explicit attempt to downplay status and hierarchy because of his assumption that good ideas can come from anyone.

He drove a small car, had an unpretentious office, dressed informally and spent many hours wandering among the employees at all levels getting to know them informally.

Criteria for allocation of rewards and status. Members of any organization learn from their own experience of promotions, performance appraisals, and discussion with the boss what the organization values and what the organization punishes.

Both the nature of the behavior rewarding and punished and the nature of the rewards and punishments themselves carry the messages.

An organization's leaders can quickly get across their own priorities, values and assumptions by consistently linking rewards and punishments to the behavior they are concerned with.

Criteria for recruitment, selection, promotion, retirement and excommunication. One of the most subtle yet most potent ways in which culture gets embedded and perpetuated is the initial selection of new members.

This cultural embedding mechanism is subtle because it operates unconsciously in most organizations.

Organizations tend to favor those candidates who resemble present members in style, assumptions, values and beliefs.

Such candidates are perceived to be the "best" people to hire and have characteristics attributed to them to justify their being hired.

Unless someone outside the organization is explicitly involved in the hiring, there is no way of knowing how much the current implicit assumptions are dominating recruiters' perceptions of the candidates.

Initial selection decisions for new members, followed by the criteria applied in the promotion system, are powerful mechanisms for embedding and perpetuating the culture, especially when combined with socialization tact designed to teach cultural assumptions.

Because the messages transmitted by these mechanisms are to a large extent implicit, conflicting messages can be sent.

Sometimes such messages result from unconscious conflicts in the message senders, and sometimes they result from conflicts among key leaders in what they believe, assume and value.

In either case, the messages are implicit, and it is therefore possible for conflicting assumptions to coexist in a group and for the group to accommodate to such inconsistencies and conflicts.

There are also secondary reinforcement mechanisms. These mechanisms are ''secondary'' because they work only if they are consistent with the primary mechanisms discussed above.

When they are consistent, they begin to build organizational ideologies and thus to formalize much of what is informally learned at the outset.

If they are inconsistent, they will either be ignored or will be a source of internal conflict.

But the operating cultural assumptions will always be manifested first in what the leaders demonstrate, not in what is written down or inferred from designs and procedures.

Organization design and structure. The design for the organization initially and the periodic reorganizations that companies go through thus provide ample opportunities for the founders/leaders to embed their deeply held assumptions about the task, the means to accomplish it, the nature of people and the right kinds of relationships to foster among people.

Organizational systems and procedures. The most visible part of life in any organization is the daily, weekly, monthly, quarterly, and annual cycle or routines, procedures, reports, forms, and other recurrent tasks that have to be performed.

The origin of such routines is often not known to participants, or sometimes even to senior management, but their existence lends structure, predictability and concreteness to an otherwise vague and ambiguous organizational world.

If founders or leaders do not design systems and procedures as reinforcement mechanisms, they open the door to historically evolved inconsistencies in the culture, or weaken their own message from the outset.

Design of physical space, facades, buildings. This encompasses all the visible features of the organization that clients, customers, vendors, new employees and visitors would encounter.

The messages that can be inferred from the physical environment are potentially reinforcing of the leader's messages, but only if they are managed to be so.

Leaders who have a clear philosophy and style often choose to embody that style in the visible manifestations of their organization.

Stories about important events and people. As a group develops and accumulates a history, some of this history becomes embodied in stories about events and leadership behavior.

Since the message to be found in the story is often highly distilled or even ambiguous, however, this form of communication is somewhat unreliable.

Formal statements of organizational philosophy, creeds, charters.
The final mechanism of reinforcement is the formal statement, the attempt by the founders or leaders to state explicitly what their values or assumptions are.

These statements highlight only a small portion of the assumption set that operates in the group and, most likely, highlight those aspects of the leaders' philosophy or ideology that lend themselves to public articulation.

Such public statements may have a value for the leader as a way of emphasizing special things to be attended to in the organization, as values around which to "rally the troops" and as reminders of fundamental assumptions not to be forgotten; but formal statements cannot be seen as a way of defining the culture of the organization.

At best, they cover a small, publicly relevant segment of the culture, those aspects that leaders find useful to publish as an ideology for the organization.

LEADERSHIP IS THE ABILITY TO MANAGE CULTURE

For the manager, the message is "give culture its due."

1) Do not oversimplify and do not confuse culture with other useful concepts, such as "climate," "values," or "corporate philosophy."

Culture operates at one level below these others and largely *determines* them.

Climate, values and philosophies *can* be managed in the traditional sense of management, but it is not at all clear whether the underlying culture can be.

But culture needs to be understood in order to determine what kinds of climate, values and philosophies are possible and desirable for a given organization.

2) Do not assume that culture applies only to the human side of an organization's functioning.

Culture determines not only the ways in which the internal system of authority, communication, and work is organized and managed but also the organization's must basic sense of mission and goals.

Focusing on how people relate to each other in the organization and labeling that aspect "the culture" can be a dangerous trap because it draws attention away from shared basic assumptions about the nature of the product, the market, the organization's mission, and other factors that may have far more influence on how effective the organization is ultimately.

3) Do not assume that culture can be manipulated like other matters under the control of managers.

Culture controls the manager—more than the manager controls culture—through the automatic filters that bias the manager's perceptions, thoughts and feelings.

As culture arises and gains strength, it becomes pervasive and influences *everything* the manager does, even his own thinking and feeling.

The point is especially important because most of the elements that the manager views as aspects of "effective" management—setting objectives, following up, controlling, giving performance feedback, and so on—are themselves culturally biased to an unknown degree in any given organization.

There is no such thing as a culture-free concept of management.

4) Do not assume that there is a "correct" or "better" culture, and do not assume that "strong" cultures are better than "weak" cultures.

What is correct or whether strength is good or bad depends on the match between cultural assumptions and environmental realities.

A strong culture can be effective at one point and ineffective at another point because external realities have changed.

5) Do not assume that all aspects of the culture are relevant to the effectiveness of the organization.

Any group with any history will have a culture, but many elements of that culture may be essentially irrelevant to that group's functioning.

Much of the time, therefore, the manager need not concern himself with culture issues; or, if problems of effectiveness arise, the manger must learn how to focus on only those cultural issues that are relevant.

Insight into the culture of one's own organization contributes another layer of explanation for why things do or do not work out.

When managers observe communication or problem-solving failures, when they cannot get people to work together effectively, they need to go beyond individual explanations.

The problem may not be their own lack of managerial skill or limitations in the personalities of the people involved.

Recognizing such cultural differences is essential so that the manager can explain how things can go wrong ever if everyone has the same good intentions to make them work. ■

How to Achieve Excellence by Managing the Culture in your Company

Heinz Weihrich

In recent years, corporate culture has been a widely discussed topic by management gurus peddling their services to organizations desperate to improve their performance. Serious managers, naturally, question whether the emphasis on corporate culture is merely a passing fad, or if it indeed has a long-term beneficial effect on the way organizations are managed. Those who look for a quick fix for making organizations effective may be disappointed. We know that societal culture develops slowly and endures for a long time. Similarly, organizational culture needs to be nurtured and managed. Culture must not be separated from what managers do; instead it must be concerned with all aspects of managing. In addition, an organization culture must also guide the relationships with claimants outside the enterprise, especially customers, but also suppliers, creditors, and even competitors who deserve an operation culture of fair play in the competitive market place.

Most managers today would probably agree that the effectiveness and efficiency of an organization are influenced by its culture. This means, in turn, that key managerial functions will be carried out differently in organizations with different cultures.

Although some management advocates would have us believe that the concepts of corporate culture represent the latest thinking in management theory; they are not. In 431 B.C., Pericles eloquently urged the Athenians, who were at war with the Spartans, to adhere to values underlying the culture-democracy, informality in communication, the importance of individual

Reprinted with permission from Industrial Management, copyright Institute of Industrial Engineers, 25 Technology Park/Atlanta, Norcross, Ga. 30092, pp. 28–32, Sept/Oct 1989.

Heinz Weihrich is author of over thirty books and 80 articles published in the United States and overseas. His current research interest is improving competitiveness, managerial excellence, and global management. Weihrich is active in management consulting as well as executive and organizational development in the United States, Europe, Africa, and Asia. He is currently Professor of Management at the University of San Francisco. He received his doctoral degree from UCLA and was a visiting scholar at the University of California at Berkeley. His research focused on managing by objectives as a comprehensive, integrative management system. Dr. Weihrich has taught at Arizona State University, the University of California at Los Angeles, and in France and Austria.

dignity, and promotion based on performance. Pericles realized that these values might mean victory or defeat. You will probably note that these values are not so different from those espoused by many U.S. companies.

As it relates to organizations, culture is the general pattern of behavior, shared beliefs, and values that members have in common. Culture can be inferred from what people say, do, think, and how they behave within an organizational setting. It involves the learning and transmitting of knowledge, beliefs, and patterns of behavior over time. This also means that an organization culture is fairly stable and does not change quickly. It often sets the tone for the company and establishes implied rules for how people should behave. Many of us have heard slogans that give us a general idea what the company stands for. For General Electric, it is "progress is our most important product." American Telephone & Telegraph Company is proud of its "universal service." DuPont makes "better things for better living through chemistry." Delta Airlines describes its internal climate with the slogan, "the Delta family feeling."

Similarly, IBM wants to be known for its service, Sears for quality and price, Caterpillar for its 24-hour parts service, Polaroid for its innovation, Maytag for its reliability, and so on. Indeed, the orientation of these companies, often expressed in slogans, contributes to the successful conduct of their businesses. But slogans must be translated into managerial behavior.

Managers, and especially top managers, create the climate for the business. Their values influence the direction of the company. Although the term "value" is used differently, we like to think of a value as a fairly permanent belief about what is appropriate and what is not that guides the actions and behavior of employees in fulfilling the organization's aims. Values form an ideology that permeates everyday decisions and behavior.

In many successful companies, value-driven corporate leaders serve as role models, set the standards for performance, motivate employees, make the company special, and serve as a symbol for the external environment. It was Edwin Land, the founder of Polaroid, who created a favorable organizational environment for research and innovation. It was Jim Treybig of Tandem in the " Silicon Valley" near San Francisco who made it a point that every person is a human being and deserves to be treated accordingly. It was William Cooper Proctor of Proctor & Gamble who ran the company with the slogan, "Do what is right." It was Theodore Vail of AT&T who addressed the needs of customers by emphasizing service.

In order to understand an organizational culture, one may look at the ways managerial functions are carried out. We will do this by contrasting two different enterprises—Enterprise X and Enterprise Y. How the key managerial activities are carried out in these enterprises is summarized in tables 1, 2, and 3.

Let us look first at the underlying corporate culture that determines the way the organization is managed overall. In a free economy, such as that of the United States, businesses cannot exist without the goodwill of their customers. Yet in certain companies, customers are seen as merely interrupting work (Enterprise X). Clearly, the long-term success of such a company may be in jeopardy. By contrast, in Enterprise Y, employees in all departments (not only those that are specially set up to handle customer complaints, or public relations departments) listen carefully to the needs of the customers. After all, they are the reason the company exists.

In Enterprise X there may be slogans of providing customer satisfaction, but there may be only vague notions that customers are served well (if, in fact, they are). Most dissatisfied customers feel that their complaints will be ignored and will not induce management to change. The sad, but often unnoticed, fact is that few, if any, of these customers will return as customers when other companies provide similar services or products. On the other hand, in a Y-Enterprise, measurable customer-satisfaction objectives are set and frequently used for evaluating customer reactions. This may be done through formal surveys or, at times, top managers may contact key customers personally. When Ross Perot, the Texas billionaire who sold his computer company to General Motors, was on the GM board, he answered all customer complaints about cars personally, rather than sending form letters.

By optimizing the operation of a department, actions may be taken that are detrimental to the total organization. A case in point may be the overzealous credit manager unduly tightening the credit policy. In an extreme case, credit losses could be reduced to zero by giving no credit at all. The negative effects on sales can only be imagined. In a well-managed enterprise (such as Enterprise Y), objectives of the various functional units are set so that the total organization can optimize its operation. In other words, managers are trained to take a systems view rather than a functional one.

Too often we hear the slogan that what really counts is the bottom line. Of course, businesses can only exist in the long run by making a profit. Unfortunately, profit orientation too often means profit in the short run with little consideration for the long-term health of the enterprise. In the past some U.S. automakers neglected quality because it appeared to be cheaper to pay for warranty claims than to build quality into the products. The loss of future sales was often not recognized as a cost. In contrast, many Japanese car manufacturers have made quality the basis for long-term profit.

Quality responsibility must not be delegated to lower-level managers or a staff person with little power. Instead, it must be a primary concern of top managers. Evidence has shown that objectives in many MBO programs focused on quantity of output, sometimes also showing the cost of producing

AN OBJECTIVE IN A STAFF POSITION

In general, it is more difficult to set verifiable objectives for staff positions than setting goals for line personnel; particularly bothersome is stating the desired quality in measurable terms. For a systems manager, such an objective might sound something like:

To install a computerized control system for department X by December 31, 1988 involving not more than 300 working hours, with the system operating with not more than 15 percent downtime during the first two months of operation.

This objective tells us what is going to be done, at what time, at what *cost,* and with the *quality* expressed in downtime.

the output. But too little attention was given to verifiable objectives relating to the quality of products and services.

People respond to those things for which they get rewarded. Few rewards are usually given for quality. In a typical organization, CEOs get rewarded for return on investment or profit improvements—seldom, if ever, for quality products or services. But quality pays in the long-run as Japanese car, camera, and electronics manufacturers have shown, In Japan, responsibility for quality and productivity is placed at the top. This, in turn, creates a culture that says: Our organization is fanatical about both productivity and quality.

After World War II the United States was the world leader in productivity. But in the late 1960s the deceleration of productivity growth began. Today the urgent need for productivity improvement is recognized by government, private industry, and universities.

Successful companies create a surplus through productive operations. Although there is not complete agreement on the true meaning of productivity, we will define it as the output-input ratio within a time period with due consideration for quality. Looking at this equation, one can see that productivity can be improved 1) by increasing outputs with the same inputs, 2) by decreasing inputs but maintaining the same outputs, or 3) by increasing outputs and decreasing inputs to change the ratio favorably. In the past, productivity improvement programs were mostly aimed at the worker level. Yet, as Peter Drucker observed, "The greatest opportunity for increasing productivity is surely to be found in knowledge work itself, and especially in management."

Productivity implies effectiveness and efficiency in individual and organizational performance. Effectiveness is the achievement of objectives. Efficiency is the achievement of the ends with the least amount of resources (often this means cost).

PEROT'S RECOMMENDATIONS FOR GENERAL MOTERS

Even once-vital organizations have, over the years, built bureaucratic barriers where adherence to bureaucratic protocol is more important than getting things done. In order to turn General Motors around, Ross Perot made the following suggestions:

1. Eliminate most committees.
2. Send senior managers to the field, visiting factories, dealers, mechanics, and customers—listen to their concerns.
3. Move executive offices to the plants where cars are produced, rather than housing key managers in the headquarters.
4. Reduce the distinction between management and labor.

Managers in effective organizations are characterized by action. This can only be done by top management commitment to breaking down rigid organization structures. It may begin with some symbolic actions such as eliminating reserved parking spaces for top-echelon managers. After all, is it not equally important that the first-line supervisor be on time to start the production line rather than circling the parking lots to find a space to park?

In an X-type organization, the culture says that people can be replaced the same way broken parts of a machine can be interchanged. In other words, people are seen simply as factors of production. Contrast this with a kind of organization in which the dignity of people is paramount—not only those at upper levels of management, but people throughout the organization. Whether a manager or a worker, all contribute toward a common aim; all have basic needs for being appreciated as persons; all have the desire to feel competent in carrying out their task, whatever it is.

While a clear mission and challenging goals have the potential to motivate organizational members to excellence, the means to achieve the ends must never be compromised. Actions and behavior must be guided by adherence to company policy, must never violate any laws, and above all, must not be unethical. In an Enterprise-Y-environment, integrity is the norm, Ethics, the discipline dealing with what is good and bad and with moral duty and obligation, may be institutionalized through 1) company policy or a code of ethics, 2) a formally appointed ethics committee, and 3) the teaching of ethics in management development programs.

The overall culture of the organization sets the tone in the enterprise of how other managerial functions will be carried out. We will therefore focus next on planning and related activities.

Planning involves selecting the organization's mission and objectives and the ways to achieve them. It also requires scanning the external environment for opportunities and threats. Finally, planning requires making decisions and innovating.

THE TEAM APPROACH AT FORD

It usually takes five years to develop a car in the United States; far too long to compete successfully in the market. Ford Motor Company shortened the development time for the Taurus model by using the team concept as opposed to the sequential approach.

In the sequential approach, the planners develop the car concept, which is then given to the engineers. The engineers, in turn, provide the specifications for manufacturing and suppliers. Manufacturing then sets up the plant and the line for production. The marketing group, the service department, and legal services also eventually get involved. If a problem is discovered at any of the developmental stages or if changes have to be made, the task has to be done by the respective group. Thus, if a problem is discovered at the manufacturing stage, designers and engineers have to be involved in correcting the problem. However, if parts are already purchased or dies have already been made, such changes are very costly or are simply not made because of the delay involved.

In contrast, the Team Taurus project illustrates a Y-environment, still using the sequential steps to some extent. But many processes are done simultaneously involving many disciplines at the outset, as illustrated in Figure 1. Planners, designers, engineers, manufacturing people, and even suppliers work together as a team. Not only do the various groups work concurrently on the project, but customers are also involved in developing the car by identifying what they like and dislike. Clearly, an autocratic organizational culture is not conducive to the team concept. Thus, team development congruent with a Y-type environment may have to precede the use of the new approach to production and operations management.

Every organization should be clear about its mission and its direction. In Enterprise X, goal-setting is considered important, but for lower-level managers only. Yet, goals at all levels must contribute to the overall aims of the company. This requires a goal-driven, integrated management system permeating the total organization. This does not imply, however a complex and rigid program, but rather a complete system without excessive bureaucratic impediments. Rather than being rigid, the effective system, such as in Enterprise Y, is flexible, and adapts to the changes in the environment. Goals need to be reviewed frequently, and modified occasionally in light of circumstances.

In an Enterprise-X environment, one may find either no objectives or too many objectives. Both situations are ineffective. Instead, a well managed enterprise has relatively few objectives, but those that do exist are crucial. Moreover, the degree of importance of these goals is stated. Certainly, some objectives demand more managerial attention than others. Too often, vague and non-verifiable objectives are more like a wish list. A goal such as "improving products and quality" has little value for measuring the effectiveness of the organization. Instead, objectives need to be challenging, yet they also must be realistic and, whenever possible, must be stated in verifiable terms. The goal of "making a reasonable profit" cannot serve as a criteria of measurement. Reason is in the eye of the beholder. However, a statement such as " Achieve a return on investment of 12 percent by the end of the current fiscal year," provides a basis for measurement.

In X-Enterprise, objectives may focus on the current operation. In contrast, the effective company pays special attention to value—adding new products or services. Thus, the emphasis shifts from maintenance objectives—to increase output of product X by S percent by the end of the year—to innovative objectives. An example may be "To develop three new products with a certain profit margin to capture S percent market share by the end of the next fiscal year." Traditional companies are preoccupied with current products that account for the needed revenues. These products are indeed important "breadwinners" and must not be ignored, but one must never forget that success does not last forever. Even the highly successful Volkswagen Beetle and Ford's Model T eventually became obsolete. Thus, action-oriented teams must search for new products and services and fill current and future customer needs. IBM, for example, set up a team for the development of the personal computer while the rest of the organization continued its regular operations.

The way objectives are set is of vital importance. In a top-down approach, upper-level managers determine the objectives for their subordinates.

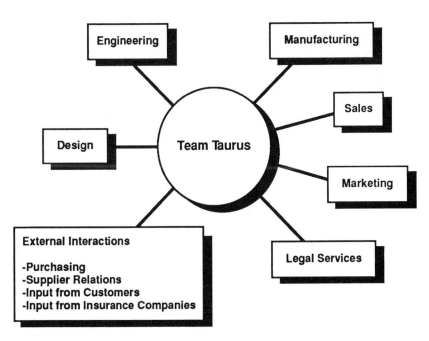

THE TEAM APPROACH TO PRODUCT DEVELOPMENT

TABLE 1

Organizational Culture as The Basis for Managing

Enterprise X
Customers seen as interrupting.
Vague notion of customer satisfaction.
Optimizing operation of the organizational unit.
Profit more important than quality.
Productivity and quality emphasis on lower organizational levels.
Rewards for quantity of output.

Enterprise Y
All departments listen to customers, who are the reason why the enterprise exists.
Specific objectives and frequent measurement of customer satisfaction.
Optimizing the operation of the whole organization.
Quality the basis for long-term profit. Verifiable objectives for quality.
Productivity and quality improvement responsibility of people at all levels.
Rewards for quantity and quality of outputs.

TABLE 2

Planning, Marketing, and Innovating

Enterprise X
Goal setting for lower-level managers only.
Complex, rigid, bureaucratic MBO program.
Rigid approach to Objective setting.
No objectives or too many objectives. Vague, non-verifiable objectives.
Cost or revenue objectives.
Emphasis on maintenance objectives.
Preoccupation with breadwinners.
Top-down objective setting.
Vague strategy

Enterprise Y
Goal-oriented management system throughout the organization.
Simple, but complete objective management system.
Flexible approach to objective setting.
Few crucial objectives with relative importance stated.
Challenging, yet realistic and verifiable objectives.
Value-added objectives for new products and services.
Focus on innovative and improvement objectives.
Establishment of action-oriented teams for new products and services.
Top-down and bottom-up mutually met objectives.
Clear and unique strategy taught and regularly evaluated. Selected resource commitment.

TABLE 3

Control and Operations Management

Enterprise X
Standards of performance set arbitarily.
Delayed feedback for control.
Sequential product planning.
Manufacturing the "stepchild."
Product development without sufficient recognition of customer needs.
Direct control based on feedback.

Enterprise Y
Challenging and verifiable goals become standards for measuring performance.
Prompt feedback and feed-forward control.
Team product planning and development.
Manufacturing a centerpiece in strategy formulation.
Customer-responsive product development.
Direct and preventive control.

This process continues down the organizational hierarchy. Proponents of the top-down approach suggest that the total organization needs direction through corporate objectives proclaimed by the chief executive officer, usually with agreement of the board of directors. On the other hand, those suggesting the bottom-up approach argue that top management needs to have information from lower-level managers presenting their objectives to their superiors. Subordinates, it is argued, are likely to be highly motivated by, and committed to, goals that they themselves initiate. My experience has shown that in most organizations the bottom-up approach is underutilized. But either approach alone is insufficient; both are essential. The emphasis depends on the situation, including factors such as the size of the organization, the organizational culture, the preferred leadership style of the executive, and the urgency of the plan.

In formulating their strategies, traditional companies may not differentiate between their successful and unsuccessful products and services and their respective contributions to profit. Progressive companies, on the other hand, focus on those adding value. Theory-Y organizations identify market niches and swiftly develop and offer products and services customers want. For this they obtain premium prices. Y-Enterprises frequently evaluate their clear and unique strategy and commit resources to the most promising products and services.

In summary, then, Y-Enterprises have a clear direction through their goal-driven management system. These organizations are characterized by genuine participation whenever such involvement in the decision-making process is appropriate. The customer-oriented strategy identifies opportunities and recognizes threats in the external environment. Even an organizational culture that emphasizes clarity and participation in planning is not sufficient. Plans must be implemented and controlled.

Controlling requires measuring performance and taking corrective action. But accurate measurement can only be made against clear plans and verifiable objectives. The control process, then, consists of three essential steps: 1) Setting standards, 2) measuring performance against these standards, and 3) correcting undesirable deviations from the standards.

These steps will be carried out differently in organization cultures such as Enterprises X and Y. Moreover, the management information system (MIS), which is an essential tool for effective control, will be different in those organizational environments. Finally, production and operations systems will also be distinct in X and Y Enterprises.

In an X-type environment, standards may be set in an arbitrary manner without consideration of situational factors. Yet the measurement of performance should give a realistic assessment of the company's performance as well as the achievements of managers. In a Y-type environment, verifiable objectives become the standards of performance. The standards, of course, should be challenging but reasonable; clear but not too detailed; and they should cover all areas in which performance is essential for the effectiveness of the enterprise, division, or department.

When feedback on performance is delayed, it may be too late to take corrective actions. New information technology facilitates real-time information that may be helpful, but is not a cure-all. There still may be a delay between identifying a deviation and taking corrective actions. Therefore, the ideal control system would be one that prevents deviations from occurring in the first place. Such a future-directed control system, also called "feed-forward control," anticipates deviation. The system, first introduced by Harold Koontz and R. W. Bradspies, monitors inputs and makes adjustment to inputs before deviations occur. A bicycle rider, for example, who wants to maintain a fairly constant speed may increase his or her effort before approaching an upcoming hill. The same principle applied to a business situation may be a company replenishing cash funds before it runs out of cash.

In the past, the term "production management" was used to refer to activities for making products. More recently, the concept of "operations management" is used for producing a product as well as delivering service. The cultural environment also influences the way operations are managed as shown by an example (see insert) from the automobile industry.

It is not uncommon to find that manufacturing is the "stepchild" of the organization. The position of operations manager does not seem to be glamorous to many MBA graduates as shown in surveys I conducted of graduate students. Yet, many successful Japanese enterprises see manufacturing as a centerpiece in formulating their strategy. Most controls are direct controls which rely on measurement and feedback, and there are also tools that help to identify probable deviations through feed-forward control. There is, however, one other control: proactive control. In the final analysis, performance depends on people. The higher the quality of people, the less need for identifying and correcting deviations. In certain situations, performance cannot be accurately measured. No one individual may be responsible for good or bad performance, mistakes may not be discovered in time to take corrective actions, and some people may not be willing or able to correct deviations. Thus, proactive control that suggests developing high-quality managers and subordinates, may be the best solution for preventing undesirable deviations. Implementing proactive control requires that managers and non-managers be willing to learn and improve their skills, and that their professional development becomes an integral part of company policy. ■

FURTHER READING

Deal, Terrence E. and Allan A. Kennedy, "Corporate Cultures," Reading, Mass.: Addison-Wesley Publishing Company, Inc., 1982.

Drucker, Peter F., "Management: Tasks, Responsibilities, Practices" New York: Harper & Row, 1973.

Koontz, H., and R. W. Bradspies, "Managing through Feedforward Control," *Business Horizons,* June 1972.

Koontz, Harold and Heinz Weihrich, "Management," 9th edition. New York: McGraw-Hill Book Company, 1988.

Littal, B., "The Corporate Culture Vultures," *Fortune,* October 17, 1983.

Luce, S. R., "Managing Corporate Culture," *Canadian Business Review,* spring 1984.

Moore, Thomas, "The GM System is Like a Blanket of Fog," *Fortune,* February 15, 1988.

Perot, Ross, "How I Would Turn Around GM," *Fortune,* February 15, 1988.

Purcell, Theodore V., and James Weber, "Institutionalizing Corporate Ethics: A Case History" New York: The Presidents Association, The Chief Executive Officers' Division of American Management Association, 1979.

Sathe, Vijay, "Some Action Implications of Corporate Culture: A Manager's Guide to Action," *Organizational Dynamics,* Autumn 1983.

Schein, Edgar H., "What You Need to Know about Organizational Culture," *Training and Development Journal,* January 1986.

Weber, James, "Institutionalizing Ethics into the Corporation," *MSU Business Topics,* Spring 1981.

Weihrich, Heinz, "Management Excellence—Productivity Through MBO," New York: McGraw-Hill Book Company, 1985.

Developing Leadership for Change

Stephen C. Schoonover
Murray M. Dalziel

"Change takes place no matter what deters it. . . . There must be measured, laborious preparation for change to avoid chaos."

—Plato

Ancient and modern pundits alike have been preoccupied with change. In all human endeavors change is inevitable. In its most raw and destructive form, change is truly "chaos"—a loss of control. When people in business initiate change or respond to it with adaptations that increase productivity, we call it innovation. But, how can change be harnessed to competitive advantage? And how can "chaos" be avoided?

In a drive to cut costs, a major old-line manufacturing company with a conservative work-force decided to institute a new manufacturing process based on the "just in time" principle. Inventories would be slashed; workers would be much more dependent on one another. Rumors about radical "Japanese-style" management spread rapidly. Japanese graffiti and sketches of top management in kimonos appeared in washrooms; unions held emergency meetings decrying the undermining of worker integrity and the "American Way."

Unfortunately, management had guaranteed a morale problem. They resisted making public knowledge the significant recent corporate losses and the vital savings on inventory. And they failed to publicize

Reprinted with permission from *Management Review*, Vol. 75, pp. 55–60, July 1986.

Steven C. Schoonover is president of Schoonover Associates and a member of the board of directors of McBer's Training Aids Division. He recently completed a product for implementing planned change for McBer called *The Change Leadership System*. Murray M. Dalziel is president and general manager of the International and Training Aid Divisions at McBer and Company. For the past several years at McBer, he has specialized in human resource development for technical professionals, and in organizational improvement.

The leadership of a large, heavy manufacturing corporation decided to introduce hand-held microprocessors for inventory control. Anticipating significant resistance, the company publicized its plans up front and then debugged the new practice with a small highly visible group of independent workers with little stake in the change process—"crane drivers" on the loading dock. Soon after introducing the new devices, the drivers became steadfast advocates of the change. Their group even developed a slogan—"The Best Is At Hand." As word spread about the ease-of-use and efficiency of the hand-held microprocessors, other workers actually requested them.

their sincere belief that corporate survival was at stake and that in-creased teamwork and tapping the energy and ingenuity of workers was a critical step in becoming competitive.

Many organizations have been victims of a poorly-planned, wrenching change experience that has caused unexpected problems. A conservative view is to "leave things as they are," but history reminds us that change is inevitable. The innovative leader *expects* it, *fosters* it, *plans* it, *directs* it, and *uses* it for competitive advantage.

WHY CHANGE?

Successful businesses must provide a stable environment for productive work. They also must adapt constantly to: new market pressures; the chang-ing composition and values of consumers: new information and technologies; and shifting practices and processes within.

In a very real sense change often is a prerequisite for organizational sur-vival. It also helps people grow: New ways of exercising and creating power are discovered; new skills are developed; new ways of sharing and teaming are made possible. In short, both individuals and organizations can profit from a spirit of exploration and growth.

Changes can rejuvenate organizations, but only when channeled to:

- Improves productivity or quality of products and services;
- Confront dissatisfaction; and
- Create new opportunities.

THE BEST CHANGE PRACTICES

Change leadership is a key role in any modern organization. It requires a range of skills that few possess naturally. Typically, simple oversights, lack of persistence, and human barriers underlie failed change efforts.

To determine the best change practices, we conducted and analyzed a series of interviews with change leaders in a variety of leading-edge com-panies. We have found that three groups of factors decide success (See figures 1–4, page 56.) They represent the critical assets or barriers in all change processes, and therefore should be the primary focus of any leader's efforts. Besides defining a framework for diagnosing vulnerabilities, we also specified effective strategies or "best practices" for overcoming barriers in each of the major dimensions of change (See figures 5–7).

Change leaders can take the chance out of change by focusing on the critical areas of modification and the best practices to guide the process. To be effective, leaders must ensure enough flexibility for creative problem-solving, enough protection to maintain work-group *esprit,* and enough control to complete specific critical tasks. In practice, four simple principles support the best change efforts:

1. Focusing on the proven critical barriers to change in organizations.
2. Choosing and enacting those selective "best practices" that fit the organizational setting.
3. Thinking about and completing any planned innovation in small, unintimidating steps.
4. Following a proven management framework that promotes understanding the change, refining appropriate implementation strategies, setting appropriate goals, formulating clear plans and completing critical action steps (See figure 8, page 60.)

Change often is a reaction to pressures or a response to innovation. However, organizations sometimes make the wrong change for wrong reasons, or the wrong change for the right reasons, or the right change in an inefficient and stressful way. Therefore, the first organizing step in planned change is to *test and specify your ideas.* By specifying change plans, a leader not only maps an initial direction, but also increases commitment.

FIVE DIMENSIONS OF ORGANIZATIONAL READINESS	**FIVE CHANGE TEAM-ROLES**
History of Change: The prior experience of the organization in accepting change.	*Inventor:* Integrates trends and data into concepts, models, and plans; envisions the "big picture" first; adapts plans.
Clarity of Expectations: The degree to which the expected results of change are shared across various levels of the organization.	*Entrepreneur:* Instinctively focuses on organizational efficiency and effectiveness; identifies critical issues and new possibilities; actively seeks advantages and opportunities.
Origin of the Problem: The degree to which those most affected by the change initiated the idea or problem the change solves.	*Integrator:* Forges alliances; gains acceptance of himself, his team, and their program; relates practical plans to strategic plans and organizational issues.
Support of Top Management: The degree to which top management sponsors the change.	*Expert:* Takes responsibility for the technical knowledge and skills required for the change; uses information skillfully and explains it in a logical way.
Compatibility with Organizational Goals: The degree to which the proposed change corresponds to past and present organizational practices and plans.	*Manager:* Simplifies, delegates, assigns priorities; develops others; gets the job done at all costs.

FIGURE 1   FIGURE 2

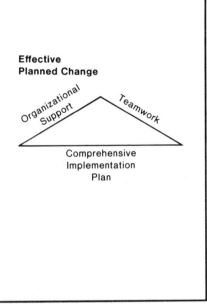

Effective
Planned Change

Organizational Support

Teamwork

Comprehensive
Implementation
Plan

FIGURE 3   FIGURE 4

INFORMATION GATHERING

Information gathering is a process that operates from the beginning to the end of the change implementation.

Leaders direct the change process as much by example as by management skills. Therefore, the first prerequisite for discovering assets and barriers to change is open-mindedness and self-questioning that results in a personal inventory of organizational practices and available people and resources.

After self-inquiry, effective change agents form wider visions of organizational vulnerabilities by assessing employee and management attitudes and practices. They gather a variety of opinions from colleagues and end-users of the change, managers from other sections of the business, and even those outside the organization who use its products or services. Short, efficient, focused discussions can yield the vital information in the normal course of a few days without disrupting the work routine.

A spirit of inquiry also fosters effective group involvement and dialogue, both among system implementors and selected groups of end users. In fact,

ORGANIZATIONAL READINESS PROBLEM SOLVING STRATEGIES

1. *History of Change*

   Inform end users fully; avoid surprises
   Make a reasonable case for change in end users' terms
   Spend more time talking
   Involve end users in diagnosing vulnerabilities
   Start Implementation with receptive workers
   Start implementation with a small part of the change for quick, visible payoff
   Publicize successes

2. *Clarity of Expectations*

   Emphasize the benefits of change—to the organization, the unit, and end users
   Avoid surprises; specify possible impact, outcomes, and problems
   Make change plans public
   Solicit formal and informal feedback

3. *Origin of the Problem*

   Specify who wants the change and why
   Clarify end users' concerns about the change
   Specify the effects of the change on day-to-day operations and work routines
   Present potential problems clearly and completely
   Set goals that confront end-user problems first
   Use feedback as a barometer of how fast to proceed with implementation plans

4. *Support of Top Management*

   Define top-management concerns
   Develop an influence network—top management allies, informal coalitions
   Implement a small part of the change for quick results and good publicity
   Develop a formal management review from top management's perspective

5. *Compatibility of the Change*

   Frame the change in terms of present organizational values and goals
   Integrate the change into ongoing procedures when possible
   Make change plans overt, common knowledge
   Start the change in an accepting environment
   Don't oversell the change

FIGURE 5

CHANGE-TEAM ROLES: IMPROVEMENT STRATEGIES

1. *Inventor*

   Make a wide search for change suggestions
   Review the common organizational and social sources of innovation
   Talk about potential future problems
   Discuss the "What-if" implications of new technologies, market changes, etc.
   Use your team to review products and services periodically.

2. *Entrepreneur*

   Work on tolerating partial answers, interim solutions, mistakes
   Practice framing ideas so that they "sell"
   Develop change resources and influence networks
   Develop planning and goal-setting skills

3. *Integrator*

   Develop interpersonal skills
   Develop informal alliances and coalitions, as well as a formal team
   Protect the change project from the usual organizational pressures
   Confront conflicts and clarify distortions
   Inform and update key personnel

4. *Expert*

   Acquire knowledge and skills, or be responsible for finding experts
   Develop skill of working with "outside" consultants(s)
   Develop presentation skills
   Update team members and end users
   Monitor change plans

5. *Manager*

   Develop coaching skills
   Set goals skillfully
   Specify, review, and revise change plans
   Delegate responsibility freely
   Take responsibility for outcomes
   Keep morale high with frequent face-to-face feedback

FIGURE 6

information-gathering is in itself an intervention—a method of comparing perceptions and confronting discrepancies among various organizational groups.

DEFINING BARRIERS TO CHANGE

Often skilled leaders instinctively focus on critical barriers to change, and then foster it by directing the attention of decision-makers and end-users to a selective group of factors. All too often, vital vulnerabilities are left unattended. The five attributes of *Organizational Readiness,* the five roles of the

---

IMPLEMENTATION PROCESS
PROBLEM-SOLVING STRATEGIES

1. *Clarifying Plans*

   Make one person responsible for implementation plans
   Formulate clear, simple, time-bound goals
   Make specific plans with milestones and outcomes
   Make plans public
   Give and solicit frequent face-to-face feedback

2. *Integrating New Practices*

   Limit the amount of change introduced at any one time
   Slow the change process
   Introduce the change to receptive users first
   Ensure that the rationale and procedure for change are well known

3. *Providing Education*

   Involve the end users and incorporate their experience
   Provide "hands-on" Training whenever possible
   Design training from end users' perspective
   Train motivated or key end users first
   Evaluate the effect of training or work practices and end-user attitudes

4. *Fostering Ownership*

   Ensure that the change improves end users' ability to accomplish work
   Provide incentives for end users applying the change
   Specify milestones for getting end-user feedback
   Incorporate end-user suggestions in the implementation plans
   Publicize end-user suggestions

5. *Giving Feedback*

   Document and communicate the expected outcomes of the change
   Ensure frequent face-to-face feedback
   Identify clear milestones
   Make sure feedback includes the large organization
   Acknowledge key success

FIGURE 7

effective *Change Team* and the five aspects of an effective *Implementation Process* provide a focus for discovering and confronting the critical vulnerabilities that interfere with planned change (See Figures 1–4.)

Hidden issues and personality conflicts inevitably influence all planned change. Leaders must confront these aspects of their organizations, but in a very special way. By making step-by-step plans the priority, while respecting the feelings and contributions of individuals, leaders can map a creative course that avoids personal issues and individual and group regression.

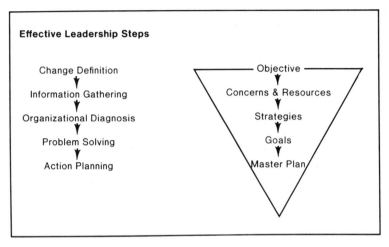

Effective Leadership Steps

Change Definition → Objective
↓
Information Gathering → Concerns & Resources
↓
Organizational Diagnosis → Strategies
↓
Problem Solving → Goals
↓
Action Planning → Master Plan

FIGURE 8

Setting priorities, however, requires more than determining selected vulnerabilities and avoiding emotional pitfalls. All barriers to change are not equally important to confront. Moreover, barriers to change are often deeply imbedded in stubborn, long-standing attitudes and practices. Trying to resolve too many problems in the context of a planned change can prove impossible if not destructive. Therefore, a leader must focus on problems that would have very significant costs to the organization if ignored, and on factors that have the most positive leverage on productivity, quality, or worker satisfaction. Most often, these priorities are clarified in discussions that try "what if" simulations for the various vulnerabilities defined as problems.

To fulfill these mandates:

- Focus on the most common barriers to change;
- Discuss behaviors, not personalities;
- Confront only a few problems that have the highest potential cost to the organization if not addressed.

In addition, remember that although the major goal may be planned change, organizational development is a frequent salutory by-product.

CONFRONTING BARRIERS

Problem-solving is a process that requires openness, creativity, and flexibility. It starts when you decide which organizational barriers to confront, and is applied during each subsequent step in the change process. Goal-setting, planning, feedback, and plan revision, although defined as separate tasks, each rely on effective problem-solving techniques.

Vulnerabilities defined by the three major dimensions of change must be translated into workable problems that are *clearly defined, small and specific in scale,* and *easily understood and accepted by implementors and end-users alike.* This requires wisdom, effort, and collaboration—and prompt action.

Once the process of discovering obstacles has begun, timely interventions are prerequisite for building or maintaining momentum. In part, the problem-solving strategies ("best practices") speed the process of confronting obstacles. By encouraging the consideration of a variety of solutions, particularly suggestions from end-users, leaders can tailor solutions to the workplace. This means visible plans, in clear terms, framed in a manner that makes sense to those who must live with them.

Beyond defining the problem in an acceptable manner, the skilled leader also provides appropriate, timely resources, such as information or education about new procedures and processes. In addition, the good leader must increase the support of employees by:

- Increasing interpersonal, group, and written communications;
- Increasing opportunities for management feedback;
- Reporting frequently on the status of the problem-solving process; and
- Rewarding each step in confronting barriers to change.

PLANNING AND IMPLEMENTING

How can a leader make and complete plans most effectively? Often projects fail because they lack focus, or because steps are ill-defined or too difficult to implement. The first key to avoiding these pitfalls is effective goal-setting. Goals, whether implicit or explicit, drive productive actions in a business setting. Moreover, evidence shows that just the act of setting goals increases the probability for goal completion and overall productivity.

In the initial planning phases of purposeful change, leaders must strike a careful balance. Specific goals are necessary for good work, but may produce opposition from anxious participants in the change process. Therefore, creative goal-setting is necessary. (See figure 9, page 60.) Leaders must:

1. Set broad performance goals in early phases of change with a great deal of dialogue to involve participants;
2. Set specific goals with short timelines covering only the initial phase of the change. This also gives immediate and probably positive feedback about the process of change.
3. Set preliminary goals focused on outcomes that are immediate concerns of end users.

HAVE YOU SET CHANGE GOALS THAT WILL WORK

Use the following checklist to rate the quality of the goals you set.
—Easy to understand.
—Simply Expressed.
—Results-oriented, not activity-oriented.
—Limited in number and scope.
—Challenging.
—Specific in their description of the following.
    —Qualities
    —Quantities
    —Responsible People
    —Constraints, and
    —Costs
—Time-bound with specific deadlines and milestones.
—Subject to measurement and feedback.

FIGURE 9

Most often, the best way to begin the goal-setting process is by asking "What results do I want?" after defining a best outcome, then ask, "What objective measures or accomplishments represent an *excellent* result?" Make sure you allow adequate dialogue about these questions within your management team and with co-workers, and that you take the time to improve goals by simplifying, objectifying, and testing them.

Well-defined goals are a prerequisite for productive action. However, they provide only one aspect of a plan—clear outcomes in the change process. they must be incorporated into a comprehensive framework—an action plan—to be truly effective. An *excellent* implementation plan:

- Assigns priorities to tasks;
- Simplifies and organizes the change process;
- Specifies responsibilities; and
- Outlines methods for measuring progress and making necessary revisions.

The plan represents a roadmap that expresses ideas and concerns in discrete, workable terms. It makes sure that you assess the critical factors that enhance or impede innovation and translate them into practical strategies and reachable goals.

MAINTAINING AND PROMOTING CHANGE

A leader's role in planned change extends well beyond the phase of implementation. By debriefing the experience, he or she refines plans and supports change as both a cultural value and a means of personal growth. In addition, the communication feedback and networking so vital for a specific project can become part of a leader's management repertoire through techniques such as:

- Periodic team meetings to discuss possible change plans;
- Larger organizational meetings with top management or other segments of the business to discuss vulnerabilities and opportunities;
- Organizational performance appraisals; or
- Consultant feedback about possible changes and barriers to change.

Change in any business system is inevitable. Competition, evolution, creativity, and even individual rebelliousness, inexorably alter the landscape of all organizations over time. Because of this inevitability *a leader's choice is not whether to change, but how.* Particularly in these turbulent times, when social, attitudinal, and technological changes are pervasive, managers must either embrace change as a normal, healthy process in the service of growth and adaptation, or perish because of their investment in the status quo. When values and knowledge undergo rapid change, people—their ideas, tolerances, skills, and idiosyncrasies—become the primary adaptive resource of organizations. In the new workplace, change must be acknowledged—even embraced—as a constant companion to be nurtured and exploited to competitive advantage. ■

Assessing the Causes of Conflicts—and Confronting the Real Issues

Peter Muniz
Peter Muniz and Company
Somerset, New Jersey
Robert Chasnoff
Kean College of New Jersey
Union, New Jersey

Philly has just offered a plan for increasing sales. John says he has a few questions about Philly's plan. But before John is finished with his "few questions," Philly's plan is dead. Everybody in the room knows that it was the conflict between Philly and John, not the merits of Philly's idea, that killed her plan.

The two clashed five years ago and never resolved the conflict and it continues to impede not only their work relationship but the performance of the department as a whole as the two work out their feelings.

As a manager, you may have to deal with conflicting subordinates. Or worse, you may have to resolve a conflict in which you are one of the parties. Your responsibility in both kinds of situations is to analyze, confront, and resolve the conflict so the detrimental effects of an unresolved conflict are avoided and the potential benefits of a properly managed conflict are received.

WHAT IS CONFLICT?

Conflict occurs when two or more parties in an organization have to interact to accomplish a task, make a decision, meet the objective, or solve a problem and (a) factors within the setting or within the parties cause self interests to clash, (b) individual parties' actions cause negative reactions in others, or (c) parties who are unable to resolve a controversy lash out at each other. Organizational results are affected as long as the conflict remains unresolved. The parties in conflict influence colleagues who begin to take sides or withdraw from the situation. In the end, the conflict adversely af-

Reprinted, by permission of the publisher, from *Supervisory Management*, March 1986 © 1986 American Management Association, New York. All rights reserved.

fects the productivity and working relationships of not only those directly involved but the whole work group.

When people tell us, "We are one big happy family and never have conflicts," we find that hard to believe.

Organizations are made up of groups of individuals. Within these groups, individuals' needs, values, goals, and methods of working are frequently at odds. This is as true in the company as a whole as in smaller work groups. The marketing, production, quality control, and personnel departments may all be a part of the same company but their self-interests may pull them in different directions.

People in organizations should admit to having conflict, even welcome it. The presence of conflict suggests that there may also be constructive controversy. And out of controversy, new ideas are born and improved.

A place where people deny that conflict exists is partially dead. In such an organization, people are too concerned with hiding conflict, perhaps out of fear of punishment from bosses or peers.

In saying that conflict should not be denied, we are not advocating that conflict be deliberately precipitated or that people be taunted into conflict. Rather, we are merely saying that a lot of energy is wasted in denying the existence of conflict that could be better used to resolve the difference.

Individual Responses

People deal with conflict in different ways. Robert Blake and Jane Mouton have defined five conflict-handling modes that individuals or groups have available when they find themselves in conflict with another party (either an individual or a group). According to this model, when you find yourself in conflict, you can avoid, accommodate, compete, compromise, or collaborate.

Avoiding is characterized by withdrawal or failure to take a position. You make no attempt to confront.

Accommodating involves neglecting your own concerns while allowing the other party to achieve what is important to him or her. There is also an attempt to de-emphasize or avoid differences and emphasize agreement. You make no attempt to confront.

Competing is characterized by the classic "win-lose" stance. When you use this mode, you are out to "win" or otherwise obtain your objectives, even if you have to do so at the expense of the other party. There is no attempt to compromise.

A **Compromise** can be reached only if each party is willing to give up a part of her or his own objective. The resolution may not fully satisfy either party or the organization, but it is considered the best way to diminish the conflict.

Collaborating consists of joint confrontation and resolution. There is mutual problem solving. Each party accepts the other's objectives, and they work together to achieve the best for both. Attempts are made to identify and resolve the issues underlying the conflict. This mode usually involves high risk because trust and openness may be required.

A word of caution is in order here. As with most models that are used to explain human behavior, this one appears to suggest positive and negative modes of handling conflict. Perhaps this is so, but the key point in selecting any mode is to consider first the possible results and consequences that may flow from the mode you select. For example, if you feel you have a good reason for competing with another party to win whatever you decide you must win, then do so. But you shouldn't forget that the other party, as a result of having lost today, may strive to win the next time you have a conflict. Thus, winning and losing may become the major agenda—not the work to be done.

You have to anticipate the possible results of the mode that you select, and more important you have to be willing to accept or deal with those consequences. So if you have made the judgment that competing is the most appropriate mode for you in a particular situation, then do so but remember that it is your decision and you are partially accountable for the work that gets done or doesn't get done because of your decision.

In another situation, you may find yourself in conflict with a party over an issue that has a low level of importance for you. You may then decide to avoid a confrontation. There is nothing wrong with this if it is based on your decision that, given the situation, avoidance is the best mode for you to adopt.

In summary, then, each mode is available to you and each has its appropriate use—and misuse. In all instances, however, it's important for you to analyze the conflict situation, make a conscious choice of which mode to use, know why that mode seems to be the best one, and accept responsibility for the results and consequences of the mode you have selected.

Confronting and Resolving Conflict

Suppose you decide that you wish to use the collaborative mode and confront the conflict. To do this, you have to understand fully the confrontation process. The images that frequently come to mind are one party shouting the other party down or telling the other party off or telling the other party that "this is the last straw" and walking away. But confrontation is something entirely different. Confrontation is a systematic process or sequence that is used by parties who are in conflict and trying together to resolve the conflict. Certain conditions contribute to the successful initiation of a confrontation. These are:

- At least one of the parties (or a third party) must be aware that conflict exists.
- One of the parties must be willing to initiate the confrontation process.
- The parties are agreeable to using a clearly defined confrontation process, a problem-solving framework, and appropriate conflict-handling modes (that is, collaboration or compromise).
- The parties expect or at least hope that the confrontation will resolve differences.

Entering into a confrontation does not guarantee automatic resolution. There is risk involved, and a key factor in assessing this risk is your lack of confidence in dealing with the other person's reaction once the confrontation is initiated.

What prevents all of us from confronting another person very often is not that we don't want to initiate the process but our own uncertainty about our ability to handle the other person's reaction to the confrontation. Moreover, some people aren't sure that a confrontation with another party will lead to a resolution, so they don't initiate the process. Others are sure that there will be no resolution or they feel that matters will worsen after a confrontation. Some people feel this way even though they have never tried to confront the other party. It would seem the most formidable barrier to the initiation of what could be a successful confrontation is our own anxiety about the possible outcome of the very act of initiating the confrontation.

Six Steps to Conflict Resolution

There are at least six major steps in confronting conflict.

Step 1. Awareness. This step is characterized by a recognition of the part of one individual or group (let us say, Party A) that conflict exists between that individual or group and another party (Party B).

Step 2. The Decision to Confront. Party A decides to initiate the confrontation with Party B.

Step 3. The Confrontation. Party A, planning to use the collaboration or compromise mode, confronts Party B. At this point, Party B may reject the confrontation or deny that conflict exists and the confrontation cannot go any further, perhaps confirming one of the fears that Party A might have had in considering the decision to confront. On the other hand, Party B may show a willingness to continue with the confrontation, perhaps even after some mild attempts at refuting or denying the seriousness of the conflict that exists between the two parties. Sometimes conflicts actually get resolved at this point. That is, at times Party B isn't aware that a conflict exists, and if the conflict is very closely related to Party B's behavior, Party B may decide to change that behavior, thus making it unnecessary to continue with the confrontation. If this agreement isn't reached, the parties must continue to step 4.

Step 4. Determining the Problem/Conflict Locus. This step involves the application of a problem-solving framework to determine the problem and its causes. The confrontation is best served by being specific about the problem(s) and by giving specific, non-judgmental feedback. People should try to describe, for example, their own opinions, feelings, reactions, and perceptions. Dumping on others, criticizing others, or tricky "pseudo-psychological analyses" of others are not useful. A crucial aspect of this step is when the parties have to decide the locus of the problem; that is, whether the problem and/or its causes lies within Party A (in which case, it would be up to Party A to make the necessary changes to eliminate the conflict), within Party B (in which case Party B would do the changing), or within both parties, in which case resolution continues in the hands of both. If the two parties cannot come to an agreement as to the locus of the problem or its causes, the confrontation has failed. If they do come to an agreement, however, the confrontation continues.

Step 5. Determining the Outcome and Further Steps. Until this step, the parties are involved in assessment and sharing information. This step requires the parties to collaborate on specific things to do in order to eliminate or at least reduce the causes of the conflict and assure productive ways to work.

Even at this step the confrontation could fail if the parties can't decide how to resolve it. Only if the parties agree on a resolution, the confrontation has succeeded.

Step 6. Follow Through. As part of the previous step both parties should agree to check at a specific time in the future to insure that their respective agreements are being kept, then the conclusion is that the conflict has been resolved. If evaluation proves that agreements have not been kept, then chances are that the conflict is continuing and the parties will have to decide whether to go back to an early step in the confrontation process to determine what went wrong or accept the continuing conflict.

If the conflict confrontation is successful, the positive outcomes will be:

- Arrival at a better solution to a problem and increased work productivity (better results) and/or improved relationships.
- Decisions that result in high levels of commitment by both parties.
- A willingness to take greater risks.

- A decrease in the time it takes to resolve future conflict.
- A more open, trusting relationship.

Although the results are admittedly worth the effort, keep in mind that you cannot confront all conflicts. People at work don't have the luxury of unlimited time and energy resources. Decisions have to be made on how to select and apportion these resources. If you go about confronting every issue without regard to value or importance, you may end up impeding your own and others' productivity and fail to change the conflict situations.

In addition, while conflict resolution is useful, **conflict prevention,** where applicable, is more productive and easier. Furthermore, conflict prevention generally requires less time and energy. For example, conflicts often arise when there is lack of definition or clarity about job roles among individuals, thereby calling for the need to confront and resolve. Definition and clarification of responsibility, authority, and accountability before individuals start working together could prevent conflict and increase organizational productivity. ■

SMR Forum:
Managing Conflict
Leonard Greenhalgh
Dartmouth College

While conflict is not necessarily "bad" or something that should be squelched (it is inherent in organizational life), it can impair relationships among people who need to interact effectively. Therefore, conflict needs to be managed. The author synthesizes much of the diverse writing on conflict management and presents a useful model that can help people diagnose a conflict situation and thus plan tactics for managing it. Ed.

Managers or change agents spend a substantial proportion of their time and energy dealing with conflict situations. Such efforts are necessary because any type of change in an organization tends to generate conflict. More specifically, conflict arises because change disrupts the existing balance of resources and power, thereby staining relations between the people involved. Since adversarial relations may impede the process of making adaptive changes in the organization, higher-level managers may have to intervene in order to implement important strategies. Their effectiveness in managing the conflict depends on how well they understand the underlying dynamics of the conflict—which may be very different from its expression—and whether they can identify the crucial tactical points for intervention.

CONFLICT MANAGEMENT

Conflict is managed when it does not substantially interfere with the on-going functional (as opposed to personal) relationships between the parties involved. For instance, two executives may agree to disagree on a number of

Reprinted from Managing Conflict by Leonard Greenhalgh, SLOAN MANAGEMENT REVIEW, Summer 1986, pp. 45–51, by permission of the publisher. Copyright © 1986 by the Sloan Management Review Association. All rights reserved.

Leonard Greenhalgh is Associate Professor at the Amos Tuck School of Business Administration, Dartmouth College. Dr. Greenhalgh holds the B.S. degree in biology and the M.B.A. degree from the University of Rhode Island, and the Ph.D. degree in organizational behavior from Cornell University. His current research and teaching interests center on the processes of power, negotiation, and conflict resolution. Dr. Greenhalgh has been working with the National Institute for Dispute Resolution in a nationwide program to develop courses and executive programs in this subject area. During the 1986–87 academic year he will be a Visiting Scholar at the School of Business Administration, Stanford University.

issues and yet be jointly committed to the course of action they have settled on. There may even be some residual hard feelings—perhaps it is too much to expect to manage feelings in addition to relationships—but as long as any resentment is at a fairly low level and does not substantially interfere with other aspects of their professional relationship, the conflict could be considered to have been managed successfully.

Conflict is not an objective, tangible phenomenon; rather, it exists in the minds of the people who are party to it. Only its manifestations, such as brooding, arguing, or fighting, are objectively real. To manage conflict, therefore, one needs to empathize, that is, to understand the situation as it is seen by the key actors involved. An important element of conflict management is persuasion, which may well involve getting participants to rethink their current views to their perspective on the situation will facilitate reconciliation rather than divisiveness.

Influencing key actors' conceptions of the conflict situation can be a powerful lever in making conflicts manageable. This approach can be used by a third party intervening in the conflict or, even more usefully, by the participants themselves. But using this perceptual lever alone will not always be sufficient. The context in which the conflict occurs, the history of the relationship between the parties, and the time available will have to be taken into account if such an approach is to be tailored to the situation. Furthermore, the conflict may prove to be simply unmanageable: one or both parties may wish to prolong the conflict or they may have reached emotional states that make constructive interaction impossible; or, perhaps the conflict is "the tip of the iceberg" and resolving it would have no significant impact on a deeply rooted antagonistic relationship.

Table 1 presents seven perceptual dimensions that form a useful diagnostic model that show what to look for in a conflict situation and pinpoints the dimensions needing high-priority attention. The model can thus be used to illuminate a way to make the conflict more manageable. The point here is that conflict becomes more negotiable between parties when a minimum number of dimensions are perceived to be at the "difficult-to-resolve" pole and a maximum number to be at the "easy-to-resolve" pole. The objective is to shift a viewpoint from the difficult-to-resolve pole to the easy-to-resolve one. At times, antagonists will deliberately resist "being more reasonable" because they see tactical advantages in taking a hard line. Nevertheless, there are strong benefits for trying to shift perspectives; these benefits should become apparent as we consider each of the dimensions in the model.

Issues in Question
People view issues on a continuum from being a matter of principle to a question of division. For example, one organization needed to change its

TABLE 1
Conflict Diagnostic Model

	Viewpoint Continuum	
Dimension	Difficult to Resolve	Easy to Resolve
Issue in Question	Matter of Principle	Divisible Issue
Size of Stakes	Large	Small
Interdependence of the Parties	Zero Sum	Positive Sum
Continuity of Interaction	Single Transaction	Long-term Relationship
Structure of the Parties	Amorphous or Fractionalized, with Weak Leadership	Cohesive, with Strong Leadership
Involvement of Third Parties	No Neutral Third Party Available	Trusted, Powerful, Prestigious, and Neutral
Perceived Progress of the Conflict	Unbalanced: One Party Feeling the More Harmed	Parties Having Done Equal Harm to Each Other

channel of distribution. The company had sold door-to-door since its founding, but the labor market was drying up and the sales force was becoming increasingly understaffed. Two factions of executive sprung up: the supporters were open to the needed change; the resisters argued that management made a commitment to the remaining sales force and, as a matter of principle, could not violate the current sales representatives' right to be the exclusive channel of distribution.

Raising principles makes conflict difficult to resolve because by definition one cannot come to a reasonable compromise; one either upholds a principle or sacrifices one's integrity. For some issues, particularly those involving ethical imperatives, such a dichotomous view may be justified. Often, however, matters of principle are raised for the purpose of solidifying a bargaining stance. Yet, this tactic may work against the party using it since it tends to invite an impasse. Once matters of principle are raised, the parties try to argue convincingly that the other's point of view is wrong. At best, this approach wastes time and saps the energy of the parties involved. A useful intervention at this point may be to have the parties acknowledge that they understand each other's view but still believe in their own, equally legitimate point of view. This acknowledgment alone often makes the parties more ready to move ahead from arguing to problem solving.

At the other extreme are divisible issues where neither side has to give in completely; the outcome may more or less favor both parties. In the door-to-door selling example, a more constructive discussion would have ensued had the parties been able to focus on the economic commitment the company had to its sales force, rather than on the moral commitment. As it was, the factions remained deadlocked until the company had suffered irrevocable losses in market share, which served no one's interests. Divisible issues in this case might have involved how much of the product line would be sold through alternative channels of distribution, the extent of exclusive territory, or how much income protection the company was willing to offer its sales force.

Size of Stakes

The greater the perceived value of what may be lost, the harder it is to manage a conflict. This point is illustrated when managers fight against acquisition attempts. If managers think their jobs are in jeopardy, they subjectively perceive the stakes as being high and are likely to fight tooth and nail against the acquisition. Contracts providing for continued economic security, so-called golden parachutes, reduce the size of the stakes for those potentially affected. Putting aside the question of whether such contracts are justifiable when viewed from other perspectives, they do tend to make acquisition conflicts more manageable.

In many cases the perceived size of the stakes can be reduced by persuasion rather than by taking concrete action. People tend to become emotionally involved in conflicts and as a result magnify the importance of what is really at stake. Their "egos" get caught up in the winning losing aspect of the conflict, and subjective values become inflated.

A good antidote is to postpone the settlement until the parties become less emotional. During this cooling-off period they can reevaluate the issues at stake, thereby restoring some objectivity to their assessments. If time does not permit a cooling off, an attempt to reassess the demands and reduce the other party's expectations may be possible: "There's no way we can give you 100 percent of what you want, so let's be realistic about what you can live with." This approach is really an attempt to induce an attitude change. In effect, the person is being persuaded to entertain the thought, "If I can get by with less than 100 percent of what I was asking for, then what is at stake must not be of paramount importance to me."

A special case of the high-stakes/low-stakes question is the issue of precedent, the stakes are seen as being higher because future conflicts will tend to be settled in terms of the current settlement. In other words, giving ground in the immediate situation is seen as giving ground for all time. This problem surfaces in settling grievances. Thus, an effective way to manage such a conflict is to emphasize the uniqueness of the situation to downplay possible precedents that could be set. Similarly, the perceived consequences of organizational changes for individuals can often be softened by explicitly downplaying the future consequences: employees are sometimes assured that the change is being made "on an experimental basis" and will later be reevaluated. The effect is to reduce the perceived risk in accepting the proposed change.

Interdependence of the Parties

The parties to a conflict can view themselves on a continuum from having "zero-sum" to "positive-sum" interdependence. Zero-sum interdependence is the perception that if one party gains in an interaction, it is at the expense of the other party. In the positive-sum case, both parties come out ahead by means of a settlement. A zero-sum relationship makes conflict difficult to resolve because it focuses attention narrowly on personal gain rather than on mutual gain through collaboration or problem solving.

Consider the example of conflict over the allocation of limited budget funds among sales and production when a new product line is introduced. The sales group fights for a large allocation to promote the product in order to build market share. The production group fights for a large allocation to provide the plant and equipment necessary to turn out high volume at high-quality levels. The funds available have a fixed ceiling, so that a gain for sales appears to be a loss for production and vice versa. From a zero-sum perspective, it makes sense to fight for the marginal dollar rather than agree on a compromise.

A positive-sum view of the same situation removes some of the urgency to win a larger share of the spoils at the outset. Attention is more usefully focused on how one party's allocation in fact helps the other. Early promotion allocations to achieve high sales volume, if successful, lead to high production volume. This in turn generates revenue that can be invested in the desired improvements to plant and equipment. Similarly, initial allocations to improve plant and equipment can make a high-quality product readily available to the sales group, and the demand for a high-quality product will foster sales.

The potential for mutual benefit is often overlooked in the scramble for scarce resources. However, if both parties can be persuaded to consider how they can both benefit from a situation, they are more likely to approach the conflict over scarce resources with more cooperative predispositions. The focus shifts from whether one party is getting a fair share of the available resources to what is the optimum initial allocation that will jointly serve the mutual long-run interests of both sales and production.

Continuity of Interaction

The continuity-of-interaction dimension concerns the time horizon over which the parties see themselves dealing with each other. If they visualize a long-term interaction—a continuous relationship—the present transaction takes on minor significance, and the conflict within that transaction tends to be easy to resolve. If, on the other hand, the transaction is viewed as a one-shot deal—and episodic relationship—the parties will have little incentive to accommodate each other, and the conflict will be difficult to resolve.

This difference in perspective is seen by contrasting how lawyers and managers approach a contract dispute. Lawyers are trained to perceive the situation as a single episode: the parties go to court, and the lawyers make the best possible case for their party in an attempt to achieve the best possible outcome. This is a "no-holds-barred" interaction in which the past and future interaction between the parties tends to be viewed as irrelevant. Thus the conflict between the parties is not really resolved; rather, an outcome is imposed by the judge.

In contrast, managers are likely to be more accommodating when the discussion of a contract is viewed as one interaction within a longer-term relationship that has both a history and a future. In such a situation, a manager is unlikely to resort to no-holds-barred tactics because he or she will have to face the other party regarding future deals. Furthermore, a continuous relationship permits the bankrolling of favors: "We helped you out on that last problem; it's your turn to work with us on this one."

Here, it is easy, even cordial, to remind the other party that a continuous relationship exists. This tactic works well because episodic situations are rare in real-world business transactions. For instance, people with substantial business experience know that a transaction is usually not completed when a contract is signed. No contract can be comprehensive enough to provide unambiguously for all possible contingencies. Thus trust and goodwill remain important long after the contract is signed. The street-fighting tactics that may seem advantageous in the context of an episodic orientation are likely to be very costly to the person who must later seek accommodation with the bruised and resentful other party.

Structure of the Parties

Conflict is easier to resolve when a party has a strong leader who can unify his or her constituency to accept and implement the agreement. If the leadership is weak rebellious subgroups who may not feel obliged to go along with the overall agreement that has been reached are likely to rise up, thereby making conflict difficult to resolve.

For example, people who deal with unions know that a strong leadership tends to be better than a weak one, especially when organizational change needs to be accomplished. A strongly led union may drive a hard bargain, but once an agreement is reached the deal is honored by union members. If a weakly led union is involved, the agreement may be undermined by factions within the union who may not like some of the details. The result may well be chronic resistance to change or even wildcat strikes. To bring peace among such factions, management may have to make further concessions that may be costly. To avoid this, managers may find themselves in a paradoxical position of needing to boost the power of union leaders.

Similar actions may be warranted when there is no union. Groups of employees often band together as informal coalitions to protect their interests in times of change. Instead of fighting or alienating a group, managers who wish to bring about change may benefit from considering ways to formalize the coalition, such as by appointing its opinion leader to a task force or steering committee. This tactic may be equivalent to cooptation, yet there is likely to be a net benefit to both the coalition and management. The coalition benefits because it is given a formal channel in which the opinion leader's viewpoint is expressed; management benefits because the spokesperson presents the conflict in a manageable form, which is much better than passive resistance or subtle sabotage.

Involvement of Third Parties

People tend to become emotionally involved in conflicts. Such involvement can have several effects: perceptions may become distorted, nonrational thought processes and arguments may arise, and unreasonable stances, impaired communication, and personal attacks may result. These effects make the conflict difficult to resolve.

The presence of a third party, even if the third party is not actively involved in the dialogue, can constrain such effects. People usually feel obliged to appear reasonable and responsible because they care more about how the neutral party is evaluating them than by how the opponent is. The more prestigious, powerful, trusted, and neutral the third party, the greater is the desire to exercise emotional restraint.

While managers often have to mediate conflicts among lower-level employees, they are rarely seen as being neutral. Therefore, consultants and change agents often end up serving a mediator role, either by design or default. This role can take several forms, ranging from an umpire supervising communication to a messenger between parties for whom face-to-face communication has become too strained. Mediation essentially involves keeping the parties interacting in a reasonable and constructive manner. Typically, however, most managers are reluctant to enlist an outsider who is a professional mediator or arbitrator, for it is very hard for them to admit openly that they are entangled in a serious conflict, much less one they cannot handle themselves.

When managers remain involved in settling disputes, they usually take a stronger role than mediators: they become arbitrators rather than mediators. As arbitrators, they arrive at a conflict-resolving judgment after hearing each party's case. In most business conflicts, mediation is preferable because the parties are helped to come to an agreement in which they have some psychological investment. Arbitration tends to be more of a judicial process in which the parties make the best possible case to support their position: this tends to further polarize rather than reconcile differences.

Managers can benefit from a third-party presence, however, without involving dispute-resolution professionals per se. For example, they can introduce a consultant into the situation, with an explicit mission that is not conflict intervention. The mere presence of this neutral witness will likely constrain the disputants' use of destructive tactics.

Alternatively, if the managers find that they themselves are party to a conflict, they can make the conflict more public and produce the same constraining effect that a third party would. They also can arrange for the presence of relatively uninvolved individuals during interactions; even having a secretary keep minutes of such interactions encourages rational behavior. If the content of the discussion cannot be disclosed to lower-level employees, a higher-level manager can be invited to sit in on the discussion, thereby discouraging dysfunctional personal attacks and unreasonable stances. To the extent that managers can be trusted to be even handed, a third-party approach can facilitate conflict management. Encouraging accommodation usually is preferable to imposing a solution that may only produce resentment of one of the parties.

PROGRESS OF THE CONFLICT

It is difficult to manage conflict when the parties are not ready to achieve a reconciliation. Thus it is important to know whether the parties believe that the conflict is escalating. The following example illustrates this point.

During a product strategy meeting, a marketing vice-president carelessly implied that the R&D group tended to overdesign products. The remark was intended to be a humorous stereotyping of the R&D function, but it was interpreted by the R&D vice-president as an attempt to pass on to his group the blame for an uncompetitive product. Later in the meeting, the R&D vice-president took advantage of an opportunity to point out that the marketing vice-president lacked the technical expertise to understand a design limitation. The marketing vice-president perceived this rejoinder as ridicule and therefore as an act of hostility. The R&D vice-president, who believed he had evened the score, was quite surprised to be denounced subsequently by the marketing vice-president, who in turn thought he was evening the score for the uncalled-for barb. These events soon led to a memo war, backbiting, and then to pressure on various employees to take sides.

The important point here is that from the first rejoinder neither party wished to escalate the conflict; each wished merely to even the score. Nonetheless, conflict resolution would have been very difficult to accomplish during this escalation phase because people do not like to disengage when they think they still "owe one" to the other party. Since an even score is subjectively defined, however, the parties need to be convinced that the overall score is approximately equal and that everyone has already suffered enough.

Developing Conflict Management Skills

Strategic decision making usually is portrayed as a unilateral process. Decision makers have some vision of where the organization needs to be headed, and they decide on the nature and timing of specific actions to achieve tangible goals. This portrayal, however, does not take into account the conflict inherent in the decision-making process; most strategic decisions are negotiated solutions to conflicts among people whose interests are affected by such decisions. Even in the uncommon case of a unilateral decision, the decision maker has to deal with the conflict that arises when he or she moves to implement the decision.

In the presence of conflict at the decision-making or decision-implementing stage, managers must focus on generating an agreement rather than a decision. A decision without agreement makes the strategic direction difficult to implement. By contrast, an agreement on a strategic direction doesn't require an explicit decision. In this context, conflict management is the process of removing cognitive barriers to agreement. Note that agreement does not imply that the conflict has "gone away." The people involved still have interests that are somewhat incompatible. Agreement implies that these people have become committed to a course of action that serves some of their interests.

People making agreements that are less than ideal from the standpoint of serving their interests when they lack the power to force others to fully comply with their wishes. On the other hand, if a manager has total power over those whose interests are affected by the outcome of a strategic decision, the manager may not care whether or not others agree, because total power implies total compliance. There are few situations in real life in which managers have influence that even approaches total power, however, and power solutions are at best unstable since most people react negatively to powerlessness per se. Thus it makes more sense to seek agreements than to seek power. Furthermore, because conflict management involves weakening or removing barriers to agreements, managers must be able to diagnose successfully such barriers. The model summarized in Table 1 identifies the primary cognitive barriers to agreement.

Competence in understanding the barriers to an agreement can be easily honed by making a pastime of conflict diagnosis. The model helps to focus attention on specific aspects of the situation that may pose obstacles to successful conflict management. This pastime transforms accounts of conflicts—from sources ranging from a spouse's response to "how was your day?" to the evening news—into a challenge in which the objective is to try to pinpoint the obstacles to agreement and to predict the success of proposed interventions.

Focusing on the underlying dynamics of the conflict makes it more likely that conflict management will tend toward resolution rather than the more familiar response of suppression. Although the conflict itself—that is, the source—will remain alive, at best, its expression will be postponed until some later occasion; at worst, it will take a less obvious and usually less manageable form.

Knowledge of and practice in using the model is only a starting point for managers and change agents. Their development as professionals requires that conflict management become an integral part of their use of power. Power is a most basic facet of organizational life, yet inevitably it generates conflict because it constricts the autonomy of those who respond to it. Anticipating precisely how the use of power will create a conflict relationship provides an enormous advantage in the ability to achieve the desired levels of control with minimal dysfunctional side effects. ■

What Managers Want to Know

Adam Radzik

The conscientious and well-meaning owner of a small business cannot seem to get his work force motivated, despite a good benefits package and pleasant working environment. "I am coming to the conclusion that it doesn't pay to be nice to people," he says. "Maybe if I fired a few of them I'd get better results."

The supervisor of a 100-employe division of a large company says his employees are demoralized; he wants to know ways to increase their motivation.

An office manager is stunned to find out that two of her best employees told another supervisor she did not like them. "They are both top performers, and I can never remember being dissatisfied with them in any way," she says, "What's happening?"

These managers are discovering that managing means managing people. In the course of consulting and column writing I have found the two major problem areas for managers are how to motivate and how to reduce conflict.

Take the owner who is contemplating firing some of his employees. It is not that he is doing something wrong by giving them a handsome benefits package and good working conditions. He is just not doing enough. If you are in his situation you should ask yourself these questions: Do your employees participate in decision making? Do they have promotion opportunities? Do they think you have made promises you have not fulfilled? Do you reward them for initiative and superior performance?

People will work for money, but except in extreme circumstances, they resist working for money alone. They also want recognition, security and opportunity. There is, accordingly, a simple solution for the supervisor of those 100 demoralized employees: Tell them "thank you."

Reprinted by permission, *Nation's Business,* August 1985, Copyright U.S. Chamber of Commerce, 1985.

Adam Radzik is a management consultant in Plainfield, N.J., and writer of "Down to Business," a twice-weekly column in the New York Post.

It is human nature to like praise and to be motivated to work for it. I often tell my clients, "Do you want to make $1,000 in five minutes? Go and give an employee a word of praise. His work rate will increase, his motivational level will rise, and he will pass along his good mood to others."

And you must be aware that all the good work and good feeling you build up can be destroyed in ways you little expect. Take the supervisor who was amazed to find out that her two best employees thought she disliked them.

It can happen like this: The manager is worried about a procurement problem. Frank, the employee, passes the manager in the corridor and greets her with a smile. The manager, engrossed in her problem, looks up briefly and mumbles a reply. Frank's mood drops. He wonders why she is angry with him, what he did, whether he is doing a good job.

The next day, the procurement problem takes a turn for the worse. Frank tries again. This time the manager does not even respond. Frank's worst fears are confirmed. And the manager does not even realize it.

Why does this happen? Employees are constantly gauging their job security and their employer's satisfaction with their performance by the expression they see on the manager's face.

Office conflict at its worst is caused by a deliberate trouble-maker. Here is a typical case:

> *"I work with a manager who constantly criticizes me and the other managers. He likes to show my boss how knowledgeable he is and how he is the only guy who can get anything done around here. The boss laps it up, and the two of them have lengthy conferences discussing all the employees. This guy is bent on climbing to the top over our bodies. What should we do?"*

These professional conflict makers create morale problems, credibility problems and eventual productivity problems. They can be cunning and vicious, but they flourish only where the boss is a willing participant.

Professional conflict makers devote so much of their energies to criticizing others' performances that their own tasks are neglected. You can find subtle ways of pointing that out to their superiors.

Worth noting is that professional conflict makers rarely confine their volleys to employees. Their highly critical appraisals usually include disparaging remarks about the boss and his management style. At the appropriate time, you might wish to share with your boss your concerns about the damage being done to the boss' own image in the eyes of the employees. By the way, bring along a witness or two. It will enhance your credibility. Keep your remarks dispassionate, and your boss will see the light.

A high level of employee motivation can make a company grow and flourish. Human conflict can reduce productivity and increase turnover. Business owners would be well advised to regularly monitor both. For a business they can spell life or death. ▪

The Control Gap
at the Top

Sumer C. Aggarwal
Vimla S. Aggarwal

What control measures apply to top management? The answer too often is, None.

In most companies, some form of control measures exist at all levels except for the top position of CEO. The chief executive, in most cases, behaves like a king.[1] Persons at the lower levels tirelessly compete for the favors of CEO. This translates into fierce competition for keeping the boss happy. The process filters down to vice presidents, whose favors must be won by departmental managers by fair means or foul. Similar competitive efforts exist at every other level, and people are constantly busy pleasing superiors at any cost. In a way, the superior-subordinate relationship style set by the CEO becomes the order of business for everyone in the organization.

At lower levels, considerable attention is paid to measures such as average productivity, staying within the allocated budgets, and the severity of complaints from the customers or from sister departments. At higher levels, unfortunately, such measures are not the primary consideration for rewards in terms of individual raises and promotions. If a person can keep the boss happy, then the boss can sugarcoat even poor scores on existing formal control measures. The boss can glorify ordinary achievements by adding adjectives, so the individual becomes a "priceless team player," "quick learner," "great firefighter," "sharp analyzer," "wonderful forecaster," or an "acute observer and identifier of individuals and opportunities."

A happy boss can always give a boost to the career of a favorite subordinate by assigning him the projects with great visibility, by asking him to make a few slick presentations in front of higher level committees, and by regularly commenting favorably in higher circles on this subordinate's great performances. Under the common rules of the game, the boss in reality is stressing that his subordinate is totally loyal, reliable, and faithful, and is not so weak in performance as to become a liability to his superior.

Business Horizons. Copyright, 1985, by the Foundation for the School of Business at Indiana University. Reprinted by permission.

Sumer C. Aggarwal is a professor of management science and operations management at The Pennsylvania State University. Vimla S. Aggarwal is a free-lance writer on administrative issues.

SELFISHNESS AND DISTORTED CONTROL

Every human is selfish and so are CEOs, VPs, departmental managers, and others. The primary objective of most top-level managers is to have subordinates who are loyal, faithful, truthful, and willing to go to great lengths to protect the boss. Mediocre performance can be tolerated or even covered up so long as the survival of the company is not in danger. Further, most top managers are often threatened by the fact that managers in competing companies promote the same type of loyalty and mediocrity; hence, they conclude that they are doing all right in relation to competition as well.

Sometimes the challenge comes from foreign competition, where actual management controls could be in terms of productivity, quality, cost, ROI, and customer service. In the face of such competition, the whole of domestic industry starts losing money. Witness what happened to U.S. car companies, TV manufacturers, sewing machine companies, photo equipment producers, and the steel industry.

Under financially stressful conditions, everyone wants to save his or her job. Realistic and scientific performance controls are put into place, and the loyalists and faithfuls (who are often second-or third-rate managers but "fat and happy") are let go by their bosses, because then "the survival of the fittest and the best" prevails.

What about obtaining the best performance from top management under ordinary conditions? The performance of CEOs is controlled only indirectly by Wall Street, where performance is reflected in the company's share price. Security analysts look primarily at accounting data, together with the prevailing external and environmental news items, but the accounting figures are prepared by the company under the guidance of the CEO. Through so-called "creative accounting," accompanied by minimization of R&D, maintenance, and replacement costs, a company can continue to satisfy Wall Street requirements for several years before its survival comes into question.

Some will argue that the board of directors is a perpetual watchdog over company affairs. But who informs the board about company performance? No one but the CEO and his loyalists, by way of reports prepared by them. Several members of the board may have been nominated by the CEO himself; others are there through personal friendships or indirect reciprocity among various boards. Boards rarely question the recommendation of the CEO: they make some suggestions or recommendations here and there, but mostly a CEO is completely free to run the company as he chooses, as long as an average or acceptable performance is there. Such conditions inadvertently make him the king, a realization that results in distorted controls.

INVERTED LOGIC

During 1982, the largest 100 publicly owned companies paid their CEOs total compensation (including salary, stocks, and nonpension plans) averaging $1.1 million per year. The smallest 25 of these largest 100 companies paid their CEOs 7 percent more than all of the others.[2] Although 55 of these 100 companies showed declining profits in 1982, most of their CEOs still got substantial raises. This can happen because the board passes on its responsibility to a compensation committee, whose members are chosen mostly by the CEO himself. When deciding on individual compensation, this committee relies heavily on the information and propositions of the CEO. Board members, particularly retired executives and minorities, want to get elected to the boards year after year. If they oppose the CEO regularly, they may never be nominated in the future to this board or any other board.

The CEO indirectly influences his own salary by suggesting higher compensation for his subordinates. These days, the main logic supporting higher compensation seems to be the urgent need for matching company payments with the average compensation levels determined by various surveys. Little consideration or weight is given to the job's contributions or the complexity of its performance requirements. There are no easy solutions to this illogical problem. This senseless throwing of money at top management indicates the near absence of controls at the top.

POWER PLAY

Power is always concentrated at the top. Often, the responsibility for detailed work is pushed down, but the subordinates are expected to push the credit upwards. Subordinates are not supposed to overcommit their boss but instead should help him stay away from mistakes. There are scarcely any objective criteria of success or performance beyond the middle management level. Accomplishments have no meaning for promotion; what really matters is a patron, a mentor, a godfather-like figure to make the employee visible to the higher echelons and to perpetually protect him or her from hostile criticisms.

Such unjustifiable criteria for promotions and rewards to middle management prevail in a host of corporations. This happens because there are no clear-cut systems for knocking down responsibility. Smart managers constantly get promoted before the consequences of some of their wrong decisions or mistakes of the past show up in the division's or department's performance. Their successors get blamed for the current poor results even when these successors had nothing to do with the actions leading to these results. The economic and status achievements of anybody beyond middle management levels are purely and simply dependent on how well the person pleases and submits to the wishes, whims, and idiosyncracies of the boss or bosses.

RESULTS-ORIENTED CONTROLS

Many organizational theories exist that suggest horizontal controls for the top management and CEOs. But how can these kingpins be made subject to the realistic efficiency and effectiveness control measures that apply to others at middle levels? It is top management who can foul up control mechanisms by sidetracking even the most efficient and creative ones if someone does not play the boss's tune, and by punishing those who dare criticize or even disagree. In the process, these inequities become the norms of the company. Eventually, the company suffers. It survives so long as its direct competition is indulging in similar manipulative and unscientific management control practices and procedures.

A few practices are available, however, that control the CEO and other top-level managers directly and are helping some companies to obtain excellent results.

EVALUATE CEOS

Senior VPs can write annual evaluations of the CEO and send copies directly and anonymously to the board chairman. A large Northwest manufacturer uses this control. If the majority of the immediate subordinates rate their boss below average two times in a row, the board investigates; if necessary, it may demote or even fire the CEO. This company has been growing fast, grossing about 20 percent before taxes for two decades, whereas its competitors recently have been struggling for survival.

INSTALL CONCURRENT EVALUATIONS BY POSITIONHOLDERS AND KNOWLEDGEHOLDERS

Intel operates through horizontal controls. "Knowledgeholders" and "positionholders" are involved in major decisions. The company provides no big offices, no private toilets, no reserved parking spaces, and no limousines. At the meetings, junior managers are treated as equal for all intents and purposes and are encouraged to participate in decision making. Intel is an example of the glorious success of "high output management." Individual raises and promotions are based on creative contributions, and productive efforts are judged by the consensus of top management and by the superiors supervising the group. There is no way a single top manager can start rewarding his loyalists and faithfuls, because the founders of the company themselves happen to be top managers. Will it continue that way after the professional managers take over? At this time the question is hypothetical, but some of the current control practices, traditions, and attitudes are likely to continue for a long time to come.

ELIMINATE TOP MANAGEMENT FEATHERBEDDING

Union featherbedding has been strongly criticized by managers and economists for causing reduced productivity and inflated labor costs. Recently, however, an increasing number of top executives are being provided "special protection" by their company boards. A case in point is the well-publicized story of past Bendix chairman William Agree and the other top 15 executives who received millions of dollars from Allied Corporation, the acquiring company, when they were released after the merger of Bendix with Allied.[3] This was an outrageous misuse of top management power. Ward Howell Associates survey reports that 60 percent of Fortune 1000 corporations have similar protection for top executives and for no one else. The yearly reward structures for most top executives have little correlation with stock price growth or with return to shareholders during the year.

PUT MAJOR EQUITYHOLDERS ON THE BOARD

In West Germany, unlike the U.S., banks are allowed by law to buy equity in corporations. Bank representatives on the company board exercise a great deal of control on CEOs. In addition, these banks often push for placement of independent technical experts on the board. Such experts not only assess closely the current state of R&D within the corporations but also analyze plans and directions as they relate to future products, services, and processes. In no way are these experts the puppets of the CEO; unlike most VPs, they are not at the mercy of the CEO for their survival and status. This way, the control gap at the top remains plugged. German companies with this control structure are quite healthy and profitable.

USE BOARD NOMINEES AS INTERNAL WATCHDOGS

Soviet industry has constantly suffered from low productivity, poor quality, and shortage problems. There are multifarious reasons for such miserable performance. One can be sure that these problems are not the result of a control gap at the top. An excellent organizational setup exerts horizontal control on the top executives of each and every organization. Each Soviet organization has a line-authority structure just like any U.S. corporation, but side by side, each of their organizations has a party control organ. The CEO must consult the party organ for all the major decisions. The party organ constantly passes judgment on current performance of the organization and also on the future plans. This organ has direct links with the minister in charge of the organization or company and also with the Central Committee. Once the plant or company organ feels strongly about inefficient performance by any top executive, it can recommend demotion, removal, or sometimes even harsh punishment by tagging him as a "people's enemy."

U.S. corporations may want to set up some control group, nominated by the board, that reports directly to the board. This group should consist of internal managers of the company and may include managers or experts from various functional areas. Their annual promotions and raises may be reviewed by the board so long as they remain members of this nominated group. These individuals should also be allowed to approach the board directly if they become victims of reprisals from superiors angered because of their participation in the board-nominated group. This sort of setup can be a very effective control on top managers and CEOs and should keep companies moving forward progressively.

DISALLOW REGULAR USE OF CONSULTANTS

Some top managers regularly use a consultant to help them make major decisions. If the consultant's recommendation does not work, executives can easily pass the blame on to the consultant.[4] But why, when top managers are paid extremely well to make major decisions, should they use so much outside help to accomplish what they are supposed to be doing themselves? Maybe the time has come when the Securities Exchange Commission will require companies to disclose the amount they spend each quarter on consultants. Boards should regularly check on how and by whom major company proposals and projects were analyzed and assessed and how much money was spent in the form of consulting fees. Such regular overview will put pressure on top managers to do what they are supposed to be doing, to be responsible for successes and failures resulting from major plans and decisions.

DON'T SUBSTITUTE STRATEGY FOR CONTROL

In management circles, there is too much talk about strategy. There is strategic management of marketing, production, finance, personnel, purchasing, facilities, and many other special areas.[5] In the process of developing and implementing strategies, top management's focus is on placing the burden on middle management. Middle managers must come up with plans, implement those strategies, and then be prepared to accept the blame for below average or poor results. In case of success, top managers can enthusiastically take the credit in the name of strategic handling of overall management activities. U.S. companies are reaching a point when this type of manipulative management endangers the very survival of the companies. Top managers must always be held accountable for poor results as well as good. They should not be allowed to find a scapegoat who can be blamed for failures or poor results. If top managers are subjected to control like everybody else, so-called strategies will take care of themselves and most companies will have good or excellent results.

BOARD CONTROLS ON TOP MANAGEMENT

Primary control mechanism would evolve automatically when the board tells the CEO that he will be held responsible for good or bad results each quarter, each year, and in the long run, irrespective of good or bad economic conditions. The CEO cannot point a finger at subordinates when the plans go awry, markets remain weak, or competition starts offering better products, prices, and services. The board must establish procedures to guard against the CEO's laziness, extreme selfishness, lack of creativity and leadership, and particularly against manipulative practices. What are some scientific measures that a board can implement to keep CEOs on the right track?

Plot aggregate productivity of the company on a quarterly and yearly basis for at least the past five years.

Let the CEO report quarterly expenses (as percent of sales) on R&D, maintenance, and on replacements and compare them with the past five years' figures for the same items.

Require the CEO to report on management development activities each quarter, giving reasons for supporting each activity.

Check regularly on the quarterly ROI plot of the past five years. Ask for the projections for the upcoming five years.

Declare that each of the ten most senior VPs will submit to the board directly and anonymously an annual evaluation report about the performance of the CEO. Each year the board may also ask a dozen or so middle managers, selected at random, to evaluate the strengths and weaknesses of the CEO's policies and procedures. Such reports, if kept both top secret and anonymous, can bring to the surface certain unknown problems that may be steering the company to a disastrous future.

If these controls are implemented sincerely and with the clear understanding that the CEO carries responsibility and authority for overall performance, be it good or bad, they will eliminate the control gap at the top. ■

NOTES

1. R. Jackall, "Moral Mazes: Bureaucracy and Managerial Work," *Harvard Business Review,* September–October 1983: 118–130.
2. A. Patton, "Why So Many Chief Executives Make Too Much," *Business Week,* October 17, 1983: 24, 26.
3. Charles A. Myers, "Top Management Featherbedding," *Sloan Management Review,* Vol. 24, No. 4, Summer 1983: 55–58.
4. "Are All These Consultants Really Necessary?" *Forbes,* October 10, 1983: 136–144.
5. G. A. Steiner, John B. Miner, and Edmund R. Gray, *Management Policy and Strategy,* 2nd ed. (New York: Macmillan, 1982).

The Human Side of Control

Waldron Berry, Ph.D.

Associate Professor of Management
College of Business Administration
University of Central Florida, Orlando

The recent progress of Japanese companies has caused managers throughout U.S. industry to take a close look at their often disappointing accomplishments as well as the declining performance of their employees. In consequence, they have placed great stress on improving productivity, usually by cutting costs and increasing controls. The short-term benefits of such crisis management have improved productivity and profits, but unless the human side of control is carefully considered, it is quite likely that productivity and profits will decline again to even lower levels in the long term.

WHY CONTROL SYSTEMS FAIL

A control system is necessary in any organization in which the activities of different divisions, departments, sections, and so on need to be coordinated and controlled.

Most control systems are past-action-oriented and consequently are inefficient or fail. For example, there is little an employee can do today to correct the results of actions completed two weeks ago. Steering controls, on the other hand, are future-oriented and allow adjustments to be made to get back on course before the control period ends. They therefore establish a more motivating climate for the employee.

What's more, although many standards or controls are simply estimates of what should occur if certain assumptions are correct, they take on a precision in today's control systems that leaves little or no margin for error. Managers would be better off establishing a range rather than a precise number and changing standards as time passes and assumptions prove erroneous. This would be fairer and would positively motivate employees.

There are three fundamental beliefs underlying most successful control systems. First, planning and control are the two most closely interrelated management functions. Second, the human side of the control process needs to be stressed as much as, if not more than, the tasks or "numbers crunching" side.

Reprinted, by permission of the publisher, from *Supervisory Management*, June 1985 © 1985 American Management Association, New York. All rights reserved.

Finally, evaluating, coaching, and rewarding are more effective in the long term than measuring, comparing, and pressure or penalizing.

PLANNING AND CONTROL

Few managers realize that a company plan must provide the framework for the company control system. If missions, goals, strategies, objectives, and plans change, then controls should change. Unfortunately, they seldom do. Although this error occurs at the top, repercussions are felt at all levels. Often, too, the standards of the control systems are derived from previous years' budgets rather than from current objectives of company plans. The result is that employees at lower levels are simply given "numbers to make" based on factors of which they have little knowledge and over which they have practically no influence.

The accompanying table shows the important interrelationship between planning and control.

As you can see, the control process does not begin after the entire planning process ends, as most managers believe.

After objectives are set in the first step of the planning process, appropriate standards should be developed for them. Standards are units of measurement established to serve as a reference base and are useful in determining time lines, sequences of activities, scheduling, and allocation of resources. For example, if objectives are set and work is planned for 18 people on an assembly line, standards or reasonable expectations of performance from each person then need to be clearly established.

The second significant interaction between planning and control occurs with the final step of the control process—taking corrective action. This can take several forms, but two of the most effective are to change the objectives or alter the plan. Managers dislike doing either; but if a positive motivational climate is to be established, these ought to be the first two corrective actions attempted. Objectives and standards are based on assumptions, but if these assumptions prove inaccurate, then objectives and standards require alteration. Thus sales quotas assigned on the premise of a booming economy can certainly be altered if, as is often the case, the economy turns sour. Likewise, if the assumptions are accurate and objectives and standards have not been met, then it is possible that the plan developed was inadequate and needs to be changed.

THE CONTROL PROCESS

Planning and organizing are two management functions that have been popular research areas in recent years. Control, the third well known

CONTROL RELATIONSHIP	
Action Planning	**Control**
1. Establish objectives	1. Establish standards
2. Determine activities	
3. Delegate	
4. Schedule	
5. Allocate resources	
6. Communicate, coordinate	
7. Provide incentives	2. Measure, compare
	3. Evaluate deviations, give feedback, and coach
	4. Take corrective action

management function, has received surprisingly little attention. This is perhaps because the task side of control is noticed and the behavioral or human side is largely overlooked. But as previously noted, managers should carefully consider the behavioral aspects of the process when designing a control system if employees are to be motivated to accomplish assigned tasks.

Step 1. Setting standards. Performance standards may be set by staff or managers, by managers and staff, or by managers with input from employees whose performance is being measured. The last method is the best because employees believe that line and staff do not have enough information about the conditions of various jobs to set realistic standards.

Managers should see that objectives and standards are measurable and that individuals are held accountable for their accomplishment. The level of difficulty should be challenging but within the capabilities of the employee. Standards set too low are usually accomplished but not exceeded, while standards set too high usually do not motivate the employee to expend much effort to reach the goal.

It is important that standards be complete; however, it is almost impossible to develop a single standard or goal that will indicate effective overall performance. For example, a few years ago an automobile dealer decided to measure salespeople's performance on the basis of the number of automobiles sold. Sales increased impressively, but it w
that many sales had been made to poor credit risks, and
had been allowed on trade-ins. Too many managers are
one magic number that will tell them how well the comj
how their employees are performing. Standards for

salespeople might have included number of sales, losses from poor credit risks, and profit on resales.

Standards should also be expressed in terms that relate to the job and are meaningful to the employee. For example, the foremen in one plant were assigned standards based on break-even analysis, although none of them had any knowledge of this analytical technique.

From a behavioral standpoint, it is extremely important that the employee be able to significantly influence or affect the standard assigned. In the early 1970s, the performance of a hotel manager in Florida was based on profit and room occupancy rates. During this period, OPEC caused a fuel crisis and relatively few tourists could travel to Florida. The hotel manager was penalized for failing to accomplish a standard over which, in this case, he had no influence.

Finally, managers should see that the number of standards assigned, like planning objectives, are limited and placed in priority order for the employee. If there are too many controls assigned, the employee will not be able to give enough attention to any of them and will become frustrated and confused.

Step 2. Measure and compare actual with planned results. As with setting standards, the objectivity of the measurement and the person who measures and compares the performance are important. Measuring and comparing can be accomplished by the person performing the task, by the boss, or by a staff person; even an automated system can measure and compare. From a behavioral standpoint, the last method is the least popular, followed by measurement by a staff person only. An employee believes an automated system, a staff person, or even the boss does not know enough about the conditions of the job to make a fair comparison between actual and planned results. Also, the employee often distrusts the staff person and sometimes even the boss. At the same time, the employee is usually not trusted enough by the company to perform the measurement and comparison alone. The best solution is to have the measurement done by the person most trusted by the employee and to allow the employee some input.

When employees have relatively low trust in a control system, they sometimes behave in various ways that are harmful to the organization. They may do what is "required" by the system. For example, when bonuses for salespeople in a department store were based on sales volume, many employees soon lost interest in customers who did not immediately purchase an item, and they spent little time helping customers, making merchandise attractive, or performing stock work.

Quite often employees will report data in such a way that performance will look good for a particular time period. Some control systems will also cause employees to report invalid or misleading data about what can be done. For example, it is not uncommon at budget time for managers to ask for larger amounts than needed if they believe their requests will be reduced. In many organizations budget-setting sessions are largely negotiating games with little effort given to establishing realistic standards. The recent advent of computer-based management information systems has also caused invalid data to be provided. These systems sometimes require historical cost, production, and other data that are simply not available and cannot be provided. When pressed, however, the data are estimated, often inaccurately.

Finally, control systems that employees view as clearly threatening will cause strong resistance. Perhaps the best example of this is automatic data systems. These systems create new experts with much power, are often not well understood, and therefore, are feared by many employees.

Step 3. Evaluate, give feedback, and coach. The third step is most effective when steering controls are selected. With these controls, forecasters of the result can also be used for early warning that specific actions may be required. For example, high morale is a popular goal but one that is difficult to measure. Forecasters such as number of accidents, absenteeism, and employee turnover may be evaluated together and serve as a surrogate measure for increasing or declining morale. Careful evaluation must be used, however. If the accident rate increases rapidly in the production area, it could suggest declining morale when a significant increase is caused by employee carelessness. However, if the cause is related to equipment that suddenly wears out, then there probably is not a relationship between accident rate and low morale. It is essential that managers carefully evaluate deviations before taking action. It is also important that they remember that deviations can be positive as well as negative and that they reward employees for positive deviations. Unfortunately, this step is often omitted and only the negative aspects of deviation received attention.

Who should receive feedback from this evaluation and how often should it be offered? The person who is accountable for accomplishing the standard should receive the information first. The employee's boss, or whoever is in a position to reward the employee, should also receive the information. The employee's boss, or whoever is in a position to reward the employee, should receive the information at about the same time or a little later. Then peers, staff people, subordinates, and other line people can receive the information. At this time, the boss ought to have some suggestions about how to get back on course if the employee needs help. The boss's most important job is coaching subordinates, and a good planning-control system provides an excellent framework for such coaching.

Feedback must be reliable, relatively frequent, and prompt. The feedback has to be reliable for the employees to be able to change the behavior or plan in order to get on course. Frequency of information has to do with the interval for which data are received. If, for instance, costs would not normally get out of control in a short period, then monthly reports might be adequate. On the other hand, a delay of six months might allow the situation to get so far out of control that it would be too late to take corrective action.

Sometimes prompt feedback can create problems. Some of today's computer-based control systems can provide feedback on an almost real time basis, but such speed can be harmful from a behavioral standpoint. This kind of speed causes undue pressure because there is no time for the manager to use discretion and make changes. A president recently described his company's "outstanding" planning-control system. He proudly explained a feedback system that provided information on a continuous basis to every employee concerning his or her progress toward a number goal. When numbers weren't being made, more pressure was applied. Employees were confused because there was no plan to change, and consequently, standards and objectives were not changed. The company had a standards-control system based on numbers; but objectives, plans, evaluation, and coaching did not exist. It is this sort of system that causes low morale and unethical and illegal behavior—all in the name of control.

Step 4. Take corrective action. Making changes as the activity is in progress is a form of corrective action. The real correction occurs when warnings raised by the forecasters or predictors are confirmed. The corrective action can be changing objectives, standards, plans, and the like, but it can also be penalizing employees when the objectives, standards, and plans are determined to be appropriate and employees have not met them. However, there usually are several alternative corrective actions that can be taken, and often more than one will prove effective. The planning-control system is not effective until corrective action is taken, and this action begins a new planning-control cycle. ■